OF PEASANTS, MIGRANTS AND PAUPERS

OF PEASANTS, MIGRANTS AND PAUPERS

Rural Labour Circulation and Capitalist Production in West India

JAN BREMAN

DELHI
OXFORD UNIVERSITY PRESS
BOMBAY CALCUTTA MADRAS
1985

Oxford University Press, Walton Street, Oxford OX2 6DP
NEW YORK TORONTO
DELHI BOMBAY CALCUTTA MADRAS KARACHI
KUALA LUMPUR SINGAPORE HONG KONG TOKYO
NAIROBI DAR ES SALAAM CAPE TOWN
MELBOURNE AUCKLAND
and associates in
BEIRUT BERLIN IBADAN MEXICO CITY NICOSIA

Typeset and printed by All India Press, Pondicherry 605 001
and published by R. Dayal, Oxford University Press
Y.M.C.A. Library Building, Jai Singh Road, New Delhi 110 001

CONTENTS

Part III

MOBILITY AND IMMOBILITY

TABLES

CHAPTER 1

CHAPTER 2

CHAPTER 3

PLATES

(following page 188)

MAPS

(pages xxvi and xxvii)

PREFACE

Between 1977 and 1982 I spent several months of each year in the Indian countryside. This book is an account of my fieldwork in the central plain of south Gujarat. It is rather unusual for empirical research to be extended over so many years, but I had no alternative. The Dutch universities have no arrangement for a sabbatical and the double work load of my posts at Erasmus University at Rotterdam and the Institute of Social Studies at the Hague precluded any possibility of pursuing my fieldwork within a shorter period of time.

Not only is there little scope for the kind of investigation which interests me, but it also has a rather low standing in the eyes of many in the profession. Fieldwork which tries to establish, in a rather detailed way and at close quarters, what is happening at the grassroot level, is time-consuming and is somewhat limited in range as a technique for collecting material. For more than one reason, the more 'distanced' kind of research—elevated, as it were, above the level of everyday reality—appears to be more highly regarded by academic and other authorities whose permission has to be obtained in order to get leave and grants. Reporting on what is happening at the bottom of a society, which I see as my chief preoccupation in research, is even more unpopular. The presumption that over the years everything that could be said about poverty has already been said, suggests a tendency to take this situation as read. It will be clear from both the method and substance of my study that I have stubbornly refused to accept this view. For me the most satisfying way of pursuing my investigations has been to live as close as possible to the people with whose situation I have been most concerned, although I have had to pay a price for this in my personal life. I am indebted to several institutions which kindly allowed me to carry out the kind of research I had in mind. A subsidy from the Netherlands Foundation for the Advancement of Tropical Research (WOTRO) enabled me to begin the study, once it was approved by the Indian Council for Social Science Research, while contributions from the Faculty of Social Sciences at Rotterdam University and from the Institute of Social Studies at The Hague, enabled me to subsequently continue my field-work. I took the opportunity to round off the empirical part of my research when the Institute of Economic Growth in Delhi (where I was a Fellow from December 1981 to April 1982) permitted me to spend much of my time in the field.

Several friends and colleagues took the trouble to read and comment on the first drafts of some of the chapters. For this I am specially thankful to Arvind Das, Harry de Haan, David Hardiman, Siem de Jong, P.C. Joshi, Ghanshyam Shah, Willem van Schendel, and Wim Wertheim. I greatly appreciated the stimulus they gave me, and needless to say, I have absorbed their criticisms as far as possible. The technical aspects of the final editing demanded much patience and dedication. Marianne Lodders and Ilse Burke prepared the manuscript for publication; Mario Rutten and V. K. Kannan helped me to compile the glossary and the index; Mr Van Dijk of the Economisch-Geografisch Instituut of Erasmus University, Rotterdam, supplied the map of the area; the photographs included in the book were taken together with Heinz Kremer. The Oxford University Press provided me with a firm but understanding editorial assistance. Finally, Enid Perlin has been more involved than anyone else in the Netherlands with the genesis of this book. She has taken far more pains, shown in the speed and skill with which she has worked, than could reasonably be expected from a translator.

Apart from the efforts of those named above the book has been made possible by the trust and friendship of a far larger number of *bhaio ane baheno* in Gujarat encountered during the course of my fieldwork, who wish to (and indeed must) remain anonymous. I will make an exception here for Praful Trivedi who, after devoting years to the cause of the poor of rural Surat, had to leave the district a short while ago. The Centre for Social Studies in Surat was much more than just a base for me from which I made sorties into the area in pursuit of my research. I shall treasure memories of the days spent there when my fieldwork was interrupted. The director Dr G. Shah and other members of the staff, left me in peace when I needed it yet were always ready to answer the questions with which I pestered them and to listen to me when I wanted to unburden my mind of recent experiences. Without in any way qualifying my appreciation of their hospitality, it was I. P. Desai above all who, both literally and metaphorically, gave me a home in Surat. The warm affection and scholarly inquisitiveness of this *eminence grise* of social sciences in India was a continuous source of inspiration for me. I. P. took keen interest in the new research which I started again in October 1984. Having completed the first round of fieldwork, I left Surat towards the end of January 1985. Only a few days later my friend passed away. An article which he urged me to write and which I dedicated to his memory will appear shortly in the *Economic and Political Weekly*.

Rotterdam/The Hague
March 1985

JAN BREMAN

INTRODUCTION

Rural India is by all accounts in a state of flux. There are, however, widely differing schools of thought on how the process of transformation should be interpreted. The cheerful tone in much of the literature on modernization, which has a strong technocratic and elite bias, can hardly be reconciled with the critical view characteristic of the on-going debate among political economists on the dominant mode of production in agriculture. Yet a common denominator in the veritable deluge of publications is the refutation of the image of immobility and stagnation in South Asia. This notion which, for a variety of reasons, has preoccupied the professionals for such a long time seems to dominate the public mind as well.

Certainly, long-term processes of change in the past appear to be slow in restrospect, resulting in an over-estimation of the tempo and impact of the more recent developments. It may be useful to observe here that the capitalist dynamic so strikingly apparent today goes back much further than to the beginning of the Green Revolution and other agrarian policies initiated only a few decades ago. Nevertheless events within the rural order in the second half of the twentieth century seem to have taken a drastic turn. The shift from quantitative to qualititative change applies as much to the development in the forces of production as to that in the relations of production.

This process took place most intensively in the Punjab which was also the first state singled out for such attention. As to be expected therefore apart from becoming an international success story, Punjab has been presented as a model which other states in India should try to emulate. Yet the progress achieved in this regime has not been as unique as it is claimed to be by various quarters. Consquently there is no reason to regard this state as an enclave of rural capitalism, a sole exception to the much more general pattern of retarded economic growth and deficient productivity caused by a persistently low capital intensity. Similar areas of concentration for the capitalist dynamic, even if on a smaller scale and more scattered than in the Punjab, exist in other parts of India as well. For instance in parts of Gujarat, Maharashtra, Uttar Pradesh, Bihar (yes, even Bihar!), Andhra Pradesh, Tamilnadu and Karnataka, to mention only the most important.

I attribute a validity to the outcome of my fieldwork which transcends the actual research setting. Although presented as a case study, my suggestion is that the situation described reflects a trend in rural development which can be found in large parts of India, although much less so in the central and eastern belt of the country.

My account relates to a region in south Gujarat which I first came to know twenty years ago. At the beginning of the 1960s I did fieldwork in a few villages on relations between landowners and agricultural labourers. On that occasion I spent time in the vicinity of Bardoli, situated in the present-day Surat District, and I have regularly returned to this region to pursue further research. Over the years I have been able to follow the impact of the process of transformation which I have discussed in this book.

My fieldwork in south Gujarat began in 1977 and lasted until the spring of 1982. Perhaps every fieldworker is prone to perceive the changes taking place at the time of his or her more or less accidental presence on the spot as being radical. I have tried to compensate for this distortion of perspective by paying a good deal of attention to the historical background of the region. The advent of canal irrigation towards the end of the 1950s and rural electrification which facilitated large-scale well irrigation, marked a sharp break between the old and the new agricultural cycle in the south Gujarat plain.

The consequences of this for the rural economy have been of the utmost importance. Concentration on only a few market crops specially on sugarcane, resulted in decreasing the area sown with food grains and increasing the capital intensity on larger holdings particularly. Transition to irrigated cultivation went hand in hand with expansion of both the physical and the organizational infrastructure.

Last but not least, the existing dependence on agriculture has given way to a much wider and more complex pattern of economic activities; a diversification in the rural economy based on agrarian surplus formation. The consequences for exchange between countryside and city, in terms of both capital, commodities, and labour, presents a separate problem which will be a subject for further research in the area.

The transition to a modern structure of production was achieved within a relatively short period of time, but this is not to say that the situation which existed previously can be described in terms of 'backwardness' and 'stagnation'. Certainly until a few decades ago an almost complete reliance on agricultural employment and income, existed side by side with a large share of the agricultural yield leaving the villages. This phenomenon went back in time for more than a century. The first part of the book is a sketch of the historical background of the region and its people. The historical perspective corrects the impression of the opening up of this peasant society only in the very recent past resulting in a rather abrupt restructuring of agriculture from one of subsistence to that of production for the world market, or, to put it differently, the transition from a 'traditional'-'feudal' order to a 'modern'-'capitalist' one.

Naturally, economic acceleration has had a strong influence on both the extent and nature of employment and on income opportunities. The limited amount of official statistical data available on the growth and composition of the working population provides a poor indication of the shift that has occurred in this pattern. Without aiming at systematic quantification at the district level—as a single researcher I had neither the means nor the time to make such an inventory—I have tried to gather as much supplementary information as possible on this subject.

What emerged logically from the central theme of my study, was the exploitation and alienation of labour due to the accumulation of capital within and outside agriculture in the rural economy of south Gujarat. A more neutral formulation of my research subject would be: the conditioning of the regional labour market by the process of transformation that is in progress in south Gujarat.

I was interested first of all in the multitude of workers who stream into the area round Bardoli each year. The statement that rural India is on the move, is meant in a literal sense as well. Remoulding the rural production structure has resulted in labour migration on a hitherto unknown scale. This mobility by itself is not a new phenomenon but in much of the relevant literature it is linked to the temporary or permanent displacement of labour moving from the countryside to the city, i.e. to the process of urbanization. Yet by far the greater part of labour migration begins and ends within the rural milieu. In the initial stage of my field research I was occupied exclusively with this type of circulation. These findings were published separately in an essay on the recruitment and employment of sugarcane cutters by the co-operative sugar factories during the harvest campaign in the central plain of Surat District.[1] An estimated 75,000 seasonal workers were already involved in this operation by the beginning of the 1980s, all coming from the regions to the east of Surat, particularly from Maharashtra. Much less striking than this tightly organized large-scale mobilization of labour coming from far away is the movement of migrants, originating from other places as well and who for several weeks or months at the peak points of the agrarian cycle head for the villages and farms in small teams, looking for work. If one includes the migrants who find work in rural industries and the rapidly expanding service sector at the busy times of the year in the district, then a total of 150,000 'guest' workers staying temporarily in the central plain of the district cannot be considered too high. Their presence, even though varying greatly in duration, has led to a significant increase in the number of rural inhabitants amounting to one and a half million, according to the 1981 census. Starting from the assumption that half this number belong to the agricultural workforce—a much higher percentage than is usually accepted—it means that during the peak periods migrants comprise at least a fifth of all the rural workers. In the leading zones of the new mode of production their percentage may even rise to 30 or 40 per cent of the total workforce or sometimes even higher than that. These figures for intra-rural migration, are derived from my impressions based on research in a limited number of locations; the approximate total size for the whole district can only be established through general-

[1] 'Seasonal migration and co-operative capitalism; the crushing of cane and of labour by the sugar factories of Bardoli, south Gujarat', published in *Economic and Political Weekly* VIII, 1978: 1317–60 and in: *The Journal of Peasant Studies* VI, 1978: 41–70 and 1979: 168–209.

ization. The government has paid scant attention to labour migration which explains why this phenomenon has remained outside official statistics.

The study of labour mobility presupposes some insight into the circumstances under which departure occurs. Although the emphasis in my study lies on the impact of the seasonal trek of the migrants on the rural order of the south Gujarat plain, I have dealt in an elementary way with the forces resulting in the periodic or permanent expulsion of these workers in the home regions.

The background to this dynamic is the way in which small cultivators slip down the agrarian ladder particularly in the dry-agriculture zones. The income earned outside during their temporary absence from home becomes indispensable for the consolidation of the small peasant holdings which have reached the level of semi-proletarianization; while the departure itself, either temporary or permanent, quite frequently helps to mask the transition to a completely landless existence among those already vulnerable. Further research is necessary in order to chart out more accurately the effects of migration on the home regions. It is however the area of departure which has, relatively speaking, attracted more attention in the few studies available on intra-rural migration. Much less is known about the accommodation of migrants in the labour regime at the place of arrival, and I have directed my fieldwork in Bardoli and its environs towards this aspect. This obviously implies the collection of data about recruiting methods, the nature and organization of work, wages, living conditions and, in a wider sense, research on the adaptation of the aliens to their temporary surroundings. But I have been concerned with other issues as well: who are the employers and since when, to what extent and why do they need additional labourers? These questions are of particular relevance in my fieldwork area because of the presence for a long time, of an extremely large local proletariat which is growing still further. It is noteworthy that those coming to the Surat countryside from other places not only monopolize a large part of the new job opportunities recently created but also oust the existing landless labourers from their traditional employment. Against the process of semi- or complete proletarianization to which the in-coming migrants are exposed in the hinterland we must place the immiserization of the local landless living in the plain.

Labour mobility and immobility are thus two sides of the same coin; both are inherent in the way in which the process of transformation has unfolded itself in rural south Gujarat.

My analysis revolves around the triangular relationship between migrants, local landless, and dominant landowners who are the principal employers.[2] The caste-class nexus obviously plays a prominent role in this configuration. I argue that class oppositions are articulated along caste lines. The old binding of a personal kind between owners of capital and landless workers was a kind of reciprocal relationship imposed from above. This has faded away and has been replaced by a new set of relations which is contractual in nature. It would be decidedly wrong to conclude that exploitation takes place only through the market forces. Jobbers and other middlemen have come to the fore as new manipulators in labour transactions, with the object of extracting docile obedience. At the same time the framework of integration which existed earlier and which made for social coherence along vertical lines has rapidly become obsolete. The growing divergence at both the top and the bottom of the rural society sets clear limits to the caste-for-itself type of social mobilization trying to instill feelings of solidarity on the basis of primordial sentiments.

A new ideology which finds support especially in the dominant rural class also emphasizes the unity of farmers and labourers against their common target, the state, which is said to show no concern for those who bear the actual burden of production but instead cares only for urban interests. The *kisans*, an all-encompassing category meant to embrace both large landowners and the landless, must work together to put an end to the neglect and subordination of 'Bharat', i.e. everything that comes from the people and that belongs to the people—as opposed to 'India'. Sharad Joshi is a prominent exponent of this rural populism. His credo is a model for the notions which Lipton gave more academic respectability several years ago. His book, *Why Poor People Stay Poor: Urban*

[2] I have written a separate fieldwork report about the trouble I had in retaining my credibility under these circumstances. This essay, entitled *Between accumulation and immiserization; the partiality of fieldwork*, will be published separately.

Bias in World Development (1977) has become an authoritative source to which Joshi refers in more polished discussions such as in a closed meeting in Surat, held on the very day that I started writing this introduction. He addresses his own following in a less unequivocal language. Joshi refuses to behave as a politician, and keeps his distance from political parties which compete for his support. He calls himself an activist in a movement giving voice to the protest 'from below'. A short while ago a camp was held in Bardoli under his leadership, to discuss the problems of the rural people. It was decided to set up a committee, consisting of the president of the powerful Farmers' Union in Gujarat and the self-styled leader of an association claiming to represent the largest agricultural labourers' caste in Surat District. The objective of the committee was to bring about 'the emotional integration of farmers and landless' (see the statement in the *Indian Express* of 26 December 1983).

Men like Sharad Joshi show a greater capability for mounting campaigns, although with variable success, than for building a standing organization. The corporatist ideology underlying his strategy does collide directly with the sharp oppositions which are increasingly being revealed between the parties at both ends of the rural system. The doctrine he preaches has an outspoken aggressive tone, and voices above all the longings of the new rural bourgeoisie for recognition and a strengthening of their power base. Yet in the last resort this is only feasible if they succeed in winning over to their side the bottom strata dependent upon them.

In spite of the use of rousing words stressing the need for unity, the leading class is totally unwilling to meet the less well endowed 'sons of the soil' even halfway in their right to exist even when the claims made in this direction are very modest indeed. The broad front envisaged stretches no further than the small farmers who produce for the market and who are inclined to let themselves be encapsulated by the dominant rural class. There is nothing to indicate, however, that the mass of landless labourers and marginal landowners are indeed willing to follow this example and behave as docile clients of their social superiors. Although these subaltern classes together constitute by far the largest proportion of the population in the district, the hegemony of the rural bourgeoisie is so unassailable that they are able to resist every pressure to allow greater freedom of action to those who have not been beneficiaries but victims of the transition to a capitalist mode of production. The reluctance to make concessions, to allow the mass of have-nots some share of the progress being made, means that there is not even the minimal convergence of interests which could provide the basis for a class reconciliation, or at least for a softening of antagonisms. On the contrary, the dynamic I have observed inclines more towards continuing the expulsion of the weak rather than their accommodation.

Is there no softening of this polarization by the state apparatus? The anti-government stance of the rural entrepreneurs should at least suggest this. In the higher echelons especially, the authorities choose to maintain that they are making efforts to bring about a more equal distribution of development costs and benefits. Leaving aside the sincerity of this often proclaimed intention, official interference has certainly not resulted in diminishing the wide disparities. The differentiation accompanying the economic transformation in the Bardoli area is not unintentional and uncontrolled: it is the logical outcome of rural development programmes initiated and directed by various bureaucratic agencies. Official action tends to benefit the owners of capital and conversely, does not only ignore those who are propertyless but also contributes to their subordination in the new social order by giving maximal priority to progressive surplus formation.

The government is obviously extremely wary of imposing regulations for the rural labour. At the same time, however, everything is done to clear away as rapidly as possible all kinds of practices which hinder the free flow of labour, such as debt and other forms of 'out-of-date' servitude. Yet legal measures such as the regulations on dismissal, right to work, health insurance etc. which might provide real protection for the large part of the rural population of India which depends upon income from wage labour, either does not exist or exists only on paper, for example the rulings on minimum wages and working hours, equal pay for men and women and the prohibition of child labour.

It has been rightly pointed out that the expansion in employment does not keep pace with population growth, a discrepancy which has much to do with the development strategy followed. The next step could be a selective population policy aimed at those who contribute least, i.e. the mass of illiterate, unskilled and floating workers whose labour productivity is often abysmally low. Although the fear of being outnumbered by inferior classes—the 'threat from below', which is a major concern of those who have something to lose—has not yet been openly translated into political action, there is reason for anxiety on another score since the state is virtually delivering the weak into the hands of the strong. During my research in the area I have often been struck by the cynical aloofness shown by bureaucrats and politicians of all ranks in confidential conversation. During my present stay in Surat I had a short meeting with the highest authority in Gujarat responsible for the upliftment of the tribal population, which includes the majority of the landless. He was very interested in what I had come to know about the going wage rate for agricultural labourers in Bardoli. When I told him that at this moment (the beginning of 1984) about Rs 5, barely half the obligatory minimum, was being paid, he nodded in confirmation as if this were the general rule. He wondered out loud how it was possible to stay alive and continue working on this amount and said he was puzzled how people were able to endure meekly such an intense degree of exploitation. At the same time he would not hesitate to defuse any labour unrest, or to suppress ruthlessly more active forms of resistance—often in retaliation against violence from the other side—for the sake of restoring 'peace and order'.

To be sure, there are other kinds of bureaucrats as well. He told me, with a hint of malice, about an I.A.S. colleague who had been his batch-mate. This man, who held a similar post in another state of India, did his best to improve the position of the rural poor by setting up camps at which they were told of their rights, by opening evening schools, and by encouraging various forms of self-organization. But due to the complaints lodged by the vested interests in the region, he was summaril re-posted elsewhere. My informant had learnt his lesson from this, he said. If ever the labourers here should insist on meeting him, which, as he conceded, was a rather unlikely occurrence, he would naturally explain their rights to them. More than that he was certainly not prepared to do. Should such examples lead us to assume that the state acts as the instrument of the ruling class in rural India? Although there is indeed at all levels some degree of collusion between those invested with formal authority and those who are actually in charge, I nevertheless do not subscribe to this rather mechanistic view, if only because in my opinion it overestimates the power of the state. A recurrent finding during my research in Surat District has been the high degree of autonomy of the rural bourgeoisie. The state tolerates and shields the mandate of the vested interests rather than enacting the rules of law, seeing to it that these apply to everyone. Authorities from top to bottom show greater negligence in protecting the majority, than in unequivocally promoting the interests of the minority. This minority in turn has to pay a price for the preferential treatment it receives.

It looked at first as though the declaration of the Emergency would lead to a break with the past. The introduction of this authoritarian regime in the mid-1970s was an attempt to give the state greater power over all sectors, segments and levels in society. But by the start of my fieldwork in 1977 I could see that the Emergency, still in force at that time, had not put an end to the hegemony of the rural bourgeoisie in the Bardoli area. The return to 'normal' conditions was justifiably explained as the restoration of civil liberties. Yet the subaltern classes remained deprived of these.

I would like to point out that the 'state of Emergency' in which the bottom strata have always lived continues unabated. Those who control their daily existence decide which rules and regulations will or will not be adhered to. Is it any wonder that the lower classes in society have pinned their hopes on outside support? Positive discrimination, public works and special target-group programmes are some of the means by which the government tries to fulfil the expectations of what have become the major votebanks of the country. Although these institutional forms of patronage have not been very successful in halting the process of polarization, they have nevertheless strengthened the notion of a benevolent state among a people who need to cling to this idea all the more stubbornly because they are defenceless and lack any other form of protection. The servility shown by those at the bottom to those at the top which used to be a characteristic feature of the social order, has completely disappeared. The changed atmosphere is expressed in the bold recklessness and indifference of those with little to lose. To the members of the class which is now dominant in the countryside, and who have often worked their way up in the recent past from a less respectable social origin, this questioning of their claim to social superiority from below, comes as a shock. They try by various means of intimidation to keep a tight rein on the have-nots, even when they are in no position to make any demands. A stream of reports from all over the country indicate the elimination of those suspected of instigating resistance. Law and order agencies invariably back up this repression, but much more remarkable than this is the privatization of violence. It will be difficult to deny that more people fall victim to the rural entrepreneurs or their mercenaries than to the revolutionary splinter groups which have been operating on a small scale in eastern and southern India in recent years. In both cases the destruction of 'class enemies' is at stake, but the entirely different meaning given to this concept explains why action from one side is perceived as an attack on the state's monopoly of violence, and if only for that reason quickly stamped out, while action from the other side is very often not redressed at all.

The prevailing climate in the central plain of south Gujarat is anti-labour, and the social-darwinist mentality of the members of the ruling class in the rural areas provides a fertile soil for an emergent brand of fascism. 'Peasants' interest' has become the social banner around which these sons of the soil rally, although their economic behaviour is that of rural entrepreneurs pure and simple. The accompanying political style has become a recognizable pattern at the regional level while traces of it can even be discerned at the national arena. It is important to establish that the direction of such fascist tendencies moves upwards from below and not the other way round. The reaction of the state to the harsh regime which is currently prevalent close to the grass roots might be a pointer to the kind of development India is likely to see in what remains of the twentieth century.

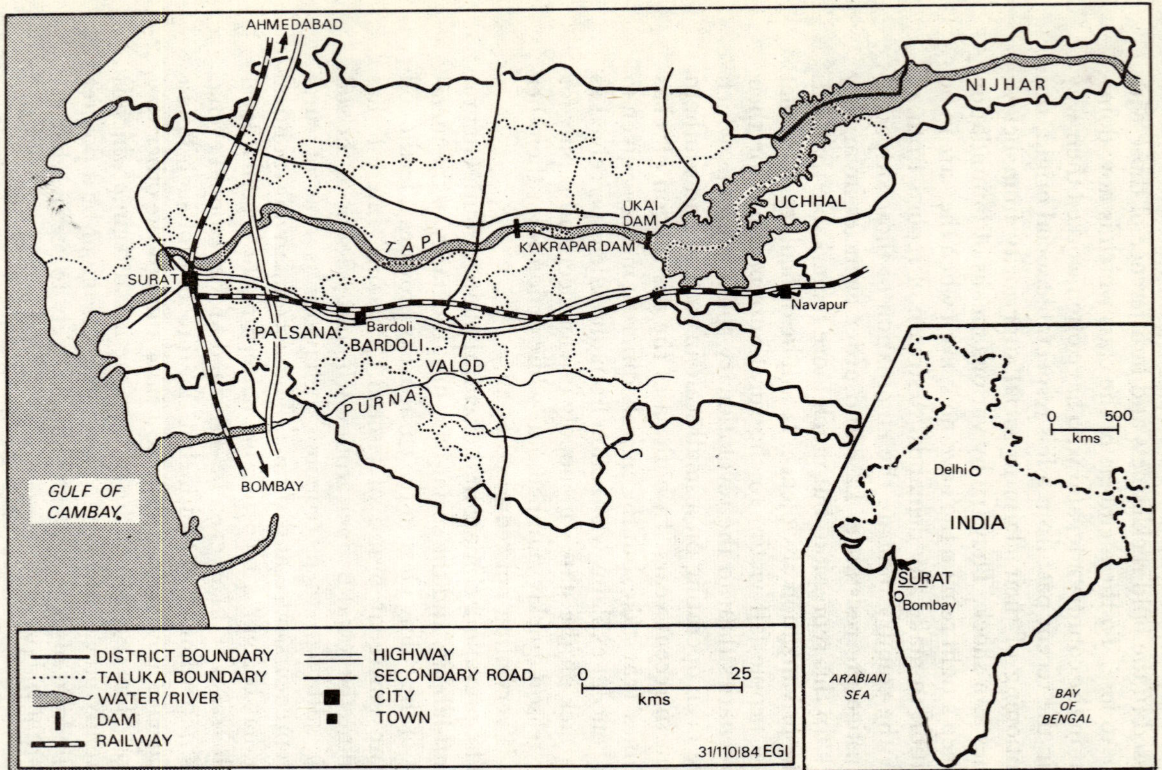

Surat district in south Gujarat

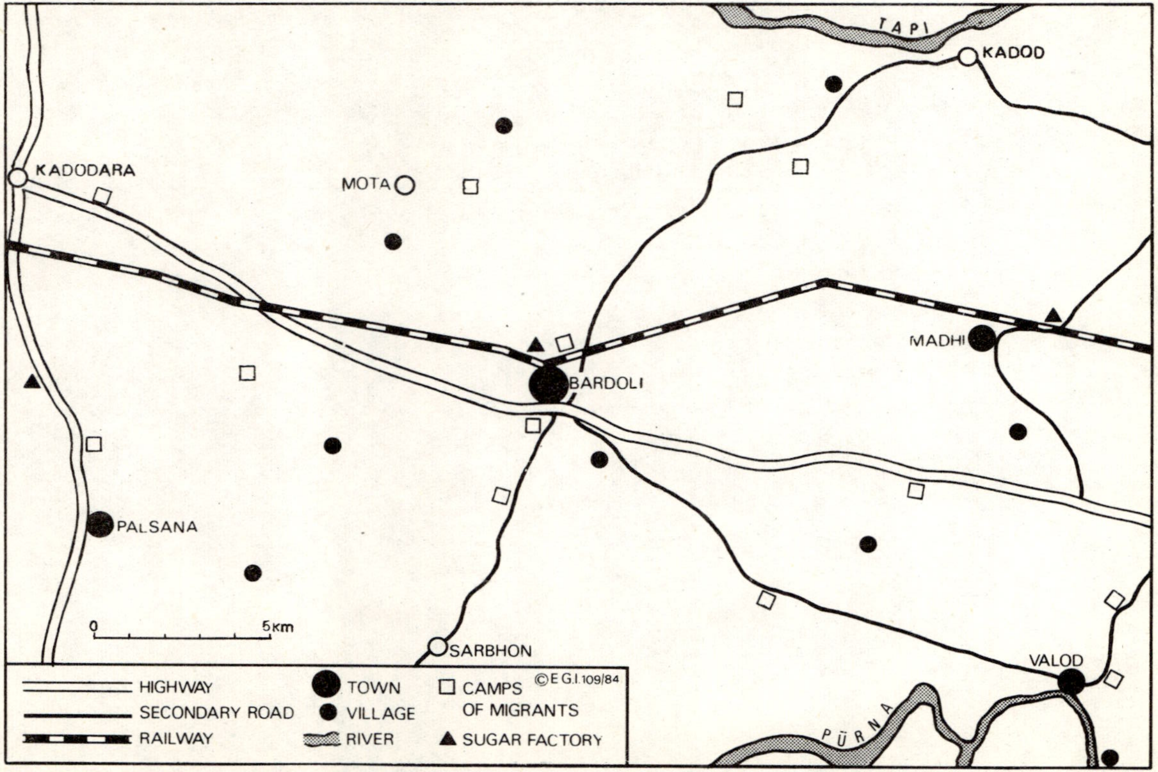

Locations of researched villages and migrant camps

Part I

TRANSITION TO RURAL CAPITALISM

1
THE AREA, ITS GEOGRAPHY AND HISTORY

Land and people

The central plain of south Gujarat is one of the regions in India where the process of modernization has pushed forward most rapidly in recent decades. My research into the impact of this transformation on rural labour relations has been carried out basically in Bardoli and environs, a fertile and densely populated area which is part of Surat District. In its present shape this district is a recent fabrication established in 1964. Some *talukas* were included in the principality of Baroda in colonial times. The incorporation of its territory—scattered around in central and south Gujarat—into Bombay State directly after independence put an end to the political and administrative fragmentation. In 1960, the splitting of Bombay into two new states, Maharashtra and Gujarat, preceded an administrative re-grouping in which the most southerly part of Surat was detached some years later in order to form the new district of Valsad.

Together with this and with Bharuch District lying to the north, Surat forms the southern part of Gujarat State, bordering in the west on the Arabian Sea and in the east on Khandesh in Maharashtra. The district is subdivided into 13 *talukas* (subdistricts) which comprise an area of 7.745 square kilometres, about 4 per cent of the state territory. There are 7 towns, varying greatly in size, and something more than 1,200 villages. Three rather large rivers—the Kim, Mindhola and Tapi, the last of which is far and away the most important—flow from the foothills of the Ghats across the alluvial plain to the sea. The climate in this coastal district is rather warm and humid; in the hot summer months between March and June the temperature rises to above 40 degrees C., but as the season advances the moderating effect of the sea wind is felt. For the same reason the temperature in the winter months (November to end of February) does not drop lower than 20–15°C. The annual precipitation reaches 107 cm. and falls almost exclusively between mid-June and the end of September. Rainfall increases from west to east but displays wide annual and local fluctuations.

As is apparent from the 1981 census, Surat District at that time had nearly two-and-a-half million inhabitants, one of the largest district populations in the state. A strikingly high percentage of the population was settled in towns—nearly 43 per cent, in contrast to less than a third in Gujarat as a whole and barely a quarter in India. In 1981 the district town of the same name had worked itself up to the position of largest-but-one city in the state, with an unparalleled decennial growth percentage of 85 per cent. Meanwhile the number of inhabitants in the conurbation Surat rose to above the million mark. This explosive growth (an average of 5.26 per cent annually between 1961 and 1971) is only a recent phenomenon, since until the mid-twentieth century the urban population was virtually stationary at a level a little above 20 per cent of the total number of inhabitants of south Gujarat (table 1.1).

Table 1.1 *Rural and urban composition of population*

unit of enumeration	population 1981			% of urban to total population		inter-censal change 1971–81 (%)		
	total	rural	urban	1971	1981	total	rural	urban
Surat district	2,491,084	1,426,374	1,064,710	33.7	42.7	39.4	20.4	76.7
Gujarat	33,960,905	23,404,474	10,556,431	28.1	31.1	27.2	21.9	40.8
India	658,140,676	501,952,169	156,188,507	19.9	23.7	20.1	14.3	43.2

Source: *Census of India 1981* Series-5, Gujarat, Provisional Population Totals. Baroda, n.d. *Census of India 1981* Series-1, India, Provisional Population Totals, New Delhi, 1981.

This high degree of urbanization has not prevented the rural population of the district from rising by 20 per cent in recent decades, an increase deviating little from the average for Gujarat.

It seems from this that in spite of urban expansion, pressure on rural sources of existence has still intensified. Demographically Surat District is experiencing a phase of exuberant growth, as we can see from recent growth in population density:

Table 1.2 *Population growth in Surat District 1961–81*

Year	*Population density per km²*		
	Surat District	Gujarat	India
1961	170	105	142
1971	231	136	178
1981	325	174	220

However, these global data need to be disaggregated, since the different parts comprising the district are not all equally well-populated. Ecologically and socio-economically, we can distinguish three zones.

In the west there is a coastal stretch along the Arabian Sea, many kilometres wide. The landscape is boggy in places and bisected by creeks which make the terrain close to the sea difficult to negotiate. The strongly salt-retaining soil allows little vegetation to grow. The population of this bleak milieu consists principally of low castes of fishermen and peasants (Kolis, Machhis, Kharvas and Muslims) living together in rather small villages situated far apart from each other. Perhaps more important than the yield of the pitifully scanty natural local resources are earnings from seafaring and smuggling. There is a large-scale illegal transit trade in all kinds of luxury consumption goods coming from the Gulf States to the interior. Contact with the outside world is thus more intensive than the marginal situation and inadequate communications—few roads and bus services—would lead one to expect. Nevertheless this remains a backward area, able to support only a scanty population.

The same applies, although in a completely different way, to the eastern part of the district which extends to the outliers of the Ghats marking the transition to the Deccan plateau, on the border with Maharashtra. Coming away from the central plain, soil fertility gradually decreases. Here also we find a landscape deeply scored by river beds and creeks becoming progressively more irregular. The process of soil erosion has been exacerbated by the nature of the terrain, largely stripped of vegetation. Although some remnants of 'jungle' still persist in the plain, very little has survived of the forests which clothed this hinterland until far into the previous century. Under the colonial regime the hinterland region was gradually opened up, a process which was accompanied by the permanent settlement of the indigenous tribal population which had previously trekked around within a large territory as shifting cultivators. The process of sedentarization accelerated with the imposition of monetary taxes based on cadastral surveys from the middle of the nineteenth century. Intruders from the plain have played an important role in this transition, a factor I shall expand upon in chapter 6. The settlements in this tribal zone consist of loose complexes of scattered living areas (*falias*) and huts, clearly different from the more concentrated village settlements customary in the plain.

The various tribal groupings, among which the Vasavas, Gamits and Chaudharis are the most important, have in the recent past increasingly adopted a caste character while retaining their earlier identity. The Scheduled Tribes, the name under which they are registered in the census reports, comprise 70 per cent of the total population in this zone, even 90 per cent in the most easterly-lying *talukas*. Cultivation of land in the hinterland is very extensive which is as much the result of inadequate cultivation as of a combination of low soil fertility and irregular rainfall. Productivity is low and in the virtual absence of employment outside agriculture this means that a large amount of land per head is necessary in order to make ends meet. What applies to the eastern part of Surat District also applies to the area on the northern bank of the Tapi river. There also an overwhelmingly tribal population leads a dreary existence as rather primitive cultivators in an unfavourable natural environment. Taken together these *talukas* occupy nearly two-thirds of the total land surface but they provide a living for barely 40 per cent of the district population. In the most peripherally situated subdistricts, population density in 1971 did not amount to more than 80 people per square kilometre.

Flanked by two marginal portions—a rather small coastal zone in the west and the thinly populated, barely productive tribal hinterland in the east—there can be no shadow of a doubt that the central plain to the south of the Tapi forms the backbone of Surat District. The fertile clay soil—the famed *kali jamin* (black soil)—which dominates the landscape, yields by far the greater part of agrarian production in south Gujarat. Even richer and moreover looser in texture is the loamy *gorat* soil which occurs in smaller concentrations and is particularly suited to the cultivation of high-value garden crops. The intensive tillage goes together with more and larger villages resulting in a population density which can rise locally to 350 per square kilometre or even higher.

Caste composition in this zone is more complex, an indication of further hardening of the division of labour and of social inequality. We also find the most important urban nuclei here. Next to the main district city already mentioned, Bardoli has also gone through a tempestuous development, although at a much lower level. With a population of not quite 10,000, this was an urban centre of very modest extent in 1951. After a population increase of 55 per cent in 1961–71 and another 45 per cent in the decade after that—a tempo of growth far above the average in Gujarat and India for localities of this size—this *taluka* town counted over 30,000 inhabitants in the last census year. Everything indicates that this expansion will continue to be maintained in the near future.

Infrastructural development has remained to a large extent limited to the central zone. This applies as much to the irrigation system—to which I shall return in more detail—as to the network of roads. Notwithstanding improved construction in recent years, road capacity is clearly insufficient for the increased economic production. In 1975 nearly 3,400 lorries were registered in the district, amounting to a doubling in ten years, and the increase since then has been even more rapid. The national Bombay–Ahmedabad highway running through the western part of the plain is vital to commodity transport and bus services over a longer distance. Parallel to this runs the railway joining Surat to Bombay and Ahmedabad/Delhi via Baroda. The link with these major market outlets in the south and north, completed in the 1860s, ushered in the economic upswing of the city.

Though once an international port on the river Tapi, Surat had lost this function by the first half of the nineteenth century; it has, however, since independence, again become an important centre of growth in western India. In other stations along the great north/south railway line a number of industrial areas came into being on government initiative, particularly after the founding of Gujarat State, which together provided space for several thousand larger and smaller enterprises in the textile, metal and chemical sector. Towards the east, along the road and railway from Surat to Bardoli constructed just before the turn of the century and from there to the rich Khandesh plain in Maharashtra, a second axis of industrialization has recently begun to emerge, albeit on a modest scale. As a result of this development the proportion of the working population outside agriculture leapt from 31 per cent in 1961 to 40 per cent in 1971 and 45 per cent in 1981.

My fieldwork was located in Bardoli and both the bordering *talukas*, Palsana and Valod in the southern river basin. This region was eminently suited to a study into the course of the agrarian dynamic and the consequences of this for relations between landowners and agricultural labourers. The characteristics of the plain, described earlier—good agricultural land, intensive cultivation, high population density, varied caste composition and the process of industrialization pressing forward along the principal lines of communication and their junctions—apply to a still greater extent to the rural heart of Surat District locally known as Bardoli Vibagh. This vaguely defined area, not forming any administrative unit and living only in the consciousness of the dominant landowners, comprises of parts of 4 *talukas*; in addition to the three mentioned earlier there is also Kamrej, not included in my field work, however. Table 1.2 reproduces demographic growth in my research area over a longer period.

Earlier fluctuations must be ascribed to a periodic high mortality (famine and plague at around the turn of the century, the influenza epidemic in 1917) and under-registration as part of

Table 1.3 *Population growth in Bardoli Vibagh, Surat District*

year	Bardoli	Valod	Palsana
1891	57,057	26,897	21,599
1901	56,907	23,751	21,647
1911	59,079	27,270	20,665
1921	61,292	26,617	26,188
1931	48,646	24,934	30,011
1941	70,595	31,629	31,162
1951	78,283	36,179	35,374
1961	90,608	42,828	41,807
1971	120,120	51,999	53,170
1981	155,274	66,281	75,875

the resistance to the colonial government in 1931. After independence there was an obvious acceleration in the tempo of growth. In the first report of the settlement survey of 1865 attention was already focussed on the high population density in parts of Bardoli Taluka—then only barely exceeded in Gujarat[1] —but this figure has been rising continually since then. In 1865 Bardoli (of which Valod also formed a part at that time) had 104 inhabitants per square kilometre (Bardoli SR 1865, para 21). A century later, in 1971, the 3 *talukas* together had 350 inhabitants per square kilometre. By leaving Bardoli town out of this calculation as the only urban centre, we can establish the rural population density, which still amounts to more than 300 inhabitants per square kilometre. While the non-agrarian population increased from 20 per cent to 23 per cent in 1961–71, the pressure on agrarian resources had also intensified due to the high rate of demographic growth.

[1] 'The late Sarbhon Taluka (note: which had become part of Bardoli Taluka) consisted of 33 Government villages comprising 38.25 square miles, or 24.515 statute acres. It contains a population of 15, 113 or so which is 398 to the square mile. This is 27 to the square mile more than Matar, the most densely populated district yet settled in Gujarat by this department. As the density of the population has so much to do with the revenue-paying capabilities of an agricultural district, and consequently one of the most important considerations in fixing maximal rates, I may remark that comparing Sarbhon with European agricultural countries the density of the population is most remarkable' (Bardoli SR. 1865, para 18).

The 3 *talukas* together occupy 12 per cent of the land surface of the district but contain 19 per cent of the district's rural population. The upper layer forms the prosperous farmer segment, who for the most part were members of the higher castes. The larger landowners among them in particular, mounted an action against the raising of the land taxes by the colonial government at the end of the 1920s, during which the name of Bardoli became known throughout the country. Referring to famed *satyagraha* of 1928 in the 1962 edition of the District Gazetteer it is proudly stated, albeit in the administrative language of the *Raj*—that: '. . . The people of Bardoli village and *taluka* are a splendid lot of citizens' (*Surat District Gazetteer* 1962: 930). This finding refers above all to the Kanbi Patidars, the dominant farmer caste in Bardoli Vibagh, who formed the vanguard for the transformation to a capitalist mode of production experienced by the countryside in the recent past. The underside of the social hierarchy consists of tribal castes—principally landless Halpatis and to a much lesser extent Gamits and Chaudharis—who comprise a little over half the total population in the 3 *talukas*.

It is striking that their proportion follows a steadily rising line. A great variety of artisan and service castes occupy the middle social level and fulfill all kinds of intermediary functions within the economic life. Since the 1931 census, statistics of the caste composition of the population have no longer been kept. Nevertheless, in order to give a fairly recent picture of social cleavages based on this principle and of the extremely uneven local concentrations into which the castes fall, I have adopted a table from a study based on agricultural-economic research into the western part of Surat District between 1967 and 1972, the area within which Bardoli Vibagh also lies. The caste configuration, as it appears in table 1.3 seems to be a good reflection of the social structure in my field work area.

Implementation of infrastructural provisions has enlarged horizons, figuratively as well as literally, for the population of the plain. Bardoli Vibagh is characterized by a great liveliness and mobility, by such intensive traffic between city and the countryside that every form of local insularity appears to have broken down. This is illustrated by comparing the frequency of bus services in this region in the mid-1970s with the restricted range of public transport in 3 *talukas* situated in the tribal

Table 1.4 *Percentage distribution of population by caste in ten villages in Surat District, 1971–2*

Name of village	Taluka	Patidar	Koli	Muslim	Rajput	Backward or Tribal	Harijan	Others	total number of inhabitants census 1971
Vanesa	Bardoli	25.06	2.70	—	0.27	61.73	2.88	6.46	2127
Umbhel	Palsana	26.25	1.72	—	—	57.64	6.20	8.19	2689
Bhamaiya	Bardoli	42.85	—	—	—	51.63	2.61	2.91	1134
Sania Hemad	Chorasi	15.52	0.28	0.56	12.42	54.30	6.21	10.71	1971
Vav	Kamrej	18.25	13.22	3.65	—	38.99	7.51	18.38	2395
Sania Kande	Chorasi	14.61	6.24	—	31.32	45.17	0.54	2.12	742
Un	Chorasi	—	18.48	38.08	6.37	20.67	15.40	1.05	1510
Masma	Chorasi	—	50.55	—	2.74	25.99	19.33	1.39	1396
Erthan	Olpad	—	43.98	—	5.74	32.03	11.95	6.30	1025
Kapura	Olpad	12.58	—	—	—	79.58	0.46	7.38	1726
Total		16.76	10.70	3.5	3.78	50.69	6.71	7.84	1671.5

Source: M. B. Desai, *Changing farm production and organization in developing agriculture.* Baroda n.d. pp. 35 and 37.

Table 1.5 *Regional distribution of bus services*

Taluka	area in sq. km.	population	total no. villages	bus connection whole year round	buses in dry season	no buses
Bardoli Palsana Valod	1,760	329,000	171	72	87	12
Songadh Ucchal Nizar	2,250	252,000	278	37	118	123

Source: compiled from G. Shah, *Socio-economic condition of Chodhras; a restudy*. Surat 1977.

hinterland (table 1.4). While buses in the plain ran to 42 per cent of the villages all year round and only 8 per cent of the villages were inaccessible, these percentages were respectively 13 per cent and 44 per cent in the tribal hinterland. I shall return to this contrast within the region at the end of this chapter.

The transition to a capitalist agricultural mode of production in the central plain and the development of the modern infrastructure connected with it, have been rooted in processes of change which go back far into the past and which have only very recently made their full impact felt. Nevertheless, it is possible to split up this long transformation into different phases indicated by some salient points of acceleration. The last of these lie in the recent past when a number of innovations began to appear—having radical consequences for the natural and social environment. As I myself have been able to confirm, the landscape of Bardoli and environs underwent a remarkable change. In 1963 I spent one month in a village in Valod Taluka verifying the outcome of my just completed field work in the present-day Valsad District in south Gujarat (Breman 1974, chapter 10).

When I arrived in the area shortly before the rainy season, the fields lay dry and deserted, the dusty roads carrying little traffic. From the figures for 1958–9, the only ones available to me at that moment, it appeared that the amount of irrigated land in the 3 *talukas* taken together covered a bare 4.5 per cent of the cultivated area. In other words agriculture was almost entirely dependent on rainfall. The agricultural calendar had a rather simple rhythm dictated by the division into a *kharif* season (June–October) and a *rabi* season (November–March). At the end of these came the harvesting of monsoon and winter crops, in turn. The crop cycle was completed by the beginning of the hot season and there followed a period in which the land lay fallow until the first rains. On returning to Bardoli Vibagh fifteen years later I encountered a completely different situation—one agreeing with the image of the kind of modern rural milieu that I have described as being typical for the central plain.

Before discussing this dynamic of the last two decades I would first like to go into the historical background in order to reach a good understanding of it. Fieldwork research—upon which my study is essentially based—easily leads to an over-emphasis on acute processes of change. It suggests a break with the past which in reality has not occurred in such an abrupt way. Still less has the volte-face been so complete that it justifies the use of sharply contrasting concepts in order to typify past and present. For instance, by discussing the situation as it is now in terms of dynamism and modernity there is probably a converse inclination to depict the past—often coinciding with the period just preceding the fieldwork—as traditional and static. Such a use of words evokes the image of a rural order marked by production for the market and by agricultural entrepreneurs where only a short time before, a stagnant agriculture and peasants producing only for their subsistence had prevailed. This last image in particular is an extremely misleading representation of affairs which can easily be refuted with the simple example that, in the region to which I first came in 1963 and which I characterized retrospectively as lacking in dynamism, the cultivation of cotton had already been the principal source of cash income for nearly a hundred years. In order to avoid being satisfied with a dichotomy old/new or traditional/modern, and to avoid the error of making this watershed coincide with the beginning of my fieldwork, it is necessary to place this rural transformation in a longer time perspective.

The central plain in historical perspective

The problem that immediately arises is the rather limited source material available in published form concerning the countryside of Surat District before the beginning of the nineteenth century. This contrasts with the many studies devoted to the history of the city and its significance as an internationally renowned trade centre as far back as the early and even precolonial period. These studies do report in detail on the long-distance movements of commodities from this principal port of the Moghul empire, but the question of how far the immediate neighbourhood was also involved is seldom systematically discussed. This is undoubtedly unjust, if only for the fact that the inhabitants of this city—strikingly big for its time—depended on the surrounding countryside for their food provisions. The manufacture of industrial products (especially textiles) for export was of a decentralized kind, with work being put out to artisan castes spread over a large area. In addition the most important through-route from Surat to the north of the country ran via Bardoli and west Khandesh. In other ways the town-country contact could not have been very intensive because of the virtual absence of roads. There was to be little or no improvement in this situation until the end of the nineteenth century. The Collector of Surat wrote in a letter in 1816 that:

> At present there is nowhere a road to be found at the distance of a mile from any principal town (Choksey 1962: 37).

Fourteen years later this complaint was repeated:

> 'There is perhaps no territory subject to the Bombay Presidency which suffers so much from want of roads as the Surat district since a line of about 100 miles in length, . . . consists of a deep, muddy soil utterly impassable by the usual conveyances of the country . . . and even by men on foot'—so the Government Secretary came to read in 1830 (Choksey 1962: 237, fn. 1).

Surat *athavisi*—the twenty-eight administrative circles into which this area was divided at the beginning of the eighteenth century—lay on the periphery of the Moghul empire and was ruled by a governor, in a rather remote way, from the city. The most important principle of government policy was the system of tax farming by which control over the peasant population was left to landed proprietors (*desais*) who settled in the larger villages and smaller market places. Sarbhon, lying to the south of Bardoli, was such a bulwark of Anavil Desais, the principal caste of landowners, and towards the end of the eighteenth century was described as being '. . . well cultivated and tolerably well peopled . . .' (Forrest 1887: 436). The same report mentioned that in this region grain (rice and millet) as well as pulses were the chief crops. However, as a consequence of continual Maratha incursions, a proportion of the inhabitants emigrated to other places. Further, in the immediate vicinity of Bardoli the land remained untilled for the same reason, and during these military expeditions many of the better houses were destroyed. Finally, according to this source little or no cultivation took place in Valod.

The turbulence mentioned resulted from the rapid fluctuations in the course of the power struggle between the Marathas, always pressing forward, and the waning power of the Moghuls in this region, in particular the power of their rather independently operating local representative in Surat. The latter was already under pressure in 1735 to surrender the levying of tribute in the district to the Marathas, who retained the system of tax farming; this spelled the end of direct control from Surat over the surrounding countryside. Increasingly it was the English who revealed themselves as the real power holders in the city, ultimately taking over formal government in 1800. With the support of the English, a vassal of the Peshwa of Poona had meanwhile succeeded in making himself independent, and at the treaty of Bassein two years later divided with them the conquered territory in south Gujarat. In the Surat District of that time Palsana, among others, formed part of the newly established principality of Baroda, which had it main basis in central Gujarat. The largest part of the hinterland of Surat—including Bardoli and Valod, originally welded into one *taluka*—passed entirely into English hands. Only after the attainment of national independence would a united and standardized administration come to exist after the inclusion of the territorially very fragmented Baroda principality.

Local lords and roving bands laid heavy impositions on the population exploiting the power vacuum in rural south Gujarat which lasted from the second half of the seventeenth century to the beginning of the nineteenth century. The people tried as far as possible to resist the pressure to hand over the maximum, and when this failed, moved away, temporarily or permanently. This explains why already, every scrap of land close to the city was under cultivation[2] while there was hardly any regular agriculture going on away from this safeguarded territory. The reports that change came to this desolate situation very rapidly after the Pax Britannica came into force, were entirely and always in accordance with the image of colonial rule. With reference to Bardoli, the Collector of Surat commented in 1819 that: 'It is fully cultivated and there are so many inhabitants that they cannot all find employment in Bardolee but engage themselves in cultivating ground in the neighbouring districts' (Collector Morison, Report 15-9-1819 and 20-9-1820: 135).

To be sure, he reported that only twenty-seven out of the sixty-two villages in Valod were inhabited—there were thick forests and tigers close by—but in contrast to this in Sarbhon (at a distance of about 25 km from here) cotton and sugar as well as grain were grown. There were therefore great variations within the region. It was obvious that optimism over a speedy recovery had been premature from the much more critical note struck by his successor in 1829–30 concerning the great turnover in population in reaction to levies fixed at too high a rate (Choksey 1962: 79–80). The farming-out of taxes was rapidly abolished in English territory in 1829[3] but the gradual introduction of the *ryatvari* system in the first half of the nineteenth century in itself brought no improvement in the position of the peasantry. Because of the high assessment imposed, the opening up or taking back into use of abandoned land certainly pro-

[2] '. . . scarcely a piece of uncultivated land is to be seen . . .', so the Dutch traveller Stavorinus described the landscape in the close neighbourhood of Surat in 1772 (Surat District Gazetteer 1962: 175, fn. 3).

[3] Bates cites sources from which it would appear that in south Gujarat *desais* (tax farmers) derived from *patels*, the original village heads (Bates 1981: 776–777 fn. 26). I am personally much more inclined to agree with A. Rogers, who reported at the end of the previous century: 'It seems doubtful whether in the villages of which the Desais settled for the revenue, there were ever any Patels (headmen) distinct from them' (Rogers 1892: 171). About the previous introduction of the *ryatvari* system in the Surat District see Rasitoy 1974: 33–4.

duced no immediate benefits. In some years the government could only forestall large-scale decampment to the neighbouring territory of Baroda principality by drastically reducing or even completely waiving the landtax. Depending on conditions, the trek could indeed even occur in the opposite direction.

It was labour, not land, that was in scarce supply in this period. 'Before 1856, the agricultural population of the State was comparatively small and the land available for cultivation was abundant' (*Report Baroda Economic Development Committee* 1920: 56).

Village autonomy, subsistence agriculture and, apart from the imposition of taxes, lack of state interference: in these words the source just cited reports on the situation in the countryside during the first half of the nineteenth century. Bardoli formed no exception to this characterization. The report of the first settlement survey dating from 1865 spoke of bad years for agriculture between 1843 and 1859. The description of the *taluka* as '. . . beautiful (and) wooded . . .' (Bardoli SR 1865, para 6) was undoubtedly connected with the economic recession in the previous period.

When I venture, as a non-historian, to summarize the development of the south Gujarat plain up to the mid-nineteenth century, the picture I derive from the limited source material I have consulted is that of a frontier territory maintaining itself over several centuries, made up by a complex of peasants with landed proprietors in their immediate neighbourhood. Some areas with dense tillage and high population pressure developed where crops such as cotton and sugar were already being produced for far-off markets. These were enclaves in an otherwise empty and uncleared region. The total area of cultivated land was moreover subject to all kinds of changes, chiefly political, on the regional level. It would be wrong to think that a permanent end to this long cycle of expansion and contraction came with the appearance of British government on the stage. In contrast to the information, for example, that between 1839 and 1866 the planted area in Bardoli increased by 45 per cent from 61,564 to 89,188 acres (Choksey 1962: 148, fn. 2), there is the statement from a somewhat later period that 'During the six years from 1870 to 1876 prices again fell, the profits of the cultivators were much reduced and a considerable area of land, once under cultivation, was abandoned' (Surat District Gazetteer 1962: 189).

It was at about this time that market mechanisms, more than shifts in political power, began to determine the fluctuations in the agrarian economy. Just before the end of the nineteenth century the central plain of Surat District had grown into one of the foremost cotton producing areas in western India. The crop had already appeared in the region much earlier, but took a rather small share in the textile industry for which Gujarat was well known long before the colonial times. Earlier on, the focal point of cultivation had lain more to the north (Choksey 1962: 127, fn. 1). In order to improve the quality of this crop the colonial government had already set up various experimental stations in the 1820s, but the experiments in Surat remained unsuccessful. After this hesitant beginning there was a considerable increase only in the second half of the last century, with particular acceleration during the American Civil War years (1861–5), when the most important source of the raw material for the English textile industry temporarily became inaccessible. To be sure, a recession followed immediately after this as colonial production was no match for the renewed American competition. But in spite of this, cotton remained the most important cash crop in Surat District.

The area planted with cotton continued to increase with the growth of a new and major outlet in East-Asia. After a rise of about 17 per cent at the beginning of the 1870s, a quarter of the total cultivable land of this region was planted with cotton, according to the revised settlement survey of Bardoli in 1895 (Bardoli RSR 1895: para 16)—much less than the two-thirds occupied at that moment by food crops, but still a clear indication of the growing importance of market production.

By bringing an increasing amount of land under cultivation it was possible to prevent the increase in commercial farming from affecting the production of foodstuffs, at least initially. Until the end of the nineteenth century not only was there a rapid growth in cotton cultivation, but there was also a considerable rise in the area under grain, particularly millet (*jovar*) grown on the dry *jarayat* land. Bardoli experienced a truly spectacular development in which the cultivated surface was tripled between 1840 and 1920 (Charlesworth 1980: 270).

According to some sources this expansion in the first decades of the twentieth century continued unabated and was even faster than demographic growth. Thus Charlesworth points out that in Surat District the cultivated area rose from 151,000 acres in 1914–15 to 876,000 acres in 1924–5 (Charlesworth 1977: 124 and appendix 1: 134–5). In contrast to this author who uses these figures as evidence of little pressure of population on available resources at the beginning of the twentieth century, I think that by this time cultivable land in the central plain around Bardoli had already become a scarce commodity. Insofar as one could still talk of an extension of the area since then, this remained to a large extent restricted to the less accessible areas in the hinterland. For instance the report of the revised settlement survey appearing in 1911 expressly stated about Palsana Taluka that after the last small amount of land had been taken into use, all reclaimable land had been exhausted since 1892–3 (Palsana RSR 1911: 3–4) and there is similar information for the other *talukas* of Bardoli Vibagh (Bardoli RSR 1895, para 22 and 63; Kamrej RSR 1910: 4 and Mahuva RSR 1916: 3). From that time on, the first period in which agriculture stood at a relatively high level, cotton became such a monoculture that its cultivation was extended at the cost of food crop production. The cultivation of millets, staple food for the majority of the population, remained important, but was shifted to less fertile areas in the hinterland of Surat District (Census of India 1921, XVII: 39). In 1914–15 cotton occupied nearly 43 per cent of the cultivated area in Surat District (Charlesworth 1977: 127). The farmers experienced a particularly good period in the First World War, with cotton prices climbing steeply as a result of the Japanese breakthrough to foreign markets for textile manufactures, for which India provided the raw material (Charlesworth 1977: 120). Attempts by the colonial government to attach a premium to grain production had little or no effect (Report Baroda Economic Development Committee: 56). The rapporteurs of an investigation committee remarked about Bardoli in this period that: 'More and more land was put under cotton, with very little regard to the proper proportion of food, grains and fodder, to the need for rotation, or even the suitability of the soil' (Broomfield and Maxwell 1929: 15).

At the beginning of the 1920s the area planted with cotton

in Bardoli was more than double the area under millet. In order to cover the shortfall, grain had to be imported from elsewhere (Bardoli RSR 1925, para 11). In order to illustrate the difficulties which were to appear shortly after the second half of this century, we find in table 1.6 a survey of the cropping pattern in Bardoli *taluka* between 1919–20 and 1923–4.

Table 1.6 *Cropping pattern of Bardoli and Valod Talukas 1919–24 (average of five years)*

crop	percentage distribution of
paddy	13.75
wheat	0.83
jowar	13.57
pulses	9.32
sugarcane	0.05
cotton	30.06
groundnut	0.05
grass	26.69
other	5.68

Source: Bardoli RSR 1925, appendix B.

In determining the trend towards commercialization in agriculture, the previous division always made between non-food and food crops rising from 28:72 to 45:54 in Gujarat between 1891 and 1938 (Choksey 1962: 88) is only a very inadequate yardstick. In Surat District the area under cotton diminished during the Second World War when the government launched the 'Grow More Food' campaign. Yet the larger part of total agrarian production did not remain behind any more in the villages. After the abolition of planting restrictions, with the independence of the country, cotton cultivation was restored at the beginning of the 1950s to more or less the pre-war level. The commercialization of agriculture, in which the relatively advanced Surat District took a lead, extended to the harvesting of food grains, a growing share of which came directly to the market in the course of the first half of the twentieth century.

Production of cash crops tells us very little about the manner in which sales were regulated. Until the late colonial period the contact between the peasantry and the market was scarcely a straightforward one. Baniyas and Parsis, operating from the larger population centres in the subdistricts, commandeered the greater part of the agricultural yield and had often secured this well in advance of harvest time. The farmers did not themselves bring the cotton to the market but sold this crop in the village to local purchasers or peripatetic merchants. Even at the beginning of the 1930s this remained the common practice. Street market transactions conducted by the producers themselves constituted less than a quarter of the total volume (Dantwala 1937: 37; Choksey 1962: 144).

> The local merchants were not content with buying up the product but rapidly took over the first processing, the ginning and pressing of the newly picked cotton in small seasonal enterprises which were set up in the market place spread over the district. It is interesting that the *dalals* (the purchasers and intermediaries) originally worked on their own account but in the course of time lost their independence, becoming sub-ordinated to trading houses and factories in Bombay and Ahmedabad, or even becoming commission agents for them. The local merchant, who is essentially a cotton trader and therefore a middleman, purchases only 25 per cent of the total arrival of seed cotton in a season, while the remaining 75 per cent is purchased either by the agents of the Bombay mills or those of foreign companies,

as stated by Dantwala in an account of his investigation during the years of crisis (Dantwala 1937: 32).

From a survey included in this study it appears that no less than 90 per cent of cotton production in Valod fell under the direct control of external or even foreign interests.

The farming population had little room for manoeuvre. The manner in which market mechanisms asserted their influence could not be disassociated from the operations of the colonial state, and this official intervention was in no way directed towards the furtherance of a greater freedom of trade. Significant in this respect was the decree promulgated by the provincial government of Bombay putting an end to the cultivation of an undesirable variety of cotton.

In 1935 the Bombay Legislative Council passed the Cotton Control Act prohibiting the growing and handling of Goghari cotton in the Surat zone. The act empowers authorised officers to enter any land or place in a controlled area, in which cultivation or mixing of Goghari cotton is suspected, and to uproot or seize such cotton. A penalty of Rs 25 for cultivation and of Rs 500 for trading in or mixing such cotton is levied (Dantwala 1937: 48).

The commercialization of agriculture proceeded in such a way that the producers were fettered rather than emancipated by this process. Only in the last phase of colonial rule did any change begin to appear in this situation, finding expression in attempts to obtain a more prominent role in the sale of the cotton yield. When a fall in prices occurred shortly after the close of the First World War, farmers in several villages in the central plain reacted by joining forces and selling their harvest collectively. The local co-operative which emerged from this initiative in 1921 was the first of its kind to be registered in Gujarat. More followed quite rapidly, although attended by many ups and downs. In 1926 came the formation of a federation which three years later acquired its own office in Surat. Of the twenty-six cotton co-operatives in Gujarat in 1936, sixteen were established in Surat District. Several of them subsequently switched to the primary processing of raw material. The first co-operative ginning and pressing factory began work in 1927 and by the mid-1930s there were already four in operation (Dantwala 1937: 27–83; Choksey 1962: 144–5). Presented in this way the development of the co-operative movement looks rather imposing but there was still no question of a real breakthrough. The economic climate in these years of Depression was too unfavourable, and moreover the competition from private trade formed too great an obstacle.

I would characterize relations of production in the south Gujarat countryside in the last phase of the colonial state in the following way: participation in the market by the mass of farmer-producers was more passive than active. They were cut off from it by a commercial capitalism which to a large extent had obtained a hold over agrarian property but which did not derive from it in a social sense. Another aspect of this was the rather low level of institutional development. In spite of increasing market production, the organizational and technical infrastructure still made little headway. Provisions for governmental administration, education and health care (insofar as these existed) continued to be concentrated in the small and relatively stationary urban centres, and the modern communications structure—posts and telegraphs and telephone connections as well as the electricity grid—remained extremely thinly spread over the district. After the turn of the century some bigger roads were indeed laid, forming links with the principal towns of the most important subdistricts, but the virtual absence of local supply roads meant that most villages were difficult to reach as well as to leave.

The members of an investigatory commission which toured the *taluka* for three months at the end of the 1920s were severely critical in their judgement of the situation.

> Not one of the old main roads, not even the road through Sarbhon to Navsari, can properly be described as *good.* There are fair stretches of them. There are also numerous patches where, if the roads were any worse than they are, they would not deserve the name of roads at all. That they are good enough for bullock carts and just passable for motorcars is about all that can be said of them. As for the by-roads and tracks between villages, it is hardly possible that they have improved much since in any worse condition they would not be usable, even by bullock carts (Broomfield and Maxwell 1929: 9).

Conditions remained exactly the same at the end of colonial rule. According to Choksey, 83 per cent of the villages in Surat District had no access roads and the black soil tract was barely passable even in the dry season (Choksey 1962: 241).

Although all cultivable land in the central plain of south Gujarat had been taken into use by the end of the last century, it was the middle of the twentieth century before this countryside really began to be opened up. After a few decades, more than half of the total land area (52 per cent) of the district was under cultivation, a percentage which was considerably higher in Bardoli Vibagh (table 1.7).

Uneven development

The agrarian dynamic and industry which are nowadays characteristic for the region around Bardoli, have brought

Table 1.7 *Cultivated and uncultivated area in Surat District 1953–4*

	total area		cultivated		uncultivated	
	ha	%	ha	%	ha	%
Bardoli	37,916	100	32,906	87	5,010	13
Palsana	20,089	100	17,981	90	2,108	10
Valod	20,228	100	17,942	89	2,286	11
Surat District*	587,112	100	411,279	70	175,833	30

* Uchhal and Nizar Talukas not yet included in Gujarat.
Source: Surat District Gazetteer 1962: 324.

progress and prosperity. Formulated in this way, we have here a success story answering to the rosiest image the green revolution can evoke. It does not take much effort to recognize a mini-Punjab in the area of my fieldwork.

Furthermore the development is strikingly visible; touring through this region, the signs of modernity obtrude inescapably on one's notice. A busy traffic dominates the roads; fully laden lorries and tractors with trailers bringing agricultural produce to the collection points for transport or processing, trains of carts carrying sugar to the factories, crowded and frequent buses which have made both countryside and city more accessible, and finally the collection of cycles, scooters, engines and private cars which emphasize the mobility permitted by modern communications. The backdrop to this lively scene is the intensively cultivated fields and the water, implements and field labour in evidence there nearly the whole year round.

The main *taluka* towns, focal points within the growing stream of goods and services, have retained and strengthened their function as centres of power and administration. They are meeting places for the agrarian entrepreneurs who come here to regulate their affairs in the government offices and other institutions established here. This applies especially to Bardoli, which in recent years has become the fastest growing place in the heartland of Surat District. The rather drowsy little town I came to know on my first visit at the beginning of the 1960s, no longer exists. Along the busy main road leading to the station many new buildings have arisen, containing offices, eating houses and shops (with display windows!). The leading residents such as doctors, advocates, bank managers and teachers, vanguard of the modern way of life, no longer practice their professions exclusively in the main *taluka* towns, but also operate in the larger villages. This is part and parcel of the way in which the countryside is being equipped with institutional provisions. For instance, further education has been greatly extended and for most pupils the secondary schools are more easily accessible either by walking or cycling. At the beginning of 1974, 80 per cent of the villages in Bardoli and Palsana and 45 per cent of those in Valod—the last *taluka* forming the transition to the tribal hinterland—were connected to the electricity grid. Water towers visible in the landscape mark the villages which have their own piped water system. Housing, with big bungalows, often with more than one storey and provided with all kinds of comforts, strikes one as being especially modern in the village centres. An increasing number and variety of daily necessities are obtainable in the village shops and the quality of this assortment has also improved.

In all this one must keep it well in mind that progress has been spatially and socially circumscribed, being to a large extent confined to the upper stratum of the population living in the central plain.[4]

The strong contrast with the bordering area of dry agriculture—a contrast that has increased in intensity—is very striking; as Shah has put it in a recent study:

> . . . one witnesses prosperity, green fields and busy factories. Well-dressed people, cars and tractors, multi-storeyed houses and electrified villages are conspicuously visible to any visitor. A few kilometres away from the central belt, one is aghast at the sharp contrast—hilly land and barren fields, small huts, rough and halfclad and half-starved people (Shah 1977: 19).

This description concerns the undeveloped part of Surat District, a poor and backward area inhabited by tribals. The social distance, particularly that between large farmers and landless labourers is, if anything, even wider in the developed part. Before a closer social and spatial analysis of the nature of this polarity there follows first a more detailed analysis of the recent transformation which the central plain has undergone.

[4] This is not all. One indication is the distribution of assets in rural Gujarat. According to a recent survey the bottom one-third of rural households possess only 4 per cent of the total assets while the top one-fifth of the households owns as much as two-thirds of all assets (*Socio-Economic Review, Gujarat State* 1982–5: 38).

2

ACCELERATION OF THE PROCESS OF RURAL TRANSFORMATION

The coming of irrigation

The construction of an extensive system of canal irrigation has been of decisive significance for the development of a modern agrarian structure. Towards the end of the 1950s the amount of irrigated land covered no more than a small percentage of the cultivated surface in the 3 *talukas* upon which my study in concentrated. The present-day farmers of Bardoli Vibagh are so given to contrasting their farming activities with the dry cultivation characterizing the life of the previous generation that it came as a great surprise to me to read that well irrigation was quite common a hundred years ago, and only fell into disuse in the last decades of the nineteenth century. In a commentary added to the report of the revised settlement survey, the Collector of Surat wrote in 1896:

> The abandoned wells in the taluka are very numerous, partly because many have fallen in owing to the looseness of the subsoil, and partly because sugarcane in some villages has ceased to be remunerative and no other crop has been found to replace it. On the whole there is no doubt there has been less and less irrigation in this part of the district (Bardoli RSR 1895: para 3).

Even taking this vanished tradition into account it does not seem too far-fetched to submit that for cultivators in the central plain the technology of water use has become more important in the past twenty years than it ever was in the past. In 1953 Kakrapar Dam on the Tapi 80 km upstream from Surat was completed, nearly a century after the first plans were laid for using this river for irrigation. In its first phase the project was modest in its aims; only a limited number of *talukas* could be irrigated and even then only seasonally. Reliance on rainfall would be reduced in this way, but it was obvious that no large changes in the cropping system had been foreseen. Increase in foodcrop production was the main objective (*Surat District Gazetter* 1962: 392–3). With the completion of the second phase in 1973—the construction of the Ukai reservoir, 36 km further upstream in the Tapi—very different estimates were made. Water flowed the whole year round along this network of main and subsidiary canals, extending over the whole plain of south Gujarat, including a part of the tribal hinterland. In order to promote proper use of the sharply increased capacity, the government decided to take upon itself the construction of and payment for, the field canals. From table 2.1 one can deduce the enormous expansion affecting the irrigated area within a short period of time.

After the first acceleration from the beginning of the 1960s a point of saturation seemed to have been reached. However, a truly spectacular growth followed as the Ukai reservoir and its channels came into operation. Although far surpassed in scope by the extensive canal system, the area irrigated by well water was also greatly extended in the same period. The landscape in the plain is sown with the pump houses for these wells, mostly hiding among the standing crops with which the fields are covered for a great part of the year.

It will occasion no surprise that the percentage of agricultural land irrigated with surface water has risen sharply in the course of the years, as we can see from the schematic view below (table 2.2). Bardoli and Palsana indicate the trend. Valod lags behind, having to profit only a short while ago from connections with the Ukai reservoir. A great deal of work was still being done on the hinterland branches of the canal system at the end of the 1970s, but now even this project has reached its final extent, the area originally planned having been increased by more than a third. The Ukai-Kakrapar command area totals 338,000 square km. Naturally it is the combination of fertile ground and an assured volume of water which, in terms of capital and labour, can be most intensively utilized and is also most productive. However, the enormous and rapid extension of the irrigated area has not been entirely without problems; interlogging and silting have appeared as the result of the sharp rise in the water table. The damage to agricultural production can only be prevented by the construction of an

Table 2.1 *Irrigated area in Surat District* (.000 acres)

Irrigation Source	Bardoli							Palsana						
	1953–4	1958–9	1962	1967	1972	1976–7	1980–1	1953–4	1958–9	1962	1967	1972	1976–7	1980–1
Canal	202	510	9,800	17,425	21,085	32,903	31,502	—	937	6,800	18,659	11,693	21,254	22,988
Tank, etc.	—	1,557	135	639	128	—	—	637	416	442	415	—	3	—
Well	1,791	1,609	891	3,095	4,250	2,275	10,888	1,403	2,550	3,410	10,189	3,600	5,194	5,602
Total	1,993	3,676	10,826	21,159	25,463	35,178	42,390	2,040	3,903	10,652	29,263	15,293	26,451	28,590

Irrigation Source	Valod							Surat District					
	1953–4	1958–9	1962	1967	1972	1976–7	1980–1	1953–4	1958–9	1962	1967	1972	1976–7
Canal	—	—	—	419	503	299	9,248		7,067	48,894	96,436	105,441	199,438
Tank, etc.	—	—	50	—	162	18	—	1,018	4,793	3,310	8,175	5,951	4,938
Well	322	415	511	543	1,513	2,248	245	12,795	13,769	13,422	26,488	45,026	52,171
Total	322	415	561	962	2,178	2,565	9,493	13,813	25,629	65,626	131,099	156,418	256,547

Table 2.2 *Percentage of net sown land under irrigation in Surat District*

Taluka	1953–4	1968–9	1976–7
Bardoli	4.5.	14	45
Palsana	9	13	62
Valod	1	1	6
Surat District	1*	13	26

* Excluding Uchhal and Nizar Talukas which in this year were still not part of Surat District.

extensive drainage system in which the farmers have not shown much interest so far.

The transition to an irrigation agriculture has brought about radical changes in the cropping system. There are still no data available at the *taluka* level for years later than those mapped out in table 2.3. The change of direction first came about in Bardoli and Palsana. Valod was beyond the range of the Kakrapar dam, with the result that the earlier cropping system was retained for much longer here, as elsewhere in Surat District. Even though the results of the new irrigation agriculture in this area were late in coming the mid-1970s, the direction of change was clear.

The factor still not adequately expressed in table 2.3 is that sugarcane in south Gujarat has become the predominant commercial crop. From the 1970s it has developed into a monoculture in the Bardoli area, completely ousting cotton. In some villages in this region, where the latter crop still occupied over 20 per cent of the cultivated area in the 1960s, it had completely vanished on my last visits in 1980 and 1981. Apart from the fact that the new irrigated crops produce higher yields, in many places the land has become too wet for the improved seed varieties which are being used in cotton cultivation. It would appear further that the production of 'status' food grains has gained in significance; this applies especially to rice which an increasing number of farmers are now growing in the hot summer months. I have the impression that the area planted with wheat has, after an initial increase, again fallen back to the previous level. The cultivation of millet (*jovar*;

Table 2.3 *Percentage distribution of area under*

crop	Bardoli				Palsana		
	1953–4	1958–9	1968–9	1977–8	1953–4	1958–9	1968–9
Paddy	13.59	12.08	16.50	18.88	6.39	5.58	8.65
Wheat	1.44	1.04	2.20	2.02	0.77	0.50	1.98
Jowar	16.71	12.13	11.04	10.54	22.79	15.07	15.31
Pulses	12.64	11.52	14.76	7.80	8.05	7.48	7.50
Sugarcane	0.01	0.65	8.95	25.75	—	1.79	4.69
Fruits + vegetables	1.88	1.05	3.61	3.37	4.01	3.90	15.17
Cotton + other fibres	29.11	38.29	17.31	3.75	29.48	39.22	16.79
Groundnut	1.18	1.05	3.00	1.15	3.56	3.64	7.00
Grass	22.06	21.54	21.31	26.19	23.92	21.36	22.14
Other crops	1.38	0.74	1.32	0.55	1.03	1.46	0.77
Gross cropped area	100.00 (36.527 ha)	100.00 (36.111 ha)	100.00 (37.084 ha)	100.00 (18.587 ha)	100.00 (18.892 ha)	100.00 (18.892 ha)	100.00 (19.102 ha)

rougher kinds of millet such as *kodra* and *nagli* had already disappeared much earlier) has declined sharply, and the same applies to pulses and groundnuts. Next to cane sugar, the cultivation of bananas has also risen in the 1960s and 1970s, with heavy concentrations in Palsana and Bardoli, but even this crop—extremely susceptible to price fluctuations—has more recently proved unable to cope with the competition from sugar. Rice and sugarcane dominate the Bardoli landscape to such an extent that, travelling along the roads in this area, one encounters scarcely any other crop.

The shift in the cultivation pattern is still going on. Apart from the results of my own fieldwork, this conclusion finds support in the few publications available on the recent rural transformation, such as for example a regional survey of the importance of off-farm employment (Kumbhar: 1981). This study refers to an area of thirty-two villages, twenty-five of which lie in Bardoli and Palsana *talukas*. In 1978–9 rice and millet occupied respectively 15 per cent and 13 per cent of the total area, and pulses occupied 8 per cent. Table 2.4 represents the increase in the area under sugarcane between 1967 and 1977 for the 3 *talukas* and the whole of Surat District. And this process is still not complete. As is apparent from my own *ajor crops in the area of research 1953–70*

	Valod				Surat District			
977–8	1953–4	1958–9	1968–9	1977–8	1953–4	1958–9	1968–9	1977–8
13.63	18.06	15.38	17.51	19.30	10.39	10.78	11.03	13.04
2.38	0.52	0.58	0.41	2.03	1.51	1.43	1.95	2.50
3.13	22.18	16.91	22.39	26.26	23.76	18.48	27.25	25.12
2.81	14.55	14.64	13.94	8.71	8.56	8.40	10.02	9.61
26.52	0.13	0.29	0.80	6.45	0.04	0.18	0.66	7.68
19.87	0.41	0.22	0.65	0.89	0.98	1.17	2.20	4.07
0.97	19.68	29.61	29.61	12.04	23.92	32.94	19.35	12.03
5.60	5.29	3.26	8.03	6.52	3.55	4.21	8.35	6.98
24.95	17.28	17.29	16.17	17.49	18.38	16.20	13.34	15.59
0.15	1.10	1.82	0.60	0.30	8.90	6.21	5.85	3.38
00.00	100.00	100.00	100.00	100.00	100.00	100.00	100.00	100.00
17.855 ha)	(19.244 ha)	(20.436 ha)	(19.602 ha)	(18.183 ha)	(348.365 ha)	(352.423 ha)	(400.057* ha)	(423.953 ha)

* The substantial increase in the area of cultivation was a consequence of the inclusion of Uchhal and Nizar Talukas

notes, the combination of rice and sugarcane in villages with the greatest irrigated surface occupied no less than two-thirds of the total cultivated area at the beginning of the 1980s.

Table 2.5 illustrates the use made of irrigation water in the mid-1970s. Needless to say I must point out that the cropping cycle on dry land—still at that time occupying half the cultivated surface even in Bardoli and Palsana—differed radically from this pattern and coincided to a much greater degree with the pattern of cultivation that was characteristic of the district earlier on.

The table below, based on a survey of thirty-two villages, is probably quite representative of agricultural production in the heart of the central plain in 1978–9.

My study is not concerned with agro-economic policies or farm management strategies and therefore passes over the question of whether such a solid concentration on one single crop, and the rapidity with which this has come about, is desirable from the point of view of the balanced development of agriculture. At all events it looks as though sugarcane, after a period of phenomenal growth, has captured a lastingly domi-

Table 2.4 *Proportion of land under sugarcane cultivation in area of research 1967–81*

Taluka	net area sown (in acres)			land under sugarcane (in acres)			percentage		
	1967–8	1976–7	1980–1	1967–8	1976–7	1980–1	1967–8	1976–7	1980–1
Bardoli	77,307	77,439	74,411	3,250	14,287	28,217	4.2	18.5	37.9
Palsana	43,998	44,094	44,082	898	8,444	16,176	2.1	19.1	36.7
Valod	44,285	44,265	42,353	186	2,500	7,417	0.04	5.6	17.5
Surat Dist.	435,206	436,280	—	5,465	37,562	—	1.2	8.6	—

nant place in the cropping scheme a century after this crop had disappeared from the district.[1]

The cultivation system displays not just regional variations, to a great extent attributable to the difference of tempo with which expansion of the irrigated area has taken place. It is further differentiated according to farm size. A report by the agricultural economist M. B. Desai, which has (unjustly) remained relatively unnoticed, is a veritable gold mine of information about the first phase of agrarian modernization. Desai undertook a highly detailed research into the changes taking place between 1968 and 1972 on 150 farms in ten villages situated in the central plain of Surat District (M. B. Desai et al., n.d.). One has to bear in mind, however, that the stratified random sample on which this study is based shows over-representation of larger landowners in the most advanced agricultural area.

Subdivided according to different farm sizes—see table 2.6—important variations in land usage can be noticed, in which, moreover, the tempo of change is clearly different. The smaller farms continue to produce relatively more food grains, while the cultivation of the new irrigated crops (sugarcane!) appears to be the preserve of the middle and large holdings. In view of these data it comes as no surprise that on the small farms

[1] Among other places Bardoli itself, then still only a village, 'yields splendid crops of sugarcane . . .' according to the first settlement survey from the mid-nineteenth century (Bardoli SR 1865, para 15). The report added that otherwise cultivation was confined to the loamy *gorat* land.

Table 2.5 *Irrigated area by major crops in area of research, 1974–5*

(in ha)

Taluka	percentage of irrigated to total cultivated land	total irrigated area	rice	wheat	jowar	other grains	pulses	sugar-cane	veget-ables and fruits	cotton	ground-nuts and other oilseeds	grass	other
Bardoli	43	14,785	5,556	1,090	—	7	3	7,089	771	112	19	125	129
Palsana	52	9,886	2,082	640	89	39	3	3,554	2,605	526	288	60	4
Valod	7	1,198	190	231	1	—	—	640	106	10	—	20	
Surat District	22	7,961	18,577	10,326	6,029	236	421	20,260	11,846	24,130	4,875	750	516

Table 2.6 *Irrigated area by major crops and size of operational holding, 1971–2*
(in percentage of total irrigated area)

size of operational holding (acres)	paddy	wheat	jowar	groundnut	cotton	sugarcane	bananas	vegetables	other	total
< 5	49.7	31.2	—	—	—	—	13.9	5.2	—	100
5–15	24.5	10.3	—	0.2	7.8	24.2	24.3	6.1	2.7	100
15–25	35.5	13.3	—	1.9	16.0	18.8	8.5	4.7	1.3	100
> 25	26.3	7.4	1.3	2.4	18.1	21.5	14.9	2.9	5.2	100

Source: M. B. Desai et al., *Changing Farm production and organisation in developing agriculture*. Baroda n.d.: 90.

the proportion of irrigated ground is also the lowest (see table 3.6).

Agrarian modernization

The cause of intensification of production cannot be reduced only to the expansion of the irrigated area, although the weight of this factor is difficult to overestimate in explaining rural dynamics. In close connection with this, the introduction of new cultivation practices has also played a very important role. In 1962–3 the 'Intensive Area District Programme' (IADP) was launched in a limited number of districts in India. Surat was one of the areas selected for making a beginning with the new agrarian strategy. It was a concentrated effort to convince the farmers of the advantages deriving from the use of improved seeds, fertilizers, better implements, and of the need for good water management, etc. To this end facilities (the inputs just mentioned, and credit) were provided on a large scale. Finally, extension services were strengthened.

The emphasis lay in the first place on boosting production of foodstuffs. On a government model farm in Vyara a team of Japanese experts was stationed for several years running; their experiments and demonstrations were intended to bring improvement to varieties of rice and to the methods of cultivation practiced by farmers in the area. It would be erroneous to suppose that advertisement of the agrarian modernization packet only began with the so-called green revolution.[2] The

[2] In Surat District the Japanese method of rice cultivation was already being propogated in 1953. In connection with the 'Grow More Food' campaign held in the mid-1940s, a village in Bardoli Taluka won the Rs 1,000 first prize in a competition held throughout Bombay State, of which Gujarat still formed part. At the beginning of the 1960s, J. M. Patel writes: 'All useful inputs as well as advanced techniques of production had been tried in this village. As an example fertilizing of the village land can be cited. The villagers used not only adequate quantities of organic chemical fertilizers, but also large quantities of green manures, sewage manures, and fishbones' (J. M. Patel 1964: 94).

In 1948–9 a programme for making compost, begun under the auspices of the Agricultural Service, was carried out in 450 villages. Even refuse from Bombay city was brought in, to be added to the fertilizer (Surat District Gazetteer 1962: 397).

use of the new agricultural practices were already being diffused and becoming familiar though on a modest scale, in the 1940s and the 1950s. It accelerated in the 1960s and in the 1970s came to be applied on a much larger scale.

Table 2.7 *Area under high yielding varieties in Surat District, 1968–74*

(area in 100 hectares)

year	paddy	wheat	cotton
1968–69	14.0	17.5	neg.
1969–70	74.1	10.2	2.8
1970–71	128.7	98.3	20.5
1971–72	140.8	99.8	27.9
1972–73	205.3	121.7	135.8
1973–74	209.2	136.0	235.6

Source: B. B. Samanta, *Planning for development of Surat district; first phase study.* Part IV *Agriculture*, n.d.: 11

'High Yielding Varieties' (H.Y.V.) were tried out in the district for the first time in 1966–7 and within a few years achieved great popularity, mainly on irrigated land. In 1974 use of H.Y.V. involved 40 per cent of the area planted with rice, 100 per cent of the wheat area and 25 per cent of the land under cotton. The application of fertilizers showed a corresponding development, the quantity used rising from 78 kg per hectare in 1970–1 to 155 kg in 1973–4. This doubling within four years compares very favourably with the average growth per acre for Gujarat State and for the country as a whole. The amount spent on insecticides and pesticides—to combat the plant diseases which increased sharply with the spread of irrigation and high quality seeds—rose drastically within a short period from Rs. 1.42 in 1968 to Rs. 13.80 in 1972. Just as in the case of the new seed varieties, fertilizers and plant protection 'medicine', as the farmers called it, were used chiefly in irrigated agriculture, in which sugarcane reached particularly high levels.

Table 2.8 *Growth of improved agricultural implements and machinery in Surat District, 1966–72*

Type	1966	1972	growth %
Iron plough	6,723	23,134	244
Improved harrow	32,393	76,907	137
Improved bored drill	14,253	18,296	28
Oil engine with pump	2,087	6,165	195
Electric motor with pump	1,043	2,722	161
Tractor	308	872	183

Source: M. B. Desai et al., tables 1.17 and 1.18.

Furthermore, the tempo of improvement in farming equipment is striking (table 2.8). Other new implements not mentioned in the list are the spraying pump and the power thresher. The switch to a new agrarian technology has continued energetically in recent years. It is indicative of the rapid strides made in mechanization that less than twenty years ago, no more than fifty tractors were registered in the whole of south Gujarat (Surat and Valsad Districts together), while during my fieldwork in 1977 and subsequent years I counted more than twenty-five tractors in several villages in the Bardoli area.

The capital intensity of agriculture has risen sharply, a development followed with great interest by the main commercial banks. In recent years these have taken to opening branches in the countryside to reach this new rural clientele, not only in order to finance farm investment but also—perhaps even especially—in order to attract the large farmers' savings. Already six different leading banks are represented in the main town, Bardoli, the largest of which—the Bank of Baroda—had six branches in 1982 and kept bi-weekly working hours in another six villages of this *taluka*. The action programme implemented in Surat District by this bank several years ago included a calculation meant to show that the purchase of a tractor was a paying proposition for a farmer with a holding of 15 acres. Armed with these figures and other propaganda material the bank officers were sent to the 'progressive farmers' to convince them of the advantages that mechanization would bring.

Table 2.9 *Production of principal crops on 150 farms in Surat District, 1969–72*

(figures in kgs. per acre)

year	paddy	wheat	jowar	beans	ground-nuts	cotton	sugar-cane	bananas	vegetables
1968–69	769	483	329	233	495	208	27,786	14,373	1,562
1969–70	942	570	258	148	451	186	27,718	9,186	3,484
1970–71	1,052	560	267	131	442	179	24,790	7,526	3,253
1971–72	1,110	584	269	169	398	273	34,978	12,673	2,451

Source: M. B. Desai et al., tables 5.23, 5.24 and 5.25.

Has intensification of agrarian production really led to a substantial rise in total yield? On the basis of currently available data a definite answer to this question can be given immediately. As an illustration, I have reproduced in table 2.9 the most important crops on the 150 farms examined in the research mentioned earlier, conducted under the guidance of M. B. Desai in the beginning of the seventies. It can be gathered from these results that the attempt to modernize agriculture has indeed been directed principally towards crops which are wholly or partly dependent upon irrigation. More traditional crops such as millet, beans and also groundnuts have lagged behind in this development.

Table 2.10 *Livestock distribution in Surat District, 1966–72*

type	Surat district 1966	Surat district 1972	Surat district growth rate %	Bardoli and Palsana 1966	Bardoli and Palsana 1972	Bardoli and Palsana growth rate %
total livestock	627,014	678,721	8	65,335	63,604	–3
bullocks	172,433	174,838	1.5	14,632	13,340	–9
cows	91,072	101,650	12	6,694	6,617	–1
buffaloes	68,196	85,722	26	11,818	14,032	19
total poultry	461,717	693,850	50	40,077	244,304	510

Source: M. B. Desai et al., tables 1.19 and 1.20.

The number of cattle has increased in these years, but this development shows differentiation (table 2.10). As might be expected, the number of draught animals have dropped in the irrigated zone where mechanization has taken place, for instance in Bardoli and Palsana, but milch cattle show a vigorous increase, especially buffaloes. The explanation for this must certainly be sought in the dairy produce co-operative Sumul in Surat, which began operations a number of years ago according to the formula which had appeared to be so successful in the model started by Amul in central Gujarat. Sumul had already been set up in 1951, but milk production was organized along modern lines only after 1968 when a refrigeration plant was established in Surat. The number of associated village societies increased to 537 at the beginning of 1982, comprising 84,000 members altogether. In order to be able to utilize the supply, new packing machinery has recently been installed which makes Bombay accessible as a market. In 1970 Sumul opened its own cattle feed factory, Sumuldan in Chalthan (Palsana).

Finally, the 'white revolution' as it is called in somewhat exaggerated jargon, also extends to poultry keeping. Chicken farms have experienced boom years, especially in the Palsana and Bardoli Talukas, from which the main urban centres are easily accessible. In order to be able to regulate egg sales more satisfactorily the Surat District Poultry Farmers' Co-operative Society was set up in 1970, and with this I come to the last aspect of the agrarian transformation—the changes in the marketing system.

With the striving towards increased productivity, farming has become still more market-oriented than it already was. From Desai's study it appears that an ever greater proportion of the total yield is sold; on average this percentage rose from 76 per cent in 1968 to 87 per cent in 1972. With regard to this I would like to observe that the division previously made between food and cash crops lost its meaning. The assumption that grains in particular were primarily or chiefly grown for personal consumption, has been out of date for a long time. The most important and most profitable crops destined for marketing are sugar, rice, bananas and cotton. The way in which the sale of these is regulated is an essential part of the agrarian transformation in Surat District, the crops being neither brought to the market by individual farmers nor bought up from the farmers by merchants. To a large extent the marketing is done via co-operatives which the most important producers have joined.

Co-operative undertakings in Surat District have a long history. This form of organization offered the farmers the opportunity of releasing themselves from the imprisoning grip of the cotton merchant/factory owner, often one and the same person. Co-operative cotton sale societies were formed for groups of villages, the historical background to which I gave in the first chapter. At the beginning of the 1970s some thirty of these associations had come into existence, incorporated into the 'Dakshina Gujarat Co-operative Cotton Marketing Union'.

While these co-operatives in the irrigated zone lead a sleepy existence due to the disappearance of cotton, for the time being this is certainly not the case with other producers' co-operatives. As I have just indicated, the same kind of federative network exists at the district level for the co-operative sale of milk and eggs. Co-operatives for the selling of vegetables and fruit had already come into existence earlier. Special mention should be made of the banana co-operatives in which farmers from the vicinity of Bardoli were involved. Cultivation of this fruit attained such huge proportions in the 1960s that sales were extended to countries abroad. The Bardoli organizations even stationed an agent in the Gulf States in this period and bought their own refrigerator boat in Europe in which to ship bananas to the Gulf.

Nevertheless the success of all these initiatives is nothing compared to the prosperous condition of production and processing of sugarcane which has been achieved entirely on a co-operative basis. For more detailed background information on this subject I refer to my study on labour relations in this branch of industry (Breman 1978–9). Mention of a few facts is enough to illustrate the changes which have come about in latter years.

In 1975–6, 11,663 farmers were connected with the three factories which came into operation a few years after the co-operatives were set up—Bardoli (1957) and Madhi (1964) in Bardoli Taluka and Chalthan (1964) in Palsana Taluka. Compared with ten years before, this meant a doubling of the membership, and the production area in the same period had risen from barely 4,000 to over 31,000 acres. For transporting the harvest from field to factory between the beginning of December and the end of May these factories employed 182 trucks and tractors as well as nearly 2,000 bullock carts. In the factories themselves nearly 2,000 men were at work, over half of whom were casual labourers who were dismissed again every year at the end of the campaign. At least 8,000 tons were processed every day. These figures, evoking an image of the stormy development process this branch of industry has gone through since the (re)introduction of sugar cultivation in the Bardoli region at the beginning of the 1960s, have meanwhile been surpassed. The total production capacity had risen at the beginning of 1982 to more than 14,000 tons a day without any marked increase in membership. The principal factory in Bardoli has developed into one of the largest co-operative-based units in India and perhaps even in the whole of Asia.

There is no better yardstick for gauging the success of this co-operative than the rising value of shares in it. Issued for Rs. 500 at the time of the establishment of the factory in 1956–7, the market price in the mid-1970s had already increased fourteen-fold and at the beginning of 1982 they were not being disposed of for less than Rs. 20,000. Two days before my last visit in the February of 1982 a record production of 8,293 tons was achieved. This concern alone offers employment to more than 40,000 cane cutters during the harvest campaign, so the manager told me on that occasion, and utilizes about 150 trucks and 100 tractors, besides a (shrinking) fleet of bullock carts. While the already existing co-operatives have managed to extend their area and capacity quite considerably, at the beginning of the 1980s two new factories also began operations in the neighbouring Mahuva and Olpad Talukas, each with an initial production capacity of 1,250 tons per day. A beginning will shortly be made on the erection of the sixth factory in Vyara. A factory in every *taluka* in the district, so the champions of this powerful lobby boast self-confidently to anyone who cares to listen. Significant in this respect is the statement in a 1971 official report about future prospects in Gujarat: 'The state can absorb 25 to 30 additional factories of which a good number could be established in the Surat District as it offers good potentiality' (Land Utilization Census 1971: 78).

The sugar factories of Bardoli are not only a result of agrarian modernization but conversely they have also very actively stimulated this process. Although the farmers themselves have a voice in decisions concerning land and production, these co-operatives have shown unmistakably that they are growing into complex agro-industries which penetrate deeply into the lives of the producers associated with them. The course of the harvest campaign immediately makes this clear. Factory processing of sugarcane in such large quantities every day is only made possible by a tight schedule based on modern principles of management and technique. In order to be able to keep track of progress being made on tasks in the fields, the planted area is subdivided into plots with which the estate manager and his staff are in regular radio contact. In addition the mechanization of transport—the purchase of an increasing number of trucks and tractors, followed by the instalment of load-lifts in the factory compound—is intended to maintain the supply of cane at a constant level.

An operation of such a high technical and organizational standard naturally does not leave farm management practices undisturbed. Even more important than this confrontation with the highly rationalized transport and processing of the crop is the direct influence on production. On the basis of its own agronomic research directed towards raising the yield per land unit (34 tons in 1977) and the sugar content of the cane (a recovery of about 11 per cent in 1980), the Department of Agriculture of each factory not only provides information about new varieties, planting methods, use of fertilizers, etc., but also keeps up a bombardment of instructions and interference throughout the growth cycle. For example, spraying with insecticides and herbicides is done from the air, for which the factories hire aircraft. While the higher factory management and board members go on visits abroad, e.g. to the USA and the Pacific, in order to keep abreast of the new production techniques, selected farmers are sent with the same object on excursions to Maharashtra. Every year members (of co-operatives) producing the highest yield are awarded prizes, which are duly recorded in the annual report.

Finally, the extension of credit is an instrument for encouraging new farming investment: land improvement, procurement of new implements and machines. In the 1980–1 season the Bank of Baroda introduced a finance scheme whereby the Bardoli factory stood guarantee for the purchase of seventy tractors (Rs. 100,000 each with trailers) and twenty-four trucks (Rs. 240,000 each). According to this scheme the selected members hired out their vehicles to the factory for the duration of the harvest campaign, the factory paying the hire purchase instalments directly to the bank. It appeared to have been such a successful formula that only a year later other factories started taking a similar initiative.

A theme that will be discussed much more fully later in this study is the dramatic effect of this new industry on employment and the prevalent labour regime. Here I am thinking not only of the much greater seasonal fluctuations that occur and the exclusive use of migrants in cane cutting, but also of the landowners' changed attitude towards labour in general as a result of the responsibility for the harvest operation which the factories themselves have continued to bear, with the displacement of the farmers as employers and even as supervisors.

The tenor of the above argument is that the introduction of irrigation agriculture in the central plain around Bardoli has resulted in changes which go much further than just the replacement of the previous cash crop (cotton) by a new one (sugarcane). The transformation that has come about is due to the combination of modern agricultural techniques—not only the extension of the irrigated land surface, but also the application of new agricultural methods and implements—and the financing of production as well as organization of market sales under farmers' control. These changes of an infrastructural, technological and organizational nature—which meant the persistence of forces already active earlier,—have resulted in a style of farm management which is conspicuously different from the conditions existing before the transition—different as much in the use of capital as in the employment of labour.

Diversification of rural production

The economic dynamic in the central plain has not remained limited to agriculture. Besides this, industry has also markedly increased, especially in and around Surat as a growth pole. In 1957 an 'industrial estate' was set up on a co-operative basis on the initiative of private entrepreneurs in Udhna, outside the city limits in order to avoid municipal ordinances and octroi levies—the *Udhna Sahakari Sangh*, 6 km to the south of Surat. After a somewhat tardy growth in the early years, by 1971 a substantial complex had already arisen offering accomodation to fully five hundred enterprises with 12,000 employees, principally in the textile, metal and chemical sectors. The expansion of activities and employment, particularly in the following years, took place at a positively feverish rate.

Arising literally outside the social boundaries, with a minimal amount of intervention from the already rather ineffective apparatus of government, an extremely harsh regime came into being here that at the same time radiated an enormous vitality. Great disorderliness, total pollution of the environment and the lack of the most elementary facilities other than industrial are typical of the location. People are here only to work and hardly have a living place they can call their own.

As Udhna has filled up—the density of industrial establishments is unprecedentedly high, in view of the low priority given to housing—the government has set up similar 'industrial estates' in other places on the city perimeter (Khatargam, Pandesara) which promise to develop and prosper in the same way.

Rising prices and other relatively high overhead costs—and here the price of labour is not the first thing that springs to mind—have encouraged a growing number of entrepreneurs to establish their workshops or factories along one of the exit roads around the district centre. Conversely, in setting up their enterprises, industrialists originating from the countryside seem inclined to make for places on the way to the city, but not quite in it. Thus the Surat-Bardoli road is beginning to stand out as an industrial overflow from the urban milieu. In recent years a concentration of new industry has come into existence particularly where this road crosses the national Bombay-Ahmedabad highway. In addition, the *taluka* main towns, Bardoli and Palsana, have developed into industrial centres. Some smaller nuclei (Madhi, Valod, Sarbhon) have also made a modest start in this direction.

It is striking that this rural industrialization is to a great extent nourished by a dynamic having its origins in the recent modernization of agriculture. Although the present scale of operations signifies a new form of the area's agro-industries,

Bardoli has for a long time had the reputation of being a centre for these. While before the turn of the century there were several large towns in the *taluka* each with its own cotton gin, in the following decades this industry came to be concentrated in the most centrally situated market places, among which Bardoli was undoubtedly the most important. At the start of the 1960s two oil presses and five ginning and pressing factories were set up here, two of the latter being farmers' co-operatives. When I began my fieldwork in 1977 these were the only enterprises left in this branch of industry. Cultivation of cotton in the immediate vicinity had declined so far that the industry could only maintain itself by transporting the cotton from Mandvi, Mangrol and other producing areas at a great distance from the irrigated zone. Since this did not appear to be a long-term paying proposition the establishments closed down in 1980–1 and the machines were sold elsewhere.

In contrast to the decay of these small-scale industries based on an earlier pattern of cultivation in the central plain, we see the rise of larger, much more capital-intensive and also technically more advanced agro-industries for processing the produce of the new irrigated crops, far and away the most important of these being the sugar factories already discussed. In addition, cattle keeping has acquired a more industrial character to which the founding of the co-operative cattle feed factory, mentioned previously, has contributed. Then there is in Bardoli a dye factory which makes henna. The paper factories—new to this area and second only to the sugar factories in significance although with a much smaller productive capacity than the latter—use the waste from rice and sugarcane as raw material. They limit their manufacture mainly to cardboard and packing paper. Out of the six enterprises—five in Bardoli and one in Valod Taluka—two are farmers' co-operatives. In addition, the new agro-industries have given a forward impulse to other branches of industry such as a local smithy in Bardoli which has grown into a much larger construction workshop specializing in the manufacture of machinery for paper factories. After having successfully fitted out several complete industrial installations in the area, this undertaking has been given assignments for supplying equipment elsewhere in Gujarat and even outside the state.

Development of the physical infrastructure in the district has given a strong impulse to the construction industry, the raw materials for which are also found on the spot. Many brick fields have sprung up along the river near Bardoli, and several quarries and stone crushing yards are operating close to Valod. In Bardoli a large roof tile manufactory has also been established and a cement factory making pipes, etc. Demand for these products—used as much in construction of roads and irrigation canals as in utilities and house building—has risen enormously. Motorization of traffic and mechanization in agriculture have led not only to an increase in technical know-how but also to the opening of workshops for maintenance and repair in the busiest centres.

At first sight the recent spread of the diamond industry over the countryside appears to be completely separate from this development. The stones come from abroad via Bombay and after being worked are exported again. A Baniya caste (the Palanpuri Jains from north Gujarat) have the monopoly of this trade and distribute the diamonds among the workshop owners. South Gujarat has in recent decades become one of the most important centres in the country for the cutting and polishing of the rough stones. Twenty-five years ago in this area there were scarcely a hundred units but, particularly from the end of the 1960s up to the mid-1970s, this branch of industry has attained huge proportions. Although progress has been interrupted by short recessions, in 1981 a total of 30,000 units were registered with about 150,000 places for workers, concentrated to a great extent in the triangle Surat-Navsari-Bardoli. The first two are still the most important locations, but this small-scale industry, which is not really bound to an urban environment, has gradually spread out over the hinterland.

Farmers' capital and the 'know-how' of the first generation of cutters—largely originating from the principal landowning class in the region—have played an important role in this trend towards ruralization. The technology is not very complicated since, apart from electricity, not much is required in order to open a workshop. Most units are accommodated in dwelling houses or small sheds with several work benches at which sit no more than ten to twenty cutters and polishers, counting the owner.[3] The data given below, derived from an official count from 1977, map out the spread of the diamond industry in the Bardoli area. According to this Economic Census the *taluka* town itself housed 85 units with 1,809 employees; 193 workshops employing 4,040 workers were established in thirty-one of the eighty-two villages in the *taluka*. I have the impression that the crisis in the diamond industry which followed some years later has led to the closure of some of the smaller workshops especially, the owners of which were financially weak and also had no direct contact with the big merchants. Although untrammeled growth appeared to be over by the end of the 1970s, in the period preceding that time a firm basis had nevertheless been laid for this industry. At the beginning of the 1980s it looked as though the countryside industries would also be able to hold their own.

What influence has economic diversification had on the composition of the working population? Between 1961 and 1981 the percentage of the labouring population outside agriculture in Surat District rose from nearly 39 per cent to 48 per cent, a growth figure considerably above the average for Gujarat State.

The picture presented in table 2.11 is, however, distorted for the district as a whole by Surat City which has developed into a conurbation with Surat which has developed with extraordinary rapidity in the last two decades, as I stated earlier. By leaving this primary nucleus of growth out of consideration it is possible to arrive at a more realistic calculation of the growth of the non-agrarian sector within the countryside itself. At the moment only the global district figures are available from the latest census but in 1971 the proportion of non-agrarian-sector workers in my 3 research *talukas* varied between 16 per cent and 27 per cent of the working population. Taking Bardoli, Palsana and Valod together, the share of the working population outside agriculture increased from 20 per cent to 23 per cent between 1961 and 1971. This still means a con-

[3] For a description of this branch of industry and a survey of labour relations within it, based upon research in Navsari in 1973, see M. Kalathil, 'Industrial relations in a small-scale industry' in: Ramaswamy (ed.) 1978.

Table 2.11 *Occupational classification of working population in Surat District, 1961–81*

administrative unit	1961					1971					1981				
	total lakhs	workers %	cultivators %	agric. labourers %	others %	total lakhs	workers %	cultivators %	agric. labourers %	others %	total lakhs	workers %	cultivators %	agric. labourers %	others %
Bardoli	0.40	100	26.87	48.47	25.16	0.49	100	15.79	56.84	27.07	0.53	100	14.89	59.41	25.70
Palsana	0.19	100	24.42	59.85	15.75	0.22	100	16.52	63.64	19.81	0.35	100	10.49	64.16	25.35
Valod	0.21	100	51.51	34.87	13.62	0.21	100	34.20	49.75	16.07	0.30	100	31.17	39.06	29.78
Surat District	5.76	100	8.26	30.98	30.76	6.64	100	27.11	33.24	39.65	9.93	100	23.68	28.31	48.01

siderable rise, especially when one considers that population growth as a whole is discounted in these figures. Furthermore, part of the growth in non-agrarian employment remains veiled because the percentages mentioned are principally based on the main source of income. The shift in the composition of rural production occurs, as far as the labour factor is concerned, in the form of industrial activity.

The outcome of two surveys carried out at the end of the 1970s suggests that this trend is still continuing. In twelve villages in Navsari Taluka—which lies in the neighbouring Valsad District but which has a socio-economic structure showing a great deal of similarity to that of Bardoli and Palsana —Naik calculated that in 1978 28.3 per cent of the working population were employed outside agriculture (K. V. Naik 1979). Khumbar also arrived at 28 per cent with a random sample of 600 households in thirty-two villages in Surat District, three-quarters of which were under the jurisdiction of Bardoli and Palsana. The rise in the last decade certainly tallies with the extension of rural industry and expansion of the services and transport sectors along the highways, at the meeting places in the *taluka* and finally even in the most isolated villages.

I conclude from this that the diversification of the economy has penetrated right to the local level. This dynamic has nevertheless not been able to prevent the vast majority of the population outside the big-city conurbation of Surat from still being dependent upon agriculture as its only or at least principal living: in 1981 these formed 79 per cent of the rural working population in the district. In an absolute sense the agricultural workforce is still increasing, from 400,000 to over 515,000 between 1971 and 1981. This trend—an increasing number of people having to make a living from the land—is the point of departure for an analysis of the processes of differentiation arising among the agrarian population in the central plain of Surat District. In the subsequent chapters I shall concentrate on the contrasts and contradictions which have arisen in rural south Gujarat as a result of a transition to an industrial mode of production both within and outside agriculture. The polarization which goes together with these dynamics is most certainly not a local phenomenon only but can be observed in other areas of Gujarat as well.

3

SOCIAL FORMATIONS WITHIN AGRARIAN PRODUCTION

Agrarian stratification

In 1971 the cultivated area in Surat District covered 430,000 hectares, amounting to 58 per cent of the total geographical surface, a percentage considerably above the average for Gujarat and indicating the steep increase in population pressure in the countryside. It appears from the 1981 census that the amount of land per head for workers in agriculture (farmers as well as agricultural labourers) is at present less than 1 hectare, and particularly in the central plain, where the present-day extent of the cultivated area was reached several decades ago, further extension is unlikely. In Bardoli Vibagh the capacity of agriculture can be increased only through intensification of tillage—more harvests each year—yet even this avenue of escape is cut off because the greater part of the irrigated area, which would be particularly fitted for such intensification, is taken up by crops with a lengthy growing cycle such as sugar and, to a lesser extent, fruit (bananas, and lately also papayas).

Naturally the distribution of land between the agrarian population is more important than these global data. When compiling table 3.1 I took as my starting point the division between marginal owners and small farmers (less than 5 acres), middle farmers (5–15 acres) and large farmers (over 15 acres). The limitations imposed on classification by this three-way division—still retained in much of the literature, nevertheless—are rather arbitrary given the great variation in access to land, soil fertility, intensity of cropping, availability of labour power and other factors of an agronomic or socio-economic nature which influence farming productivity. This does not detract from the fact that, in defining a small farmer's holding, the boundary is usually fixed at a farmed extent of less than 5 acres. Below this amount the cash value of the yield clearly remains beneath the level regarded as acceptable for a minimal livelihood, especially where unirrigated land is involved.[1] The amount of land middle farmers have at their disposal is enough to live on. They make regular use of non-household labour and produce a large market surplus based on the higher capital intensity of their holdings. They do not lead the way in the process of agrarian transformation but take every available opportunity of keeping up with imported modern technology, i.e. they have access to the new facilities and can find the wherewithal for the necessary investment in them, and can moreover derive from them a profit commensurate with their outlay. The fixing of the upper limit for this class at 15 acres marks the transition to a type of agrarian proprietor who forms the vanguard of the capitalist mode of production which has gained dominance. Here I am alluding to the class of large farmers providing the initiative for the technological and organizational transformation mentioned earlier. They are the first to make use of the infrastructural and institutional provisions offered on such a generous scale by the government and, as is evident from their cumulative economic capacity, they also derive the most advantage from the modernizing of the rural order.

As a result of the increasing productivity of agriculture deriving from extension of the irrigated area and from application of new production techniques, much less land is necessary nowadays for providing an adequate living. One result of this has been the gradual lowering of the upper limit on the amount of agrarian property which a farmer's household is allowed to possess. A programme of land reform beginning with the abolition of tenancy towards the end of the 1950s (see Baks 1969) merged, at the beginning of the 1970s, into the fixing of a ceiling of 13–19 acres for irrigated land and 26–39 acres for dry land. This implied a substantial scaling down (to 48 acres) of the ceiling on which the Congress movement had agreed after

[1] M. B. Desai, in the economic study already mentioned, calculated that the gross value of the yield per hectare for small farmers in Surat District in 1971–2 amounted to only Rs. 1,200, much less than they needed for a livelihood at that time. See also Samanta, n.d.: 24.

long discussions in the 1940s (Wood: 250). For the area round Bardoli the maximum for irrigated land was lowered again some years ago to 10 acres after years of obstruction from the larger landowners. With this figure in mind, a holding of 15 acres or more seems an acceptable yardstick for defining a large farm in my research area.

Now we turn to the interpretation of table 3.1. To begin with I would like to point out that careful and restricted use of these figures is required. Statements concerning ownership (which, as experience teaches us, are seldom to be trusted) leave much to be desired when they are made against the background of government regulations which those who have most at stake perceive as damaging to their position. Thus under-registration, especially of the larger holdings, with an eye to imminent land reform, undoubtedly explains the decline in the total area of cultivated land registered for 1960. Land can actually be lost in official statistics. At a subsequent stocktaking, methods had in the meantime been found for getting rid of the 'surplus' in other ways. The rapid rise of the middle farmer class especially, results from the need to satisfy, at least on paper, the legal construct which permits no ownership above the established ceiling. A logical outcome of this is fictionalization of the agrarian middle level as a result of spurious subdivision among relatives.

If we accept this distortion—which is almost impossible to eliminate as long as the government apparatus systematically continues to put the interests of the propertied classes first, at the local level as well as above this—the principal features of the agrarian order and the direction of change can both be summarized as follows: firstly, the extremely high percentage of small landowners; secondly, the concentration of by far the greatest share of agrarian property in the hands of middle and large farmers.

These phenomena are revealed against the background of a real drop in landownership throughout the whole length of the agrarian ladder, although the same relative distribution existing earlier between small landowners on the one hand and middle and large farmers on the other has been more or less maintained. I shall now examine each of these classes separately.

The class of small owners

According to the Agricultural Census for Gujarat for 1970–1, more than half of the farming population in Surat District owned less than a quarter of the total amount of available land. In the region of advanced agriculture around Bardoli this discrepancy was even more marked, as table 3.2 shows clearly.

Furthermore, upon splitting up this most extensive class of landowners still further into its component parts we can see the preponderance of marginal owners within it (less than 2 acres). The disproportion between their numbers (32.33 per cent) and their share (5.53 per cent) in the agrarian property structure within my area of research not only illustrates the perilous insecurity of their existence but also suggests that they really should not be reduced to one common denominator with the other owning classes. These are not farmers, but workers who have a small piece of land in addition to their incomes from wage labour.

The question immediately presenting itself is whether this congestion at the base of landownership results from regression—loss of agrarian capital—linked with the process of modernization which has been taking place in the central plain in recent decades. Did small owners in Gujarat lose their land to middle and large farmers? This was the pertinent question posed by Vyas several years ago (1975); his own answer to this was that they had not. According to this view the number and proportion of small farmers did increase, but the same could be said for the area they cultivated, with the result that the average farm size remained more or less constant. It is interesting that this author himself mentions Surat District as a possible exception to this finding, indicating in this context the study by M. B. Desai which states that between 1965 and 1971 small-scale landownership was somewhat reduced. However, Vyas' general conclusion is that the class of small farmers is undergoing a process of impoverishment (*Verdelendung*) but not proletarianization. The picture he sketches fits in with the mechanism of fragmentation—a continual subdivision of property within each succeeding generation—described in particular detail in the literature on the late colonial period. On the other hand there are indications that the number of members within a household to whom land is allotted has

Table 3.1 *Size of landholdings in Surat District, 1952–70*

size of holding	1952–3*				1960*				1970			
	number of holdings	per-cent	area in acres	per-cent	number of holdings	per-cent	area in acres	per-cent	number of holdings	per-cent	area in acres	per-cent
5 acres	54,871	54.77	160,142	15.95	60,881	52.76	208,143	23.02	88,450	55.07	n.a.	—
5–15 acres	28,159	28.11	253,613	25.26	37,959	32.89	290,070	32.08	56,871	35.40	n.a.	—
15 acres	17,159	17.13	590,292	58.79	16,558	14.35	405,875	44.89	15,314	9.53	n.a.	—
total	100,189	100	1,004,047	100	115,398	100	904,088	100	160,635	100	n.a.	—

Source: Surat District Gazetteer 1962 and Agricultural Census 1970–1, Gujarat.
*Uchhal and Nizar Talukas not yet included in Gujarat.

Table 3.2 *Distribution of holdings in area of research 1970*

administrative unit	up to 2 acres				2–5 acres				more than 5 acres				total			
	number of holdings	per-cent	area in acres	per-cent	number of holdings	per-cent	area in acres	per-cent	number of holdings	per-cent	area in acres	per-cent	number of holdings	per-cent	area in acres	per-cent
Bardoli	4,830	34.72	4,428	5.47	3,327	23.83	14,348	17.73	5,741	41.46	62,145	76.80	13,918	100	80,921	100
Palsana	1,791	24.26	17,404	4.93	2,220	30.07	8,032	22.77	3,372	45.67	25,501	72.30	7,383	100	35,273	100
Valod	2,772	35.77	2,582	6.14	2.213	28.55	7,548	17.95	2,765	35.68	31,914	75.91	7,750	100	42,044	100
total of three *talukas*	9,393	32.35	24,414	5.53	7,760	26.73	29,928	18.91	11,878	40.99	119,560	75.56	29,031	100	158,238	100

remained constant over a long period, as Pandit has argued on the strength of a number of case studies partly located in south Gujarat (1969).

When I place the earliest-known and the most recent data for Bardoli Taluka together side by side (table 3.3) then there appears to have been no drastic alteration in the division of the landowning population within the compass of half a century—at least so far as the division between small farmers on the one hand and middle and large farmers on the other is concerned.

Table 3.3 *Pattern of land distribution in Bardoli Taluka, 1920–78*

size of holding	1920*		1924*		1970–1**		1977–8**	
	holdings %	area %	holdings %	area %	holdings %	area %	holdings %	area %
5 acres	61.30	n.a.	62.49	n.a.	61.31	23.20	63.34	25.65
5–15 acres	34.43	n.a.	35.14	n.a.	31.28	48.94	31.20	51.78
15 acres	4.26	n.a.	4.36	n.a.	7.41	27.88	5.46	22.57

Source: *Bardoli RSR 1925
**Report of the Gujarat State Land Commission 1979.

A good deal of caution is necessary in the use of these figures, based on source material which does nothing to diminish the distortion and for that reason alone can lead to dubious conclusions. Further, it is certainly not my intention to suggest that the agrarian order has remained static. Truly radical institutional changes in property relations are hidden behind the percentages, but the fact that roughly 60 per cent of the farmers are small landowners is a remarkably constant datum. Towards the end of this period they had at most a quarter of the total cultivated area at their disposal, and there is no reason to assume that this state of affairs was very different in the past.

So—no proletarianization? As would appear from a general survey article appearing a short while ago, Byres subscribes to a different view, certainly as far as the most recent past is concerned. After discussing the findings of a number of studies concerning various parts of India he cautiously draws up the balance sheet as follows:

> I would interpret the foregoing as, indeed, signifying the operation of a process of proletarianization of the peasantry, or depeasantization: one that is complex, but as yet partial in its impact. The 'new technology' has produced conditions in which, by a variety of means, the poor peasantry has lost an increasing share of the operated area to rich peasants. Not only that, but the poor peasantry is, in different ways, being transformed more and more into a rural proletariat (Byres 1981: 430).

Where small landowners or even agricultural labourers previously made their appearance as share croppers on land belonging to bigger farmers, now the phenomenon is reversed. The incomplete proletarianization that Byres describes boils down to the fact that increasingly more small owners surrender the working of their properties to larger farmers without giving up their own rights in them. Since this fell outside my research scope I did not systematically collect information on this aspect, but during my fieldwork in various villages in Bardoli and its environs I did repeatedly come across similar cases. Nearly always they involved marginal landowners who, because of implements, capital or even lack of time, were in general no longer in a position to cultivate their lands themselves. As part of debt relations in which they were usually already involved, they ceded the use of their plots to bigger farmers who were frequently at the same time owners of neighbouring fields. This is an impressionistic picture without factual support, but for which I find quantitative confirmation in M. B. Desai's study. On the basis of his random sample of 150 farms distributed over Surat District he calculated that the average surface area worked by small owners dropped from 3.2 acres to 2.99 acres between 1967 and 1972 as a result of the leasing out of land, particularly to farmers in possession of 15 to 25 acres. As a result of this transfer of land the area cultivated by the latter class of owners rose by only 3 per cent net, but the area which small farmers kept for their own use dropped by at least 20 per cent (Desai tables 4.19 and 4.20).

Without deriving too drastic a conclusion from these findings —the non-representative character of the random sample upon which Desai's study is based does not permit generalization—I nevertheless think that Vyas, in rejecting the thesis of proletarianization, has too easily passed over the phenomenon of the reversal of traditional tenancy relationships. For the rest, it is not entirely impossible that proletarianization remains incomplete as a result of the bigger farmers' fear of a more scrupulous application of land reform legislation in the future.

When taking as my point of departure a real loss of land among the agrarian class owning the least property, I do so with the reservation that this decline arises primarily among marginal landowners as far as the central plain is concerned. In anticipation of matters to be discussed in chapter 6, I would like to observe that retreat down the agrarian ladder in the tribal hinterland of Surat District is a more all-embracing process. However, in the area around Bardoli the class of small farmers, in the precise sense attached to this definition —all owners of between 2 and 5 acres, according to governmental classification—appear in general to have been able to maintain the size of their holdings. How is this to be explained?

In the first place by more intensive land usage; the percentage of land harvested more than once a year is significantly higher than on larger farms. In the second place, in addition to growing food grains and pulses—providing for the needs of one's own household being an absolute priority—crops which do require a good deal of labour but which also guarantee a high yield, for instance, bananas, chillies, tomatoes and other vegetables are also grown. Nevertheless there is a limit to this labour-intensive strategy, a limit determined by the small farmers' lack of capital strength. Above all, the productivity of their farms remains lower than that of the larger farmers' holdings because they cannot permit themselves the investment that is part and parcel of the new agrarian technology. As Desai's report demonstrates with a wealth of detail, the small farmers' unfavourable starting position—only small amounts of land, of an inferior kind and of which a smaller proportion is irrigated—bears a cumulative disadvantage. They have fewer work implements (traditional or modern) and not the financial means to utilize the new agrarian inputs; they remain to a great extent deprived of all kinds of facilities which are available to the classes of larger owners. Because of this they achieve a lower yield per unit of land, expressed in terms of both weight and money; they dispose of a smaller part of their production in the market and as a consequence of all these factors they are barely able to accumulate any savings.

The example of sugar production shows that not only a

structural handicap is involved but also a conscious exclusion of the small farmers by the agrarian upper stratum. The few small farmers who have turned to the cultivation of sugar in Bardoli Vibagh—the majority cannot afford to make land available for this over such a long period or to make the necessary outlay—have no direct entry to the co-operative factories. They have to sell their harvest via the larger landowners who are members of the co-operatives, a mediation for which there is naturally a price to pay. The frequently expressed prediction that the benefits of the new technology would after some time fall within their reach as well, leading to a more equal distribution, has not by and large been borne out. It is an expectation prompted more by wishful thinking than by sober analysis.

In order to put an end to the backwardness of this part of the farming population a special service has been created on the initiative of central government: the Small Farmer's Development Agency. Its office in Surat, one of the first in Gujarat, was opened in 1971. Almost immediately this organization extended its services to marginal landowners, a broadening of assignment which went even further from 1974 onwards by including agricultural labourers in the programme of activities. Nevertheless this effort remained principally directed towards the original target group and consisted of little more than the granting of modest subsidies for farm investment (soil improvement, irrigation, purchase of working implements, etc.), the size of which decreased as the amount of property increased.

Results in the first years were disappointing, as one can see from evaluation studies.[2] Since then little has happened to permit a more positive judgement. The main reasons for this failure are lack of an adequate framework with a budget attuned to it, as well as weakening of the personal objective by the way in which it is attained. The mutual backscratching between the agrarian elite and the government bureaucracy blocks the small owners' way to the institutional provisions which have been created as part of the process of agrarian modernization in the central plain. When small farmers have been able nevertheless to hold their own, this has certainly

[2] See among others *An assessment of the performance of SFDA, Surat District, 1971–1972 to 1973–1974.* Directorate of Evaluation, Government of Gujarat, Ahmedabad n.d.

never, or hardly ever, been thanks to any co-operation they have enjoyed from the official side. A short time ago a new national scheme was launched with the objective of stimulating employment and income opportunities of households living below the poverty line (Rs. 3,500 per year in 1983). The implementation of this Integrated Rural Development Programme has been entrusted to an agency which operates at the district level. According to a first evaluation report the result of activities carried out so far in Surat District are very promising (Jan. 1983). I must add, however, that I myself have not been able to find any solid evidence for such an optimistic view.

As a result of their inability to derive a proportionate profit from a capitalistic mode of production, the distance between these small cultivators and the larger landowners has greatly increased. Yet the statement that the division between these agrarian classes has acquired sharper contours does not mean that the small farmers in the region around Bardoli have also been impoverished in an absolute sense.

The rise of non-agrarian industry in my research area or at a short distance from it in the centre of growth at Surat, has encouraged the majority of them to seize the opportunity of temporarily or partially supplementing the yield from their own farms with outside work. In the same manner subdivision of land among the new generation is avoided as far as possible by equipping one or more sons for an existence outside agriculture by means of education. Probably for no other rural class does non-agrarian employment form such an important source of livelihood as for the small landowners, and in no other class are such a high percentage of the working members of the household dependent—perhaps completely so—upon this kind of employment. The benefits of agrarian modernization continue to elude the majority of them even where they have not actually sustained damage from it, but they do profit from the diversification of the rural economy which has in the long run stemmed from this transformation.

The social origins of most small farmers lie within the lower or middle castes. Besides Kolis and Muslims I also include in these the cultivators from upwardly mobile tribal castes, particularly the Chaudharis in the northern part of the central plain and the Dhodhias in the southern part. And beyond these, all kinds of artisan and service castes, including Harijans, whose traditional occupations in the past gave their members access to ownership of land as long as this was not in short supply and as long as commercialized agriculture remained undeveloped. This segment of the population especially has a pronounced non-agrarian occupational tradition, embracing a very diverse conglomeration of castes. Although small in numbers they are not distributed over all the villages in the plain but usually live together in larger concentrations (see also table 1.3).

Members of these castes are considered primarily suitable for filling all kinds of lower posts within the formal employment structure of factories and workshops, in government agencies, in the service sector etc. Where they do not already possess non-agrarian occupational skills they have had the chance of qualifying, through education, for the somewhat more skilled labour which requires some training, for which a great need has developed.

By underlining the importance of the employment which has come to exist as a result of diversification in the rural economy, I do not want to suggest that the heightened chances for small landowners of escaping in this direction is to be equated with a rise in socio-economic status. Members of these households practically never break through to the higher echelons of rural and urban employment outside agriculture. They are unable either to raise the capital for the education and other kinds of investment necessary for this, or to acquire the contacts which are indispensible for an introduction into the higher circuits of the regional labour market. They do manage however to keep their heads above water with the help of external earnings, or—to put it in another way—thanks to the yield of the land they own, a large proportion of small farmers have succeeded in obtaining an entry to employment outside agriculture in accordance with their station in life, in their own area or in the urban centres along the western railway line. Conversely the outflow of this labour, whether temporary, partial or permanent, and the return inflow of at least a part of the resulting earnings, have become essential for the maintenance of the small farmers' holdings.

For this class I would characterize the probable outcome of the sum total of agrarian modernization, rural industrialization and a general diversification of the central plain's economy as neither more or less than consolidation. The social attitude that goes with this is a very defensive one; on the one hand the insight that economic improvement and social progress are difficult to attain, and on the other the consciousness of the vulnerability of one's livelihood. The little that one has is soon lost and there is great anxiety about slipping downwards. Not daring to take any risks yet at the same time having to seek new openings: this combination is characteristic of the precarious strategy small landowners are compelled to adopt. They play no active role in the expansion undergone by the regional economy, nor do they experience this process as helpless victims. In this respect the small farmers differ from the classes between which they are socially and economically pinched—above them the bigger landowners and below them the landless labourers.

This assessment should not create the impression that rural stratification can be reduced to a simple three-way division. In the foregoing pages I have examined in detail the situation and the problem of the smaller landowners, because in my view they are not the principal actors in the social dynamic which has arisen, and for this reason they will be largely left out of consideration in the remainder of this study. Although institutional and structural transformation has not entirely passed them by, I regard the term 'peasants' as still being appropriate to this class because of their hesitant and defensive reaction to the situation which has come into being. Without much hope of improvement, they try as far as possible to protect themselves from the negative consequences of this process of change, and on the whole they have been reasonably successful in this.

As distinct from this wide intermediate layer I am devoting attention to the classes who have been either the entrepreneurs of rural transformation in Surat District or, on a large scale, the main victims of it. Both these strata form the exclusive focus of my research.

This top and bottom of the agrarian hierarchy are split up yet again into different classes. The differentiation between large and middle farmers has already been discussed earlier, and the landless proletariat form even less of an homogeneous mass. In anticipation of a much more detailed discussion in both the following chapters over the origin and background of the communities with which these classes can be identified in the remainder of this chapter I shall briefly examine their extent and social significance.

The class of middle and large farmers

According to the most recent data, roughly three-quarters of all cultivable land is concentrated in the hands of owners of middle and large holdings, who comprise about a third of the farming population. It is not impossible that both the percentages on which this proportion is based follow a dipping graph line, as table 3.4 for Bardoli Taluka illustrates. If there is any question of this—even ignoring the dubious reliability of all the sources on which I am obliged to rely,—then the decline, viewed over a rather long stretch of time, can hardly be called startling.

Table 3.4 *Concentration of land above 5 acres in Bardoli Taluka, 1920–78.*

year	% of farms	% of cultivable land	source
1920	38.69	n.a.	Bardoli RSR 1925
1924	37.50	n.a.	ibid.
1952–53	43.60	83.27	Gazetteer Surat District 1962
1960	41.81	71.13	ibid.
1970	40.99	75.56	Agricultural Census Gujarat 1970–71
1970–71	38.69	76.82	Report of the Gujarat State Land Commission 1977
1977–78	36.66	74.35	ibid.

The mutual displacement which has arisen between the propertied classes in the upper brackets has been undoubtedly more radical. The proportion of holdings extending to more than 25 acres in the *taluka*—still 6.5 per cent of the total at the beginning of the 1950s, which embraced about a third of the cultivated area—had by the end of the 1970s dwindled to barely 1 per cent of all holdings, occupying only 6.5 per cent of the cultivated area; i.e. the proportion decreased both absolutely and relatively. It would be incorrect to conclude that this category of landownership is of little further significance. In the first place the deterioration is less than these numbers suggest; the introduction of a legal maximum in the intervening years, however much this might be disregarded in practice, leads unavoidably to under-registration of agrarian property above the maximum. In the second place I would like to point out that, even taking into consideration the statistical distortion which for these reasons has come about, large holdings still always cover a greater amount of land than that which marginal owners, forming a third of the total, can command.

These marginal notes do not however detract from my conclusion that the centre of gravity in the agrarian order has moved to the owners of about 15 acres. As I have already said, I draw the dividing line here between the classes of middle and large farmers, in whose social position there has been considerable improvement as the result of institutional change in the agrarian framework which until now has not been taken into account. I am alluding here to the abolition of tenancy. It is not a mere coincidence that the restructuring of ownership rights preceded technological modernization. In the hinterland of Surat District especially, leasing had become a mode of exploitation which persisted until the beginning of the Second World War. Through indebtedness a great many of the tribal producers fell into the bondage of dependence on money lenders and merchants—principally Baniyas, Brahmins and Parsis usually established in the larger villages and market centres—who had no personal interest in working the land but only in what it yielded. For that matter, many farmers even from higher castes in the central plain had in a similar way become tenants on their own farms, and in the mid-1920s half of the land was not being worked by its owners, according to the Bombay Settlement Commissioner (Charlesworth 1980: 271). The first protective regulations enacted on the strength of the Bombay Tenancy Act of 1939 appear to have had an immediate effect. 'The money lending classes unloaded part of their land possessions during the war period probably with a view to realise the best price, or to get rid of an asset which had come to be an object for social disapproval in their case and had become the target for many restricting Government laws' (C.H. Shah 1952: 559).

Yet at the beginning of the 1950s about a quarter of the total cultivable area in Surat District was still in the hands of absentee landowners (Gazetteer Surat District 1962: 407). However, the abolition of tenancy, carried through in 1957, to a large extent put an end to this practice, i.e. the concentration of land in the possession of non-cultivators. Transfer to the actual cultivators did not necessarily mean, however, that the land was returned directly to the original owners or their heirs. A large proportion of the original tribal property in the central plain ultimately fell into the hands of middle and larger farmers from higher castes, through the leasing mechanism and mediated through a commercial capitalism holding its own up to the middle of this century.

The land reform legislation of which abolition of tenancy formed a part, was based on the premise that 18 acres of dry land, 8 acres of seasonally irrigated or 4 acres of permanently irrigated land was necessary for a viable farm holding. Although even at that time a somewhat smaller amount would probably have been sufficient—Baks (1969: 17) referring to local research, worked it out at 10 acres *jarayal* (dry land) and 3 acres *kyari* (monsoon-irrigated land)—the lowering of the economic holding since then to 5 acres at the completion of my fieldwork illustrates the increased value and productivity of this basic agrarian asset. The factor which has had the greatest influence on this achievement has undoubtedly been the extension of the irrigated area, and M. B. Desai's study makes it clear that the spread of irrigation has necessarily remained limited to middle and large farms, with the result that the existing inequality within the farming population has increased still further (table 3.5).

In the years that have passed since the introduction of the Land Ceiling Act (1960 and amended in 1974, when the ceiling was further lowered) the irrigated surface area in the central plain has also increased still further, but I cannot see any policy in favour of the small farms to compensate for the arrears into which they have fallen.

Just as the realization of a system of canal irrigation preceded a more intensive land usage, so also the abolition of tenancy made it possible and attractive for some of the producers to

Table 3.5 *Irrigated area per farm and per acre by size of operational holding, 1971–2*

size of operational holding	percentage to gross cropped area	*irrigated area* per farm	per acre
5 acres	25.65	0.91	0.26
5–15 acres	40.64	4.54	0.41
15–25 acres	30.36	6.91	0.31
25 acres	38.34	16.82	0.38

Source: M. B. Desai et al., table 4.8.

change over to the capital investments required or the application of the new agrarian technology. These infrastructural and institutional changes were necessary but at the same time were not in themselves sufficient conditions for raising productive capacity. Thus, those with less than an economic size of holding remained to a large extent deprived of irrigation facilities, and moreover these small owners could not afford the expenditure necessary for the modernization of their farming practice. Table 3.6 brings clearly into focus the growing distance between the different agrarian classes.

Because of the non-selective character of the random sample, with a great under-representation of both the smallest and the largest holdings, I have not included the averages for these economic indices. The first and last vertical columns represent the most significant jumps in the division of the propertied classes in agriculture. This fits in with the findings of other publications which take a limit of between 5 and 25 acres as their starting point. As I have argued in the foregoing pages however, in my view the sharp rise in productivity which has been achieved on a great deal of the cultivated land in the plain in the past twenty years, is a convincing argument for retaining a lower limit of 15 acres for a large farm holding. The upper stratum holding more than this forms an agrarian elite that has provided the lead in the process of agrarian transformation, and has also been seeking ways of investing the new capital outside agriculture, in education and in rural or even urban industry.

In taking these initiatives they can count on the support and imitation of middle farmers who, as will shortly become

Table 3.6 *Economic status by size of operational holding based on a sample of 150 households in Surat District, 1971–2*

size of operational holding	number of family members		number of earners		rate of illiteracy of family members	average house value in Rs	value of traditional and modern implements in Rs		savings and investment in Rs	value of durable consumer goods in Rs	gross income in Rs		cash receipts in Rs		proportion of cash receipts to gross output
	per farm	per acre	per farm	per acre			per farm	per acre	per farm	per farm	per farm	per acre	per farm	per acre	
< 5 acres	7.04	2.35	2.28	0.76	48.65%	2,377	82.43	27.59	23.95	435	1,688	475	526	148	31.15%
5–15 acres	8.70	0.90	2.17	0.22	25.95%	14,982	513.28	53.45	603.44	2,145	9,125	817	8,029	719	87.98%
15–25 acres	9.22	0.48	1.65	0.08	21.96%	15,209	780.23	40.70	1388.60	2,658	12,949	569	10,728	471	82.84%
> 25 acres	10.34	0.27	1.56	0.04	20.17%	27,212	1482.69	39.65	3768.24	5,017	36,376	829	32,272	735	88.71%

Source: compounded on the basis of various tables in M. B. Desai et al.

apparent, originate to a large extent from the same social milieu. The latter form the largest propertied class among cultivators if one does not include the marginal owners within the ranks of farming classes. The proprietors of these middle-sized holdings constitute nearly a third of the total farming population and monopolize half of all cultivable land in my research area (see table 3.3). The great interest they display in industry and work outside agriculture in the region, is connected with the need for launching a proportion of the new generation in other directions, avoiding in this way the subdivision of holdings. On the basis of their wider financial opportunities and higher social status as well as the more influential outside contacts accompanying these, they succeed in penetrating to the higher circuits of off-farm employment but nevertheless agriculture continues to be the chief source of livelihood for the majority of these households. Together with the bigger landowners, I count these middle farmers among the prosperous agrarian classes which throughout the whole plain of south Gujarat have gained a dominant position in the capitalist mode of production.

The landless proletariat

The landless proletariat in Surat District is not only greater in size than each propertied class in agriculture individually but is greater than all these classes put together (see table 3.7). Their annual increase between 1961 and 1981 has been no less than 2.3 per cent, a growth figure higher than that for the agrarian population as a whole. In consequence their proportion within this latter had likewise risen from 44.5 per cent in 1961 to 54.5 per cent in 1981. A change in the definition of 'worker' in 1971 has probably led to the acceptance of an exaggerated increase for labourers in the whole of India. The slight drop in the percentage of the landless shown in 1981 does not therefore indicate a real decline but must be explained as a statistical correction to the over-registration which resulted from the change of definitions in the previous census.[3] The increase, absolute and

[3] Changes in the counting procedure was one of the reasons for a steep rise in the percentage of agricultural labourers in West Bengal also, between 1961 and 1971 (Bandyopadhyaya 1977: A114).

Table 3.7 *Percentage distribution of working population in agriculture in Surat District, 1951–81.*

administrative unit	1951			1961		
	agricultural population	cultivators	agricultural labourers	agricultural population	cultivators	agricultural labourers
Bardoli	100	49.58	50.42	100	35.24	64.76
Palsana	100	47.28	50.72	100	28.98	71.02
Valod	100	74.60	25.40	100	59.62	40.38
Surat District	100	71.35	28.65	100	55.45	44.55

Percentage distribution of working population in Surat District, 1951–81

administrative unit	1971			1981		
	agricultural population	cultivators	agricultural labourers	agricultural population	cultivators	agricultural labourers
Bardoli	100	21.74	78.26	100	20.04	79.96
Palsana	100	20.60	79.40	100	14.05	85.95
Valod	100	40.75	59.25	100	44.38	55.62
Surat District	100	44.91	55.09	100	45.54	54.46

proportional, in the landless proletariat is a phenomenon that also appears in other parts of the country, even though usually on a much lower level. There are few other places in Gujarat or elsewhere in India where the numbers of agricultural labourers has exceeded those of the landowners.[4] The relative exception formed by this agrarian configuration of Surat District and, to a more extreme degree still, of its heartland, can be gathered from table 3.8.

Combined with the extremely high percentage of marginal owners and small farmers, the enormous size of the landless proletariat illustrates the great extent to which pressure on agrarian sources of livelihood has intensified. A calculation based on a farm management study in Surat District dating from the end of the 1960s demonstrates that the number of working days per hectare of cultivable land amounted at that time to 171 per annum. Taking an average of 300 working days as our starting point, this produces an estimated need for 260,000 employees in agriculture, but as is apparent from the 1971 census, the agrarian population already included a total work force of about 400,000, from which we can deduce a surplus of 150,000 (Samanta n.d.: 56–7). In other words, ten years ago about a third of the available manpower in agriculture was already in fact superfluous. Since then the supply of labour has increased faster than demand for it, and under the influence of the raising of agrarian productivity this disparity has intensified. Personally speaking, I am sceptical about this kind of arithmetical exercise which in my view shows evidence of a much too mechanistic representation of reality. For instance, it is naive to postulate the uniform participation of the different classes in the execution of agricultural operations and job incomes from off-farm employment are moreover, quite wrongly left out of consideration. Nonetheless, this finding is useful for providing an approximate indication of the high number of labourers engaged in agricultural work.

What also come clearly to the fore in tables 3.7 and 3.8 is the unequal distribution of agricultural labour over Surat

[4] Tanjore District in Tamilnadu was an example of such an area, where in 1971 agricultural labourers comprised 42 per cent of the total working population and 59 per cent of the agrarian occupational population. In the years since then this percentage has risen still further (Gough 1978: 47).

Table 3.8 *Change in the proportion between cultivators and agricultural labourers, 1951–81*

territory	1951	1961	1971	1981
	cultivators : agricultural labourers	cultivators : agricultural labourers	cultivators : agricultural labourers	cultivators : agricultural labourers
India	4.60 : 1	3.16 : 1	1.68 : 1	n.a.
Gujarat	2.49 : 1	3.61 : 1	1.95 : 1	1.65 : 1
Surat district	n.a.	1.24 : 1	0.82 : 1	0.84 : 1
Bardoli, Palsana and Valod *talukas*	1.26 : 1	0.69 : 1	0.26 : 1	0.32 : 1

Source: Population Census Reports 1951, 1961, 1971, 1981.

District. While in the comparatively thinly populated and remote eastern *talukas*, tenancy was the institution whereby the tribals living there were exploited—the majority of them continued until after independence to be maintained as dependent peasants on their own land. The largest tribal grouping in the western *talukas* had already from early times been denied access to land. Besides being notable for an extremely high population density and the best arable land, Bardoli Vibagh stands out particularly as an area with a concentration of agricultural labourers. According to the findings of the 1971 census (the figures for 1981 are so far lacking) 74 out of every 100 agrarian workers in Bardoli, Palsana and Valod Talukas belong to this class—a truly unprecedented percentage, resulting from an extremely rapid increase in the previous years. As far as the plain in south Gujarat is concerned this finding signifies a refutation of Bardhan's conclusion (1977: A38) that in the period 1961–71 there had been little or no change in the size of the rural proletariat.

Vyas, in his article (mentioned earlier) on the dislocation which has taken place in the agrarian structure of Gujarat, names four factors in explanation of this dynamic:

- an accelerated demographic growth of the social categories from which the agricultural labourers originate
- loss of land among small farmers
- the expulsion of superfluous members of small farmers' households
- the decline of traditional employment for artisan and service castes

How do these arguments measure up to the situation in south Gujarat? To begin with there are no signs of an extra-rapid growth of the caste of Halpatis, from which the vast majority of agricultural labourers are recruited; increase among this caste of tribal origin in the central plain is even below the growth figure for the landless proletariat in Surat District.[5]

[5] The 19.74 per cent increase among the Halpatis between 1961 and 1971 was outstripped by the relatively higher growth figure, 26 per cent, among the tribal castes. This is probably attributable to under-registration as a result of wrong classification (Murthy 1978: 7 and 14). Otherwise, the increase in numbers of Halpatis in Bardoli Taluka from 28,021 to 36,060 approaches the average rise in tribal population. Nonetheless the population of agricultural labourers in the Halpatis' living area increased

As far as the second factor is concerned, Vyas denies that the numbers of landless labourers are replenished from above by descent down the agrarian ladder. Except for the marginal landowners, of whom a proportion no longer appear to be able to hold their own in working the land themselves, I am inclined to endorse this conclusion for Bardoli and neighbourhood, at least as far as the small farmers living there are concerned, as I stated in the previous section. Vyas argues 'It is really the third and fourth possibilities, namely, the influx of surplus members from the small farmers' households and artisans and other workers in rural areas, which can explain the bulk of the increase in the number and proportion of agricultural labourers in the rural work force' (1975: 7).

However, even this last explanation is not adequate for an understanding of change in the composition of the agrarian population in Surat District, because it is precisely in this area that a dynamic appears which is lacking elsewhere in Gujarat. This according to Vyas is a diversification of the rural economy and with it the possibility of escaping to urban employment at not too great a distance.

In the central plain it is precisely the members of small-farmer and of artisan and service castes who seize the chance of taking refuge in the new employment opportunities, and the majority of them thus manage reasonably successfully to avoid being reduced to an agricultural labourer's existence. The fact that, proletarianization on a large scale is nonetheless, also going on in Surat District is connected with the influx, temporary or permanent, of peasants and landless labourers from the tribal hinterland and even from neighbouring Maharashtra, into the central plain. This wholesale displacement of labour is a comparatively recent phenomenon (one which has occupied a central place in my research and to which I shall return in detail in chapters 6 and 7) and is associated with an accelerating process of differentiation among the tribal farming population in the hinterland. Here I will content myself with the observation that this geographical mobility within the district or over the district borders has performed the function of masking downward social mobility. Nevertheless, for

---

much faster between 1961 and 1971 than the demographic growth of this 'Scheduled Tribe'.

an explanation of the movement of labour it is not enough to point to processes of socio-economic change in the area of origin. Of greater importance still—and this phenomenon has been decisive for the location and direction of my research—is the demand for this outside labour which has arisen in the south Gujarat plain. As I shall argue, this need is very closely connected with the increasing dominance of the capitalist mode of production.

While making this *leitmotiv* clear in my fieldwork and source-materials study, I do not wish to create the impression that the existence of an extensive landless proletariat in Bardoli and neighbourhood originated in the accelerated transformation of the rural economy in recent decades.

This conclusion would be a serious misunderstanding of the nature of the rural order which has always characterized Surat District. The essential feature of this was not a rather homogeneous mass of cultivating farmers, but rather a population which separated out into classes of the landowners and the landless, the latter for the large part bound to the former in an unfree state. This division within the agricultural population was mentioned even in the earliest colonial writings. Considering the chief preoccupation of the rulers, namely the question of how to tax the yield from the land, it is hardly surprising that little systematic attention was paid to the landless class until the end of the British rule. However, it is evident from the cadastral surveys carried out during the second half of the nineteenth century in this *taluka* that a considerable proportion of the agrarian population were landless labourers in Bardoli and its neighbourhood. In the correspondence which followed the presentation of the first report in 1865, farm servants were mentioned, although with no details of numbers or of their relations towards employers.[6] However, from an enclosure in the report of the revised survey of the same *taluka* dating from 1895 it appears that the classes of farmers and labourers were much the same in size: 45 per cent of the total

[6] Comments by A. Rogers, Revenue Commissioner, on the Settlement Report for Bardoli Taluka 1865, 23 January 1866, sections 25 and 28.

population were farmers (tenants as well as owners), 32 per cent were agricultural labourers, while the rest (nearly a quarter) were non-agrarian workers (Bardoli RSR 1897, appendix D). Bardoli formed no exception in the plain; the identical report from 1911 on Palsana Taluka, which formed part of the principality of Baroda, gave the information that 5,972 of the 12,649 male inhabitants—i.e. nearly half—were agricultural labourers without land (Palsana RSR 1911: 5). It is certainly not permissible to generalize for the whole of Surat District on the basis of this information. Once again I must point out that agricultural labour occurred much less frequently in the earlier period in the tribal hinterland. Conversely landlessness in the plain was probably a phenomenon that could not be separated from the manner in which the land was originally brought under cultivation many centuries ago.

When confining my attention to the context of this chapter, I maintain that the presence of an extensive landless proletariat in Bardoli Vibagh several generations ago indicates a property structure and, in line with this, labour relations which crystallized long before the processes of firstly, commercialization in the nineteenth century and secondly, modernization of the agricultural economy in the twentieth century were set in motion.

My conclusion that present-day social formations within the agrarian order have their roots in a bygone mode of production does not mean that the nature, size and composition of the rural proletariat have remained unchanged. In any case I would not willingly take upon myself this thesis of social continuity in view of the transformation which has come about in rural south Gujarat. The vast majority of the indigenous agricultural labourers in my research area are descendents of agricultural labourers and have been so for many generations already, but in no way does it follow from this that they lead the same life as their forefathers. Apart from the fact that fundamental modifications have taken place in the quality of landless existence, the size of this class has increased significantly. Finally, this growth to approximately three-quarters of the agrarian population in the heartland of the plain during the last few decades has occurred chiefly through the influx from other places, which to an important extent involves tribal cultivators who are unable to make a sufficient living from their own land or who have gradually lost this land completely. The consequence of this is that the composition of the landless proletariat in the area of destination has recently become more heterogeneous.

Conclusion

The entire agrarian population is involved in the transition to the new agrarian order of production, as I have made clear in this chapter. Nonetheless this process has been most visible in the change that has come about in relations between larger landowners (in my terminology, middle and large farmers) on the one hand and landless labourers on the other. These classes have also been the object of my research not because I think, along with Rudra, that they make up the total structure of agrarian stratification, as this economist stated some years ago:

> It is our thesis that, in Indian agriculture today, one can distinguish only two classes . . . a class of big landowners and a class of agricultural labourers (including landless labourers, landed labourers, and poor tenants who do not hire other labourers). There are members of the working population in agriculture who do not belong to these two classes. In our view, they do not constitute or belong to any class or classes. That is because, farmers so placed have on the one hand contradictions among themselves; on the other, they do not have clear-cut contradictions with members belonging to the two classes defined above (Rudra 1978: 1001).

His notion that the small landowners, especially, form neither a seperate class nor a part of any other, leads in fact to a declassing, i.e. the spiriting away of a considerable part of the farming population. Outclassed—so we could call these segments by analogy with a similar reasoning of a more sociological stamp which denies to some castes a place in the *varna* system. Rudra's reduction of a complex reality to a simple social duality is decidedly not the beginning point for my argument. Yet it is precisely these diametrically opposed classes which also occupy the forefront of my research. This is not because I begin with their exclusive existence in an objective or subjective sense (class-for-itself or class-in-itself) but because it is my impression that their mutual relationship sets the tone of the social dynamic in the central plain. The transition to a capitalist mode of production can best be explained through the analysis of the relations maintained by the larger farmers with landless labourers.

What patterns of coalition form the basis of this primary social opposition, and what are their social contours? The middle and large farmers who have put their own stamp on the importation of the new agrarian technology and the rural industry which has come into existence in line with it are for the most part Patidars. Members of this caste form a dominant category in the central plain. Their economic interests run parallel as a rule and the common social identity accents this still further. The boundaries between these two upper classes become blurred in the appeal to caste solidarity and in the manipulation of these primordial sentiments, in many cases very appropriately, as a principle of social organization.

They do not find themselves facing a united front of small cultivators and a landless proletariat, classes which together comprise some four-fifths of the agrarian population in Surat District. In Bardoli Vibagh this percentage is even higher. The smaller farmers in particular, however, separate out into a great diversity of middle and lower castes especially, and their economic interests are furthermore largely divorced from, if not actually in opposition to, those of the mass of agricultural labourers, who belong for the most part to the landless Halpati caste. The subordinated classes within the rural order thus do not only function within seperate economic circuits but also originate from different social milieus, and thus even from the beginning the chance of joining together to make a common stand against the agrarian upper strata has to be regarded as extremely unlikely.

The already existing inequality of access to resources and facilities is unquestionably exacerbated by the differential course of population growth according to agrarian class. Although not detached from this demographic dynamic, the forward march of the capitalist mode of production in recent decades has put tremendous pressure on the rural order and has laid a new foundation for the extreme inequality and fierce opposition arising from it.

By identifying the social nature of the extremities of the agrarian hierarchy, and by tracing their history, it is possible to bring to light the connection, or lack of one, between caste and class. This starting point leads, in the following chapters, first to a discussion of both Patidars and Halpatis, castes which to a great extent form the bulk of the classes of dominant landowners and agricultural labourers respectively in the plain of Surat District. After that I shall devote attention in a seperate chapter to the situation in the hinterland, where a process of differentiation has taken place that results in the expulsion of a proportion of the tribals to the plain where they add, temporarily or permanently, to the number of the landless proletariat already there.

Part II
SOCIAL FORMATIONS IN SOUTH GUJARAT

4
THE DOMINANT LANDOWNERS

Regional dominance

The rural upper stratum of middle and large farmers consists primarily of Kanbi Patidars, a caste which is concentrated in the central belt of the famous black soil. Data on their present-day numerical extent are lacking because no statistics on caste composition have been compiled for many decades. According to the 1872 census this farmer caste comprised 7.50 per cent of the total population in south Gujarat—a figure which reveals little in itself but which nevertheless stands out in sharper relief when we mention that they far exceed in number the Anavil Brahmins, who are, in the traditional status hierarchy, the superiors of the Kanbi Patidars. The proportion of population formed by what was at that time the most eminent rural caste, the top layer of which consisted of feudal landlords, only amounted to 5 per cent.

The territory inhabited by both these castes of landowners in south Gujarat is divided. It rarely happens that many households from different castes live together in the same villages. When Surat District (dating from 1964 in its present form) came into existence, the aspirations of members of the largest farmer caste were not difficult to understand; they ultimately succeeded in giving a territorial content to their increased social influence and control, after devoting many years to this end.

Bardoli Vibagh is undoubtedly the Patidars' most important power base and in this region the proportion of its population reaches approximately 12 per cent. This figure is the same as that at the beginning of this century as we can see from the the 1901 census—with wide local variations in distribution. In four of the ten villages of which M. B. Desai based his study of agrarian modernization they are generally absent. Kolis,

Muslims and Rajputs are the landowners here. In the six other villages their concentration varies from 13 per cent to 43 per cent. Thus, they form a substantial minority, who have control of by far the largest share of land, the prime yardstick for judging rural dominance. It was no accident that Desai, in his research among large farmers, came up with particularly large members from this caste. On the basis of a household survey of ten villages which are more or less representative of conditions in the central plain as a whole, a stratified random sample was made but was so constituted that the number of middle and large farms has been greatly over-represented. Thus it strikes one immediately that over half of this random sample of landowners consists of Kanbi Patidars, while they comprise only 17 per cent of the caste population as a whole. Furthermore only members of this caste are under-represented in the category of small farmers. Their relative importance increases along with farm size, as table 4.1 shows.

Table 4.1 ***Proportion of Kanbi Patidars among the landowning castes in ten villages in Surat District.***

extent of holding	Kanbi Patidars a	Other castes b	total c	ratio a : c
small farmers (< 5 acres)	3	18	21	14%
middle farmers (5–15 acres)	19	26	45	42%
large farmers (> 15 acres)	53	28	81	65%
total number of farmers	75	72	147	51%

Source: M. B. Desai n.d., table 3.6.

Three fairly recent monographs, in which the Patidars appear as the principal landowning caste, make their local hegemony even clearer than do these aggregate but highly selective data. Forming between a sixth and a third of the local population, they control between three-quarters and nearly all of the arable land in these villages (see table 4.2).

Table 4.2 *Patidar dominance in three localities of south Gujarat.*

village	year of research	total population	proportion of Patidars % of population	% of land
Afawa	1961–2*	255 households	32.5	95
"Nevapor"	1963**	244 inhabitants	16.5	96
Sisodra	1973–4***	785 households	20.5	75

[1] Source: * R. M. Patel, *Afawa (Surat District, Gujarat): an advanced village in traditional setting.* Vallabh Vidyanagar 1966.

** C. Baks *Afschaffing van pacht.* (Abolition of tenancy) Diss. Univ. of Amsterdam 1969.

*** M. Kalathil, *The sociological implications of industrialisation in a locality in Gujarat.* Diss. University of Delhi 1979.

The Kanbi Patidars belong to that part of the population which until recently was referred to as *ujliparaj*, 'the fair skinned' a collective name for all those social categories distinguished from the *kaliparaj* registered as 'scheduled tribes' in official statistics. Although representing the 'better part' of a social dichotomy which still operates semi-officially, they separate out into a large number of smaller groupings characterized by a high degree of socio-economic inequality. Several other elite castes occupy a position within the agrarian hierarchy corresponding to that of the Patidars, particularly Anavil Brahmins, Rajputs and Vohras who live in smaller concentrations dispersed throughout the district and who are the dominant landowners in a few villages. Such enclaves do not, however, detract from the Kanbi Patidar's hegemony in the central plain; most of the villages in Bardoli, Palsana and Valod being

[1] A later study (1973) concentrated on the landowners in this village provides the following image of the division, according to size, of the 75 farm holdings:

marginal and small holdings	(< 5 acres)	:	21 farms
medium holdings	(5-15 acreas)	:	37 farms
large holdings	(> 15 acres)	:	17 farms

The owners from both these last categories were all Patidars, who were represented by 71 families (32 per cent of the population) (R. D. Patel 1973).

their territory. The roads leading to anyone of these villages invariably pass by their fields where they supervise the work being carried out by others, over which their tractors ride and on which their motor pumps stand, and on to the village centre, where their homes are the biggest and finest buildings. Local key positions such as those of village headman, police *patel* or secretary of the co-operative, are controlled even when not actually held by members of this caste.

However, in the extension of scale which has also manifested itself in the exercise of power, the villages are no more than bases for the Patidars' sorties into a wider world. Their influence has penetrated right through to the district level in the socio-organizational infrastructure. One encounters them with remarkable frequency, or so it seems, along the road, by the bus stops, in shops and in government offices in the main *taluka* towns. The members of this minority are accustomed to making their presence clearly felt and to expressing their 'surplus value' emphatically in word and deed, but in the formal sense as well they govern public life throughout the whole area. Businesses and agricultural co-operatives bear their caste name; official posts within the various political parties are in their hands, and they decide matters on school boards and in socio-cultural associations. In every respect this heartland of Surat District is Patidar land.

Origin and composition

The Kanbi Patidars have not always held this position of power. In colonial times they enjoyed the reputation of being simple and hardworking peasants of relatively low descent.[2] Several early government reports give the impression that they were of tribal stock, originally, and became Hinduized in the not so distant past. 'The Aborigines of the plains have, to a great extent, adopted the religious and social customs of the Hindus among whom they live . . . The Kanbis are now wholly submissive to Brahmanical Institutes; and are ranged as the

[2] '. . . sober, peaceful, hardworking, hospitable, independent, thrifty . . .' (*Gazetteer Bombay Presidency*, 1877: 52); '. . . the Kanbis . . . retain their good name for their hard work and industry' (Jalalpur RSR 1899: appendix R, 9),

fourth estate of the Indian community' (Census 1881 Baroda Territories 1883: 92). Several sources liken them to the Kolis—the main low peasant caste whose members populate the coastal tract of south Gujarat and adjacent Maharashtra—for whom the process of de-tribalization is historically easier to demonstrate. We certainly cannot completely rule out such a 'dark' past for these genuine 'sons of the soil' who are regarded as founders of villages and the first to have brought the land under cultivation. In contrast to the theory of local origin, there is another and more accepted school of thought which attributes the opening up of Surat District to colonists who came to the area from elsewhere. It is difficult to know who the original inhabitants of Tundi (note: a village in Bardoli Taluka) were but it is probable that around A.D. 1800 today's peasant castes arrived from outside and settled in Tundi. Patidars and Anavils cleared the surrounding forests and prepared the land for agriculture. The Patidars had migrated from Kheda and Baroda districts, (P. Patel 1982: 4). Members of the dominant caste themselves maintain that their forebears came originally from the north and spread out from there over the Surat plain. A story about the founders of a village a short distance to the south-east of Bardoli shows that the Patidars cannot always claim for themselves the right of first clearance.

> Afawa village is an old settlement though its history is obscure. The village is supposed to have come into existence about 500 years back. The geneologists residing in the nearby area say that the first settlers of this village were two murderers who had come to hide themselves in the bushes of this area. But the first regular inhabitors were Kolis. It is said that during a severe famine they left this village. During the survey period there was no Koli household in the village, though they were in the neighbouring villages. Patels of Broach area who came as later migrants, cleared the jungles and made land suitable for agriculture. It is reported that these Patels were attracted by the local administrators who wanted to use them to control the local adivasi population (R. M. Patel 1966: 6).

As the Kanbi Patidars in Surat District began to improve their social position, since the end of the last century their past history was adjusted to the new conditions. Their not-very-respectable background became hidden behind the claim to kinship with the caste of the same name in Kheda District in central Gujarat. In this area to the north several prominent sections (the Patidars) had in the course of the nineteenth century already gone through a process of upward social mobility which ultimately also benefitted Kanbis living elsewhere.

Is the claim about migration from the north merely an invention? Indeed not, at least for part of them. In the area of ascribed descent itself there are sufficient indications of the early emigration of the Kanbis to north Gujarat among other places, where they also established themselves as reclaimers of land (G. Shah 1975: 24–5). The trek to the south probably occurred in several waves which can be explained chiefly in terms of economic need. Thus the Levas of Surat District—the biggest sub-caste among the Kanbi Patidars—trace their arrival in the area back to the famine that prevailed in Charotar (central Gujarat) in 1786–7. After receiving favourable reports from those who had left, many others followed (Mahuva RSR 1916: appendix D). It has become a standard and frequently repeated story that . . . they (Leva Patidars) are in majority in this taluka (Bardoli) and they mostly migrated from Charotar and surrounding villages' (S. D. Patel 1965). Informants from smaller Patidar sub-castes—for example Bhakta, Kadva and Anjana—whom I met in Surat District, told me that they had originated from north Gujarat. In none of these cases could they confirm their claim by showing existing family ties with the area of descent. For the rest, geographical origins are not the only dividing line along which the various sections of Kanbi Patidars separate out. While the Levas have been Vaishnavas from of old, the Matias adhered in the past to all kinds of Muslim practices from which they have increasingly disassociated themselves. During a recent anthropological research an informant gave the following explanation for this:

> Our community got influenced by Islam because we were not well-versed in our own cultural heritage. We did not know what we had. Now that many of us are educated, we find that our original culture is superior to what we adopted in ignorance. Hence we are resuming our ancient practices and discarding the accretions from Islam (Kalathil: 40–1).

The Matias, who are found only in south Gujarat, also trace their origin back to Charotar. If this really is the case then they probably took part in a rather early wave of migration. A colonial report mentions that the Matias in Sisodra (probably the same village where the anthropological research, quoted above, was carried out) were towards the end of the eighteenth century already attempting to improve their status by means of 'acts of religious piety'.[3]

The self-image of the Kanbi Patidars in south Gujarat is that of a colonizing caste from which a great number migrated here in previous generations in order to found villages and to take the initiative in opening up new lands. Caste leaders maintained that the cradle of their caste was in the Punjab or even in Central Asia, from whence they migrated long ago to what is now Gujarat. This tale about their descent enables them to claim kinship with the Jats, the corresponding farmer-caste dominant in the north-western plain.[4] After arriving in their present area of domicile they split up, for all kinds of reasons. These divisions resulted in a restricted social interchange, with the exclusion of marriage alliances. Only during the last decades has change again taken place under the influence of all kinds of modernizing tendencies, and the earlier unity gradually restored, at least externally.

This Kanbi lore needs to be modified for a number of reasons. In the first place it seems credible that small groups of peasants should migrate from the north over a long period, a migration in which economic motives—scarcity of land as well as acute crises such as periodic famines—played an important role. In so far as these colonizers brought new land under cultivation they did so as ordinary cultivators and not as a non-working landlord elite. Secondly I think it is unlikely that the migration took place collectively by caste groups. As a matter of fact the Kolis are also said to belong originally to north Gujarat, from whence they drifted south over a long period of time (A. M. Shah 1982: 12). The newcomers mingled with the local population of tribals, which I would regard as an expression of their rather low social origin. As is evident from several sources until the end of the nineteenth century it remained the custom to take women from low castes, Kolis and Dublas, for instance (Toothi; Census of India 1921, XVII, 328).

In the third place I think that there can be no valid reason

[3] Bates 1981: 788. This author refers to a colonial report maintaining that the name Matia goes back to *muth* = monastery.

[4] *Gujaratne Rajkiya* . . . 1972: 466. See also Pocock 1972: 15[8], footnote 1.

to speculate that there was one original caste of which all Kanbis formed a part. Rather there were a number of peasant groupings which enjoying approximate equality in economic position, sought mutual kinship on a social level also. The differences in life styles which developed with the amalgamation of castes were maintained for a long time and until the beginning of this century were still perceptible even to outsiders.

Until far into the nineteenth century the Kanbis in Bardoli Vibagh were subordinated to Brahmin castes of landlords and tax farmers who held a dominant position here (Anavils in Sarbhon, Motalas in Mota). In the earlier period the Kanbis were only able to advance where this rural elite was lacking, such as in the village of Afawa, where according to the first settlement survey of Bardoli in 1865 they were the chief landowners (Bardoli SR 1865, section 39). The treatment they received at the hands of the tax farmers in the principality, who made exorbitant demands on the farmers, illustrates their lowly position:

> We, Brahmins (n.b. it appears from the context that it concerns Bhatelas, the cultivating sub-caste among the Anavils), declining to pay, were kept in custoday in the chowri for one or two days, our cattle were tied up, & c. The Kanbis suffered more. They were made to stand touching their toes, with stones on their backs, and so forth, and in this way the tax was levied from us (Baroda Enquiry Commission, I: 400).

Until the beginning of the twentieth century they occupied only a modest proportion of the total cultivable land, no more than 13 per cent in Kamrej and Mahuva, according to the reports of the revised settlement surveys of these *talukas* (Kamrej RSR 1910: 15; Mahuva RSR 1916: 7). According to these reports the best land along the river was in the hands of the Anavils, who were the first to establish themselves in the area. The Kanbis who came after them occupied the largest share of the black soil, and only the worst land was left for the tribal farmers.

This formulation creates the erroneous impression that a more or less empty territory was opened up by the colonists. What in fact happened was that the tribals living here lost increasingly more land, beginning with the best of it, to the invading members of the higher castes. In this way the process of colonization that was still forging ahead around the turn of the century took shape. In Mahuva, *ujliparaj* from the surrounding *talukas*—the Kanbis from Bardoli were particularly mentioned in this context—marched in and made themselves masters of the tribal land, the colonial government taking an active interest in driving out the original owners. The official charged with carrying out the settlement survey, claimed that the members of the cultivating castes, finding an outlet for their energy would provide an example to the tribals (Mahuva RSR 1916). The Kanbis did not renounce their tradition as a caste of colonists. When resources in the plain were exhausted they pressed further into the hinterland. Information about this migration, due to a lack of cultivable land which became more marked at the end of the century, dates from as early as the beginning of the nineteenth century (Collector Morison's Report, 1812: 135).

> In many parts of the taluka, there is no room for further increase; and the emigration of cultivators to places as far out as Nandurbar is not unknown (Bardoli RSR 1895, para 22).

At the end of the nineteenth century one would have been able to typify the Kanbi Patidars in Bardoli Vibagh as simple middle peasants cultivating their land themselves and spending their lives as ordinary Shudras. In contrast to the Anavil Brahmins who as a rural elite could afford to keep farm servants, the Kanbis were mainly, if not exclusively, dependent on the labour power of their own household.

> 'Bhatella Brahmins are, if anything, superior to Koonbees; because, in addition to better status, they have the privilege of free labour from their Hallees or bondsmen, who are as a body devoted to their master's interest, and reside on the farm, a circumstance which accounts for the Bhatella holdings being generally more attended to, and worked to the best advantage', according to the report of the cadastral survey in Jalalpur taluka 1868–69 (Jalalpur RSR 1899: appendix R.8).

Even in this period it was not exceptional for Kanbis to be compelled to obtain a livelihood by working on the land of other cultivators. Members of the tribal Chaudhari caste in Valod Taluka told me that Kanbis, shortly after their arrival in the area, worked alongside them in the fields only two generations ago. In other words the Kanbis had worked with the grandparents of the present generation of tribal Chaudharis. The relationship of dependence which then existed, as a result of Kanbis labouring for tribal cultivators, was reversed in the previous generation, the same kind of social reversal also occurring elsewhere. Pocock writes about the Bareias in Kheda District—a low caste of ex-landowners who now work as agricultural labourers—that 'They once sent food to the Patidars' (Pocock 1973: 75).

Economic growth

The Kanbis have profited like no other caste from the extension of large-scale cotton cultivation. This crop has laid the basis for their rise to the position of a respectable caste of gentlemen farmers in the mid-twentieth century.

Cotton was seldom found in the region until the mid-nineteenth century. Around Navsari, for instance, it was only grown for the personal needs of the farming population (Jalalpur RSR 1899: appendix R.6) and there was little to show for early attempts by the colonial government to extend production in Surat District. Change came only after the outbreak of the American Civil War, when increased demand functioned as a catalyst. Within a few decades cotton became the principal cash crop in the central plain and the farmers' most important source of income. However, as I established in Chapter 1, it was the merchants and money lenders who profited, rather than the producers. Buyers who were themselves owners of the cotton gins newly opened in the area and who acted as agents for the trading houses in Bombay, were guilty of all kinds of dishonest practices.

> Poor farmers sold their cotton in advance before the crop was ready, thus losing the opportunity to sell it when the prices were favourable. *Dalals* made the farmers sign a contract (*Kabala*) which was binding on the cultivator but could be broken by the gin owner, under the pretence of the cotton being inferior at the time of the delivery. After the contract was signed by the farmer, if the cotton went down, the gin owner troubled the farmer in several ways. He refused to take the cotton under the pretext that it was of an inferior quality. If accepted, the farmer who had no knowledge of

> weighing, was invariably cheated on delivery of his goods. When the gin owner withholds immediate payment he adulterated the cotton; and when he received a lesser price for such adulterated cotton he paid the farmer a much lower price. This opportunity to cheat the farmer was due to most of the cotton being sold in the villages. Seldom was it brought to the market.[5]

The risk accompanying production for the market led to an increasing indebtedness to money lenders (*savkars*) and merchants, with the result that these commercial classes took over an increasingly larger share of the cultivable area. Registration of landownership in six villages of Kamrej on the occasion of the revised cadastral survey in this *taluka* in 1909, brought to light the fact that Baniyas and Parsis had acquired 62 per cent of all agrarian property. The Kanbis had only 13 per cent of the land, which was less than their proportion of the farming population (Kamrej RSR 1910: 15), but in contrast to the tribal farmers they had been able to hold their own in the process of commercialization. More than that, as middle farmers they were now better able to withstand the buyers' manipulations, and they were also considered to be more efficient producers. They were able to extend their landownership gradually at the cost of the tribal owners regarded as being inferior cultivators. The yields from cotton therefore brought advantages to the Kanbis, albeit tardily and sporadically rather than continuously. The cultivation of cotton enlarged their market orientation in terms of both production and consumption, and there were signs of greater prosperity, but to speak of 'unmixed prosperity' as did the reporter of the cadastral survey in Bardoli shortly before the close of the nineteenth century, was going much too far in the Collector of Surat's view. In a rather tart commentary in the revised Survey and Settlement Report he indicated the increasing indebtedness of the high caste farmers.

> . . . the present men as they live less labourious lives, . . . have more expensive tastes than their forbears, and to gratify them will refer to the savkar, if there is no money in the house. Formerly the ordinary cultivators to a man wore more country cloth; now they must have it of finer texture from Manchester. Cheap local rice,

[5] Choksey 1968: 144. For a more extensive treatment of these kinds of fraudulent practices see Dantwala, chapter 3.

> dal and gul were enough for the daily food; now vegetables, imported rice and refined sugar are in demand. A more luxurious generation seeks after *pan-supari*, chiroots, hired servants, sweetmeats, and American watches, and will borrow money to get them.[6]

Part of the transition to a new, more respectable life style was the struggle to protect themselves as far as possible against having to perform agricultural labour. After a long period of time the large majority of the members of the dominant caste ultimately succeeded in distancing themselves from the heavy manual labour accompanying the farmers' life. Although as early as a century ago they were regarded as belonging to the higher and better-endowed classes of *ujliparaj*, as simple middle peasants, they were still obliged to recognize the Anavil Brahmins (who formed the rural elite in south Gujarat) as their superiors. The economic supremacy of this landlord caste was reinforced by their behaviour as patrons towards landless labourers who worked for them as bonded farm servants (*halis*). The highest section among them especially—the Desais, who fulfilled the function of tax farmers—led a splendid existence in the countryside on a more or less feudal pattern. Only a small number of Kanbis could measure up to them, namely those living in the more southerly-lying 'garden'-land villages where sugarcane, the cash crop of that period, was grown.

> There is no part of Guzerat in which the sugarcane is cultivated to the same extent and perfection as in our own and the Guikwar districts in the attaveesy (n.b. this term refers to the territorial division of pre-colonial south Gujarat into twenty-eight administrative units). In a few villages of the Guikwars the assessment is I believe as high as Rupees 100 a beega on sugarcane, and there are some Coonbees in our villages who consume all the other produce of their farms themselves, and pay their entire Revenue from jagree and who are as rich people in their way as any I have ever met with, indeed they may be called Planters as they have 30 to 40 bond servants and cattle in proportion under them (Letter of Collector of Surat, W.J. Lumsden, 9-4-1823: 4816).

As we have intimated, this sort of story nearly always applied to a small top layer among the landlords. The majority of

[6] Thus the reaction of the Collector of Surat directed towards the Commissioner, Northern Division, on 27 January 1896 (Bardoli RSR 1897: para. 6).

Kanbis in Bardoli Vibagh lived in an extremely modest fashion and little or no change was to enter this situation in the course of the nineteenth century. Whenever they commanded the labour of farm servants they themselves worked beside them on the land, but since elsewhere in Gujarat the landowners as a rule had to be satisfied with household labour, the use in that period of outside labour (farm servants or day labourers) was viewed as an ostentatious luxury. In the report of the revised cadastral survey of Palsana, the custom among the high caste farmers in south Gujarat of keeping *halis* was attributed to the climate.

> The cultivators, owing to laziness or want of vigour, do not themselves do all that is done by their brethren in Kadi, Amreli and Baroda Divisions. The average Kunbi of the Navsari Division is much inferior in strength and vigour to the average Kunbi of Amreli (Palsana RSR 1911: 6).

Even though they may not have done 'all that is done by their brethren', what they did do was quite sufficient to keep intact their local reputation for industriousness and hard work, at least for the time being. The economic dependence on middlemen established the Kanbis' position as that of a solid middle caste, and until the end of the first half of this century most members of the caste led a relatively simple life. Cattle were kept inside the houses and Kanbi women shared in the work on the land. This latter detail is not without importance when one thinks of a proverb regarding the rural elite of that time, about the Anavil women's shameful habit of openly carrying food to their menfolk in the fields (in Bozzadaille 1874; Desai 1930: 131).

In order to succeed in establishing a claim to higher status it was necessary in the beginning for the Kanbis to disengage themselves from the pressure of the elite castes and to shape a freer social space for themselves. This was made easier by the creation of a new *taluka* in 1861 of which Bardoli became the administrative headquarters. Together with the abolition of the tax farming system, which had continued in the territory of the princely state of Baroda, this bureaucratic realignment signified an undermining of the power of the ruling Brahmin castes which had their domain in Sarbhon (the Anavils) and Mota (the Motalas). The colonial government contributed to the inevitable dislocation of the old feudal elite in the south Gujarat countryside by promoting production for the market and thus reorienting its economic policies from those who appropriated agricultural surplus to those who actually produced it. As the older centres lost their importance a number of Brahmin households left the area, the Anavils in particular joined the colonial bureaucracy in cadre positions. On their departure from Sarbhon they transferred the landownership to the Kanbis.[7]

Release from isolation was necessary for measuring up to the new yardstick for gauging progress. Lack of roads made the area to the east to Surat difficult to reach and on these grounds the population there was considered to be backward. Improvement was only very gradual as would appear from the report of the revised settlement survey in 1895 for instance. 'The road from Surat to Bardoli was, up to the beginning of last year, no better than it was 30 years ago; for Colonel Prescott's description of it, that, ' "nothing more execrable than it could be conceived, and that to travel on it broke the heart of man and beast", suited it exactly' (Bardoli SRR 1895: para 19). The construction of the Tapi Valley Railway from Surat to west Maharashtra shortly before the turn of the century was especially important in consolidating the economic and administrative function of Bardoli.

Towards the end of the nineteenth century expressions of satisfaction with the hardworking and thrifty Kanbis in the colonial reports began to give way to complaints about the more extravagant life members of this farmer caste were beginning to lead. Better housing, richer diet, more expensive consumption goods and, last but not least, the tendency to take on more farm servants, were not only seen as an indication of material progress but merited special attention in order to justify the raising of the land tax.

The famine of 1899–1900 that ravaged Gujarat also interrupted the process of economic growth in Surat District and created acute distress among large sections of the population.

[7] S. D. Patel 1965: 54. For a description of the changes in the Anavil caste see Van der Veen 1972.

However, for most Kanbi farmers this set-back was only temporary, and they even derived indirect advantages from this crisis, since during this period especially, the tribals—who lived closer to the minimum livelihood and who for this reason alone were already much more vulnerable—lost a large part of their property to money lenders, for whom they still continued to work as tenants for the time being. Once alienated, in the following decades this land ultimately came into the hands of the dominant caste especially in the central plain.

The rise in land prices a few years after the turn of the century was one of the signs pointing to a rapid economic recovery. 'In Bardoli and Jalalpor the jarayat land sometimes fetches more than what it does in Charotar', wrote the Deputy Collector of Surat in 1908 (Choksey: 180). And his superior had already noticed before that in spite of the recent calamity '... cultivators no higher than the middle class now enjoy little luxuries, such as tea which were formerly unknown to them' (Bates 1981 : 805). In the light of this information the thesis of proletarianization of the middle peasants from the beginning of this century, as originally formulated by Hardiman (1976: 369) strikes one as being unconvincing, as Charlesworth and Bates have argued (Charlesworth 1980 and 1982; Bates 1981 : 809). I think, with the latter, that at the beginning of the twentieth century there was an acceleration in the commercialization of economic production which was carried through by middle peasants particularly, such as the Kanbis in Bardoli Vibagh (Bates 1981: 808). The rise in cotton prices between 1890 and 1924, led albeit with great fluctuations, to a steadily increasing extension of cultivation. In the last year of this period this crop occupied a third of the total cultivated area of Bardoli Taluka, a 50 per cent rise compared with the last decade of the nineteenth century (Charlesworth 1880: 270).

Especially during and shortly after the First World War, demand increased so much that one can speak of a real cotton 'boom' in these years. In Bardoli, Palsana and Valod this staple crop occupied the same place of importance as does sugarcane to-day. The ousting of millet as the most important food grain was an irreversable consequence of this boom. 'The period of commercial agriculture' was the significant description in the report of the Baroda Economic Development Committee for these years (1920: 56). In the first quarter of the twentieth century a clear rise in living standards was to be seen among the chief agricultural producers in the central plain. The official commission set up in 1928 to investigate complaints about the increase in the land tax in Bardoli Taluka stated that since the last revision (1895) in the villages, many new houses had been built:

> . . . the population of these *talukas* is fairly well housed, at any rate so far as the better class cultivators, Kunbis, Anavils, etc. are concerned. The appearance of the average village in which people of these classes reside suggests, if not prosperity, at any rate a decent competence (Broomfield and Maxwell 1929: 14).

At the same time the indebtedness already existing increased still further, this was due not only to speculation—the expectation of a further rise in the price of cotton encouraged farmers to grow more cotton than market conditions permitted—but also particularly to the bad habits in which those farmers who had achieved relative prosperity indulged in to excess: 'lavish expenditure in marriages, dowries, caste dinners and the like' (Broomfield and Maxwell 1929: 65). Although castigated as extravagance and prodigality this investment in caste status and caste cohesion had significance not only for consumption: the growing unity on the basis of caste facilitated the Kanbis' interest in setting up agricultural co-operatives. The setting up of these alliances of common interest shortly after the First World War ended the trade monopoly of the Baniya and Parsi middlemen, commercial agents who, towards the end of the nineteenth century, had provided the initiative for the first industrial processing of agrarian products—cotton gins and presses, oil presses, rice hulling and milling establishments, etc. From market places such as Bardoli, Madhi, Mota, Sarbhon and Valod the owners of these small undertakings bound the farmers in the surrounding villages to them by means of advances. Originally the new co-operatives confined their activities to the buying of cotton. In a subsequent phase several cotton gins were also either taken over from the previous owners or founded independently, (e.g. Patidar Ginning and Pressing in Bardoli in 1927, Baben in 1933). The private merchants' and moneylenders' hold, therefore, at least over the middle farmers, gradually relaxed. As I established in chapter 1, the co-operative movement with regard to cotton production was imported into western India via Surat District, and the Kanbis were notable as its initiators. In 1926, also under their leadership, a federation of local alliances came into being with its own office in Surat, a condition for the further consolidation of the producers' interests. The number and also the diversity of co-operatives increased sharply in the following decades, a successful development that has remained a relative exception in India. The formula for the success is intimately connected with the prominent, even exclusive role taken by the Kanbis, who have used this new form of organization to bring to fruition their economic dominance.

Upward social mobility and political action

Shortly after the turn of the century a movement for emancipation, beginning among the younger generation, put an end to the localized existence of the Kanbis and freed them from the stigma of backwardness accompanying that isolation. The derogatory term 'Kanbi' gradually fell into disuse and by dissociating themselves from the villified *bhabha* behaviour—a term referring to the coarse and simple lifestyle of the peasant—and by adopting the new caste name of Patidar they gave themselves the respect they thought due to them and compelled others to follow suit.

The most important instrument of this reform movement was the Patidar Yuvak Mandal founded in 1908 (Bhatt 1970 and G. Shah 1974), the leaders of which had, as young men, been greatly impressed by the militant ideas of the Arya Samaj and had disseminated them among their caste fellows by means of their own periodical *Patidar Hitechhu*. Education was an important cornerstone of the self-improvement programme. In order to make secondary education more accessible a hostel was set up in Surat for Patidar boys in 1911 and, as an *ashram*, this institution continued to be a 'nursery' for the organization of activities. A social worker (*updeshak*) was appointed to go round the villages of the district propagating the new purity, adaptation to the life rules of a higher caste. Undoubtedly it was at this time that there came an end to objectionable customs such as that of taking women from lower castes, social practices belonging to a less polished life style.

Public meetings were held for demonstrating the Patidars' new power and unity, and a blurring of internal lines of division also fittled a strategy directed towards social homogenization. For the Matias this meant abandoning Muslim practices such as that of burying their dead, and their women abandoning the *kachhada* manner of wearing saris, i.e. tied between the legs to facilitate working on the land.

They made great efforts to be accepted as orthodox Vaishnavas by building temples (e.g. S. D. Patel 1965: 59). In this manner their differences from the ostensibly superior Levas were gradually eroded, at least in the eyes of outsiders. The process of upwards mobility had already begun earlier among the Kanbis in Kheda District, and they provided the reference group for their caste fellows in Surat District. 'Whereas in the early nineteenth century they were locally ranked as Sudras, they now stood with the Vanias in ritual status, and reinforced their economic success with those signs of ritual purity, like the prohibition of widow marriage, essential to a caste claiming high status' (Brown 1972: 89). In the 1931 census the Kanbis of Kheda District themselves officially registered as Patidars, and from then on the members of the dominant caste in Surat District also wanted to be known by this name. At the beginning of the twentieth century the word Patidar hardly ever occurred in south Gujarat, and even in school registers they were recorded as Kanbis, a custom to which the Mandal put an end (Bhatt 1970: 318).

The process of social mobilization implied an enlargement of scale which found expression in the emphasis on solidarity with corresponding peasant castes elsewhere. Initially this search for unity remained confined to Gujarat and by tightening bonds with caste fellows in Kheda District and Saurashtra there was a consolidation of power within the Patidar Parishad. This alliance acquired its own mouthpiece in the *Patel Bandhu* which absorbed the periodical published earlier in Surat. The first conference of the Gujarat Patidars took place as early as 1910 and when this gathering was held outside Surat District for the first time in 1917, about 8,000 people took part.

There was, however, also a consciousness of having interests in common with rising peasant castes elsewhere. As early as 1913 the leader of the Patidar Yuvak Mandal visited the 'All India Kurmi Parishad' and in the same year an article appeared in *Patel Bandhu* pleading for natural unity on the basis of shared identity. 'Marathas of Maharashtra, Vokalingas of Mysore, Reddis of Andhra, Naidus of Madras, are all Patidars' according to the slogan that was raised. (Bhatt 1970: 310). Despite opposition from the Brahmins, participation in a more extensive emancipation movement helped the Patidars to shed their Shudra past completely and to claim a higher place in the caste hierarchy.

In a subsequent phase of mobilization the new consciousness and social importance was converted into political hegemony. Work for social reform within the caste receded somewhat into the background and gave way to an increasing combativeness towards the outside world, an appropriate platform for this being the nationalist movement with which affiliation was sought. The Bardoli *satyagraha* of 1928 both confirmed this tendency and rewarded it with success. The militant peasant campaign against the 22 per cent increase in the land tax at a time when market prices were dropping sharply was largely a Patidar affair, their leaders urging the selection of Bardoli Taluka for this action, and Patidars played a decisive role in carrying it out. At first sight this political mobilization seems to have been organized along particularistic lines. The Patidars were exhorted to conduct themselves like true Kshatriyas on pain of expulsion and degradation to untouchable status. In calling for disobedience, other castes were also mobilized by appealing to their own code of conduct. The members had to keep to the specific 'do's and don'ts' which applied to them. Village and caste councils formed the lowest level in the network of organizational activities, and traditional values were articulated through the *Satyagraha Patrika*—the daily bulletin with a circulation of over 10,000 among the farmers in Bardoli Vibagh (Dhanagare 1980). The rare individual who ventured to criticize this strengthening of communalist tendencies and the legitimization of the inequality that was part and parcel of it, was given to understand that results could be obtained only in this way. For a more detailed exposition of the instrumental use of caste sentiments during the course of the campaign, I refer readers to the well documented articles by Bhatt, Shah and Dhanagare.

The main issue in this struggle was the landowners' interest but even more, the interests of the dominant caste. In my view Hardiman, in his discussion with Charlesworth, rightly concludes that: 'Patidar discontent was in other words long-term and political rather than short-term and narrowly economic' (Hardiman 1981: 375). Dhanagare also sees in this the motive for the *satyagraha*: 'What angered Patidars and particularly the Patidar elite, was the fact that their dominance, so visible in local social hierarchy was not acknowledged by the government' (Dhanagare: 1983: 94). This interpretation contradicts the current notion that the initiative for the peasants' mobilization stemmed from the Congress movement. Rather, the Patidars who had achieved the standing of independent cultivators in their struggle for social confirmation of their newly acquired status, accommodated themselves to the nationalist movement. It goes without saying that the Patidars assumed a key position in the front which was formed, and the vast majority of the cadre came from this caste. The simplicity and docility of their following was in fact an important consideration in the decision to mount the action in this region. As one leader wrote: 'It is fortunate that there is no intellectualism in the people of Bardoli, as they do most of the work on faith, otherwise they would not have followed us without questioning' (Bhatt 1970: 329).

A successful agitation would have been inconceivable without the Patidars, but conversely the *satyagraha* consolidated their progress and even assured them national recognition. The emancipation of this caste to a position of rural dominance coincided with the attempt by the nationalist movement to broaden its social base and to extend its activities to the countryside, a process in which caste organization and class formation became closely intertwined. Yet solidarity based on primary loyalties was by definition not enough for accomplishing an all-encompassing and fundamental unity. By using the term *khedut* and stretching it to include agricultural labourers and tenants as well as landowners, it was possible to create the impression of a peasant movement which the entire agrarian population supported and in which all participated out of common interest. Thus, in accordance with Gandhi's teachings, the notion of caste acquired an all-encompassing content.

However, the Patidars' leading role remained clearly visible behind this rural idiom. Although they gave the impression of striving to cross caste barriers through a significant degree of secularization and a common peasant front, little came of it in practice. In order to confirm this with one example, in 1920 the regulation which barred access to the Surat *ashram* to everyone but Patidar boys was abolished, but between 1911 and 1950 (the years for which data are available) out of a total of 1,744 students, only a quarter belonged to other castes, most of these also *ujliparaj*, and during this entire period there were only thirteen tribal students. In other words, the half of the district population belonging to the low tribal castes was represented by barely 1 per cent of the intake in this 'emancipated' institution. Another salient datum is that in 1936 not a single student from any of the untouchable castes was admitted to the *ashrams* and hostels of the Patidar Mandal in the Bardoli area.

The position of leadership occupied by the Patidars in the process of rural transformation in south Gujarat in the post colonial era was in line with their hegemony as the chief landowning class since the beginning of the twentieth century. At the 1917 conference the Patidars had taken the *khedut* as their caste symbol. 'It was argued that all Patidars were peasants by occupation and the well-being of the peasants was therefore the well-being of the Patidars' (Bhatt 1970: 308). Vallabhbhai Patel, subsequently nicknamed the 'Lion of Bardoli', did a great deal to inspire and manage the *satyagraha*, glorifying his caste fellows as the indigenous Indian peasants and priding himself on being a 'son of the soil'.

> By education, family background, style and selfproclamation, the Sardar identified with the landed peasantry of Gujarat, and they with him. Patel, not Gandhi, is credited with making this organizational breakthrough . . . Patidars were called the real producers of India; land tax was their issue and caste solidarity their weapon (Spodek 1975: 1934).

These *bhumiputra* sentiments, used by the Gandhian movement in a popularistic manner in the freedom struggle, have since then become more systematically embedded into the ideology of the new *kulak* class.

It is important here that, in connection with recent developments in Bardoli Vibagh, the members of the dominant caste—

already open to an appeal to self-esteem and self-importance—steeled themselves for an anti-authoritarian stance in the battle for lower land taxes. The *satyagraha* and also the other actions following upon it fulfilled the function of a training school in the resistance to government interference which was to erupt again with great violence a few decades after independence under the leadership of the Patidar-controlled peasant union, the Khedut Samaj. An important instance was the *hijrat* of 1930, when 10,000 peasants from 188 villages in Surat District took refuge in the territory of Baroda during the district's resistance to the colonial government (Hardiman 1977: 62). Thus after first having liberated themselves from social inferiority the Patidars adopted a new formula for the promotion of self-interest, based on their common interest as producers. One could thus sum up the history of the rise of these middle peasants as a transition from caste organization to a class movement. This sequence can be taken for granted, but it still does not take sufficient account of the class elements already present at the consolidation of power. Conversely, it will be clear that even caste consciousness continues to be the active principle of class organization. Referring mainly to Gujarat, Hardiman has observed, quite rightly, that this movement of middle castes was in fact a class movement, to which I would however add that its origins must be sought in economic improvement rather than in deterioration. The political mobilization of the Patidars was not a defensive reaction, but resulted from their progress in producing for the agrarian market.

The effects of emigration

The development of agriculture, and in particular the cultivation of cotton as a principal cash crop, was not the only source of prosperity for the Patidars. Their mobility even took them abroad, and the earnings derived from emigration have contributed to the material progress of the households of this caste in the area. The arduous movement abroad began in the coastal area where the population (Muslims, especially) had from of old maintained overseas links. It is not unlikely that there was an acceleration during the period of economic deterioration around the turn of the century, but even in the years before that the Kanbis were among those who ventured the leap in the dark. Those going away had a low economic standing, but had to be able to pay for the journey at least, as appears from information given by the Collector of Surat in 1899.

> In the early years the trip place in grim conditions, as I was told by Mochis in the village where I carried out my first field work in 1962. Where many of them were concerned, nothing was ever heard of them again after their departure, since a substantial number of them never reached the African coast, the crossing being made by sailing boat (*dhow*) with inadequate navigational means and little food on board. Even K. M., an elderly leader of the Patidar movement in Bardoli, told me that his father first walked to Bombay from Vankaner at the beginning of the 1890s and then crossed from there by sailing ship. He himself was one of the first to make the journey by steam ship. (Jalalpur RSR 1899: 85).

It was no accident that, among the Patidars, it was the Matias who left first. Most of them were small peasants who, in the face of economic progress of their stronger caste fellows the Levas, were in danger of falling still further behind. Moreover, in contrast to the Levas the Matias were not hampered by religious orthodoxy. By seeking their fortune abroad they could try to limit the extent of their backwardness. In my research area I was able to trace the first emigrants to the village of Vankanar, a Matia bulwark halfway between Bardoli and Valod.

Restrictive conditions were rather rapidly imposed in the receiving countries. In South Africa, for instance, from 1914 on, would-be immigrants had to show a clear connection with family members already resident. It would seem that at the end of the 1920s a growing number of caste members followed the example of these pioneers.

> The number of people earning their living in foreign parts is quite considerable in the Sarbhon group of villages, Sarbhon (79), Supa (74), Ambheti (200) also in Vankaner (142), Varad (100), Singod (39), Bamni (45): and probably in others which we did not see. The figure for Bamni, a small village, represents one at least from almost every Kunbi family residing there (Broomfield and Maxwell 1929: 13).

Permanent settlement was hindered, and this explains why the laborious movement overseas—originally to South Africa and

New Zealand in particular—for a long time preserved the character of circulation, but in addition the poverty and insecurity of the migrants, as well as their determination at that point to return eventually to their home area, played an important role in this. Only younger men, usually married, left the village for a period of many years, sometimes in repetitive cycles, while the remaining members of the household stayed behind to take care of the land and other agrarian property. Mention has already been made of the use of diverse savings for the purchase of land (Kamrej RSR 1910: 18, Broomfield and Maxwell 1929: 46–7).

The Levas' success in agriculture delayed their participation in the migration process. 'Unlike Matia Patidars, whatever prosperity that we witness in their villages is entirely due to agriculture and not due to any money brought by them from foreign countries' (S. D. Patel 1965: 58). Yet the higher section of the caste was gradually outstripped by the returning Matia emigrants who brought with them new consumer goods and habits as well as savings from abroad. As one facet of better housing they introduced modern comforts (outside toilet, separate kitchens and bathing corners), while the cattle were banished to a stall outside the house. With 'novelties' such as clocks and radios, etc., living arrangements were adapted to the new taste. Equipped with a water tower, electricity, a temple, a big school and sometimes even a library, the migrants' village became easily recognizable to the researcher. These community facilities are at least partly paid for by collections made overseas and are principally destined for the caste fellows of these openhanded Patidars. It is ususally only the Patidars' houses which are connected to piped water and the electricity grid. Another direct consequence of emigration was the growing interest in education, for girls as well as boys, and the foundation in later years of several secondary schools, among which there is even an English-medium school and a college in Bardoli, thanks to financial support from abroad.

When a sizeable migration resulted from the opening up of new destinations after the Second World War—East Africa, England and (for the more highly trained) the United States—the Levas no longer stayed behind; now they too were ripe for *bahar-gam* (living outside). Narsi Patel mentioned in an autobiographical account published in 1972 that in his own village, where indeed the process had already begun earlier on, perhaps more than half the young men of the village had left for England (N. Patel 1972; see also Baks: 144). This latter emigration however, rapidly decreased with the rigorous restrictions imposed in the former mother country. A new wave has the U.S.A. as its destination, this country having become very popular in recent years. There are many, more particularly among the younger generation, who hope to go there. This wish is not so unrealistic because 40 per cent of the Indian community in the U.S.A. comes from Gujarat (*Indian Express*, 21.3.1982) including many Patidars from Surat District. These are found in particularly large numbers on the West Coast, where a sizeable proportion of the motels are in their hands; 'Hotels, motels and Patels', so reads the heading of an article devoted to the Patidars some years ago in a popular English-language weekly (*Illustrated Weekly*). My attention was repeatedly drawn to this article, emphatically and with pride, and this topic was far more exciting for my informants than my inquisitive probing into their earlier background. The reserve displayed over and again by members of this caste when I brought up the past—the vagueness was not simulated but derived from genuine ignorance on the subject—often gave way to enthusiasm as soon as the conversation turned to emigration. 'We are more interested in future than in past generations', so one of them explained this striking contrast.

The character of migration has changed greatly in the last decade, a change which has had drastic consequences for both migrants and those left behind. More and more often the temporary absence of the migrants has changed into permanent departure, and a significant expression of this has been the shifting of family reunions to overseas. In Narsi Patel's words:

> There is a growing awareness in my village that emigrants have changed. Earlier emigrants used to go abroad alone, come back with their savings and go back alone, whereas nowadays the younger emigrants keep their immediate families with them all the time they can manage it. The villagers cannot understand why they invest their money abroad rather than in their birthplace, why they visit home like tourists and show a greater attachment to the

> foreign country and put their deeper roots there. They complain about how they spoil their children, who behave strangely, talk back and do not know good Gujarati (N. Patel 1972: 63).

The existence of a different migration pattern is a subject for separate study and falls outside the scope of my argument. If I limit my observations to the consequences of the Patidar migration upon their position within the regional economy, particularly during the first phase of circulation, then I would draw the following conclusions:

1. —the departure of some of the young men has served the interests of the households remaining behind:
2. —the differential course of migration among Matias and Levas initially furthered their 'standarization' as members of the same caste;
3. — the return of migrants at an earlier stage led to acceleration of the process of agrarian modernization in the Bardoli area.

Each of these points requires further elucidation. Beginning with the first point, the long and often repeated absence of part of the younger generation of men prevents a premature splitting of the family properly into smaller and thus less remunerative holdings. This of itself reduces the pressure on land, but the effect is still further strengthened by the use of savings transmitted from abroad for the purchase of new plots of land to be added to the family holding. In this way the landownership of the dominant caste has been extended.

It is interesting that the status of a 'migrant' does not of itself bestow prestige. Indeed the opposite is true to a certain extent. Without open discussion of the matter, there is nevertheless a feeling that living in a foreign country all too often does not accord with the newly-won dignity of being a Patidar. Certainly in the beginning, when skill and higher occupational experience were still lacking, migrants were dependent upon unskilled and low-prestige work and in the colonial milieu in which they usually found themselves overseas they were at the mercy of the economic and social discrimination practiced by white employers. This degrading existence in an alien environment was however a sacrifice that had to be made in the interests of those remaining at home, and only on his return did the migrant become 'successful', at any rate if he could provide the material proof of success. Even then his prestige was only relative. Narsi Patel, who in the course of his story about his family devoted attention to these aspects, very perceptively remarked that:

> Yet my uncle commanded greater respect than my father among villagers and relatives, for he was always there in their midst in an endless exchange of favors and obligations; father was aware of this consequence of emigration, and it hurt his pride. While he liked the way uncle had managed everything in his absence, he could not forget that his role as an elder brother and as a member of the kinship, caste and village community was compromised. His self-chosen exile for 11 years was a matchless sacrifice for the joint family. But he became quickly reconciled to the idea that he could save it by going abroad once more (N. Patel 1972: 28).

As we have said, the Matias migrated before the Levas. In South Africa they became familiar with Gandhi's ideas which they put into practice on their return to south Gujarat. They formed an important part of the cadre which led the political action in Surat District (Spodek 1975: 1931). This progressive vanguard role in the campaign ended the social inferiority of the subcastes to which they belonged, and with the help of their overseas earnings the Matias were able to eradicate their initial economic backwardness. The way in which they succeeded in catching up created a greater material conformity within the dominant caste, based on the modern lifestyle held up to all the members as a model. For the rest this modernity was not directed solely towards consumption, but was also significant for production.

> With the foreign money they acquired plots of land and utilized their talent, intelligence and money in making agriculture a prosperous occupation. They did not stop there but they introduced mechanisation in agriculture and cultivated land in most modern techniques and produced more yield than other farmers. They were the first in irrigating land with the help of pumps. They were also the first in introducing shift system in farming, utilising chemical fertilisers in agriculture, using tractors in place of indigenous methods and thus brought about a revolution in the system of agriculture (S. D. Patel 1952: 59).

This quotation on the Matias' economic behaviour at the same time illustrates my last conclusion, that migration has hastened the process of agrarian modernization. It is striking that the leading positions in the co-operative organizations still continue to be reserved for the Leva Patidars (S. D. Patel 1965: 56). The earlier temporary absence and the later permanent departure of the younger generation has not prevented the Patidar caste from remaining rooted in agriculture. As we have indicated, the cause of departure in the first place was not not the desire to escape from a rural existence, but to strengthen their position in the countryside by buying up land. 'They are so attached to the land that even when they migrate to foreign countries, they are reluctant to alienate the land. Some of the migrants try to keep a member of their family in the village to take care of the ancestral house and landed property', according to Kalathil (1979: 41).

According to the 1921 census, 800 out of every 1,000 Patidars returned to their traditional caste occupation as agriculturists. With the growth of urban employment and the rise in educational levels since then, this ratio had undoubtedly dropped steadily, yet their urban orientation is much less obvious than that of the Anavil Brahmins in the more southerly and westerly *talukas* of south Gujarat. The preference for 'service', the professions and, in general, a non-agrarian sphere of work, had already appeared among the latter caste at an early stage. For a growing proportion of its members this preference has led to a process of urbanization with a corresponding weakening of their hegemony within the village order, to the extent that one can even ask whether the Anavil Brahmins can still be described as a dominant caste in their living area. The way in which this concept of dominance has found acceptance is linked with a rural environment, a position of power anchored in ownership of land, and a life style in which agriculture is not perceived as degrading. In all these respects the Patidars have never repudiated their background as a caste of cultivators, and among my Patidar informants several are returned as migrants who, have again in recent years, become active agriculturalists.

The emergence of a new life style

The Patidars have climbed from a rather inferior status as

simple Shudras to follow the Brahmins in the ritual hierarchy. But what precisely is their place within this order? At the beginning of this century it looked as though they would be guided by the *Kshatriya* ideal (Bhatt 1970: 318), and also at the time of the *satyagraha* this behaviour was held up to the Patidars as a model (G. Shah 1974: 99). But in imitation of their more illustrious caste fellows in central Gujarat, the Surat Patidars later took the Vaniyas as their model and became mostly orthodox Vaishnavas. As one would expect from a mobile caste, the social ideal in this model emphasized assertive traits such as the striving for self-improvement (*sudharavun*) and superiority to others—in short, a pattern of norms displaying a resemblance to the Protestant ethic, as Bates has observed (1981: 795 and 813).

The Patidars' economic behaviour was described already in the beginning of the colonial period in terms of industriousness and frugality. A strongly developed self-respect taught these rural capitalists that they must endeavour to avoid situations in which they were subordinated to others. This conduct stimulated them to establish themselves as independent entrepreneurs, both within agriculture and outside it.

> The prospect of working in the neighbourhood of their village as a factory hand has little attraction to Patel youths. One of them said: 'It is loss of status. *Patels are wage givers, not wage earners*' (my italics). When I pointed out to the person that there were many Patel diamond workers in Navsari, he replied: 'Patel diamond workers invariably aspire to become factory owners. The time they spend as workers is considered as a necessary training rather than mere workers. Had they no hope of becoming factory owners, they would quit the work.' The researcher cites a Patidar informant who explained why management is attractive: 'A manager is one who can work independently in his factory. All the others are dependent on him. Success in managing a factory is sure proof of being mentally sharp and intelligent' (Khalatil 1979: 111–113).

With this, the 'sanskritization' of the Patidars' seems to be rounded off. Inspired by the Vaniya model, the Patidars in south Gujarat are said to have adopted an ethic that outfitted them for successful entrepreneurship within the rural economy. In some respects this interpretation is rather crude and mechanistic. The reason begins with the rigidity of an hierarchical schema, according to which a low group, becoming collectively socially mobile of necessity adopts the complex of attitudes and behavioural traits of a more highly placed caste. In contrast to this I would like to point out that not all traits can be explained in terms of emulation or imitation. As I have argued elsewhere (Breman 1974: 54), every dominant caste is characterized by a number of qualities outside those belonging to the specific caste model to which its members adhere. First of all I regard a territorial principle as fundamental to this, i.e. the tendency to regard the living area as a personal domain, and to disregard the claims of others to that territory, even if these cannot be refuted. The insistence on autonomy which emerges from this is also displayed in a social sense: the refusal to submit to others and, conversely, the desire to reduce others to submission.

In contrast to the Anavil Brahmins in south Gujarat who, holding to a feudally tinged ideal, aspire to the life of rustic landlords and patrons assuming responsibility for the livelihood of their subordinates, the Patidars are guided by a different economic spirit. They have never been rulers of their area but do regard themselves as its owners. The Patidars are active managers of their farm business as much in the public as in the private sense, without feeling the need to be accountable to others or to recognize obligations to them. This behaviour accords with a capitalist mentality within which self-interest is accepted, takes precedence and is accompained by a life style in which the *homo economicus* is easier to recognize than the *homo hierarchicus* from a bygone mode of production.

In the second place the members of the dominant caste distinguish themselves from others by an outspokenly secular behaviour pattern. Despite the religious orthodoxy which has secured a higher place in the traditional hierarchy for the Patidars, the vast majority of the new generation lead a remarkably worldly existence. In social interchanges with others their attitude is characterized by bluntness and arrogance and by their refusal to allow themselves, as typical 'sons of the soil', to be overawed by the urbane or sophisticated forms of social intercourse among those who think they are better than the Patidars. Conversely they show a brutal indifference or even callousness towards those classed as being socially lower. If as Kanbis they were famed earlier for their industriousness and sobriety, as Patidars they have exchanged the sobre qualities which governed the lives of previous generations for conspicuous leisure and consumption. Many of them live in landlords' comfort, no longer themselves working on the land and deriving an often handsome income from their agrarian business. Their cultural style, however, continues to be that of middle farmers, expressed in a rather pedestrain materialism. The Anavil Brahmins, as an old elite of largely faded glory, are inclined to speak with a mixture of jealousy and disdain about these upstarts.

The yearning for outward show is not limited to the building of costly and over-large houses, but also shows itself in, for instance, the rapid expansion in the number of tractors in the area. It is not only business-like considerations that underlie the decision to purchase these machines; when a marriage is arranged, the presence of a tractor serves as a symbol of prosperity in much the same way as did a horse or motor car previously. Typical of the frankly vulgar behaviour of some of the big farmers are the chicken-and-whisky parties in which they indulge when away from home, but even among the less well-to-do the earlier simplicity and thrift—'we only ate rice if there were guests'—has given way to more consumption-orientated and comfort-loving behaviour. As members of the dominant caste they feel obliged to make this kind of display without its diminishing their social assertiveness in which the striving for economic success is foremost.

The unmistakeable economic progress in which most Patidars have shared, albeit in different degrees, is the result of a longlasting process and of a combination of factors. These are the introduction of cotton cultivation, the profits from emigration, land reforms (particularly the abolition of tenancy shortly after independence), the transition to irrigation agriculture in recent decades and, in the long run, a diversification of the rural economy. To an increasing extent the villages in Bardoli Vibagh have become springboards for economic activities directed outwards, and the Patidars' sphere of operations has undergone a significant extension in both space and content. The Patidars have pushed their way through to the urban order and in doing so have enlarged their commercial and industrial interests. The economic aggressiveness persistently encouraged as caste style is displayed in a new capacity for enterprise, which at the same time underlines the transition to Vaisya status. After completing a college education in Bardoli or Surat, increasingly more of the younger generation are taking to commerce, with a clear preference for dealing in modern production and consumption commodities or else they set up business as owners/partners of the new industrial undertakings in Surat, Udhna, Navsari or Bardoli. Besides this, the many diamond polishing workshops which have been opened in recent years in the villages surrounding Bardoli, have been almost exclusively floated by Patidar youngsters.

What must be stressed first and foremost is that economic expansion and the economic dynamic have not progressed at the expense of this caste's position in the villages and in agriculture. The vast majority of its members still continue to lead a definitely rural existence. It was no accident that as early as the first caste conference, held in 1910 in Surat District, there was a plea for the institution of an agricultural college. However, the solid link with the farming life to which this plea bears witness, has changed its character in the course of time. As we have observed, the upper layer of Patidars has developed into a class of gentleman farmers and even the less well-to-do try as far as possible to conform to this ideal. Around 1930 it was still very common for Patidar women to take part in fieldwork, but this has been carefully expunged from memories even as a custom from the past. Also, the share taken by the Patidar men in manual work has been sharply reduced since then, and is now preferably restricted to the role of supervisor. Social dignity and a position as larger landowners have enabled the Patidars to acquire the status of supervising farmers and they are recognized as such today. We shall encounter them as principal users of others' labour power in agriculture, and in fact this is the chief reason I have concentrated my fieldwork where employers are concerned, on the members of the dominant caste.

It is not unusual for dynamic castes in the countryside of India to be labelled in a collective way—'progressive farmers' in government terminology or the 'new class of *kulaks*' from a completely different viewpoint. Both terms are however too broad to embrace all landowners with more than 5 acres. As I explained earlier, they separate out into middle and large farmers, two categories to which the majority of the dominant class belongs. They themselves argue, with a certain amount of exaggeration, that the currently permitted ownership of 10 acres of irrigated land corresponds to a minimal economic holding, allowing for bare subsistence only. My own view is that the image of the successful Patidar farmers, who are in a position to behave as modern agrarian entrepreneurs, has this size of holding as its lower limit. From this level upwards, there is active participation in the broadening of the regional economy by investment of part of the agrarian profit in new economic activities (industry trade and the profession) in which a growing proportion of well educated Patidar youngsters are taking part.

I have presented the Patidars as the principal landowners in the central plain, who together form a broad base for the transformation to a capitalist mode of production in agriculture. This process has pushed forward with an accelerated tempo in recent years, but is rooted in the past, and there can be no question of a sudden upheaval. Both the rise in production and the improvement in living standards is the result of a long-lasting development with, a change-over to commercial crops, the adaptation to new techniques of agriculture and the appearance of new forms of market organization. All this has been made possible over a long period by investment in land accumulated partly locally and partly with money earned elsewhere, but agriculture itself has also become increasingly more profitable, particularly since the transition to the cultivation of irrigated crops.

Here, sugar in particular has served to create the prosperity and comfort enjoyed by members of the dominant caste. By leaving responsibility for cultivation of this crop to the co-operative factories the Patidars have been able to set themselves up as gentleman farmers, with the result that the yield—both in tonnage per unit of land and in net profit per ton—has risen sharply in the course of the years. Accumulation was created largely via the co-operatives which, certainly in Bardoli Vibagh, are almost entirely in the hands of Patidars. In the three factories in this area the affiliated members had, by 1976–7, already built up a sum of 112 *lakhs* of rupees in obligatory savings, while they had raised credit for 152 *lakhs*. On the basis of research in ten villages in Bardoli and environs,

Parmar, from whom I have derived these data, established that the amount of obligatory savings varied, according to the capital supplied, between 3,000 and 6,000 rupees per member in this year alone. In order to illustrate the difference in prosperity he compared 54 farmers who cultivated sugarcane (all bigger landowners and members of higher castes, especially Patidars) with 8 farmers who did not (mostly small landowners and members of low and tribal castes). In table 4.3. I have adopted a condensed form of this survey.

Table 4.3 *Socio-economic conditions of sugarcane growing and non-sugarcane growing farmers in ten villages of Bardoli Vibagh, 1976–7.*

indicator	sugarcane growing farmers (54)	non-sugarcane growing farmers (8)
standard of living	they live in brick-houses, put on decent dresses, enjoy luxuries. 28 have motor-cycles, 4 farmers have scooters, 8 have Luna motorcycles, 6 have motorcars, 4 have bicycles, 6 have refrigerators, 2 have T.V. sets, 32 have tape recorders, 46 have radio sets, 34 have modern sanitary facilities.	they live in ordinary houses; 4 farmers have bicycles, 1 has a motorcycle, 1 has a Luna motor cycle, 2 have no vehicles at all. 6 farmers have radio-sets, 1 with tape recorder. All of them are without sanitary facilities, but they do have electricity.
re-investment	re-investment in farming is possible due to their membership in the sugar cooperative societies	re-investment is negligible.
debt position	they are not really in debt but 47 farmers have obtained loans from sugar cooperative societies	all farmers are indebted to private money lenders
modern technology	virtually, every farmer is making an attempt to adopt modern technology.	they are not able to utilise modern technology even though they are aware of it.

Source: Parmar 1978: 62–3

In this way it is possible to present the middle and large farmers among the Patidars as a closed front, since the differential course of the process of agrarian growth entails growing income disparities within the dominant caste. Among the Patidars there are countless smaller landowners who, as a result of their small-sized holdings, are less able to produce, save and invest, and who live in the shadow of their more illustrious caste fellows. They make less use of hired labourers, they have to work in the fields themselves, and they are in no position to conform in their behaviour to the new norms and values of the social milieu to which they consider themselves bound. Even though their livelihood has not actually deteriorated compared with that of the previous generation, they have little reason for satisfaction, but the Patidars who suffer poverty in silence hope for the support and intercession of their more successful caste fellows. Thanks to this lead, even the smaller farmers among them are able to maintain their holdings and to derive sufficient surplus from them to provide the more promising among the younger generation with access to non-agrarian employment. They then have to be content with lower-cadre functions in the paper and sugar factories and with modest clerical positions in the regional government bureaucracy—jobs which offer no more than Rs 300 to 500 a month, and for which the bigger farmers' sons consider themselves too good, but which are at least jobs in the so-called formal sector, with a relatively certain and secure income, from which a great many of the working population are excluded right from the start.

Compared with the growing opposition between the economically strong and weak within the dominant caste, the earlier lines of social division have lost much of their significance, but they have still not disappeared entirely. As before, the Leva Patidars continue to set the tone, and have united in the Leva Patidar Samaj, a rather loosely knit caste association of nine regional sections is south Gujarat, the leaders of which appear to be co-opted. They meet each other at gatherings which are held at least once a year, usually in the building of one of the co-operative societies in Bardoli where they dominate. All kinds of life-rules are discussed at these gatherings.

Marriages between sub-castes are still rare, but the internal divisions remain hidden behind the image of a united front presented to the outside world. Mutual differences are nevertheless discussed in a good-humoured way.

The organization of the Patidars' dominance rests on the principle of unity within diversity. The consciousness of being numerically a minority and of being in opposition to a largely tribal population who are gradually preparing to escape from the supremacy of the *ujliparaj* and to win back the territory lost to them, inclines the Patidars to keep their ranks solidly closed. Moreover, educational and other institutions in which the socially powerful meet together, exercise an homogenizing effect. Thus the college opened several decades ago in Bardoli is a veritable Patidar bastion, in which this caste forms a large proportion of the 1300 students. It is interesting to observe their order of preference in the three lines of study: commerce and science first, with arts taking last place. They have only recently begun to take to higher education—much later than the Anavil Brahmins who, with a tradition as local rulers, sought entry to the (colonial) bureaucracy much earlier, and who were also driven to compensate in this way for having lost control of the south Gujarat countryside. In comparison the Patidars have continued to be solidly anchored in the agrarian order. To be sure, the rural upper layer are not recruited exclusively from the dominant caste and conversely not all its members belong to the rural upper layer. However, the link is so significant that I have no scruples about identifying the Patidars as the major adversaries of the agricultural labourers. The large farmers thus form a vanguard which determines the importance of the whole caste as much as the direction in which its members are moving. Their gradual penetration into the urban economy as entrepreneurs is a subject beyond the scope of the remainder of this study.

5

THE LANDLESS PROLETARIAT

Agricultural labour as a tribal phenomenon

Agricultural labourers in Surat District are nearly all tribals, a section of the population known earlier as *kaliparaj* (dark coloured). This loaded term, embodying a social stigma, has now fallen into disuse and is being replaced by Adivasis, a term which has no pejorative meaning and which, in its sense of 'original inhabitants', has become the official collective name for all categories of tribals. In contrast to the higher castes, such groups are distinguished as Scheduled Tribes in every census. The purpose of this registration is to put an end to their socio-economic backwardness and the discrimination to which they are subjected, by means of protective regulations and preferential policies of all kinds.

While roughly 7 per cent of the population in India as a whole consists of tribals, this percentage is doubled in Gujarat, the southern part of this state having a pronounced tribal character. In Valsad, Surat and Broach districts, the Adivasis form nearly half, and sometimes more, of the total population while in the inaccessible and largely unreclaimed Dhangs District, more than 90 per cent of the inhabitants are Adivasis.

A small minority of the tribals in south Gujarat live in urban centres—only 7 per cent in Surat District in 1971. Although this proportion has increased since then, the vast majority continue to be part of the rural order, and 90 per cent of the economically active among the tribal population are dependent upon agriculture for their livelihood. Agricultural wage labourers predominate among them; 87 per cent of all agricultural labourers in Surat District belong to this tribal category, i.e. 193,072 out of 220,909 of these labourers in 1971. Although most agricultural labourers are tribals, the converse is not true. In the same census report a little over a third (36 per cent) of the tribal working population are registered as peasant cultivators. Growing differentiation among landowners and the proletarianization which involves a substantial proportion of them forms the theme of the following chapter and serves as an introduction to the phenomenon of migrant labour.

53 per cent of the tribal working population are landless agricultural labourers. They comprise a rural class which, as we observed above, is for the most part attached to the fertile middle belt of Surat District.

The Adivasis can be divided into several groups which live more or less territorially separated from each other. The Halpatis inhabit the central plain of south Gujarat. With a total number of 387,533 in 1971 they comprised 11 per cent of the tribal population at that time, and in Gujarat they are outnumbered only by the Bhils. Approximately 90 per cent of the Halpatis are concentrated in Surat and Valsad, and within these densely populated districts there are also a number of *talukas* with strikingly high concentrations of this tribal caste. This applies especially to the Bardoli area; 18 per cent of all the Halpatis in south Gujarat live in Bardoli, Palsana and Valod, and Halpatis comprise 30 per cent of the population in these *talukas* taken together, thus forming the largest social category locally. The results of local research show that in a great number of villages in the central plain of Surat District, Halpatis constitute half or even more than half of the population (see table 5.1).

Table 5.1 *Number of Halpatis in Surat District, 1951–71*

year	1951		1961		1971	
Taluka	Halpatis	% of total population	Halpatis	% of total population	Halpatis	% of total population
Bardoli	27,938	35.7	n.a.	n.a.	39,430	32.8
Palsana	11,610	32.8	n.a.	n.a.	20,984	39.5
Valod	5,475	15.1	7.085	16.5	8,516	16.4
Surat District	104,179	10.7	n.a.	n.a.	179,112	10.2

The main cities in south Gujarat are situated in the area inhabited by the Halpatis, and the immediate proximity of these cities explains why Halpatis are somewhat over-represented in the urban centres compared with most other tribals. Nevertheless Halpatis, representing 13 per cent of the urban population in 1971, lag far behind higher castes in the process of urbanization which has been steadily gathering momentum in the plain. The vast majority of Halpatis—87 per cent in 1971—continue to live an obviously rural existence (Shah 1978: 16).

Most of the agricultural labourers in Surat District are recruited from among members of this tribal caste. Halpatis form the vast majority (86 per cent in 1971 according to Shah's estimate) of those Adivasis for whom agricultural labour is the principal, if not the only, source of livelihood. Even in the earliest colonial reports from the beginning of the previous century this was the Halpatis' economic status, and has remained so up to the present. Out of all members of this tribal caste in the Surat District 78 per cent worked as agricultural labourers in 1961. The identification of Halpatis with the occupation of agricultural labourer can be illustrated further with the help of more locally directed studies. For instance, there is the research carried out by the rural economist J. M. Patel in the village of Afwa (Bardoli Taluka) at the beginning of the 1960s. It appears from his findings that 145 out of the 255 households studied lived mainly by agricultural labour. This was by far the most important source of employment for the Halpatis, who with 166 households comprised about two-thirds of the village population; 142 households, in other words 86 per cent of the number representing this caste, obtained their living in this way. This percentage had remained nearly constant in the previous twenty years. Put in another way, 142 of the 145 agricultural labourers' households, or 98 per cent of them, belonged to the Halpati caste. Spread over the twelve villages in the bordering Navsari Taluka, Naik established towards the end of the 1970s that with the exception of four households all were Halpatis (Naik 1979).

The same picture emerges from two other monographs based on village studies. In 'Nevapor', also situated in Bardoli Taluka, Baks confirmed in the same period that the Halpatis, the caste to which 52 per cent of all inhabitants belonged, were almost exclusively employed as agricultural labourers. In the following decade there was to be little change in this situation; according to Kalathil's study, dating from the beginning of the 1970s, 350 of the 425 Halpati households in Sisodra (56 per cent of all inhabitants and 82 per cent of all Halpatis) were mainly dependent upon agricultural labour. In the slack times they maintained themselves by casual labour outside agriculture, in the adjacent town of Navsari. In spite of its closeness only a small minority of Halpatis (a total of 51) had succeeded in penetrating the sphere of industrial employment which had come into existence in this centre of growth. As a predominantly agricultural labourers' caste the Halpatis largely depend on the larger landowners for employment and livelihood. There is a conspicuous connection between the concentration of this landless proletariat in the plain of south Gujarat and the dominant farmer castes living there. In all the households of the substantial farmers—those of Patidars or other high caste landowners—in my research area, there were two to three Halpatis attached to each farmer in a casual or permanent working relationship. This relation is thrown into still sharper relief when one considers that the difference on the material plane means that a much larger proportion of the members of a landless household are economically active than in a household possessing more land. Discounting the difference in size of family this ratio is at least double that in a farmer's household of the middle or higher category. M. B. Desai discovered during his research that over half of the landowning households had one working member, while only a small minority had three or more working members, a percentage that declines further as the extent of landownership increases (Desai n.d.: 167). In village A the number of working members averaged 2.7 agricultural labourers per household (J. M. Patel 1964: 98). In a random sample taken from among households of agricultural labourers in Navsari Taluka fifteen years later, Naik arrived at an even higher figure—no less than 3.1 active members from among an average number of 5.05 members per household (Naik 1979). As we can see from table 5.2 based on the three village monographs already mentioned, in my research area, agrarian relations of production are to a large extent determined by the presence of Patidars—the chief employers, as dominant landowners—and the Halpatis, who are their main employees as landless labourers.

Table 5.2 *Proportionate share of castes of dominant landowners and of agricultural labourers in three villages of Surat District*

	village		
caste	Afawa	'Nevapor'**	Sisodra
Patidars	33%	17%	21%
Halpatis	57–61%	52%	56%

Source: R. M. Patel (Afawa); Baks (Nevapor) and Kalathil (Sisodra). According to the findings of the first author* in 1961–62 57 per cent of all inhabitants belonged to the Halpatis caste. Ten years later R. D. Patel reported that their share in the population of Afawa had increased to 61 per cent.

The numerical weight of both these castes which together constitute from two-thirds to more than three-quarters of the population in a great many villages in my research area, and the majority of whom are respectively farmers and landless labourers, has led me to concentrate my study on the relationship between these top and bottom strata. In other words, my research into recent changes in the labour order of Bardoli and its neighbourhood has been focused on the extremities of the rural production structure. I have identified these by concentrating my analysis on the Patidars as the dominant caste and the Halpatis as the caste dominated by them. In the plain of Surat District the agricultural labourers' existence binds the Halpatis to the Patidars, in whose hands lies by far the greatest share of the land.

To an increasing extent members of the landless caste are experiencing competition from outsiders in the struggle for a livelihood. These newcomers in recent decades have been penetrating the area in ever larger numbers. This subject will be discussed extensively in the following chapter, while in this chapter I shall confine my attention to the Halpatis, the origin and background of the landless proletariat which has for many centuries formed part of the social order in my research area.

Halpatis: social origins and ranking within the caste order

Considering the numerical proportion of the two castes one could predict that the area around Bardoli would be considered not as Patidar land but as the Halpatis' territory. However, just as the Patidars' position of eminence bestows upon them a 'surplus value' far surpassing the size of the caste, so conversely the numerical dominance of the Halpatis is nullified by their immense poverty and the social inferiority accompanying it.

As a rule the Halpatis live outside the village centres in separate, dispersed hutment areas, which are the worst locations in the region, difficult to reach and rarely visited by outsiders. After all, who would want to go there? A large proportion of them are defined as socially redundant, and in a sense they are expected to demonstrate this inferiority by living an inconspicuous and withdrawn existence. The farmyards and fields are full of them but otherwise one only comes across them on their way to or from work. They have little or no business in the village itself, except in the farmer's house. Local facilities such as shops, temples, schools, clinics and so on, are not for them, and only very few manage to gain entry to these places. On the supra-local level, as well in the buses, in market places and government offices—they are less visible than their numbers would lead one to expect. Entirely in accordance with their under-representation in public life, when outside their own surroundings the Halpatis, especially the older generation, behave with great diffidence out of an apparent consciousness that their very presence in itself gives offence. They rarely if ever play any role in formal organizations such as co-operatives and political parties.

One story has it that when Gandhi was preparing a civil disobedience campaign in Bardoli at the beginning of the 1920s he showed great concern over the rather low number of people which could be mobilized. But in the estimates he had been given only the *ujliparaj* were included. The other half of the population, as the farmers added reassuringly, consisted of *kaliparaj*, and therefore need not be counted. This anecdote is interesting not only because it shows that the Halpatis did not 'count' but also because it shows that even then higher castes could not rely on the Halpatis for support in their actions. With all the changes that have taken place since then in the behaviour of the Halpatis and in attitudes towards them, it seems that the low esteem in which they have been held by those higher up has remained unaltered. The social isolation of the Halpatis and the idea that they are a well-nigh intolerable burden on society are both greater than ever today. Like the untouchables, who stood outside the traditional caste society, the Halpatis are, naturally, not really redundant in the present day order of things. Their relationship to it is one of the central themes of this study, and I shall return to it later. In the remainder of this chapter I will provide more information about the Halpatis' ranking within the social hierarchy in the past, their bonds of service with the Patidars and other farmer castes as these obtained until several decades ago, and the half-hearted and not very successful attempts by well-meaning outsiders to improve their socio-economic condition. For a more detailed treatment of precisely these historical aspects I refer the reader to a publication based on earlier research devoted to changes in the relationship between high caste farmers (Anavil Brahmins) and agricultural labourers (Halpatis) in the more southerly Valsad District (Breman 1974).

Little can be stated with certainty about the Halpatis or Dublas, as they were formerly called. The latter caste name has fallen increasingly into disuse. It is important to note that, in contrast to most other tribal groupings, they have no known history as hunters/gatherers or primitive cultivators, i.e., as original claimants to land within a more or less defined territorial domain. The only notice taken of them in the recorded past has been as a shadow force in the presence of the most important landowning castes. The Halpatis' territory in south Gujarat corresponds largely with that of the Anavil Brahmins and the Patidars whom they have always served as landless labourers. In the regional myth of origin—written down with the recording of the rural elite's traditional rights in the mid-nineteenth century—the Halpatis are represented as farm servants who, when villages were founded under high caste leadership, ploughed the soil and brought the land under cultivation.

> Each village was originally founded by a family, or association of families of the cultivating caste—Rajputs, Kunbees, Vohoras or

> Batthelas, all apparently belonging to kindred tribes. These people, with their servants and 'Halis', fixed the village site, dug the well and bank, planted the groves, built the village temple, and then exercised the right of possession. They then induced artisans to settle in their village, who were the servants of the community, and to whom they gave houses, bits of land rent-free, grain cesses, & c. Other cultivators, mostly of inferior castes, were in process of time attracted to the village, and the proprietory body permitted them to cultivate such land as they did not want themselves, but gave them no proprietory rights (Robertson 1865: 29; Enthoven 1920: 347).

Yet the phenomenon of landowning Halpatis is not completely unknown. I have noted such cases in several parts of south Gujarat during fieldwork over the last two decades. They often involved individual households who in the past were remunerated for village services with a plot of ground withdrawn from communal land. Or the Halpati landowners were descendants of farm servants to whom generous masters had given pieces of land, perhaps in reward for years of faithful service. However, a number of times I came across concentrations of Halpati cultivators who lived in separate hamlets and whose holdings always lay at a greater distance from the village centre. Are these the last vestiges of a process of regression down the agrarian ladder occuring in the recent past? The lack of a peasant tradition—for example, reminiscences such as one finds among most tribal castes about ownership rights which were taken away—makes this seem unlikely. When today we find a handful of Halpatis belonging to the category of small or marginal cultivators (and we are talking here about an absolutely minimal number) this does not mean that their number and share was greater in the previous generation. Infertile *jarayat* land is nearly always involved, land abandoned in the late colonial period by peasants from higher castes in order to escape increased land taxes. Besides this, during the cotton growing boom even Halpati agricultural labourers were installed as sharecroppers by landlords (Broomfield and Maxwell 1929: 15 and 21). In a still more remote past the Halpatis had already been denied access to land, for which Kosambi has given the following explanation:

> Many tribal people had fallen into servitude in times of famine

and one step away were the tribal castes or poorest cultivators who had at the same time incurred a debt which could not be repaid by generation after generation. This accounts for the lower retained castes such as the Cheruman in Malabar, the Koltas of Jaunsar-Bawar in the Himalayan foothills near Almora, the Halis of Gujarat, and the like (Kosambi 1956: 353).

The Halpatis are associated to such an extent with landlessness that even the hypothetical ability to lead a peasant's life is denied to them. The ethnography devoted to them reproduces the stereotype which flourishes among the high landowning castes and which is even cultivated, not without ulterior motives. They seem to have neither the capacity nor the tendency to live as a self-sufficient autonomous body. They are usually employed as landless labourers and even if they were landholders in the distant past, they have lost that position (Shah 1958: 12). The author mentions a discussion among the main propertied class over the question of whether Dublas deserved a share of the land which would be made available under the Bhoodan programme. Shah regarded it as quite likely that the Halpatis, in the remote past, had circulated as primitive peasants within the region they inhabited, but had already lost their rights to land in precolonial times (Shah 1958: 172–6).

Following Kosambi, up to now I have described the Halpatis as a tribal caste, this term being an expression of their ambiguous position within the social order of south Gujarat. The Halpatis in the plain, living in immediate proximity to high castes for many generations, were Hinduized much earlier as a result of this longlasting association. Because of this they are distinguished socially from other tribal groupings inhabiting the eastern part of south Gujarat. While the latter were still regarded as animists a hundred years ago, the Halpatis were already being referred to as 'backward' or 'semi-Hindus' in the first census reports Census 1881, III, app. H; (Gazetteer IX, 1901: 317; Census 1911, XVI: 169, 271; Enthoven 1920: 347; Toothi 1935: 116). In spite of their low economic status, compared with those outside the caste system they were regarded as being less coarse and less uncivilized. However, they were accommodated within the caste system at the lowest level possible. The new social echelon that came to exist at the bottom of the society, offered refuge to those from higher up who were no longer accepted within their own caste, particularly because of sexual transgressions. '. . . tribes like Dublas, Dhodhias and Bhils admit people freely (sometimes only at the cost of a feast) from other races and even from higher Hindu castes as well. Kanbis are known to affiliate themselves into the Dubla class. . . .' (Census 1921, XVII: 328).

The Halpatis and other tribal groupings have tried to escape the stigma of impurity and inadequacy by abandoning various kinds of unacceptable practices and in general following as closely as possible the example set by higher castes. Religious purification came about through the influence of movements arising unexpectedly then disappearing again, which flowed like waves through the area, inspired by a small vanguard from among the tribals who preached vegetarianism, abstention from alcohol, and other forms of 'pure' behaviour. This kind of campaign, such as the Devi or Mata movement in Surat District at the beginning of the 1920s, not only introduced a model for being a 'better' Hindu but also contained elements of resistance to the low ranking of the tribals within the social hierarchy in the plain and to their exploitation by non-tribals.[1] One such movement among a subgroup of Halpatis in Broach District in 1885 called for emancipation from domination along with the promise, which was to be revived later, that the goddess Mata would make the enemies' bullets melt (Dosabhai 1894: 299, 301; Hunter 1892: 413).

Incorporation into the caste system was naturally not a matter of free choice but was imposed by the social order of which the Halpatis formed a part. Elements of the original tribal classification were preserved at the transition from tribe to caste, particularly the division along clan lines which was accompanied by a certain territorial separation as well as by marriage circles. The earlier clans appeared to assume the character of subcastes, with a hierarchical relationship developing between them. The Talavias tried in this way to separate themselves from the Halpatis by claiming to be

[1] The commentary on the 1931 census gave detailed attention to the Mata Movement which reached its peak in 1923 (Census of India 1931, XIX: 386). The report of the 1941 census mentioned that this Mata Movement gained particular support among those tribals, such as the Dublas, who had already had a longstanding contact with caste Hindus (Census of India 1941, XVII: 62–63).

descendants of the Rajputs in northern Gujarat, a vaguely defined area from which they were assumed to have fled as a result of war or famine (Census 1921, XVII: 328). Their attempts to win a higher status as Rathods and to maintain only hypergamous relations with those in lower levels, failed as increasing numbers of Halpatis began to pass themselves off as Talavias.

The fact that economic differentiation did not occur prevented the subcastes from being able to crystallize out along the dividing lines of the social structure dating back to their tribal past. Instead of putting internal divisions in the forefront, the emphasis came to lie on collective upward mobility within the dominant scheme of stratification. This is obvious from the adoption of sanctions employed by the higher castes, and a telling example of this is the refusal of Halpati farm servants to have anything more to do with progressive members of the Patidar caste when these answered Gandhi's call to receive the untouchable Dheds in their homes.[2]

Conformity with the official 'rules of the game' still did not mean that the Halpatis lost their low social rank. However, the Halpatis were thwarted to a significant degree in their efforts to 'sanskritize' by the poverty which in practice excluded conformity with the prescribed rules of behaviour. The fact that poverty compelled them to bury their dead tells us a great deal (Census 1931 XIX: 463). Instead of being able to abandon conduct considered to be inferior, they are forced through economic need to sell their services and thus free others from onerous tasks, thereby establishing both the superiority of those they serve and at the same time their own lack of respectability. Halpatis who worked for Muslim cultivators stood in

[2] 'Reports vary as to the results of the special campaign against untouchability. It is stated that in South Gujarat, where this part of the programme was seriously pursued, even the Dublas refused to have anything to do with the Kanbis after the latter decided to let in the Dheds to their houses' (Census of India 1922, XVII: 134).

Although not in themselves untouchable, the Halpatis were also allotted a place at the bottom within the caste system. Up to a point, their servitude made the presence of large numbers of Untouchables superfluous. It is certainly no more coincidence that where they and other similar groups from a tribal background in Gujarat also performed household services for members of higher castes, the genuinely untouchable castes were poorly represented.

lower esteem and were shunned by their caste fellows, indicating that it was not the kind of service as such, but the person for whom this was performed, which formed the criterion for social ranking.

The Halpatis were incorporated within the caste system earlier than other tribals, but as a consequence of their landlessness and its attendant servitude they remained locked in the lowest regions of the system. The economic condition of the Adivasis in the eastern part of Surat District has been affected by the process of penetration, resulting in large-scale indebtedness and alienation of land, but they have been able more or less to support themselves in their own territory, if not as independent farmers then at least as tenants or share-croppers. As a result these latecomers to the process of Hinduization have not only been better able to preserve their own identity, but have also succeeded in catching up with the Halpatis in the social ranking order and even overtaking them. If one takes acceptance or refusal of food as a criterion of mutual assessment, then it would appear that Halpatis are regarded as having the lowest standing among the tribal castes. The Chaudharis, for instance, who according to Enthoven were still the social inferiors of the Halpatis some fifty years ago, nowadays look down on them and shun social contacts with them (Enthoven 1920: 345). Compared with these landowning tribals, who are currently involved in a process of upwards social mobility similar to that of the Kolis in the plain of south Gujarat several generations ago, the Halpatis as a landless caste were hopelessly 'déclassé' from the moment they entered the caste order.

Ultimately the members of this caste are unable to profit from their enormous numbers. The region where the Halpatis live, the central plain, has long been non-Adivasi territory, and no matter how numerous they may be locally, in none of the *talukas* of the south Gujarat plain do they form a majority of the population. This means that the Halpatis can derive only limited economic and political advantage from their status as a 'scheduled tribe'. In this respect they are also subordinated to the tribal castes who have much more of a personal territory in the hinterland of Surat District and who are also numerically dominant there. As always the Halpatis have to live in the shadow of powerful and prominent landowning castes.

The earlier relationship

The agricultural labourers' existence led by the Halpatis was formerly institutionalized in the *halipratha*, a form of servitude which imprisoned them in a state of poverty and inferiority.

Hali was the name given to a farm servant who had bound himself by indebtedness to a farmer, and in exchange for his subsistence performed any task given him in field and household. Debt-bondage was essential to the service relationship from the beginning. Attachment usually arose when a farmer advanced the means for the agricultural labourer's marriage by paying all the costs involved, the payments being mostly in kind and consisting primarily of food for the marriage party. The cash equivalent of such credit involved no more than Rs 30–50 in the second half of the nineteenth century, approximately Rs 100–250 between the two world wars, and Rs 200–400 in the first years after independence. Apart from the *hali* himself providing agricultural labour, the master usually also commanded the services of his *hali*'s wife who was employed as a household maidservant, and his *hali*'s growing children among whom the pre-adolescent sons particularly (those from 8 to 10 years onwards) tended the livestock. Together and with a good deal of mutual substitutability they carried out all the tasks which had to be performed on the land, in the house, and around the farmer's compound. There was no question of fixed working hours in this: they were at their master's beck and call not only during the day but in the evenings as house servants, and if necessary at night as well. Conversely the farmer was responsible for meeting his subordinates' subsistence needs. In addition to a daily grain ration this entailed all kinds of additional emoluments such as a morning or midday meal, some tobacco, a little drinking money now and then, a cup of tea (after this new consumption habit began to be common around the turn of the century), firewood, clothing and shoes every year, medicine in the event of sickness, a hut in the master's compound or on his land with the material, such as roofing, for its maintenance—in short, everything necessary for a bare living. This often included a plot of ground (*vavla*) which the farm servant could cultivate for himself. The all-encompassing nature of this service relationship meant that neither the wages, kind of work nor working hours were specified contractually, although there did exist a kind of cultural standard by which the 'good behaviour' of master and farm servant toward each other were defined.

The *hali*'s bondage was partly preserved by giving the subsistence allowance—an absolute minimum—in the form of an advance on work yet to be done, the loan which marked the beginning of the servitude being only one aspect of this. The daily allowance received by the *hali* was so low that he had no means of holding his own against all kinds of crises which regularly afflicted him in his life of poverty. Time and again he was forced to ask for his master's help, which could be granted as a favour or withheld at the farmer's pleasure. Moreover there was not always work for the *hali* and even the grain ration given to him on these workless days was registered as a loan.

Most of the earnings from the extra exertions the *hali* and his family had to make in busy times were deducted from this balance. The result was that over a long stretch of years the total size of the debt remained constant at the very least, but more often it increased, because the master charged interest on the sum owing. In the context of *halipratha*, however, notions of 'loan', 'advance' and 'interest' had only a nominal significance since neither party tried to end the servitude by redeeming the debt. The system of bondage was attractive to the landowners because it guaranteed them cheap and permanent labour, while the agricultural labourers preferred it because it assured them of at least a minimal security. From early colonial reports it appears that unattached labourers were less numerous, economically worse off, and lower in social standing.

The combination of the lowest possible subsistence wage and payment by advance loan reinforced by an abundant labour supply—arising from the exclusion of the landless part of the agrarian population from free access to land—in fact compelled labourers to submit to voluntary bondage. Consequently labourers entered into servitude for an indefinite period and mostly for life. It was moreover not only the right but the duty of the farmer to take his *hali*'s son into service. The youth who had previously worked as a cow-boy was subsequently given the opportunity to marry by his father's master, and only with the latter's permission could he offer his services to another party. Thus by means of the *halipratha* the households of agricultural labourers and landowners could remain firmly bound to each other for successive generations. Transfer to a new master occurred only when another landowner was prepared to take over the *hali*'s debts. Although the farm servant entered into the relationship voluntarily he could not himself end the contract except by running away. The masters had armed themselves against such escapes by mutual agreement not to employ runaway *halis*, and anyone doing so was fined. In addition lower government officials were helpful in tracking down and bringing back runaway farm servants.

In all these respects *halipratha* must be regarded as a system of unfree labour, but this is not the whole story. As I have argued elsewhere, the master-farm servant relationship was also characterized to a significant extent by elements of patronage. The master who was under obligation to guarantee a subsistence livelihood to his farm servant and to protect him against third parties, could conversely claim unconditional loyalty and total submission from his client. By emphasizing the personal character of this vertical relationship, which could extend to mutual intimacy and the warmly affectionate feelings which household members of succeeding generations of masters and farm servants felt for each other, a much too idyllic image of the *hali* system could easily be created. Reciprocity existed only as an ideal. The high-handedness permitted to the patron in his treatment of landless clients underlined the inequality of the parties. This institution was based on coercion and exploitation. The surplus value extracted from the farm servant by forcing him down to a level of bare survival was not only economic in the limited meaning of this word. The docility and deference to which the *hali* was bound heightened his master's sense of superiority and to this extent patronage must be understood as the socio-political dimension of a pre-capitalistic relation of exploitation.

It is obvious that there is a connection between the disintegration of *halipratha* and the emergence of a capitalist mode of production in the south Gujarat countryside. The question of whether or not this process has also led to the disappearance of bonded labour will be left to a later chapter. In this chapter I would like to point out that this servitude cannot be considered as having been static and uniform even in the past. Its more recent dynamic forms part of the process of change arising between landowners and agricultural labourers from the beginning of this century. Apart from a small number originating from other lower agrarian castes, the overwhelming majority of farm servants in Bardoli and its environs, as elsewhere in south Gujarat, were Halpatis. So closely was servitude connected with this largest landless category that *hali* was even used as a caste name. Historical sources give the impression of a centuries-old institution which remained more or less unchanged. Thus the report from the 1895 revision of the settlement survey of Bardoli mentions that:

> . . . the Dubla caste, whose men, for ages, have been content to serve as agricultural servants to anyone who will help to marry them. A Dubla marriage costs within Rs 40 and, as the couple will never dream of being able to repay the sum, they offer their life servitude in exchange for the money. From all enquiries, I learn that they are always well treated; for they get food and clothing throughout the year, and are not neglected in times of illness. At first sight this arrangement scarcely appears an economical one to the masters; but they have assured me that, everything considered, it is financially better than keeping no farm servants, and engaging labourers when they are wanted. For, when any of the principal agricultural operations, such as ploughing, reaping, & c., are in full swing, the demand for labourers is often far greater than the supply; and not to have sufficient hands at such seasons must mean a heavy loss. In the dull season these servants, or halis (cultivators) as they are called, are employed in various ways, such as repairing and building rice embankments, converting jirayat into rice land, carting manure, & c. (Bardoli RSR 1897: 7).

For whom did the *halis* work? Only the largest landowners could afford to take agricultural labourers into permanent service and were also obliged by caste status to do so. The upper section of the Anavil Brahmins especially—predominantly landlords in south Gujarat—made use of farm servants and in several early colonial reports they were the only landlords to be mentioned specifically.[3] *Halipratha* as a feudal institution is linked much more with them than with the Kanbi Patidars. As stated in the previous chapter, in the nineteenth century the latter enjoyed the reputation of being hardworking peasant farmers mainly dependent on family labour. Still, already at the beginning of the nineteenth century Kanbis were specifically mentioned as masters of Halpati servants.[4] Probably only the top few could afford the luxury of more farm servants and insofar as their less well-to-do caste fellows had extra labourers at their disposal, they worked alongside them on the land. The distance separating the Kanbis from the Dublas was usually much less than in the case of the Desai landlords, and the memory of this has been preserved down to the present generation of landowners and agricultural labourers in the Bardoli area. The increasing prosperity which resulted from the extension of cotton cultivation towards the end of the nineteenth century enabled increasingly more peasant farmers to employ agricultural labourers in permanent service. Even the desire to limit their need to work on the land themselves would have been an important stimulus to turn to the cultivation of the new crop. 'It is even asserted by careful observers that the keenness of cultivators to grow cotton is due not only to the fact that they can usually make good profits from it, but also to the fact that it is an easy crop to grow and leaves them plenty of leisure', thus Keatinge observed.[5]

It would seem from the above that the relation between the emergence of a capitalist mode of production and the disappearance of unfree labour is not so automatic and direct as one would assume. An important effect of the extension of cotton cultivation was that more and more farmers could

[3] The Halee Dooblas are entirely distinct from a class of slaves of Koolee origin, existing in considerable numbers in the Pargunnas to the southward and eastward of Surat under Desaee and Patel masters', thus goes an official memorandum in 1822 (quoted in Mehta & Mehta 1966: 77, fn 10).

[4] Thus for instance the letter dated 8-8-1825 in which W. J. Lumsden, as Collector and Magistrate of Surat, answered a government circular of 30-6-1825 enquiring into the incidence of unfree labour (Correspondence . . . etc., on Slavery: 433).

[5] Keatinge 1921: 145–6. The author draws attention to a publication according to which 300,000 men from the current generation among the landowning castes in south Gujarat (the Patidars being foremost among these) no longer performed agricultural labour.

afford to maintain more and more *halis*, as Shukla established in his village research in the early 1930s (Shukla 1937: 124). The question of whether or not this kind of servitude was an attractive economic proposition at the time, cannot be answered simply by determining the additional profit from labour. An important factor in this was the transition to a different behaviour pattern among the Patidars as dominant caste, which prescribed liberation from menial labour, first for the women and after that for the men. Farm servants catered for their masters' conspicuous leisure and the latters' prestige was moreover enhanced by the conspicuous consumption linked with the keeping of one or more of these underlings. The Anavil Brahmins were the outstanding example of landlords who strove for prestige by making others dependent upon them. For them *halipratha* was an age-old investment in people, aimed at reinforcing their eminent position in south Gujarat.

Compared with this old elite the Patidar case was different. Although their socio-economic progress gave rise to elements of rural patronage this has remained much more in the background as a more general caste style. The fact that the Patidars' ascent was achieved in a period in which the capitalist mode of production was beginning to emerge was not without its effect. It was appropriate to the more feudal orientation of the Anavil Brahmins that they attempted to lead a seigneurial kind of life for which a large number of *halis* was necessary. The Patidars have never aspired to such a lordly existence. They have, it is true, succeeded in gradually working their way up to gentleman-farmer status, but even in this they still remain more farmers than gentlemen. The different economic spirit guiding them finds expression in a much more active orientation towards commercialism, among other things. Apart from their more direct involvement in agriculture I also regard the increase in their livestock as an indication of a firmer rooting in a peasant way of life. The Patidars are credited with the qualities of a typical peasant caste: good business sense, cunning, and coarse manners, and they have acquired a reputation for being hard and demanding employers. Conversely the agricultural labourers in Bardoli refer scornfully to the humble origins of their superiors, the older generation of which still worked on the land beside their labourers.[6]

[6] That the Patidars in central Gujarat behaved in a similar manner can be inferred

The *hali* system is too easily associated with a more or less closed village economy, a feudal mode of production which would as a matter of course come to an end with the linkage to external markets for commodities and labour. This was a mistaken assumption, as Weber concluded in his interesting study on agricultural labourers in the countryside of eastern Germany towards the end of the nineteenth century. He points out that the *Instmann*—more or less comparable with the *hali*—was not a semi-feudal relic but the product of more recent changes taking place in agriculture.[7] Under the influence of the intensification of agrarian production in the first decades of the twentieth century unfree labour did not disappear immediately and completely. In a feudal atmosphere of patronage there was still some sense in retaining the emphasis on personal bond marking the relation between master and farm servant in the past, however exaggerated it might be. It is therefore striking that even at an early period the landowners of Bardoli and surrounding *talukas* gave evidence of an outspokenly instrumental attitude towards their farm servants. Where production for the world market was the furthest advanced, the affection and care with which the master had treated his *halis* earlier on, an affection which colonial government reports had emphasized (not without some exaggeration) gave way to coldness and even ruthlessness. Shukla, in his research on a village in Surat District in the early 1930s, established that 'If the master's work does not suffer in the event of the Hali's sickness, he may be allowed to rot in his cottage' (Shukla 1937: 123). A striking example of this "*Verdinglichung*" (instrumentalization) of labour can be found in the report of the official investigation following upon the *satyagraha* of 1928. In an attempt to find a better basis for the imposition of land taxes in each of the villages visited, the investigating commission collected information of the costs of agriculture, during

---

from the following quotation: 'In Kheda, however, the superior Patidars had never been inhibited by the responsibilities of patronage to the same extent and evolved a subtle exploitative relationship with the *kaliparaj*, or lower castes, at an earlier date. An important feature of this was the exploitation of debt, and in the field of money lending generally the superior Patidars came to the fore, both as borrowers and usurers, as the century advanced' (Bates 1981 : 796).

[7] Weber 1924. See also footnote 2 of the English version of this article provided by K. Tribe in *Economy and Society* 1979.

which they also obtained calculations from the farmers on how much it costs each year to maintain a Dubla. This amount, totalling Rs 140–150, largely involved food, clothing and an occasional small gratuity in cash or kind, but also included interest on the debt and an entry for 'depreciation'. The Dubla was thus evaluated in the same way as a commodity and was accordingly subject to wear and tear, as we can see from the statement of farming costs submitted to the commission in each of the villages visited.

> . . . the cost of cultivation for the unit under the heads maintenance of bullocks, maintenance of Dubla, wages paid to labourers other than the Dubla (or the wages which would be paid, assuming that the cultivator and his family did not work themselves), seeds, manure, repairs of dead stock and depreciation (of stock implements and Dubla), and interest (on price of stock and implements and on money advanced to the Dubla) (Broomfield and Maxwell 1929: 57).

One must ask whether there could be any question of truly harmonious relationships between farmers and agricultural labourers in such a social climate. In any case, it is not surprising that the same report mentions a growing recalcitrance among the Dublas.[8] Yet it would be premature to infer the disintegration of the *hali* system from this kind of information. The imminent demise was, it is true, announced in all kinds of official publications long before Independence on the basis of village research carried out in the middle of the 1930s but Shukla thought that such talk was premature (Shukla 1937: 132). More and more cultivators were substituting *hali* labour power with their own. They reacted sharply to the increasing 'untrustworthiness' of the *halis* by putting pressure on the government to sanction this form of unfree labour. They argued that the farm servants had entered into a labour contract by which they were obliged to work for as long as they failed to repay the advance loan received.

> To remedy this evil (i.e. the running away of farm servants who

[8] '. . . the Dublas are undoubtedly becoming more independent and more capable of combining in defence of their rights or interests. If they think they are stinted of their food ration or not paid a fair wage they will desert the village in a body, as happened this year in Afwa, Vankaner, Timberva and other places' (Broomfield and Maxwell 1929: 15).

> had debts), some of the witnesses suggested that the special legislation should be enacted by which the man could be prevented from avoiding the contract and that some kind of reciprocity may be established between the adjoining States by which these men could be brought back and made to fulfil the rest of their contract (*Report Baroda Economic Development Committee* . . . 1920: 131–2).

Years later, in a memorandum from the Deputy Director of Agriculture, Gujarat to the Royal Commission on Agriculture, the plea was still being made for the introduction of an identity card system.[9] To be sure, the government turned a deaf ear to this pressure from the employers' side, but this did not mean that the end of bondage was in sight. As long as alternative employment was lacking, servitude was sought for the security of living it offered. As a consequence of a certain degree of internalization of their dependency, the labourers themselves appear to have derived some prestige from their *hali* status. The famed social worker Jugatram Dave remarked in his description of *halipratha* in Bardoli and environs, written in the mid-1940s, that: 'As a woman without having married a husband has no prestige in the society, similarly a Halpati without a Dhaniama (landlord) as his master has no prestige in his community' (Dave 1946: 18; *my translation*).

From this and other publications it appears that the working of the *hali* system in an area where already by the end of the nineteenth century a considerable share of agrarian production had been destined for the world market, did not deviate fundamentally from the way in which this system of bondage had functioned in the previous century. The only difference lay in the fact that, in the central plain of Surat District, the mitigating elements of patronage in servitude were less in evidence. It is unclear whether the explanation for this must be sought in the varied caste background of the masters or in the different tempo with which the capitalist mode of production began to penetrate the countryside. Of course, a direct link between these two variables cannot be excluded.

There appeared to be no foreseeable end to the *hali* system and, even shortly after independence, its continuing exist-

[9] Memorandum Rao Sahib B. M. Desai in Royal Commission on Agriculture in India. vol. II, part 1 Evidence taken in the Bombay Presidency London 1927: 577 and 601.

ence was confirmed in a report by the official commission of investigation which has never been released for publication (Report Hali Labour Enquiry Committee 1950). No attempt on the part of officialdom undertaken in the colonial period to abolish *hali* servitude as a form of unfree labour, had any effect. Certainly, it was no longer permitted to use the machinery of government for tracking down runaway *halis* and bringing them back, but unofficially the farmers were still assured of co-operation from lower government personnel. For the same reason the ban on engaging new *halis* proclaimed in 1923 in the part of south Gujarat belonging to the State of Baroda, had little effect.[10] The refusal to interfere in social matters in favour of the landless class, lasted until after independence. Thus, the government failed to enforce legal regulations based on the recommendations of the Hali Labour Enquiry Committee, which was itself hardly radical. Two motives for this surprising decision were mentioned in a press report.[11] What had never been approved, said the government of the State of Bombay as it then was, did not need to be forbidden. Even passing over this obviously ridiculous argument, the fact still remains that an official prohibition was regarded as unnecessary because farmers and labourers in Bardoli had, with the mediation of Morarji Desai and Gulzarilal Nanda (respectively Minister for Home Affairs and Minister for Labour in Bombay State) reached an agreement in which they solemnly foreswore the *hali* system. The presence of two such eminent office holders guaranteed, so it was suggested, that with this meeting the foundation for a new labour order was to be considered as binding throughout south Gujarat. How realistic was this official interpretation? The answer to this question requires a more detailed discussion of action carried out over a period of several decades by Gandhian social workers in the area round Bardoli, with the aim of eliminating *hali-pratha*.

10 'In July 1923 the Government of the State by proclamation declared the whole system of forced indenture as illegal and allowed the Kaliparaj serf to repudiate it if he chose to. But the intentions of the Government were not properly interpreted by subordinate revenue officials and the operation of the government's order is therefore not effective' (Census of India 1931, XIX: 255).

11 This newspaper item is included in the book mentioned earlier by P. G. Shah: 210–11.

Social uplift, the Gandhian way

From the very beginning the struggle of the Gandhian movement to end bondage as a form of tied labour was concentrated upon Bardoli and environs. In preparation for the *satyagraha* which was originally planned for 1924, several of Gandhi's co-workers came from Ahmedabad to launch a consciousness-raising campaign among the rural population. From the Sarbhon *ashram*, the centre of their activities set up in 1923, they visited Halpati neighbourhoods in nearby villages to preach 'purity' and to set up *bhajan* groups. They very soon met with opposition from the landowners who were outraged that these outsiders should approach the farm servants directly instead of through them. There was open conflict when the social workers started an evening school to teach the alphabet and some simple arithmetic as well as the *bhajans*. The farmers put an end to this teaching by prohibiting their dependents, under threat of punishment, from taking part in the evening gatherings. The leader of the action group, Narhibhai Parikh, reacted to this by beginning a hunger strike (M. Desai 1929: 7). The farmers refused to give in, and the arrival of Vallabhbhai Patel was necessary before the issue could be resolved.

The compromise reached included the farmers' approval of the evening school, but the Halpatis had become so frightened that the re-opening of the school failed to materialize. The lesson derived from this incident by the Gandhian workers was that action among the agricultural labourers must be relinquished for the time being. The solution to the Halpati problem required reform on the part of their masters. This was also the opinion of Jugatram Dave, the social worker who was highly respected right from the start and who was Gandhi's most prominent disciple in south Gujarat. 'We must first gain the confidence of the landlord's class slowly and patiently. It would only be after serving them for a long time that we could hope to inspire in them the feeling of kindness and fairness. Therefore, we, the social workers, did not touch this question even unintentionally during the period from 1924 to 1938' (Dave 1946: 35; *my translation*).

Thus Gandhi's viewpoint that the struggle against foreign domination was only justified if the lack of freedom within

Indian society was also abolished did not yield any positive result. Gandhi in this context, had even mentioned *halipratha* by name.[12] On the contrary, Sardar Patel resolutely put an end to attempts made by the more radical side to mobilize the tribal population on their own initiative.[13] Consequently, agricultural labourers took no part in the 1928 *satyagraha*, and this campaign served none of their interests. It was obvious that the colonial government tried to use the Halpatis to break their masters' resistance. In order to avoid this danger, leaders such as Vallabhbhai Patel impressed upon the Halpatis that their *dharma* was to serve their masters loyally (Shah 1974: 101 and Dhanagare 1980). This appeal to obedience according to traditional norms signified a confirmation of the landless labourers' servitude to the dominant caste of landowners. A meeting of the National Congress in 1938 in the village of Haripura in Bardoli Taluka, seemed to promise change when an agreement was reached which would mean the end of the *hali* system in the region. The initiative for this came from Vallabhbhai Patel who enjoyed the unconditional trust of the peasant farmers. Dave described how the Halpatis, enticed by the slogan of *swaraj* (freedom) streamed in from the surrounding villages and offered by the hundreds to prepare the camp where the conference was to be held in Haripura. Under the supervision of Congress movement cadre members the Halpatis dug latrines and performed all the other heavy and menial tasks. The farmers, who saw their authority being threatened, were opposed to this, but did not dare to protest openly. The Sardar was so impressed by the Halpatis' zeal that he promised the abolition of their bondage in the future, on condition that the Halpatis took an oath to foreswear alcohol. That at least is the Gandhian reading, which however is not undisputed. '. . . in 1938 when Indulal Yagnik led 10,000 indentured servants of South Gujarat, "halipatis", into the Congress annual session in Haripura, a session specifically organized by the Sardar, Patel was enraged at this direct confrontation with Congress authority on the part of a class based organization' (Spodek 1975: 1932).

[12] See the introduction by N. Parikh in Dave 1946.

[13] 'Dinker Mehta reports that when he, Mehta, chose to work with tribals of Surat district while the Bardoli satyagraha of 1928 was in progress, Sardar called him and told him that the first priority was the satyagraha; organising tribals would have to wait' (Spodek 1975: 1932).

As a result of this pressure from below Sardar Patel had to accept a settlement. Under his leadership a committee was set up with the task of developing new guidelines for labour conditions, of which the most important specifications were that:

— daily wages were to be fixed at 4 annas and 2 pice a day. Farm servants employed on a yearly basis were to receive Rs 50. This did not mean that the price of labour was increased, but only that payment in kind was converted into cash payment. The labourers would no longer accept meals in the farmer's house, and all other emoluments and perquisites would lapse;
— any farm servant who had served his master for twelve years or longer would have his debt remitted. For a shorter length of service the debt would be reduced by one-twelfth for every year served. Repayment of the remainder would be achieved by withholding one anna from the daily wage;
— maidservant's wages would be fixed at Re 1 per month for every daily working hour;
— the working day would be 8 hours long as a rule, but could be extended to 10 hours;
— settlement of disputes would be made through the arbitration commission that had to be set up in each village.

At a meeting held in Bardoli on 26 January 1939, at which Gandhi and Nehru among others were present, this agreement was solemnly sealed. In the speech which Gandhi delivered on this occasion he replaced the pejorative term 'Dubla' with the new caste name 'Halpati' and reproached the farmers over the fact that the decisions taken were one-sided in being only to their advantage. He maintained that justice had not been done to the agricultural labourers, and thus the compromise must be adjusted further to include a wage rise to 8 annas. But even the low wage rate agreed upon was not acceptable to the landowners. Agricultural labourers worked for a few days but were not paid. After much hesitation the Patidars in one village showed some readiness to meet these demands, on the condition that social workers should ring a bell early in the morning and in the evening to mark the beginning and end of the working day. In other words they feared that the Halpatis would evade their obligations, by coming late and leaving early, a complaint heard to this day. Ultimately even in this village the Patidars were unwilling to abide by the agreements because they were afraid of arousing the wrath of their caste fellows in the region. There was not a single village in which the farmers seemed prepared to sit with Halpatis on the local arbitration committee (*panch*) entrusted with supervising the fulfilment of the Bardoli agreement.

In reaction to this total unwillingness to comply, the agricultural labourers went on strike in some places, but this had little or no effect; this being the slack period in the agrarian cycle. Interestingly, there came a change when the Halpatis' womenfolk in some villages stayed at home. The farmers gave in under this pressure, but only reluctantly and without really complying with all the conditions. Tension continued because the Gandhian workers now began to extend their social action again to the Halpatis. At several *ashrams* set up especially for this landless caste, the formation of *bhajan mandlis* was encouraged for the singing of semi-religious songs and the propagation of the spinning wheel. The discontent already present among the Patidars was stimulated further by this 'meddling'. They considered it insupportable that outsiders should concern themselves with those whom the Patidars regarded as their personal chattels and wherever possible they opposed Gandhian activities.

There came a temporary end to this unpromising beginning to the emancipation struggle when a new phase in the fight for national independence began in 1942. Even the cadres of the Gandhian movement, when not already in prison, had to concentrate on this issue, and the work among the Halpatis was dropped. Much more important, however, was the sudden rise in food prices resulting from the threat of imminent war, with wages lagging far behind. It had become impossible to live on 4½ annas a day, and even this amount was not paid everywhere. Furthermore, it appeared that some additional emoluments given earlier, particularly food, were essential supplements to wages. It became quite common to revert back again to the former payment in kind, but old practices were not restored in every case. One important outcome which adversely affected the Halpatis was that during the war years, with the effect of food scarcity and the resulting high grain prices, the custom of giving *halis* a plot of land for personal cultivation was ended (C. H. Shah 1952: 450).

The relationship of dependence endured but was being increasingly stripped of the security of living which had accompanied it earlier; this was the inescapable conclusion forced upon the social workers. In 1946 the Halpati Mahajan, a communal association modelled on the famous Gandhian labour union in Ahmedabad, was set up under the chairmanship of Jugatram Dave. It was a loosely structured, rather artificial organization managed from the *ashrams* in Bardoli and Valod, consisting of only a few staff and with no clear basis. The programme was no different from that of earlier activities and remained primarily directed towards bringing social reform into the lives of the Halpatis. After the coming of independence, however, the government was pressured to effect the advancement of the Halpatis by (a) prohibiting the *hali* system, (b) introducing a minimum wage for agricultural labourers; (c) improving their economic and social condition by creating employment opportunities, and providing for education, housing and health care.

It was probably as a result of this pressure that the government of the State of Bombay established the 'Hali Labour Enquiry Committee' in May 1947, with the assignment of: '. . . suggesting measures necessary for rehabilitating this class of agricultural labourers and for enabling them to live a life consistent with human dignity and self-respect' ('Notes and comments' in: *Indian Journal of Agricultural Economics*, September 1948). The report of this committee, never released for publication, affirmed that *halipratha* was a form of unfree labour. An interesting indication of change in the social climate was that even the farmers who were questioned claimed to place no value on maintaining the *hali* system any longer. They did however impress upon the committee that an alternative should at least include the obligation to provide labour power in the busy season, arguing that otherwise agrarian production would suffer. This proposal to give labour ties a modern contractual basis was in line with the argument put forward by the farmers' representatives on various occasions in the past, for the introduction of a system of identity cards in order to put an end to the evil of runaway *halis*. According to this line of thought, government intervention in social life was permissible only when it was necessary to protect the interests of the farmers. The reasoning was that the raising of agrarian production was an important national priority and it was therefore the duty of the government to ensure that enough cheap labour would be available.

The proposal of this investigating committee to prohibit the *hali* system and to punish infringement of the ban was coupled with a number of recommendations, the most important of which were:

— the declaration of a minimum wage of Re 1 per day for day labourers and an annual Rs 275 for farm servants. In both cases all other emoluments were to be discontinued;
— cancellation of all debts older than three years;
— the founding of an obligatory savings fund created from wage deductions. The capital accumulated to be used as a source of credit for consumption purposes in times of need, to be paid out to members by local co-operatives of the landless;
— housing for Halpatis on land of their own, making building materials available and thereby reducing dependence on the farmers;
— the formation of local labour tribunals presided over by a government welfare officer.

The wage proposal was based on a calculation of a minimum subsistence, for which the committee took as its starting point the calculation that an agricultural labourer's family needed 8 *seers* of grain a day—6 *seers* of food as an absolute minimum and the equivalent of 2 *seers* for other necessities. According to prices then current, this meant a sum of Re 1 per day. By linking the daily wage to the retail price of food grain, maintenance of the agricultural labourer's real income could be guaranteed. The committee noted further that this sum was the minimum necessary for sheer survival.[14] The payment of a 'fair' wage would have to wait until agriculture became more profitable.

There was no official response to this report and no attempt was made to implement its recommendations. As we have already observed, the government was under the impression

[14] Disunity reigned within the commission. One of the report makers felt that the recommendations, already less than generous, still went too far. He proposed a lower minimum wage and was clearly opposed to the idea of cancellation of debts. M. B. Desai, Minute of Dissent in: *Report HLEC*.

that the Bardoli agreement between farmers and agricultural labourers made in the presence of Morarji Desai in 1948 had rendered a formal prohibition of the *hali* system superfluous. In fact this was a repetition of the events of 1939. Although in this settlement the farmers' interests were even more prominent than in the recommendations of the investigating committee, nevertheless the Patidars evaded putting it into practice (M. B. Desai and C. H. Shah 1950: 71). The strikes which agricultural labourers again mounted in several villages had little or no result during the harvest period.

From the discussion of the current situation it will be clear that labour relations have changed drastically over the last few decades. The changes that have taken place have to a large extent occurred autonomously, i.e., they have resulted from an accelerated transition to a new mode of production in agriculture, and not from government intervention aimed at the protection of labour. Although the Gandhian movement has traditionally been concentrated in Bardoli and its environs, the social action it has undertaken has had only a marginal impact in this area.

The cause of the failure to emancipate the agricultural labourers must be sought in the way in which Gandhian workers have judged the rural situation in south Gujarat from the very beginning: not as a conflict between classes with contradictory interests but as a moral problem within the existing social order. This attitude reverberates throughout the booklet on the *hali* system published by Jugatram Dave in 1946. It is a fierce attack on bonded labour which reduces the Halpati to the level of an animal. Yet, says the writer, it is the masters who suffer greater damage, since they rob themselves of human feelings.[15] The strategy underlying this point of view was that abolition of the *hali* system must be fought for by convincing the landowners of its injustice rather than by mobilizing the

[15] Dave, op.cit. 30. The author rebuked the farmers who had rejected personal physical labour in the same wording used by Gandhi in his romantic depiction of the good old days of his youth in Saurashtra: '. . . there was more lustre in people's eyes, and more life in their limbs, than there is today', in: *Harijan*, September 1941, quoted by Lipton 1977: 382 (footnote 122).

Halpatis to resist it. Given the idea that only gradual change from within could bring a solution to the problem, the emphasis in the social movement lay on harmony and mediation. Any form of direct action which stimulated the agricultural labourers' belligerence still further and which advocated confrontation with the farmers, was vehemently rejected by the Gandhian doctrine. Narhari Parikh, the same man who in 1924 carried out a seven-day hunger strike in a vain attempt to break the Patidars' opposition to social work among the agricultural labourers, wrote in the introduction to Dave's publication:

> Some old social workers of the Bardoli taluka sense an attempt to create class conflict in the activities of the workers to bring about an awakening among the Halpatis. But Jugatrambhai has made one thing very clear in this booklet, that efforts to secure human treatment and justice to the Halpatis should be made on the basis of truth and non-violence and in no way in a manner that would breed class conflict (Dave 1946: 10).

A large proportion of the social workers who have been active in this struggle over the past few decades belong to the elite castes either within or outside the region. It would be only too easy to attribute the fear of far-reaching reforms to class prejudice *per se*, but this does not alter the fact that the view of society as a community governing the Gandhian movement has in essence contributed to the perpetuation of the Patidars' hegemony as the leading peasant caste. The preference for such principles as moderation and reconciliation have from the outset precluded more than a marginal correction to the existing inequality. The possibility that growing opposition would inevitably result from the agricultural labourers' increased consciousness has never really been faced. Insofar as this has happened (about which we will write more later), opposition has had unintended and even deplorable consequences. Clashes with the farmers have therefore been systematically avoided. It was characteristic of the Bardoli campaign that, according to Dhanagare, the subjection of the agricultural labourers to the Patidar landowners was utilized in order to carry out the struggle against the colonial government more effectively (Dhanagare 1980). When government officials came to confiscate the possessions of the cultivators who had failed to pay their land tax, the Halpatis refused to help them even when offered the prospect of an adequate wage in exchange for their co-operation. One must ask whether the Halpatis' fidelity and obedience was really so complete as the contemporary historiography suggests. It was intimidation and fear of heavy sanctions, rather than unquestioning loyalty, that most probably deterred many farm servants from collaborating with the colonial government. One indication of the dissension already existing were the agricultural labourers' strikes which, in the season after the action, broke out in several villages of Bardoli Taluka (Broomfield and Maxwell 1929: 15).

The Gandhian workers proved to be unequal to the pressure put on them. The most important leader left the area for the *ashram* in Valod, an area where the percentage of agricultural labourers was still low and where the Halpatis formed a minority. This desertion made it possible to evade the necessity for greater militance in taking the part of the socially weak and making a stand against the rural upper stratum. It was much easier to avoid this choice by giving high priority to the eastern *talukas* where the tribals had retained a greater independence as farmers. The Adivasi area was an attractive sphere of operations for the Gandhian movement, which gave priority to Hinduization in its programme, and most of the movement's new action centres were established here in the 1950s and 1960s.

The Gandhian ideology offered an alternative for all those who believed that the *hali* system did not belong in the India which had freed itself from foreign domination, but who were otherwise averse to a far-reaching social reconstruction. Thus, the report of the Hali Labour Enquiry Committee spoke warmly of the patriotic social workers who, while striving to improve the agricultural labourers' condition, never lost sight of the national interest. Conversely, disquiet was expressed over the agitation carried out in south Gujarat by the communist Kisan Sabha. With an ominous reference to the revolt against bonded labour which broke out among the Adivasis in Thana District shortly after the Second World War[16] the report continues:

[16] For this see the lively account by Godavari Parulekar from 1975. The author was himself involved, as political activist, in this tribal movement.

> If things proceed along the line pursued today in which poisonous propaganda is being dinned into the ears of the Halpatis without putting the entire question in its proper perspective before them, the conclusion is irresistible that a violent class conflict leading to considerable destruction might be in store. If this were unfortunately to happen it will embitter the relationship between the farmers and the Halis and will be calamitous for the progress of agriculture in the district. It is highly improper to further political motives under the pretext of fighting for the emancipation of the working class. An effort should, therefore, be made to properly appreciate the achievements through constructive efforts by selfless workers in Bardoli and Valod whose life's mission is the service of the down-trodden in the true Gandhian way (Report HLEC 1950: 51).

No other way but the Gandhian way. This was also the message which Morarji—who had himself originated from south Gujarat and who had meanwhile risen to the post of Minister of Finance in the central government—impressed upon the Halpatis at a meeting held in Sarbhon in May 1963. During that year I was carrying out research among agricultural labourers in several villages of south Gujarat, and this was the first time that I had taken part in such a politically coloured demonstration. The meeting was held in a mango orchard belonging to a large farmer who was at the same time a well-known social worker. Those present were meticulously divided up into several categories, just as at a large wedding, with different eating lines for different castes. Seated in front were the politicians, high officials and other outsiders who underlined the importance of the affair by their presence. Thereafter followed many rows of local social workers, recognizeable by their *khadi* clothing. Behind these were seated a few well-meaning Gandhian landowners. At some distance, at the edge of the orchard, the Halpatis drummed up from nearby villages watched the proceedings like a lukewarm audience who were only moderately interested in the play. Some of their leaders had been allotted a small role, reading aloud the text of the resolutions unanimously adopted by the social workers—or rather, since they were illiterate, repeating the text word for word as prompted.

The tenor of these final resolutions had already been revealed by Morarji Desai in his introductory speech. The *hali* system, he said, arose out of the loans contracted by the Halpatis for their marriages, and the system was maintained by their partiality for liquor. He called on them to free themselves from their bondage by avoiding indebtedness in future, and abandoning bad habits, particularly drinking. The total amount of land was insufficient to allow the Halpatis to profit from land reform. Therefore he counselled them to ask for higher wages. However, they were not to go on strike or even stage go-slows, since by doing so they would harm not only the farmers but also themselves, and he urged his audience to have patience and not to listen to agitators, but to put their trust in the Congress Party.

The meeting was the occasion of the second anniversary of the Surat Jilla Halpati Seva Sangh which had continued the activities of the Mahajan. From an organizational point of view this signalled the beginning of a new phase. Under the new leadership, with Jugatram Dave continuing as the honorary chairman and with a growing number of staff, the work was continued on a much larger scale than before. Ten years later, when branch offices were also opened outside the district, it was obvious that the name should be changed to Halpati Seva Sangh. From the first annual report covering the period from the end of September 1961 (the date of its official foundation) to May 1963, it would appear that the organization consisted of a vanguard of social workers, half of whom were identifiable as belonging to the most prominent landowning castes in the region (12 Patidars, 12 Anavils) and only a bare quarter coming from the target group itself (11 out of a total of 48). Admission to this cadre required fulfilment of the following criteria: the wearing of *khadi*, abstention from alcohol, experience of having worked among the Halpatis for at least five years, and an annual contribution of one day's wages and one day's production of thread hand-spun by the applicant. Apart from two donors, one of whom was Morarji Desai, there were 7,723 members who were each expected to pay 10 new *paise* (cents) a year. Ten years later the membership was said to have risen to nearly 20,000 Halpatis, who were theoretically supposed to make the same symbolic contribution but whose membership had only a minimal significance. The increase in membership mainly served to display the Halpati Seva Sangh to the outside world as a mass movement and as the only representative organization of agricultural labourers to gain official recognition. From the outset the work of the organization, along with overhead costs such as office expenses, staff salaries, etc., was to a large extent if not exclusively financed by government subsidies. The strong basis of the Gandhian movement, centred on *ashrams* within a surrounding network of helpers and sympathizers, and the solid coalition of Congress Party and bureaucracy in the region, made the Bardoli countryside an almost impregnable stronghold against other competing organizations interested in the emancipation of landless labourers.

Over the years there has been little change in the nature of the programme. Housing, education and socio-cultural activities have remained the chief components. A number of projects for the building of improved huts had already been launched in previous years[17] and this programme was greatly expanded after the extensive flooding of 1968. Land had already been made available to the landless in many villages but owing to the farmers' opposition they were usually allotted the worst sites: uneven, with insufficient drainage in the monsoon, far removed from the real village centre and difficult to reach. The materials (wood, roof tiles) were made available to the local building co-operatives either cheaply or free of cost, and the Halpatis themselves supplied the labour. The Halpatis live, isolated from others, in the localities built up in this way.

The *ashrams* in Surat District have increasingly assumed the character of educational institutions in which children are disciplined in the Gandhian way of life. In addition, several lower and middle-level boarding schools have been established throughout the district, especially for Halpati youth, in which the teaching follows Gandhian principles. To prevent the new generation from remaining dependent on agricultural labour, technical training is also provided, aiming at artisan occupations such as tailoring and bricklaying, and at new skills such as diamond cutting/polishing, and driving. Over the years the ambitious programme of activities followed by the Halpati Seva Sangh has met with only moderate success, and in fact a

[17] A beginning was first made with this in the 1950s. For a similar project in Bardoli Taluka see *Privileges Provided by Bombay State Government for Backward Classes*. Bombay 1955: 56.

fundamental motive in the organization's work has been the affirmation of the agricultural labourers' inferiority. The starting point and also the lesson sytematically drilled into the Halpatis was that they must gain respectability by adapting to Hindu norms and higher-caste customs. The purification of social life entailed adherence to a number of hygienic-ritual precepts such as the taking of morning baths, but it was also necessary for the Halpatis to discard a number of practices regarded as objectionable by the caste Hindus, even though they were basic to the tribal identity of the Halpati and were counterpoints to the dominant values imposed from above. Such a counterpoint culture might have played an important role in the Halpatis' social mobilization. However, the kind of emancipation pursued by the Halpati Seva Sangh was one of upliftment, not through resistance to the existing social order, but through accommodation to that order. For the acquisition of human dignity in this way, however, some minimal economic and political pre-conditions had to be met, in particular those relating to their state of poverty and oppression. By and large this idea has never been properly developed in Gandhian teaching or practice, with the result that, even when measured by its own objectives, the outcome of the movement's efforts in Bardoli was rather disappointing (Breman 1974b).

Transition to the contemporary situation

During the first half of the twentieth century there was no real improvement in the agricultural labourers' socio-economic condition in the plain of south Gujarat. The *hali* system did indeed gradually disintegrate, a process in which the transition to an agrarian order based on market production was of decisive importance. However, with the disappearance of the farm servant's bondage, the limited security of livelihood inherent in this form of bonded labour was lost. In spite of the transition to a capitalist economy which created a freer labour regime, the landless of south Gujarat remained confined to a living standard that made survival barely possible.

Yet in the first decades of this century particularly, reports appeared suggesting real progress as the result of a putative scarcity of labourers. Demographic, social and economic factors, alternately or in combination, were held responsible for this state of affairs. Famine following drought and plague around the turn of the century found many victims, especially among the landless of Gujarat. The extremely high mortality among the low castes led to a rise in wages in the years following.[18] The influenza epidemic which broke out at the end of the First World War had the same result (Census of India 1921, XVII: 37). A socially determined motive for the growing demand for labourers lay in the changing life-style of the employers. The larger farmers showed themselves increasingly reluctant to take part in agricultural work. It is worth mentioning here that the growth of industrial employment, particularly at the time of the First World War, also exerted an upwards pressure on wages (Gazetteer Baroda State, I, 1923: 253,300; Mehta 1932: 126). We may well ask, however, whether the rural proletariat profited from this. Insofar as people living at some distance being recruited for industrial employment were concerned in this phase of early industrialization, this remained mainly limited to members of the artisan and service castes. It was to be several decades before landless labourers could obtain entry to the urban labour market, and even then only to a modest extent. *Halis* did, with increasing frequency, run away, more in the hope of finding a better master than of trying to gain access to employment outside agriculture.[19] Geographical mobility among agricultural labourers and also seasonal migration to urban industries were absent in the village which Shukla studied in the early 1930s. Only within the area was there any exchange of labour between villages with either shortages or surpluses of labour (Shukla 1937: 129). Some publications bearing on this period give the impression that the number of agricultural labourers

[18] '. . . continued high prices, both of food and labour. Depopulation by famine and plague is the main cause, which has contributed to the rise in the volume of labour' (Census of India 1911, XVI: 32, 333–4). For information on the differential impact of these disasters see Census of India 1901, XVIII: 72–3 and 513; *Report of famine operations* . . . 1900: 3, 12.

[19] 'The labourers run away not because they get better terms elsewhere but because the treatment given to them is not at all sympathetic. Most of the labourers are Dublas and Dhankas, members of the aboriginal classes, illiterate and ignorant. The employers sometimes maltreat them and to avoid further trouble they run away to some other place. To force these people would be cruel', in: *Report Baroda Economic Development Committee* 1920: 131–2.

decreased, not so much under the influence of growing urban employment but because some of the landless moved up into the landowning class. Charlesworth seeks the explanation for this upwards rise within the agrarian order in the continuing extension of the cultivated area and the way in which labourers were allowed to lease land intended for cotton cultivation.

> Even those who remained simply labourers may have benefitted from rising real wages—certainly a constant complaint of cash crop producers in this period—as the expansion of cotton with its thirst for labour pressed on traditional resources. Bardoli was now an economy where agricultural commercialization was much more broadly established and where, therefore, in conditions of rapid expension [*sic*], manipulation of production for the market by a narrow proprietory elite was arguably no longer possible (Charlesworth 1980).

According to this author, who has repeated his idea more emphatically in a recent article, access to land in the vicinity of Bardoli was to remain open to non-owning classes for a long while yet. '. . . during the first quarter of the twentieth century a more flexible agricultural economy and agrarian social structure was emerging in areas like Bardoli. Categorizations like "landowner", "tenant", "labourer" and "smallholder" had become far from clear-cut (Charlesworth 1982: 269).

This thesis now appears to me to be an exaggerated representation of the social dynamic in the countryside of the south Gujarat plain. To be sure, there are indications that here and there landless people had acquired some land, either as owners or as tenant cultivators, but this always involved, in the first place, a marginal amount of land, and in the second, land which was barely productive and in which the farmer castes had no interest.[20]

The Halpatis have had probably even less opportunity than other landless castes to work their way up to ownership of land. To be sure, Mukhtyar did mention this phenomenon in his village study in south Gujarat at the end of the 1920s (Mukh-

[20] 'There is very little of cultivable land left unoccupied in the State; the best cultivators would not usually care for it, and as each additional acre is leased for cultivation, there being less and less demand from the real agriculturists, more and more these landless labourers drift in to take it up' (Census of India 1921, XVII: 367).

It is not without significance that, in the summary of castes following this, the Kolis (from of old a caste of cultivators) are mentioned while the Halpatis are not.

tyar 1930: 160) but Shukla stated specifically that in the course of his research he had not encountered a single Halpati with a patch of ground or who had become a tenant (Shukla 1937: 128).

The thesis that upward mobility led to a decrease in the size of the landless class seems to me to be an untenable proposition, yet this is one of the explanations for the rise in real wages in the first decades of the twentieth century. Charlesworth, who takes this as his starting point, agrees with the official sources he cites, according to which it was the agricultural labourers rather than the farmers, who profited from the commercialization of agrarian production.[21] It is perhaps possible to support this proposition with factual data derived from colonial statistics, but I find it difficult to recognize the social reality in this view, and in particular the dynamic of rural class relations in south Gujarat. As far as the first decade of this century is concerned, it is not entirely out of the question that the increase in agricultural labourers' wages did not lag behind the rise in the cost of living, but this certainly does apply to the following years, as we can see from other government publications.[22] Even Charlesworth seems to have retreated from his earlier standpoint, indicating in a recent publication devoted to the levying of land taxes under the *ryatvari* system that, while landowners were to a certain extent spared, the landless had to produce an increasingly larger share of the taxes:

> The major shift from land towards consumption taxes between 1880 and the 1920s adversely affected rural labourers and some tenants . . . the actual tax paid by the landless agricultural la-

[21] '. . . the general result seems to be a rise in the prosperity of the labouring classes in rural areas', but 'the farmer producing market crops and employing labour largely in his work has suffered badly'; and '. . . By the late 1920s it was clear that the class of the agricultural population which has suffered most is the big cultivator employing hired labour on a large scale inproducing his crop. . .', Charlesworth 1979: 132 and 133–4. McAlpin had drawn a similar conclusion: 'If there was any shift in the relative-factor returns, it probably occurred in favor of labor. The area was close to Bombay and may have fed labor into both the Bombay and Ahmedabad mills. If this occurred, it would have minimized population pressure on land and, therefore, would have helped to maintain the level of wages' (1975: 298).

[22] For the period 1900–22 see Shirras 1924. According to the 1931 census report, agricultural labourers' wages decreased in Gujarat between 1921 and 1931 (Census of India 1931 XIX: 269).

bourers doubled between the periods 1911–14 and 1922–25, slightly more than the average increase in prices (Charlesworth 1981: 21).

At the end of the colonial period there was no real change in this trend. The raising of the wage for agricultural labour during and shortly after the Second World War followed behind the rise in the prices of daily food and other bare necessities, and did not move ahead of them.[23]

In the first half of the twentieth century there was an increase in the share of the agricultural labourer's wage paid in cash, influenced by changes in the agrarian mode of production. The gradual increase in this money sum did not, however, indicate an improvement in labour conditions brought about by an insufficient supply of labour.

Convincing evidence is lacking for this last proposition also, wrongly deduced from the growing stability of the master-servant relationship. By constantly keeping wages for agricultural labour at the lowest possible level, landowners who employed landless labourers avoided the need to redistribute the growing surplus. Without raising the level of real wages, an increase in their money value was necessary in order to guarantee the reproduction of labour to a sufficient extent. Nevertheless remuneration never went above a level that merely permitted survival.

In the mid-twentieth century the Halpatis' position within the process of socio-economic change in the Surat countryside was already an unfavourable one, and as an inferior class they have fallen still further behind since then. There has been no room for them within the strategy of modernization followed since independence. In fact they have been penalized by this policy and have not received the governmental attention to which they should be entitled, in view of their number and threatened livelihoods.

[23] 'The farm labourer was of course adversely affected due to uneven rises in wages and prices, but the increase in indebtedness was only partly due to shortfall in incomes but was mainly due to other expenses'. . . . 'In the case of both the contract and the casual labourers expenses for social ceremonies featured prominently among the causes for incurring fresh debts' (C. H. Shah 1952: 455 and 460. For the early post-war years see Desai and Shah 1950: 57 ff. and 71).

The limited efforts made by official authorities to offer protection and extra opportunities to disadvantaged groupings have to a large extent bypassed the landless labourers. There are several reasons for this. In the first place, most of these compensation programmes begin by dividing the population along social lines rather than economic ones. In the rural policy followed by both the Indian government and the government of Gujarat, the agricultural labourers—forming a growing proportion of the working population—are systematically overlooked. This can also be said of more recent years, in which programmes for agrarian reform and redistribution of land appear to have become more intensive. The surplus land which should have been released with land reform has never been intended for the landless, and even less have they been able to profit from more recent schemes enabling small and marginal farmers to participate in the modernization of agrarian production. The issue here is not that these measures have been implemented only half-heartedly if at all, but rather that a considerable proportion of the agrarian population have from the outset been ignored as an object of concern in policy making. The principal exception to this has been the attempt to introduce a minimum wage for agricultural labour. The effect of this intervention will be discussed at length later in this study.

As a 'backward' social category the Halpatis have in recent years been included in the programmes intended for tribal castes, but they have derived relatively little profit even from these. A large number of groupings are clubbed together under the collective term 'tribal', even when they display wide differences in their relative social positions. In the competition with landowning Adivasis in the region, the landless Halpatis have not succeeded in capturing a proportionate share of the various facilities—scholarships, lower-level government posts, agrarian or commercial credit, technical training—which the government has made available for the benefit of these vulnerable categories. One important factor contributing to this is that Halpatis do not form a majority anywhere in the *talukas* of south Gujarat, although they are the largest tribal caste in that region. The lack of numerical ascendancy within a concentrated territorial domain ensures that the Halpatis have little say in district councils, while they also have almost no political leaders of their own to champion their cause at higher levels. The paternalist approach characteristic of the Gandhian method means that their dependence, formerly institutionalized on an individual basis in servitude, is now simply perpetuated in a collective form in their clientage to the Halpati Seva Sangh. In an earlier publication I compared the leader of this organization to a *dhaniyamo*, a traditional master from the landlord caste, from which he does, in fact, originate (Breman 1974b: 494).

In contrast to several other tribal castes such as Chaudharis and Gamits, the Halpatis are markedly under-represented in occupations such as teaching and the civil service, i.e. jobs which should fall within their reach and which moreover function as channels for upward mobility. The vicious circle of social isolation and poor education forces most of the younger generation into the dead-end existence of agricultural labour. The Halpatis' low degree of participation in education is striking, given the way in which social workers have given pride of place to this in all their activities. In the schools especially instituted for Halpatis, the majority of pupils often belong to other tribal castes. In 1971 only 13.725 per cent of the Halpatis in Surat District were literate, a percentage clearly far below the average of 39.3 per cent for the total population, and lower even than that of 17.1 per cent for all the tribal castes taken together. In this respect it is significant that in Bardoli Taluka an area with a very high density of schools, a long tradition of education and a large Halpati population—the percentage of literates among the tribal population is lower than in several other *talukas* where educational facilities began later and are spread much more thinly. The following example is taken rather arbitrarily from the research undertaken by Patel in Afwa at the beginning of the sixties. 97 per cent of higher-caste village children attend the village school (instituted in 1867) of which only 7 per cent are Halpati. Literacy among the adults is 83 per cent for higher castes and 11 per cent for Halpatis (R. M. Patel 1966: 76 and 80). To round off this picture, between 1961 and 1971 the literacy rate among this agricultural labourers' caste rose less rapidly than the rate for all tribals taken together. Their retarded participation in education means that the Halpatis' low rank in the traditional hierarchy has been carried over into the new order.

The suggestion of structural continuity emerging from this diagnosis has a reifying effect, in that we cannot take it for granted that the social dynamic follows the division of the population along caste lines. It is precisely because the strength of this type of collectivity is taken for granted in much social science research—expressed in a conventional but very negatively loaded stereotyping of the lowest castes—that extra caution is needed in analysing processes of change based on a social stigma which was linked with an earlier hierarchical configuration. In other words, by labelling the Halpatis as exclusively agricultural labourers, and agricultural labourers as exclusively Halpatis, on the one hand we lose sight of the differentiation existing even among this caste, and on the other hand we ignore the growing supply of agricultural labour from other castes.

To begin with the first proposition: a small Halpati vanguard has succeeded in finding a livelihood outside agriculture and their numbers are increasing, especially among the younger generation. Access to non-agricultural employment is admittedly hampered by the Halpatis' unfavourable social milieu, but on the other hand it is precisely their main home region, the western part of Surat District, which has seen rapid economic growth. A growing number of Halpatis are profiting from expanding employment in nearby urban centres, where their greatest chances for social advancement lie. Although still proportionately under-represented, growing numbers are penetrating the lower regions of the urban economy. Compared with social groups able to enter this arena at a higher level, the Halpatis' position is hardly enviable, but their handicap as unskilled labour does not alter the fact that in the urban setting they have gained a higher living standard than the majority of their caste fellows in the rural areas. This contrast is clearly evident in the case of Halpatis with permanent jobs as factory workers or class IV (lowest level) government employees outside the village, but who still live in the village. From a material point of view these households are identifiable by better housing, better food and the possession of durable consumer goods. They form a vanguard which, in a sociocultural sense, conforms to the behaviour expected of those who are working their way upwards; for example, their children, especially the boys, go to school. The diamond cutters and polishers also belong to this privileged category which has succeeded in distancing itself from the agricultural labourer's existence. This branch of industry has experienced an explosive development in recent years in Surat District. Workshops have been opened in a number of villages and expansion has been so rapid that the Patidar owners have been forced to recruit some of the polishers needed from among the Halpatis. However, only a limited proportion of Halpatis have been able to profit from this new industry, i.e. those able to find the money needed for the obligatory apprenticeship.

I shall return later to a fuller discussion of the mechanisms and effects of this process of differentiation among the Halpatis. Nevertheless I would like, for the sake of clarity, to reaffirm that in spite of the diversification which has taken place in the regional economy the vast majority of Halpatis have to still earn their living by agricultural labour. According to the findings of the 1961 Census 78 per cent of the working population among this caste were dependent on this employment. My impression (and it can be no more than an impression, given the lack of quantified data) is that this percentage has dropped since 1961, albeit not to any spectacular degree.

Against horizontal mobility, i.e. those who have been able to escape to other occupations, there stands the fact of demographic growth, with more Halpatis than ever before living as agricultural labourers. On the other hand, the percentage of agricultural labourers in the central Surat plain is much higher than the proportion of Halpatis in the population would suggest. It is relevant to note here that in agricultural labourers' households the highest possible number—on average, three out of five family members—are available for participation in the labour process.[24] Virtually everyone on their feet—children from seven or eight years old, to the more or less able-bodied old—must in principle provide the labour power for their own subsistence. This contrasts sharply with landowning families. In other words, the socio-economic status of those households living on the income derived from agriculture bears an inverse proportion to their representation in the labour force. This finding forms a partial explanation for the disproportionate

[24] Working children under the age of ten years are not counted in this figure. *Report HLEC* 1950: 28.

number of agricultural labourers among the agrarian population. The overwhelming majority are still Halpatis, but the continuing expansion of the agricultural-labourer population can certainly not be attributed solely or even mainly to the demographic growth of this caste. Rather, the cause is an economic one and must be sought in the growing supply of agricultural labour drawn from other castes who try to distinguish themselves from the Halpatis by virtue of their past history as peasant cultivators. This supply for the most part takes the form of migrant labour and is linked with the dynamic which has emerged in the hinterland of Surat District. As mostly small landowners they occupy an intermediate position between the larger landowners on the one hand and the landless labourers on the other. The historical background of this social class and the growing differentiation within it, will be the subject of the following chapter.

6

COLONIZATION OF THE TRIBAL HINTERLAND

Development in dependence

Tribal peasant castes predominate in the eastern *talukas* of Surat District. This bleak natural environment of infertile soil in a terrain seriously affected by surface erosion is the living area of Chaudharis, Gamits, Vasavas (Bhils) and several smaller Adivasi groups, which together constitute some 70 per cent to 90 per cent of the total population. There is a clear relationship between ecological conditions and the composition of the population, Valod Taluka forming a transitional zone between the tribal landscape and the more westerly belt of black soil, most of which belongs to 'superior' castes.

In contrast to the fertile plain where agriculture had already been developed long before the beginning of the colonial period, the area beyond Bardoli had barely been opened up by the mid-nineteenth century (see Forrester 1887: 434–8). Colonial officials described Surat's hinterland as little more than a jungle, sparsely populated by semi-nomad tribes practicing a primitive agriculture and cultivating only a few varieties of rough millets. The tribals were not concentrated in villages but lived dispersed in hamlets (*falias*). These small nuclei, each limited to a few huts and lying at several kilometres distance from each other, together make up village life until the present day. The inhabitants were subordinated to pre-colonial lords (Rajput *gerasias*) who with their armed bands made regular raids on the area from surrounding power centres, in order to collect tribute. When there was a death in the family, when a harvest failed or when some other crisis arose, the peasants left their primitive huts to establish themselves temporarily somewhere else within the vaguely defined boundaries of the tribal territory and to take new land into cultivation.

> A patch of forest land was cleared by the cultivators, and grass, weeds and wild plants were collected and burnt on the spot thus preparing the seed-beds. Grains of previous years were scattered after the first showers of rain, and the aboriginal was satisfied with harvesting a crop of coarse cereal, usually *kodra* (paspalum sero biculatum) or *nagli* (eleusine coracana)' (Mehta 1934: 316; also Gazetteer Bombay Presidency II, 1877: 62–3).

Colonial reports give the impression that the opening up of this backward region resulted from the Pax Britannica. Although this is correct in broad outline, the region's earlier isolation should not be exaggerated. The trade route from the port of Surat via Khandesh to central and northern India passed through the Tapi river basin, but it is questionable whether this through-road had much impact on the immediate vicinity. The small irrigation works in the eastern parts of the present-day Surat District were probably more important for contacts with the outside world. These *bandharas* formed the basis for the cultivation of several superior food crops, including rice, which were exported through Surat even to countries overseas in pre-colonial times (Vyara RSR 1907: 6).

However, this small-scale infrastructure of a higher technological level did not survive the Marathas' plundering at the end of the eighteenth century. Although it is sufficiently clear from various reports that there is no reason to take it for granted that the region was found unsettled and uninhabited at the beginning of colonial rule, the introduction of colonial government indisputably led to a more systematic development of the area. In the first place the cadastral survey begun in the second half of the nineteenth century was of crucial importance. This registration formed the basis for taxation and also signified that land was henceforth firmly established as private property, thus ending the existing tribal practice of allotting rights of usufruct for unoccupied land by mutual agreement. 'The families did not occupy any definite piece of land, but moved about from village to village, cultivating their crops on any available piece of land within the tribal area. The aborigines maintain that until about 1870 they selected sites for cultivation by mutual agreement, and all differences were finally settled by their *karbhari* (head)' (Mehta 1934: 316). Thus the government dictated the transition to a more sedentary form of agriculture, which made larger settlements possible. The distinction formerly made between *rasti* villages in the plain, inhabited by a variety of castes which as a body were subject to regular tax collection, and the *rani* villages in the east where tribal cultivators led a rather unsettled life, gradually became obsolete.

There was further evidence of the opening up of the area on the arrival of shopkeepers, moneylenders and distillers from the western plain, who plied their exploitative trades among the tribals from their bases in the main villages and market places which had come into being partly as a result of their advent. The imposition of taxes in cash was an important mechanism for skimming off the surplus, which allowed Baniyas, Brahmins and Parsis, especially, to act as intermediaries between the *kaliparaj* on the one hand and, on the other, the market forces conjured up by the colonial government. Even before the end of the nineteenth century the population was in debt to these interlopers. The introduction of land taxes forced the peasants to set aside part of their product for sale in the market (with which they were otherwise linked only indirectly) via their creditors. On the one hand there were the fluctuations in the harvest yield resulting from the low level of agrarian technology and, on the other, a fixed assessment imposed by the colonial regime on the land held by each peasant household. The discrepancy between the total yield on the one hand, and subsistence needs and the share earmarked for taxes on the other, made borrowing inevitable.[1] The high interest charged by the Baniya merchants led to a relationship of dependence, which was perpetuated in a vicious circle through obligatory delivery of part of the harvest, and conversely the extension of credit for consumption purposes and for seeds at the beginning of the new rainy season as well.

> Their illiteracy and guilelessness have made them slaves of the money-lenders who are either the Vanias, the Marvaris or the

[1] 'They rarely taste rice and live on the coarsest grain in the shape of porridge washed down with toddy. Even kodra and nagli fail and by the end of June they beg of the sowcar for grains which they have to return at 1.5 maunds per maund lent, a clear loss of 50 per cent (*Census of India* 1901, XVIII: 501).

> Parsi liquor-sellers. They work against these simpletons in the following way. When corn is ready in the fields, the *sowcar* goes to his client and takes away a greater portion of it as past payment of his debt, keeping only so much with the debtor as would last him till the end of the winter season. When this is over the poor debtor is forced to him again and borrow as much corn as will make him pull through to the next harvest time. He borrows seeds when the monsoon comes, the first bar is known as khavti (food) and the second as bivda (seeds); for the former, the debtor has to return the quantity taken plus half the quantity, and for the latter double the quantity. Thus calculated the rate of the interest these poor people have to pay comes to 50 per cent and cent per cent respectively, per annum. In addition to this they impose upon them in measuring the corn, and in charging a higher price when lending and a lower price when receiving the corn.
>
> From what has been said above as regards the habits of these people we can never expect them to be prudent enough to keep in stock corn and other eatables ready for use on a rainy and rainless day. Hence in summer and the monsoon, most of those who have no credit with the *sowcars* have to content themselves with only one meal a day and that too on wild roots, flowers and creepers. Some of these are so bad for food that they bring about nausea and stomach complaints, if taken by those not gradually accustomed to it (Census of India 1901, XVIII, part 1: 501).

This transaction with the *kaliparaj* was in kind, but the net effect was of a progressive indebtedness registered in cash.

This process of exploitation was reinforced further by colonial policy which prohibited the distilling of liquor for private use. The right to distill liquor was confined to those with government licenses, which were periodically auctioned, usually to Parsis who, with an eye to this lucrative business in the tribal region, had settled there and had maintained their monopoly of alcohol distilling by ensuring that the law was strictly enforced. In this case too the provision of credit to addicted tribals took on the character of a debt relation, as a rule expressed in monetary terms merely for bookkeeping purposes. There was only a modest amount of cash circulation, and in this it is erroneous (taking things at face value) to consider the indebtedness of the *kaliparaj* as being due to the moneylending activities of merchants and distillers. This only came about later when the market economy penetrated the sphere of consumption.

The merchants and distillers were not primarily interested in acquiring land, although they were inscribed in the local registers as owners, having actually paid taxes which were often in arrears (Vyara RSR 1907: 9). Their first interest lay in the peasants' labour, i.e. in seizing control of the agrarian product. Land was thus a security accepted as a means of making the obligation to supply produce and additional personal services a binding one. The merchants and shopkeepers, settled in local market places for the most part, did not develop into a class of agrarian entrepreneurs with their own farm holdings. The cadastral surveys and population growth had, however, made free access to new land impossible. In other words the region's agrarian resources were closed off, with the result that the intrinsic value of land as a capital commodity increased. It was no longer possible to escape one's creditors by simply moving away and taking new land elsewhere into cultivation (Gazetteer Bombay Presidency II, 1877: 195–6). Gradually the situation emerged in which approximately half the cultivated area was being leased by the original owners, who cultivated their former holdings as mere sharecroppers. With periodic crises, such as the famine at the turn of the century, this agrarian regression accelerated. The result, judging from village research at the beginning of the 1930s, was that the share of cultivable land owned by absentee landlords had risen to 60 per cent (B. M. Mehta 1934). Tenancy, not agricultural labour, was the institution which determined the tribal population's economic bondage to an invading vanguard of the *ujliparaj* in the east of Surat District.[2] The socio-economic context in which agrarian production took place made the choice of renting out newly acquired land, rather than working it with hired labour, a logical consequence of the way in which the area had been opened up.

Although the *kaliparaj* were unable to defend themselves against the erosion of their autonomy, they were well aware of the mechanisms used to attack their property rights. In 1871, for example, a British government official noted that:

> They have the most astonishing power of memory; 99 out of 100 of these men will tell you what instalments of revenue they have

[2] For a detailed description of this historical process in the northern part of Valod Taluka see Baks 1974, Chapter IV.

> paid to the talatis even to the annas and pies, during the last 10 years. The mamlatdar asked me to test the fact, which I did, indiscriminately selecting the most idiotic in appearance, and in no instance found them wrong (N. B. Beijts, Revenue Officer 1871 in: Choksey 1968: 56–57).

Did the government offer no protection at all against the alienation of tribal land? The colonial machine had penetrated the tribal area in order to impose heavy taxation and it appeared easier to collect these taxes either directly from, or through, economic intermediaries. It is true that there was some attempt at an early stage to make allowances for the vulnerability of the original cultivators by the introduction of a lower tax rate, but because this concession provided extra profit for the money lenders, this well intentioned measure accelerated rather than retarded the loss of land (Mahuva RSR 1916: 20; Bardoli RSR 1895: 10). A very common reaction on the part of government was to blame the bad economic condition of the *kaliparaj* on their own backwardness. 'These people have not availed themselves of the lenient treatment given to them in the original settlement but they have abused it and consequently lost much of their lands, and became mere tenants of will of their Sahukars' (Mahuva RSR 1916).

The residential pattern of scattered habitations going back to the tribal past of shifting cultivation was ascribed in the colonial interpretation to addiction to alcohol which made it possible to exaggerate the significance of this vice until it became the ostensible main cause of their miserable existence.

> One of the results of their drunken habits is the straggling nature of their villages, however large. Every house, or rather hut of wattle and daub with thatched roofing seems to stand as isolated as it can so that a large Chodra village is merely a conglomeration of several small irregular villages. The reason for this is evident: they each dread that his neighbours will set fire not only to his hut but that of his neighbour as well in one of his drunken moments. Even in the hills where the tiger and the panther roam at night, the huts of the smallest villages are scattered, so it would appear, and they acknowledge it, that they fear their own kind more than the wild beast of the forest. The only way to save the Chodra from his low stage of moral and physical degradation into a thrifty and intelligent cultivator is to reduce the source of his liquor supply (I. J. Prescott, Revenue Officer 1872, in: Choksey 1968: 58).

Even the scattered pattern of living of the tribals has been explained by reference to their addiction to alchohol. The officer in charge of the cadastral survey of Bardoli Taluka in 1895 commented on the

> . . . gypsy-like instincts of the Kali Paraj, which prevent them from living in large communities. One local cause has certainly nurtured these instincts for ages, and that is the more than liberal way in which nature has endorsed these districts with the means of intoxication in the date trees. Before the present strict Abkari regime began the ordinary condition of these people was one of intoxication, and as their houses were built of such combustible materials as dry twigs and leaves, they naturally preferred to live in isolation (Bardoli RSR 1895: 16).

I. P. Desai has rightly indicated the inadequacy of this explanation. While the *kaliparaj* have always been accustomed to drinking, it was only after the advent of the colonial government that they began to lose their land. There was official sanction for the hostile attitude of merchants, shopkeepers and other local notables towards the temperance movement which emerged among the tribals in the early 1920s, indicating that there was scarcely any question of the regional government taking an honest interest in improving the lot of the *kaliparaj*. According to one local source, the attempt to break the movement included force-feeding those who refused alcohol, by holding their mouths open and pouring drink down their throats, in much the same way as castor oil is administered to oxen (I. P. Desai 1977: 47). Abolition meetings were prohibited and participants were treated roughly by the police. When social workers from the western plain wanted to come into the area to help the tribals, they were refused entry by the Government of the State of Baroda.

> These orders have been issued to the persons concerned, because it is believed that these persons intend to carry on the movement among the Adivasis to stop drinking liquor and to attempt to create conflict between communities and to ruin the Parsis (G. Shah 1977: 35).

The only solution was for the *kaliparaj* to die out, as a highly placed government official had already once remarked (Mahuva RSR 1916: 9). From this social-Darwinist viewpoint their supplanting by the *ujliparaj* was seen as a positive development which would ultimately serve the interests of progress in the district. In one case a local *maharajah* took the initiative in promoting colonization by *ujliparaj* in order to accelerate the opening up of the area; the ruler of the small state of Bansda encouraged the migration of Kanbis from the plain by land grants and the supply of cheap credit (Mahuva RSR 1916, app. D: 5). More commonly there was a spontaneous infiltration from the densely populated plain, with several Kanbi households establishing themselves in the transitional zone. Gradually the newcomers succeeded in obtaining the most fertile land and thus gaining control over the village. This was the pattern of penetration into Valod Taluka, for example, where the Kanbis brought their own Dubla agricultural labourers with them and where the tribal inhabitants still have a vivid memory of the ancestral lands lost to them only one or two generations ago. Where *ujliparaj* from the plain estabblished themselves as cultivators in this transitional area, land was probably wrested more permanently from the indigenous population. The fact that this process of alienation did not spread further to the east is due not only to an unfavourable natural environment and the post-independence national agrarian policy but also to the onset of the struggle for social and economic improvement among the *kaliparaj* and their gradually increasing consciousness of their separate identity which surfaced several decades before the ending of colonial rule.

Tribal subordination: accommodation and resistance

The penetration of the *ujliparaj* from the plain into the eastern part of Surat District assumed the character of a complete subjection of the *kaliparaj*. The emergent ideology was the socio-cultural expression of this process of subordination. The accommodation of the tribal population into the larger social system of which they became a part, has been described mainly in terms of adaptation. The image which emerges from the literature is that of a gradual embedding in the caste system to the extent that the accompanying scale of values was accepted.

Education has been an important instrument of this encapsulation. Even before the end of the last century a number of schools were opened throughout the eastern *talukas*, functioning as outposts of Hindu civilization. Students at the boarding school for tribal youths in Songhad—the first in the area and founded in 1885 by the progressive Maharajah of Baroda—requested the right to register as Hindus in the census (Census of India 1911, XVI: 54).

From approximately this time on tribal history began to be rewritten with suggestions of descent from, or at least mythical ties with, Rajput groupings in the north of Gujarat, and with the transformation of separate tribal entities (Chaudharis, Gamits, Bhils, etc.) into as many castes. Kosambi's dictum that 'the entire course of Indian history shows tribal elements being fused into a general history' (1956: 25) certainly applies to the population in the eastern *talukas* during the past hundred years. *Bhakti* principles embodied in ritual and in songs had already gained some acceptance in the past, through travelling *sadhus* who came into the tribal area. The indigenous *bhagats*, as religious leaders, popularized the new practices and adapted them to local custom. The new code of behaviour included the observance of Hindu ceremonies and festivities, different marriage customs, more rigid man/woman relationships, the taking of a morning bath to dispel pollution, and abstention from alcohol and meat. A small circle of advocates of this new life style (*ehda*) emerged, who set the example in purification of behaviour and who preached the new code in a sectarian manner. These innovators, called *varjelas*, who had foresworn the tribal gods, kept themselves apart from the much larger group of *sarjelas*, who continued to cling to the old customs and ideas. However, the conversion to the new life style periodically underwent a convulsive acceleration as a result of shortlived campaigns mounted in the tribal area. One example is the Devi or Mata Movement which spread from Khandesh in Maharashtra to the east of Surat District in the early 1920s. The followers of this movement formed a vanguard among the tribals, as I. P. Desai makes clear in a reconstruction based on the testimonies of several participants (1977: 49–50).

Certainly, such reform movements could easily be explained as deriving from the need to adapt to the values of a dominant culture. In fact detribalization amounted to absorption into the lowest echelon of the caste hierarchy and led to stigmatization as 'backward Hindus'. The process of Hinduization inevitably created a certain ambivalence, and this mean that purification of behaviour should be seen rather as a struggle for emancipation, insofar as it expressed a protest against the social degradation imposed on them. According to a contemporary commentary on the progress of the Devi Movement in 1922–3, this resistance had a secular foundation, even though the religious content was dominant.

> Agitation became more and more violent, but the religious interest was organised on a more permanent basis under Hindu influence. Bhajan meetings were held everywhere and became a regular feature of aboriginal life: attempts to give *dikshu* to educated tribesmen were made and advantage was taken of the anti-drink movement to introduce changes in food, dress, habit, etc. While the anti-drink fury and the class-war subsided, as they were bound to, these changes in religion and social attitude have persisted and tended to become permanent (Census of India 1931, XIX: 386).

In retrospect, I. P. Desai reaches a somewhat different conclusion in which the element of contest is still further emphasized and converted into resentments arising from economic exploitation and social subservience. He describes how the tribals held their own meetings, trying by means of this isolation to make themselves immune to outside influences in order to win self-esteem and to fight for equality.

> The Adivasis knew the non-Adivasis through the exploiters only, viz. the moneylenders, the police and other government officers, and the liquor shop owners. They therefore distrusted all non-Adivasis. They did not want any 'outsider' to be present at their meetings and made a rule that if any 'outsider' came to the meeting the proceedings should stop. The 'outsider' was actually the exploiter primarily. The 'Ujaliak' was disliked because he was an exploiter first, non-Adivasi next (I. P. Desai 1977: 52).

Desai demonstrates that the tribals did not passively suffer their integration at an inferior level in Hindu society, but were themselves the first to take action against the consumption of alcohol and other practices regarded as unacceptable by contemporary standards, practices upon which discrimination against the tribals was based.

Attracted by the abolition movement, Gandhian workers tried to establish contact with the tribal reformers and on the basis of the Gandhian fight against the colonial government, gradully succeeded in winning the trust of the tribal vanguard. They introduced the term Adivasis (the original people) in place of the perjorative name *kaliparaj* (literally, 'dark skinned') a definition which was untenable even as an ethnic distinction.

The spreading of Gandhian ideology over the tribal hinterland began from the Swaraj *ashram* in Bardoli founded in 1922, and soon there were small centres elsewhere, offshoots of the parent institution in Bardoli. The Vedchhi *ashram* near Valod was founded as early as 1924, and when Jugatram Dave settled there several years later this became the foremost action centre for work among the Adivasis in the east of Surat District. From the very beginning the Gandhian leadership in the region applied itself to social reform, educating its clientele to be better Hindus. In the programme, emphasis lay on teetotalism, vegetarianism, the propagation of ideas on hygiene, and other 'proper' rules of behaviour. Through an expanding group of supporters among the Adivasis a network of voluntary agents was created, centred on the *ashrams* and extending to the villages. The most active among them were commissioned as extension workers operating from the action centres. They held meetings for providing information and education, and stimulated the establishment of *bhajan mandalis*—small neighbourhood groups which met regularly to sing socio-religious songs—which spread the new ideas and values.

Efforts to improve the economic condition of the tribal population were subordinated to the foremost objective, which was their social upgrading. Here also a clear choice was made in favour of omitting changes in the structure of production, although from a strategic viewpoint the political and economic risks of siding with the lower castes was much smaller than in the plain. The combination of merchant/distiller/large landowner unmistakeably represented an alien element of coercion in this overwhelmingly tribal area, an element which for all practical purposes acted as an extension of the colonial government. In this early period however there was still no question of the Gandhian movement promoting material interests.

> The Gandhian leaders of Bardoli sought to defuse the *adivasi* agitation by converting it into a movement of mild reform. *Adivasi* meetings were held at which the stress was placed on abstention from liquor, on the need to wear handspun cloth and the need for *adivasi* education. The antilandlord aspect of the movement was played down. Special Gandhian ashrams were established in various parts of the *taluka* to implement this programme. To a large extent the Chodras were won over to this approach. As a result the Mata movement was turned into reformist channels. But even reformism had its dangers for the dominant class, and then Gandhians were only able to operate as they did because the landlords were Vaniyas and Parsis rather than Patidars (Hardiman 1981: 376).

Only towards the end of the 1930s was any attention paid to the need for ending indebtedness and reforming tenancy relations. The fact that these issues were not pushed to the fore earlier and more emphatically in the programme of activities is undoubtedly connected with Gandhian teaching which excluded a radical and militant stance on these questions. Thus it came about that the leadership of this reform movement consisted of Brahmins and members of other high castes who believed that Hinduization of their clientele was a necessary, if not a sufficient, condition for over-all improvement.

To pass a negative judgement on this attitude after the event would show a deficient historical consciousness. When one agrees that the Gandhian workers shrank from a real confrontation with the non-Adivasi elite in the eastern *talukas* one must at the same time observe that, without their presence among the tribals, the exploitation and repression of the latter would have been considerably worse. However paternalist in style and tenor, still a solidarity with the local population lay at the root of the behaviour of these activists which gained further content from their simple way of life. Thanks to their efforts the Adivasis were put on the region's social map, and were found to be important rank and file members of the organization of the nationalist movement. *Khadi* was a very essential part of the educational activities and the workers formed a cadre in the organization of the widespread participation in the frequent disobedience campaigns. Had not Gandhi himself said that 'without their support half of our body is paralyzed'? (Bhatt 1970: 326).

This mobilization within the framework of the independence struggle raised the consciousness of the Adivasis, promoted the emergence of a tribal elite and contributed to their emancipation as a social collectivity. The result was that (as this is so meaningfully expressed in Gandhian jargon) they united with the mainstream of social intercourse.

The Hinduization of the Adivasis not only meant that their subordination to the *ujliparaj* was now formalized within the regional caste composition as well, but also entailed the need to specify a ranking order among the tribal castes. It is important to observe here that there was an obvious connection between social rank and the degree of dependence. The Adivasis who have at least partly succeeded in maintaining their autonomy and who are less weighed down by the presence of higher castes, have a higher social status, while those who, as landless labourers, have become subjugated having been deprived of a collective identity of their own in the more remote past, have a low status. The difference in the type of integration into the caste system explains, for example, the inferior position of Halpatis in relation to the Chaudharis. 'No aboriginal touches a Dubla or enters his house, water becomes polluted at his touch. He attends the Chodhra marriage but sits at a distance and does not join the dances', thus Mehta states at the beginning of the thirties. Concerning the present, Shah adds: 'Even today, Chaudhris do not like to share food with other Adivasis whom they consider inferior. They look down upon Halpatis and avoid social relations with them' (Shah 1977: 118).

The conversion into tribal castes continues into the present through the proselytizing of sects such as the Moksh Marg, which is extremely active. The followers of this sect belong to the better-off among their grouping, holding up their 'purity' and devotion to the other members as an ideal.

Even after independence the Gandhian movement continued to be a major factor. The number of *ashrams* in the eastern *talukas* increased still further and, besides being centres of social action, these also became (perhaps above all) educational institution. This process began shortly before World War II when, as part of provincial autonomy, a Congress government was installed in Bombay. In 1939 Bardoli and Valod were selected for an experiment in which nineteen schools based on Gandhian principles of education, were opened, and this programme has been pushed through on a much bigger scale throughout the whole region in recent decades. The establishment of boarding schools made it possible to recruit pupils from remote villages who for a long time had been deprived of education, and the concentrated effort to make the Adivasis literate after 1950 is largely due to the work of the Gandhian institutions organized under the umbrella of the Raniparaj Seva Sabha. The picture becomes less positive when we consider that the kind of education which has been given has led to the systematic destruction of tribal culture. Indoctrination of the young with Gandhian principles has had only a limited success, but has certainly succeeded in inculcating contempt for their own background and past.

Leadership of the movement has remained firmly in the hands of the *ujliparaj*. Acting with the conscious superiority of Hinduism, they have never considered the possibility of protecting tribal identity, even in an adapted form, or using it as a catalyst for social mobilization. Jugatram Dave, the hallowed 'conscience' of the movement, sternly rejected the suggestion made by a protagonist of tribal art to preserve what remained of the region's material culture. 'You want us to preserve what we want to forget. To you this may be just forms, to us they are a symbol of their orgies and bouts of animal sacrifices and drinking' (Shah 1977: 38).

This reform policy has resulted in an unsatisfactory halfway situation in which the tribal castes have on the one hand been detached from their own traditions and life style, but on the other have not been acknowledged as equals by the outsiders held up to them as a reference group. I shall return in a later chapter to the social tensions which this alienation has created among the younger generation.

It would in any case be rash to assume that the encapsulation of the Adivasis within the larger social order has taken place in silence. An undercurrent of protest against the combination of economic exploitation and social subordination has remained continually audible. The authentic manifestations of this protest in, for instance, the Devi movement, have been largely absorbed and rendered harmless by the Gandhian *ashrams*, but alternative forms of collective resistance have regularly appeared outside the Gandhian context. In the tribal area to the north of the Tapi river, the influence of a Kisan Sabha core is still discernible. This is a residue of the radical movement under the leadership of Dattu Pangarkar which, even before independence, enjoyed strong support among the tribal population of the bordering Broach District and which, towards the end of the 1960s, appeared to gain a new lease of life in the Dakshin Gujarat Adivasi Swayat Raj under CPI(M) leadership (Desai 1977: 75). A completely different movement, which emphasized a unique ethnic identity and held the Hindu system responsible for the Adivasis' economic backwardness, emerged in Vyara Taluka in the mid 1950s (Desai 1977-12-13). Under the leadership of the Gamit, Khesri Singh, a fierce stand was made against outsiders, both *ujliparaj* and Gandhian workers. The search for its own road to emancipation gave the movement—locally known as *satti-patti*—a markedly sectarian character with a number of revivalist features. A procession in Valod which ended with police firing, and other violent clashes occurring near the border with Maharashtra, led to the prosecution of the leaders, which spelt the untimely end of the movement. However, the memory of this Adimjati Mahasabha, one of whose most popular demands was for the return of lost land, still lives on. As I found out some years ago, there are still some remnants of the movement here and there, and it is likely that its organizational structure has remained more or less intact. A revival of the movement under a new and better educated leadership is certainly not entirely out of the question given the steadily growing resentment against the Gandhian Movement, in spite of its honourable aims. This is especially true of the youths who meet in *yuvak mandals* and who feel that their own aspirations are being blocked by the higher non-Adivasi cadres, thus providing a fertile soil for such a revival.

The dynamic of the tribal castes must, however, be judged above all against the background of the economic changes which have taken place since independence in the eastern part of Surat District. As part of agrarian reform, tenancy was abolished in 1957 in Bombay State, of which Gujarat formed part at that time. As elsewhere in India, both the explicit aim and the actual result of this legislation was the development of prosperous peasantry which could be entrusted with the task of an increasing agrarian production. 'Land to the tiller' in the eastern *talukas* meant that the tribal peasants who had become share-croppers regained their earlier property rights. The real effect of this reform on the rural order has definitely been much greater than that of establishing land ceilings in 1960 and 1972, legislation that was weakened right from the start in Surat District, as elsewhere, by the many loopholes it contained. For the rest, enforcement of the law has been so lax as to prevent any fundamental change in the distribution of agrarian property. But the abolition of tenancy was also subject to some important restrictions. By making use of the clause stating that land personally cultivated by the owner did not have to be handed over, in many cases the former landowners succeeded in preventing transfer of their best land by working it themselves or by allowing trusted family members to manage it. In the second place it would be rash to assume that tenancy in fact disappeared with the 1957 law. Baks, in his research in the early 1960s, encountered a new form of sharecropping, and Shah also shows that concealed tenancy arrangements, often concluded only by word of mouth, still occurred in many guises at the village level. Besides sharecropping there is also *bani*, a form of mortgage in which the right to cultivate land is temporarily surrendered in exchange for a cash loan (Shah 1977: 54). Ultimately, Patidars and members of other self-cultivating castes have not as a rule lost any land and have even succeeded in profiting by the legislation on tenancy by extending their holdings still further, at the expense of the Adivasis' claims, in both the plain and the transitional zone to the east which they have penetrated. While they have been registered as the new owners of leased land, they have blocked the transfer of the land they have leased out to others.

Nevertheless, the category of absentee landowners who formerly controlled a large part of total agrarian production in the tribal area has virtually disappeared. This means that the power of Baniyas, Brahmins and Parsis in particular, has been for the most part broken in the eastern *talukas*. Shah rightly asserts that: 'A Chaudhri tenant cultivator who used to give a part of his product as rent on sharecropping in 1930, has now become owner of his own land. He can now consume or sell off his product freely in the market. An intermediary exploiter between Chaudhri and the market is removed, providing incentive to the farmer for developing his agriculture' (Shah 1977: 54). The return of the land to its former owners was not the result of active struggle started by the Adivasis themselves. Still, their rehabilitation reinforced their self-confidence. What has been the economic effect of these social dynamics?

Differentiation within the tribal castes

The unequal distribution of land among members of the tribal castes is not only an indication of the rapidly growing economic contradictions but is at the same time the main cause of this process of differentiation. In order to make the contrast with the current agrarian stratification even clearer, there is a tendency to place a strong emphasis on the earlier homogeneity of the Adivasis. Even before the end of the nineteenth century, the communal character of the tribal order had been eroded, and although subjection to external forces suggests the emergence of a dualistic order, there has always been an internal dynamic as well. In other words, the image of the tribal population as an undifferentiated mass of small peasants right up to the present generation, is very misleading. In a village study dating from 1930–1, undertaken in the Chaudharis' home area, Mehta stated that: 'the enrichment of some meant the impoverishment of the less fortunate, and the latter supplied the growing demand for labour' (Mehta 1934: 5–30). The author supports this conclusion with figures which show that approximately one-third of the households studied had little or no land (< 5 acres); nearly one-third occupied a middle position (5–15 acres) and one-third formed an upper stratum (>15 acres). He mentions that tribals with substantial holdings even employed *halis*, usually orphans or unmarried youths from poor households, who were taken on as farm servants on a yearly basis. Even small cultivators regularly worked on the lands of their better-endowed caste fellows. At the same time he hastens to add that the differences between extremes on the agrarian ladder were not of a fundamental nature, and in everyday life these differences were obscured by a common life style. One gains the impression from his study that the beginnings of economic differentiation were already present, but that they had not yet completely hardened into structural stratification. A majority of households cultivated the land with their own labour, but exchanges of labour were also made, usually between family members or between inhabitants of the same *falia* (Blankenberg 1981).

The process of differentiation was retarded still further by a number of levelling mechanisms. Undoubtedly the most important of these was tenancy relations themselves. A large part of the cultivable area had been withdrawn from free circulation among the Adivasis, and the share of the yield handed over to the landlord—usually a non-Adivasi—was so large that this form of lease offered barely any opportunity of accumulation. Conversely the sharecropping arrangement, often combined with a privately owned plot of land, enabled the less well endowed to secure a livelihood without being compelled to hire themselves out permanently as almost landless labourers. The institution of *khandhadio* also had some redistributive effect and worked against the creation of a permanently landless category. *Khandhadio* is the name for a son-in-law who lives with his wife in her father's house. Instead of payment of a bride price the bride's father paid the wedding costs. The latter thus gained an extra pair of hands on the holding and in exchange for this he was obliged to provide his son-in-law with a subsistence and as a rule also gave him a plot of land for himself (*vavlu*). The contract stemmed from poverty, on the one hand—and for that reason was regarded with contempt—and on the other, from the need for extra labour power on the holding. In fact, where a family lacked marriageable sons, it was a form of adoption. Although *khandhadio* marriages still occur, they are less frequent because of the widespread opposition to the system among the young generation (Shah 1977: 133–7).

The social climate in which these levelling mechanisms operated has disappeared and there is now clearly a much greater degree of economic differentiation. The emergence of class stratification is a logical outcome of this process (Bose 1981:

191–6; Pathy 1983: 165–89). To begin with, population pressure on land has increased sharply in recent decades. It is striking that the tribal castes have grown proportionately faster than the non-Adivasis since 1951, which means that the high percentage formed by the scheduled tribes in the total population of south Gujarat, already quite high, has risen still further. In spite of this differential pattern of demographic growth it seems unlikely that in the short run there will be any fundamental change in the unequal distribution of population over Surat District. Density per sq. km. in the eastern *talukas* inhabited by tribals is much lower than in the central plain. On the other hand the harsh environment of the hinterland gives a much lower productivity per capita and per unit of land. The heavier pressure on agrarian resources caused by population growth can be illustrated from the restudy by Ganshyam Shah a few years ago of the village where Mehta carried out his research in the 1930s (Shah 1977). While the population of the sample villages had more than doubled in the intervening period, the cultivable area had remained virtually unchanged. Accordingly the amount of land available to each household unit was halved from 11.87 acres in 1930 to 5.39 acres in 1974.

The erosion of the material basis of existence indicated by these figures has to a certain extent been ameliorated by institutional reforms of which the most important is the reinstatement of tribal cultivators as landowners. Shah mentions that in 1974, 148 Chaudhari tenants had been given (back) a total of 484 acres, a substantial amount in view of the average holding available to a household. The surplus that formerly had to be handed over to the landlord can now be either used for personal cultivation or sold, thus removing an important hindrance to intensification of agriculture. Increasing agrarian production has been further stimulated by the gradual introduction of the modern technology which has already created such radical changes in the plain. In spite of the stubbornness with which the traditional cropping system is maintained—a high percentage of food crops, followed by cotton and groundnuts—it would seem that cultivators are gradually beginning to emulate the transformation which has taken place in the plain.

Part of this eastern region lies within reach of the Ukhai

reservoir. Construction of the distribution channels is now almost finished and as soon as this latest phase of the largest irrigation project in south Gujarat comes into operation there will definitely be an acceleration in the process of modernization. The extension of the area irrigated by wells has already anticipated this next stage, and the spread of new agricultural practices such as the use of fertilizers and high-yielding seeds, motor pumps and new implements, and the growing importance of dairying, should also be seen as part of the approaching transformation. Parallel with this are improvements in the technical and organizational infrastructure: road construction, storage sheds, and co-operatives for ensuring credit, distribution of inputs, the sale of produce, etc.

It goes without saying that not all Adivasis derive equal profit from these institutional developments. The differences already existing in socio-economic position have been exacerbated still further by the pressure of population growth. Inheritance rights dictate the equal division of holdings among sons, and without attaching an autonomous effect to this factor, there are significant consequences for the distribution of property among the various agrarian classes. From the data relating to the village re-studied by Shah it would appear that there is only a small minority of large cultivators, the stratum of middle cultivators has remained constant in size, while the landless and the small cultivators are becoming the vast majority. This accumulation at the base of the agrarian hierarchy is confirmed by a survey carried out at the same time among Chaudharis in twenty-one other villages in the tribal area and reported in Shah's study:

little or no land	($<$ 1 acre)	24%
small cultivators	(1–5 acres)	37%
middle cultivators	(5–15 acres)	33%
large cultivators	($>$ 15 acres)	5%

In addition to population pressure the differential results inherent in the course of modernization strongly reinforce the increasing socio-economic divergence in this bleak and backward environment. The bottom strata to which two-thirds of the tribal cultivators belong have lagged even further behind as a result of this process, small cultivators forming the largest category with 37 per cent. Their holdings (1–5 acres) yield too little for subsistence; according to the kind of market-economy calculation which has little bearing on the rationale of the small cultivator's life, 6 acres is the minimum necessary for subsistence in Surat District, as the recent agro-economic standards indicate (Samanta n.d.: 24). Here as elsewhere, use of the new agrarian technology which is making great strides seems to be closely linked with the size of holding, and the small landowners do not possess the means for increasing productivity through capital investment. Both Shah's study and the report by M. B. Desai mentioned earlier confirm that it is structurally impossible for the largest tribal segment to break out of the vicious circle of poverty by their own efforts alone. The small cultivators still work their land with only a few old-fashioned implements, planting mostly traditional crops. Only a handful have scraped enough money together to sink a well and purchase the water pump necessary for cultivating the much more profitable new irrigated crops such as sugar and bananas. They have come to rely on the use of fertilizers, the most important of all modern inputs, but are always last in line where the distribution of these through official channels, is concerned and cannot afford the higher price demanded on the open market. As a result they use only 20 to 25 per cent of the overall average applied. There is a widespread idea that small cultivators own a relatively high number of livestock and that the sale of milk through the rapidly expanding dairy co-operatives constitutes an important source of extra income. This assumption is not supported by the actual data at present available (Shah 1977: 66–7). The small cultivators have fewer draught animals and those they do possess are of inferior quality; the number of milch cows and buffaloes they keep is still more limited and decreased even further in the early 1970s, according to M. B. Desai. There appears to be a shift towards cheaper livestock such as goats and chickens. The survival strategy which small cultivators have to adopt explains why food crops—rice, but more particularly *jovar* and pulses—always occupy more than half their land.

Yet it would be wrong to regard them exclusively as subsistence producers. In principle the output is certainly intended for their own consumption, but after the harvest many of them are compelled to sell part of it, usually to private traders, in order to pay off debts and to satisfy other requirements which cannot wait. Small landowners still continue to exchange labour with each other in order to avoid having to hire extra labourers during the busy seasons, and all their household members—men, women and children—regularly work in the fields of bigger landowners to supplement their incomes. They are also employed as unskilled labour on road and canal construction and in the other infrastructural activities in the region which indicate an acceleration in the modernization of the rural economy.

For those with no land, or hardly any at all (< 1 acre) life is even more precarious. These virtually landless families have lost all the cultivator's independence, no longer possessing any tools, so that land is usually not even leased out to them. They even appear to have lost the usufruct of a personal plot of land as *khandhadio* (Shah 1977: 133–7). This category is forced to live almost exclusively by selling their labour, depending primarily on more substantial landowners for employment. Nowadays it has become more advantageous for middle and large cultivators to pay their labourers in cash rather than in kind. For better or worse the landless also seek seasonal work outside agriculture, but opportunities for this are extremely limited in the immediate vicinity, consisting of wood cutting, stone quarrying, stone crushing, transport, road maintenance and other construction work, illegal distilling, etc. The total demand for labour is far exceeded by supply, and this discrepancy will widen still further since a proportion of the small cultivators are unable to consolidate their position.

A variety of causes underlie the small cultivator's loss of land, a phenomenon documented by M. B. Desai in his report on Surat District in the early 1970s. Firstly, economic regression among members of this vulnerable agrarian class is the result of indebtedness. The high percentage of land rented out by members of this category may indicate the tendency to slide down on the agrarian ladder. While among middle and large cultivators hardly any land was rented, either by them or to them, the small cultivators from Desai's random sample had leased out 20 per cent of their property to others. (Desai n.d.: 99). As Shah makes clear, in order to qualify for a loan the small cultivators are either reduced to being sharecroppers on their own land or have to surrender it as security for the loan (Shah 1977: 54). As the long history behind this type of transaction shows, it is often concluded with wealtheir family members belonging to the category of larger cultivators, and usually ends with permanent loss of the land by their poor relatives. This mechanism of impoverishment cannot be separated from the phenomenon of demographic pressure, a factor which carries its own independent weight. In the case of families with several sons among the present generation the transition from an existence as small cultivator to being nearly or wholly landless is well-nigh inevitable. In the course of my fieldwork I have gained the impression (which I cannot, alas, substantiate with quantitative data) that this process of decline results in differentiation within the next generation, i.e., in many cases where the patrimonial holding is less than the crucial 2–3 acres, the land is not divided further. This results in a situation in which after most of the brothers have separated, one brother obtains both the right to work the land and the farming implements, in return for which he is expected to surrender part of the harvest to the others. Certainly, if the cultivating brother can find enough labour within his own household for working the holding, then this arrangement is liable to rapid erosion in such an impoverished context. But, regardless of whether regression in the younger generation results from equal distribution or from differentiation, the consequences are the same: the proportion of wholly or nearly landless increases.

Government policy and progressive inequality

The lackadaisical attempts so far made by the government to diminish the growing economic distance between the various agrarian categories have produced few results in Surat District. When the central government announced in 1970 that a special effort would be made to help the rural poor, Surat was one of the forty-six districts in India where a Small Farmers' Development Agency (SFDA) was established. Although since 1974 the brief of this target group programme has been extended, in a vague way, to include marginal landowners (> 2 acres) and landless labourers, the primary aim remains an increase in the productive capacity of small cultivators (2–5 acres). A first evaluation of results shows that the project has touched only the margins of the target groups in Surat and even then in a way which has not accounted for their distribution over the area. Only a quarter of the organization's clients live in the plain but it is precisely in this privileged zone, where the small cultivators mostly belong to non-tribal castes, that the organization has been most active (I. D. Desai 1974). It remains to be seen whether the Integrated Rural Development Programme, which has recently replaced the SFDA will be more successful. As far as the landless proletariat is concerned this is more than doubtful.

In comparison with the massive lower class the middle and large cultivators lead a much less insecure life. It is these categories especially which have derived profit from the abolition of tenancy. In addition to this institutional change in the structure of agrarian production, the advent of canal irrigation in the tribal *talukas* contributes significantly to the further strengthening of their position. Only 5 per cent of all households have more than 15 acres, but this category exerts an influence far exceeding its numerical weight, since it is the large landowners who spread the new technology among the other Adivasis. They can afford the investment necessary for raising the productivity of their holdings, and know how to obtain the new inputs such as fertilizers. According to Shah, in 1974 a third of them had wells and a quarter had motor pumps, usually obtained with government help. The quantity and quality of their farming implements and livestock was well above average. These large farmers were the first to switch to the cultivation of new irrigated crops; they sell their produce largely through co-operatives and display a sensitivity to price fluctuations in planning their cropping schemes.

They set the example for the middle cultivators, who form a third of all Adivasi households. The process of agrarian modernization appears to have taken firm hold among this substantial class, and they are its most important representatives. Together with the large cultivators they occupy the key positions in the social infrastructure, especially in the village and district councils where the middle stratum exercises a dominant influence (Shah 1977: 185). By virtually monopolizing access to governmental institutions they have succeeded in grabbing the lion's share of the facilities and subsidies provided for the scheduled tribes. Among the leading categories of the various tribal castes there is overdistribution of these benefits; in the east of Surat District this inter-tribal rivalry occurs particularly between Chaudharis and Gamits, a rivalry in which the Vasavas take hardly any part as yet. Finally, an important indication of growing differentiation is that members of households belonging to the upper class are no longer willing to provide agricultural labour for others. Moreover, they increasingly use the labour of small cultivators and landless labourers for the tilling of their own land. In this way they can permit themselves the luxury of replacing their own labour by that of outsiders. The emergence of an open labour market goes hand in hand with a more business-like attitude on the part of employers, as the following quotation from Shah indicates: 'The Chaudhri landowners who have more than five acres of land, pumpset plus some education, look down upon labourers of their tribe. They have begun to treat manual labour with contempt. Being conscious of the market they want more work for less wages from the labourers. They therefore started grumbling about inefficiency of the labourers' (G. Shah 1977: 82).

The stratification already existing among the tribal cultivators has crystallized still further with the influence of modernization of the agrarian economy. With the disappearance of *ujliparaj* middlemen, Adivasi cultivators have acquired a direct linkage with market mechanisms. In the case of middle and large landowners this has led to a rise in the surplus produced and in farming profits generally. In table 4.1 we can see the extent to which the small cultivators, whether Advasi or not, have been left behind in this development. Their integration into the market economy is of a much more defensive kind. Although they grow mostly food grains for their own consumption they are forced by need and indebtedness to sell a portion of their harvest to shopkeepers, money lenders and wholesalers. While they are dependent on these private dealers, the middle and large landowners on the other hand market their cash crops through the co-operatives (M. B. Desai n.d.: 163; Shah 1977: 71). In this way unequal participation in agrarian production is further exacerbated by the manner in which the sale of produce is organized.

Small cultivators are dependent on the market for selling their own labour power, and the same applies to landless labourers in a much more absolute sense. As landowners and landless have continued to separate out into ever more distinct classes, the interaction between members of the two strata has increasingly assumed the character of a pure labour relationship.

However, this does not mean that tribal society has hardened into rigid compartments with this on-going stratification. Within certain limits upward mobility and, more especially, downward mobility do occur, and the various positions within the agrarian hierarchy have still only to a very marginal extent led to vertical confrontation. As Shah puts it:

> The rich Chaudhri cultivator has become calculating like his non-Adivasi counterpart. The labourers do not get enough quantity of foodgrains from the amount they get as wages. They are dissatisfied with the rates, but they are helpless. They are not organised and cannot press for their demand. Most of them do not know about regarding minimum wages fixed by government. They believe that their wages can be increased by doing more work, or by the kindness of the village elders who decide the rate of wage in the village (Shah 1977: 78).

The growth of a more antagonistic relationship which would accord with the employers' changing interpretation of the labour utility of dependent households, is held in check by family ties, personal mediation, and other primary loyalties which both bind and protect the weaker party in the vertical relationship. This relationship is however prejudiced still further by the discrepancy between an overabundant and still rapidly growing supply of labour on the one hand, and a limited and temporary demand for labour on the other.

The growing pressure on agrarian resources is assuming serious proportions, especially for households in the tribal lower strata. The chances of escape to urban employment in the western part of the district are insignificant as yet; in 1971 only 2.6 per cent of the Chaudharis lived outside the rural environment, and the degree of urbanization among Gamits and Vasavas must be lower still. The amount of off-farm employment in the region is gradually growing, but this expansion tends to strengthen rather than weaken the socio-economic differences already existing between upper and lower strata, since access to the ranks of the non-agrarian working population largely depends on one's original socio-economic position.

The majority of uneducated children of landless labourers and small cultivators, like adults, are nearly always considered fit only for low-paid and irregular work demanding great physical exertion. They are almost all day labourers, *chhuta*, a word denoting both the low quality of their work in agriculture or outside it, and their impoverished life. Only a small number succeed in pushing a way through to the very lowest government jobs, as peons, sweepers, watchmen, postmen, etc., and even for these jobs a primary-school certificate is nowadays required as a minimum requirement. There is a clear link between the size of holding and the level of education reached. However, the most highly prized jobs are the better paid and influential white-collar occupations of a teacher, *gram sevak* (extension worker), *talati* (village accountant), policeman, clerk in one of the government agencies in the chief *taluka* town, bookkeeper in a co-operative, bus conductor, etc. It is the children of middle and large landowners who succeed in gaining prestige in terms of the new social values by acquiring a secondary-school or even college education. Thus equipped they occupy the formal key positions through which are distributed the facilities provided by the government for the Scheduled Tribes. Given this kind of virtual monopoly along with the political hegemony enjoyed by the upper class, it is hardly any wonder that the scholarships, jobs and cheap credit intended to allow backward groups to catch up, barely ever reach the small cultivators, let alone the landless labourers.

This unequal distribution of benefits also has an inter-tribal dimension. The relative lead taken by the Chaudharis in recent decades means that Gamit and Vasava interests are overshadowed. The way in which a vanguard from among these groups is currently fighting for a proportionate share of positions of power and government benefits follows a familiar pattern: the process of catching up is accompanied inevitably by an increasing differentiation among these tribal castes.

While alternative employment is necessary for supplementing the incomes of poor cultivators and such extra income is almost exclusively spent on consumption, for the propertied households it has a more productive function. Middle and large landowners use the income and influence won outside agriculture in order to obtain knowledge about new agrarian technology and its inputs, and to increase the capital intensiveness of their holdings, which permits structural improvement. The new off-farm elite which has emerged remains closely tied to the rural milieu. They use their savings to open village stores, lend money or buy land. In other words, the dynamic in the structure of agrarian production is reinforced by the differential access to off-farm employment.

As we have already stated, this process of cumulative inequality has not yet crystallized out into a rigid class stratification. This does not alter the fact that to an increasing degree the separate strata are beginning to distinguish themselves from each other by their life styles and living conditions. Shah indicates that differences in material position create sharply diverging patterns of consumption in food, dress, housing, etc., and also parallel differences in, for instance, the level of education, religious orientation and preferences in political (Shah 1977: 164, 197). While the lower strata are condemned by their poverty to following traditional behaviour patterns, the upper strata model their life styles on those of the dominant non-Adivasi farmers of the plain. Everything points to an eventual structural hardening of this divergence in life styles within the tribal castes. A large proportion of landowners with more than 5 acres, barely 40 per cent of the tribal population in the eastern *talukas*, will profit from the continuing modernization of agrarian production, and from this class in particular will come the future occupants of the skilled and permanent posts created by the limited diversification of the rural economy. Thus the more substantial landowners will benefit both directly and indirectly.

In contrast, the already vulnerable position of the small cultivators and landless labourers is being weakened still further. Modernization is not a levelling or even a neutralizing process of innovation, but is accomplished at the expense of this lower segment which had already been created by the interaction between internal dynamic and external change in preceding decades. This agrarian underclass, which today comprises 60 per cent of the members of tribal castes, lags behind economically, socially and politically. They can only react defensively to the transformation of the rural order and a significant proportion of them are gradually becoming uprooted from the regional economy, since in their home area there are simply not enough ways of making a living for this lower stratum, which is rapidly growing in numbers. The carrying capacity of the predominantly dry agriculture is too little to provide them with employment the whole year round, either on their own land or as hired labourers on some other cultivator's land. On the other hand it is precisely these poor and landless peasants who, for a number of economic and geographical reasons, are denied access to relatively permanent employment opportunities elsewhere in the western plain of the district or even further away. In short, continued residence in their home area is impossible, but permanent out-migration even more so.

This dilemma is formulated by Shah as follows: 'They do not migrate not because they get enough labour in the village; in fact they do not get labour around the year, and they do not get sufficient wages to maintain themselves. They do not settle outside permanently as they are not assured of longterm work' (Shah 1977: 92). The survival strategy which poor households are forced to adopt dictates that one or more members leave the area for longer or shorter periods. After the harvest is over at the end of the rainy season, an enormous migration of labour to the irrigated zone in Surat District begins, which continues throughout the following dry months. Over the past twenty years this seasonal migration has resulted in a substantial expansion of the work force in the central plain.

ıts of the local landless.

alpati colony. Electricity lines, typically, bypass it.

A typical scene—the migrants are certainly around.

Rural transients.

ural transients taking shelter.

handeshis on their way to the sugarcane fields in the early morning.

A Khandeshi woman and girl at work in the sugarcane fields.

Sugarcane being cut by migrant workers.

Two Halpati girls. Both work. The younger one is a cowherd.

;rant children guarding the belongings of their parents while they are away at work.

Khandeshi harvest workers setting up a camp some distance away from huts of the local landless.

Camp of sugarcane workers with farmers' houses in the background.

ımp of sugarcane cutters.

igation canals and sugarcane fields in the central plain of south Gujarat.
co-operative sugarcane mill can be seen in the background.

The dwelling of a migrant worker.

A typical newly-built *haveli* in the village.

Part III
MOBILITY AND IMMOBILITY

7
OUT-MIGRATION

Background

It is virtually taken for granted that those who work in an area also belong there, and moreover that the social pattern existing today can be traced back to the past. The myth of an immobile peasantry persists, not only in anthropological literature, but just as much in common usage. In contrast to the lower social strata whose past remains obscure and to whom the consciousness of a past history with its concomitant rights has often been denied, members of the higher castes tend to present themselves as the original 'sons of the soil'. According to the dominant myth, under their leadership a social system has been disseminated over the region—exactly in what manner remains unclear—which since then has been reproduced from generation to generation.

Village studies have contributed to a similar reification of the past by emphasizing the closed nature and the continuity of the local order, and by paying little or no attention, generally speaking, to migration which assumes the character of a displacement of labour. The under-illumination of intra-rural mobility as an important economic phenomenon is also apparent in contemporary rural studies. In many publications peasant society is still presented as extremely static. At best, migration is merely mentioned and even then nearly always in connection with urbanization. Those who come to the village to work are hardly noticed, especially when their presence is only temporary. The scale on which this phenomenon is occurring today in Bardoli and its environs indicates an acceleration in the socio-economic dynamic. Without underestimating the open character of the agrarian system in south Gujarat's past, it must nevertheless still be noted that a new situation has arisen with the periodic influx of labour into the central plain in recent years.

Intra-rural migration is more important than ever as a subject of study, even though not all levels of the population are involved to the same extent or in the same way. There is an obvious connection between the type of mobility and socio-economic stratification. In my own work I have concentrated principally on the seasonal circulation of unskilled labour, demonstrably the most striking form of migration within the rural milieu. Nearly the whole year round, except for the months of heaviest rainfall, I encountered a wide variety of this type of migrant in my research area. Time and again in my daily round I came upon different categories of migrants: pastoral nomads from north Gujarat with their flocks; donkey drivers from the same area; 'navvies' from Saurashtra; road workers from Panch Mahals; quarry workers from Bharuch District; and cane cutters from neighbouring Maharashtra State. They are easily recognizable as foreign elements, as much from the specific work they perform (usually in groups) as from their dress and dialect. They live a segregated existence in their own camps by the roadside or in the fields.

In contrast to these obvious outsiders a very large proportion of seasonal migrants do not cross the boundaries of their own district, i.e. most of them come from the immediate vicinity, within a radius of up to 80 km. As we saw in the previous chapter, tribals from the eastern *talukas* of Surat District provide agricultural labour on a large scale in the irrigated zone round Bardoli. They travel around the villages in small groups seeking work, returning again to their home bases after a span of time varying from a few weeks to a whole season. The relatively short distance facilitates such a movement back and forth, and consequently many make the journey several times a year. Neither in outward appearance nor in their manner of working are they markedly distinguishable from the agricultural labourer population in the actual area. Although they form the largest category among the intruders, they are much less conspicuous than the migrants coming from far away.

A pool of surplus labour rapidly growing in size and mobility in the tribal hinterland of Surat District, competes for agricultural work with the local landless in the central plain. In order to understand the presence of this outside labour however, a basic knowledge of the situation in the villages from which migrants originate is also necessary. With this in mind I made repeated visits in the course of my fieldwork to the migrants' home regions. Their close proximity—even under the most unfavourable circumstances the trip from Bardoli could be made in less than a day—enabled me to collect this information. The results of this part of my research are presented in this chapter.

One result of the priority I attached to research in the plain was that I could not allow my stay there to be interrupted for any length of time. Of course the short trips I made, never more than a few days at a time, did not offer an opportunity for a thorough study of one or more home villages. Instead, therefore, I took advantage of rather accidental meetings in the area of departure and was able to gather data from some sixty migrants and members of their households. I did not record these cases in an entirely haphazard manner. I tried to avoid the disadvantages of an overly fragmented representation of reality, which meant a concentration on individual migrant households spread in an arbitrary way over the tribal hinterland—by limiting my research instead to random samples in two *talukas* which together present a more or less representative situation. One case involves an area bordering directly on the irrigated zone, and the other an area lying further away; thus the choice fell on the southern part of Valod Taluka and the western part of Uchhal Taluka. In both these regions I visited a total of seven villages, some of them more often than others. In a number of cases I was able to make use of introductions from people in the plain. On the basis of information collected from households in these villages, it was possible gradually to build up a more coherent picture of the manner in which seasonal migration had begun, its significance for the local economy, and so forth.

Besides enabling me to gather information about those remaining at home, this method was also very important in allowing me to meet the migrant labourers in a safe and trusted environment. I can confirm the definite difference this made to the quality of information I was able to elicit from those I had interviewed in the plain and then in their homes. Where research is concerned it would have been even better to have joined the migrants in their trek, literally following in their footsteps to the plain and back, but I did not succeed in doing so.

The home villages

The tribal area begins just behind Bardoli. This part of Surat District is distinguished by its rolling terrain composed largely of dry land that is much less intensively cultivated than the plain. Settlements are fewer in number and smaller in size, an indication of relatively low population density. The area's infrastructure is decidedly underdeveloped: few roads carrying little traffic, few electricity lines, brick buildings or other signs of modernity. Even the main *taluka* towns functioning as regional centres create a very bucolic impression and nearly all of them are considerably smaller than the average town in the central plain of Gujarat. At best the villages have very few facilities: a simple school, with here and there a house frontage converted into a 'shop' with a very modest display of goods. They are spread over dispersed hamlets (*falias*) each composed of similarly scattered mud huts. Towards the east the landscape gradually becomes more hilly, dusty, desolate and above all poor.

As I explained in chapter 1, Valod forms a transitional zone between this area and the plain, in an ecological as well as a socio-economic sense. This relationship is partly the consequence of the presence of peasant castes—primarily Kanbi Patidars but also Anavil Brahmins and Rajputs—who spread in small groups throughout the *taluka* only a few generations ago. The places where these households settled have developed into the most important villages in the area. These concentrations have clear residential nuclei, the domain of the *ujliparaj*, and are provided with more and better facilities. Memories of the past are treasured among the tribals, perhaps precisely because the outsiders' recent entry contrasts so sharply with the position of power they now occupy. Several informants were able to recount how Kanbis, supposedly driven from their previous homes by famine, arrived in Valod poor and without any possession. Some of them were compelled to earn their living as agricultural labourers for tribal cultivators and even received advance grain allowances from the latter in order to tide over the lean season. Within half a century the newcomers had succeeded in gaining control over the largest and best portion of the cultivable land. Several informants were able to state precisely when, how and to whom their families had lost their lands, thus emphasizing the untrustworthiness and greed of the interlopers. While I was collecting information in 1962 on a tribal protest movement (*sati-pati*) which has reached its peak a few years before, it was interesting to note that in a number of places quite detailed arrangements had been made for re-allocating the holdings of the *ujliparaj* after they had been expelled, to the descendants of their original owners.

The use of oral history makes it possible to refute the Patidars' claim that, as colonists in a relatively empty region, they were the first to have cleared and cultivated the land.

In villages where higher caste cultivators live, seasonal migration to the plain is relatively less frequent. It is true that canal irrigation has only recently been introduced into this region. At the beginning of my field work in 1977 the older commercial crops—especially cotton and groundnuts—were still being extensively cultivated. Agriculture binds the local labourers to the *ujliparaj* farmers in the villages, who nowadays are just as reluctant as their caste fellows in the plain to work on the land themselves. The demand for labour even makes it necessary to bring in extra labour from outside in the harvest period.

The situation is different in villages where there are few or no higher caste households, which is not to say that tribal peasants here have retained complete autonomy. Land alienation on a large scale also occurred here in the past but, as I explained in the previous chapter, tenancy legislation broke the power of absentee landowners (Parsis and Baniyas), who operated as merchants and moneylenders from bases in the larger villages. The poor soil and low capital intensity of the average tribal small-holding has resulted in a simpler cropping pattern: there is less cultivation of cotton and groundnuts while relatively more attention is given to production of food grains. For a long time there has been no question of a real subsistence economy. Part of the harvest is sold from sheer need. Such sales are dictated by a defensive strategy rather than by a conscious market orientation. The yield from one's own plot of land, however small, remains the basis of subsistence among the tribal population of the area, but in most cases this yield needs to be supplemented by outside earnings, because the fulfilment of elementary needs increasingly requires some cash income. However, off-farm employment within the region remains restricted to a few stone quarries and crushing plants along the river, road work and maintenance connected with public works, and lastly a modest service sector and a few small industries in the *taluka* town, established partly on the initiative of Gandhian workers active in the area. Given these circumstances, seasonal migration in the slack season is one of the few available opportunities by which small households can maintain themselves.

In obtaining more detailed information about the trek to the plain I have concentrated on three villages in the southern part of the *taluka*, lying at roughly one hour's walking distance from the town, Valod. In one of these villages, with an homogeneous tribal population of Chaudharis, a village-level worker conducted a basic household survey under my supervision, in order to map out the pattern of external employment and to establish the significance of this for the local economy. The results show that nearly every household has to fall back, to a greater or lesser extent, on supplementary earnings from outside the village. In this area bordering on the plain, progress due to infra-structural development is as much a cause as a consequence of out-migration.

As the distance from the plain increases, access to it becomes more difficult because of the weak structure of communication. Travelling eastwards from Valod one encounters fewer and fewer fields and dwellings. The land here has suffered severe surface erosion. As one approaches the foothills of the Ghats, tree cover increases and because of this it is still customary to discribe this area as jungle, which is a gross exaggeration. It is in fact a completely inappropriate term for this dry, sparsely forested landscape, but the pejorative characterization 'jungle' is primarily intended to emphasis the backwardness of the area and its population.

As one approaches the area bordering on Maharashtra the proportion of Chaudharis and Gamits among the tribal inhabitants decreases while the number of Vasavas increases. The latter are counted as Bhils, one of the largest Adivasi groups in western India. Non-tribals form only a small minority and live for the most part in several market centres; thus Ukai, where a reservoir has been built, can be regarded as a modern enclave within an otherwise tribal area. The climate is no worse than in the central part of south Gujarat and is probably even better, but the remoteness of the area and the preponderance of a population regarded as inferior, ensures it a bad reputation. High-level government officials only come here for the briefest of visits, while those at a lower level regard being stationed in the area as a punishment. The road and railway line which run through the Tapi plain to Maharashtra pass the border near Navapur. To the north of this lie Uchhal and Nizar, two *talukas* which still form part of Surat District. The explanation for the marked eccentricity of their inclusion in that district is that this area, originally part of Maharashtra, was added to Gujarat when the original Bombay State was split up in 1960, in order to facilitate construction of the Ukai reservoir.

Inhabitants of the northern part of Uchhal which disappeared beneath the waters, were resettled on higher ground at some distance from the reservoir. New land was allotted to them, albeit not as much as they had lost in their former home. The government also tried to provide accommodation for them, but without taking into account the particular way of life, based on rational principles, of tribal cultivators. A number of concentrated settlements arose consisting of several rows of dwellings symmetrically spaced out along the main road, which are remarkable for their bare ugliness.

In this arid and broken terrain, agriculture is practiced in the most primitive of ways. Cultivators still occasionally told me the size of their holdings in terms of the amount of land tax they had to pay, or the size of harvest yield. Inferior food grains predominate here. Some rice is still grown on lowlying ground, but this is sown directly in the fields rather than transplanted. Cash crops are not grown. The agrarian cycle lasts no longer than four months. The slack season follows the harvest at the end of the monsoons. Forestry work is one of the few sources of employment outside agriculture; exploitation of the tribals by private lumber merchants, often with the connivance of government officials, was ended a few decades ago. After independence forestry co-operatives were established on the initiative of the Gandhian Movement, although the tribal population has generally had little 'say' in these concerns. More important, however, is the fact that the economic significance of this source of income has declined sharply as a result of deforestation during the last century. The fact that tree felling and log transportation nevertheless offer the best prospects of supplementary employment—apart from the illegal distilling of alcohol—tells us something about the scarcity of off-farm employment in the area. Although this region is the source of the extensive irrigation network which provides water to much of south Gujarat, the area itself derives no profit from it. Even a small number of local channels, which cost little but would be greatly to the advantage of the tribal cultivators, had still not been completed at the time of my fieldwork in 1977. Just as the water from the upper reaches of the Tapi river is being put to productive use in the agriculture of the central plain, so labour from the hinterland is being mobilized for deployment to this already privileged area, and the two factors are connected. None of the water that is thus tapped comes back and, as we shall see, the same could be said of the surplus value of labour which is drawn from the region.

Origin and magnitude of seasonal migration

Temporary migrant labour is a comparatively recent phenomenon in the plain. When reading earlier reports one is left with the impression that most of the cultivators used to work their land themselves, along with farm servants, and that agrarian operations such as cotton picking and sugarcane cutting, which would later on be largely, or even exclusively, performed by migrants, were still the monopoly of the local Halpatis. This pattern began to change in the 1960s. During his field work in a village close to Bardoli in 1962, Baks observed that the Patidars had for several years been recruiting harvest labourers in the surrounding tribal *talukas*. He wrote that as recently as 1955 outside labourers had only very occasionally been used in the fields. His observations agree with my own experience during the same period in the countryside a little further to the south. There I regularly encountered seasonal migrants from Saurashtra, transients travelling from village to village. These Kathiawadis, the term based on the old name for their native area, had earned a name for themselves throughout south Gujarat as industrious, sturdy and reliable workers. A study made in 1962 of agricultural labour in the village of Afwa, close to Bardoli, mentions their arrival at the time of the cotton harvest. There were also a limited number of cane cutters from Maharashtra already working on the sugarcane crop, imported by a Bardoli sugar factory, established a short while before. However, the author immediately added that these outside labourers stayed only a short time and that their numbers were insignificant (Patel 1964: 98). Until this period, agricultural labour in the plain was still very localized in the sense that workers were usually tied to the village they inhabited. Yet this does not imply that agricultural labourers were immobile. The proletarian past of the Halpatis in south Gujarat is obvious from, among other factors, the high degree of mobility which has always characterized this landless caste. On the basis of continuing research I have carried out among Halpatis in several villages, which also included data on previous generations, it can be demonstrated that a markedly high percentage originated from other places. *Ghar jamai* status—that of a man settling in his wife's village—offers the opportunity for extricating oneself from overly oppressive labour relationships in one's own village, or conversely for seeking the protection of a better patron. The Halpatis' past dependence on the most prominent landowning castes—institutionalized in the *halipratha*—meant that one's place of residence usually coincided with one's place of employment. The movement of casual labour, in so far as this existed, occurred within a small radius and was limited to neighbouring villages.

Over the past two decades the villages in the Bardoli area have absorbed increasing numbers of outside labourers, for longer or shorter periods. I have been visiting this area almost every year for varying lengths of time since 1971, and as a result I have been able to follow the rapid growth of the migrant labour phenomenon quite closely. Convinced of its importance, I decided to give central place to this subject in my fieldwork. The mobility of labour assumes a dynamic in the area of departure as well as in the area of destination. The demand for labour arising on the employers' side—the causes of which will be discussed in subsequent chapters—must of itself evoke a reaction somewhere else in the offer to supply labour. What were the circumstances which resulted in seasonal migration from the tribal hinterland, the principal recruitment area for additional manpower in the plain? In answering this question we must turn our immediate attention to a difference between the initial situation in Valod and that in Uchhal.

Valod has clearly derived an advantage from its location in the transitional zone close to the more developed part of Surat District. This area was affected sooner than the more distant *talukas* by the social changes intruding from the west; the penetration and gradual dominance of a money economy and of market mechanisms, improvements in the infrastructure, the rising standard of facilities as well as the differential effects of all these processes. As we have already observed, this relatively early opening-up of the area led to the establishment of some non-agrarian employment in the region, and to a situation which would later on lead to labour circulation on a wide scale. I was repeatedly told that out-migration—permanent escape to other places—was still infrequent, and because of this I shall not discuss here the few such cases I did record. The table below offers a sketch of the pattern of external earnings in a village in the southern part of the *taluka*. The data are drawn from material collected, under my supervision, from 131 households.

Table 7.1 *Pattern of off-farm earnings in a village in Valod Taluka*

number of households investigated (with an average of 5.4 persons per household)	131
households in which one or more members are employed outside the village	126
a) in the home area	
— for the whole year	16
— over the year intermittently	64
b) as seasonal migrants to other places	
— in cotton gins in Bardoli town	76
— in villages in the plain	198

Source: fieldwork data

These results indicate that survival without off-farm earnings has become inconceivable. In contrast to the five households which can manage without external earnings there are the remaining 126 households in which usually more than one member contributes, with incomes earned outside the village, to the securing of the household's material subsistence. A total of sixteen households have government jobs or more or less regular work in the neighbourhood: 2 school teachers, a postman, a bus conductor, a lorry driver, a tailor, a welder, 5 factory workers, and two shop assistants. A larger number of members of households, 64, work as off-farm casual labourers in the area: 16 in road and irrigation canal construction and maintenance, 9 in building, 9 in a recently opened carpet factory in Valod, 2 in logging, 2 in toddy tapping, 2 in a brick-field, and 17 in unspecified casual labour. All this concerns unskilled work tied to the dry winter and summer months, but even then with marked fluctuations in extent. The basis for the selection is previous work experience and this explains the clustering of specific work activities round a limited number of households, although this has not solidified into an occupational exclusiveness—the labour specialization is too elementary for such exclusiveness. In fact, the concise questionnaire necessary to guarantee a reasonably reliable survey cannot do justice to the complexity of the actual employment pattern. For example, by pressing respondents to state only the principle source of external earnings over the preceding year, the individual variation in, or even combination of occupations is concealed.

Although there is certainly no lack of a local demand for off-farm labour, demand falls far behind the supply. In 78 per cent of households the migration of one or more family members to the plain at least once a year has become unavoidable in making ends meet. An exceptionally large number of inhabitants, 71 in 1977, go to work at two cotton ginning factories in Bardoli. The connection began many years ago when one of the ginneries in Valod closed down and the Baniya proprietor managed to secure a place in the Bardoli ginnery belonging to his relative for a resident of the village who had always worked for him. Through this first opening and with an obvious concentration of gin workers in several *falias*—again, an indication of the strongly particularistic character of labour recruitment—employment in this seasonal industry has shown a sharp increase over the years. The element of chance plays an important role in establishing contacts with a source of extra-local employment. In a situation of scarcity migrants obviously try as far as possible to fill the jobs available within their network of contacts, with members of their own households and *falias*. Outsiders, and certainly inhabitants of other villages count as such, only occasionally obtain entry to these networks.

The season opens slowly with the beginning of the cotton harvest at the end of February and lasts until May, in all, approximately three months. Women also take part in the migration to the Bardoli cotton ginneries, and it would appear from my data that women even comprise the majority of migrants. This contrasts sharply with alternative employment in their own region which, apart from agricultural labour, remains a principally male preserve. However, seasonal migration with this destination in view appears to be coming to an end since, although Bardoli developed into an important centre for the primary processing of cotton in the first half of this century, only two of the ginning factories established here have survived. Even these can only be kept in operation by transporting cotton from more distant production areas in the western and northern part of the district. In the plain around Bardoli, cotton cultivation has been completely replaced by the new irrigated crops, while the soil and climate of south Gujarat are too humid for the new varieties of cotton which have come into favour in recent years.

However, the consequences for seasonal migrants of this industry's decline have been more than compensated by the cyclical movement of agricultural labour out to the plain. This process is less selective, reflecting a much more general dynamic which leaves practically no village in Valod untouched. Labour migration of this kind, still unknown in the previous generation, has emerged within a short time—the connection between migration and the advent of canal irrigation in the plain is indeed undeniable and is even obvious to informants—and is growing in extent with every year. Generally speaking, absences from home remain limited to periods of one week to a month, but these occur several times a year. Many informants remain away for the harvesting of successive crops or for other operations requiring intensive labour. Valod is favourably situated—at a short distance and easy of access—for repeated short-term excursions to villages in the plain where there is agricultural work. The real explanation for this periodic migration is, of course, that the local economy—the profits from agriculture together with employment opportunities outside it—can no longer provide a sufficient basis for subsistence.

In the villages of Uchhal this process has come about in a much more abrupt fashion. Inadequate infrastructure accompanies limited diversification in the rural economy. Forestry work provides more or less the only opportunity for obtaining an income outside agriculture in this backward region. Now and then one encounters processions of oxcarts laden with tree trunks, on their way to the jungle-co-operative depots. This transport is particularly striking because, except for a single bus and a few cars belonging to government agencies, there is no other traffic on the only proper road in the region. Cultivating land, however extensive and short-term, is for the vast majority of inhabitants the principal, if not the only source of local employment and offers only the most meagre of subsistences. Measured in terms of the level of agrarian development, Uchhal occupies 172nd place compared to other *talukas* of Gujarat, according to a socio-economic study carried out several years ago (*Classification of Backward Areas*, 1968). This was one of the lowest placings of all the *talukas* in the southern part of the state, and there appears to have been little change since then.

Until a few decades ago the tribal population had little reason to look beyond the borders of their own area. The peripheral location of Uchhal contributed to its high degree of isolation and, in so far as contacts with the outside world were maintained, these were directed towards western Maharashtra of which it also formed a part. 'Going to Gujarat' is still the way in which inhabitants of the area refer to their migration to the villages surrounding Bardoli; conversely they are called Khandeshis in this alien milieu.

Even more than in the case of Valod where at least there had been some tradition of migration, the seasonal flow of labour to the plain of south Gujarat is attributable to the construction of the extensive system of irrigation canals which has

Uchhal as its starting point. The tribals who fell victim to the construction of the Ukai reservoir when they were driven off their lands, have also been the first to join the current of movement to the plain because in the new villages in which they were resettled, there was insufficient employment for them. Only full compensation for lost land would have restored them to their previous economic level, which was already too low in any case, but there has never been any question of such compensation. The new settlements have been allocated very little land, a maximum of 4 acres per household only, far less than the victims had in their previous homes. Only those cultivators registered as owners have received any land at all, and this is much less and of poorer quality than the land they had lost. Tenants and illegal occupants of government lands received no compensation. The new economic order which came into existence—founded on agriculture alone—immediately excluded a segment of the 'rehabilitated' tribals from ownership of land. For the remainder, claims for lost holdings were settled only in cash. With only the slightest acquaintance with money dealings, the illiterate tribals very soon parted with these cash sums to government officials, Gandhian social workers and shopkeepers. It is hardly surprising that outsiders are viewed with thorough mistrust, as I experienced for myself in the new settlements. In these new locations several of those present at the time avoided meeting me, or took refuge in vague, empty answers to my questions. However, during my stay I came to the conclusion that the inhabitants maintained a great distance in their mutual contacts as well and could even show marked hostility to each other. As partners in misfortune they have been living since their resettlement in a socially amorphous climate in which the tradition of communal life has been lost. Competition for the meagre 'survival opportunities' seems to have thwarted the development of even a minimal level of social cohesion. The shortsightedness, indifference and corruption characterizing this type of 'rehabilitation' scheme is a scandal which merits a thorough investigation. Information which has become available so far (see Mankodi and Gangopadhayay 1983) suggests that the same process may repeat itself in other parts of Gujarat and the rest of India. At all events, in Uchhal it has made seasonal migration even more acute.

If local people had been employed on construction of the reservoir and irrigation canals, this might have provided some temporary relief for the loss of agrarian sources of livelihood, but even this indirect profit was not realized. Certainly where large-scale projects are concerned, the practice of farming out public works to private contractors means that practically no use is made of available local labour. Most of the labourers needed for construction of the Kakrapar and Ukai dams and the main and secondary canals were transported from a great distance, mainly from Saurashtra and even partly from Andhra Pradesh.[1]

For the Uchhal tribals there was little choice but to move elsewhere. An unknown number of those who had supposedly been 'resettled' were unable to support themselves in the new milieu and left the area for good. I came across some of them again in a semi-permanent camp consisting of a collection of improvised huts which sprang up on the outskirts of Bardoli. Over the past few years others will have found their way to the slum areas of Surat City, lying on both sides of the railway line along the southern bank of the river and in the vicinity of industrial enclaves. The size of this floating segment is difficult to establish since they have never officially 'arrived' anywhere but have at the same time been written off in the home area, and often remain unrecorded in attempts to register those absent. From the outset some of them were unable to weather the shock of relocation, while others were able to postpone permanent departure until new disasters struck, such as the great floods of 1968 or the period of prolonged drought in 1974.

Crises of this kind have certainly also contributed to periodic migration to the plain. In the four villages of this *taluka* where I collected information, key informants (village headmen, school teachers, shopkeepers) estimated that, respectively for each village, 30 per cent, 40 per cent, 75 per cent and 85 per cent of households had sent out one or more members during

[1] 'The Kakrapar before and the Ukai now employs labour which is mostly from Saurashtra and partly from Andhra' (*Report MWAC* 1966: 43). The report, without any further discussion of the matter, attributes this preference for labourers from outside to their better work performance.

the current year. These figures are corroborated by estimates mentioned in a later report based on a village survey in the same area (Mankodi 1983: 17). According to figures provided by the Taluka Panchayat nearly half of the total population of Uchhal participates in the seasonal migration (Mankodi and Gangopadhayay 1983: 89). The report from which I derive this information mentions that of the twenty-five pupils in a small village school fifteen children had left together with their parents for the duration of the season. While mobility is still greatest in the new settlements, other villages have also been pulled into this process. Relatives are taken along for the first time by family members who have made the trek before, and subsequently act as recruitment agents in their own localities. In this way I have been able to trace the beginning of migratory labour in several villages to a rehabilitation colony. In a situation of scarcity, seasonal migration is a self-accelerating process. Once it is realized that there is an opportunity for temporary escape, and a growing number of people come to know the route, there is also an increasing possibility of weathering all kinds of crises, whether big or small, arising at the household or village level. The plain is a good deal less accessible from this area than it is from Valod. A relatively longer distance has to be bridged, firstly by several hours of walking and then by an expensive bus or train journey to Bardoli. Lack of savings from agriculture or outside it nevertheless compels a growing number of people to undertake the journey periodically.

Survival in the tribal hinterland of Surat has come to depend on the regular migration of labour to the plain. According to my data, one half to two-thirds of members (both productive and non-productive) of households involved in the migration process, remain behind.

The situation which I have described is anything but unique, as becomes clear from another study on labour migration from the tribal Panch Mahals District to the central Gujarat plain. Already at the beginning of the 1970s seasonal circulation was massive in scale. In 93 per cent of the households investigated at least one member had gone out in the preceding year for a shorter or a longer period (Bulletin of Economics and Statistics, Gujarat 1974: 1).

Differential participation and its effects

However massive in scale, seasonal migration remains a selective process. Age, educational level, sex and economic status are some of the obvious factors to which differential results are ascribed in the literature on migration.

As one would expect, it is primarily young people who are mobile. According to my data at least half the migrants belong to the fifteen to thirty age group, with a decided concentration of twenty-year-olds. Mobility falls away sharply at forty years of age and over. The migrants' existence is a hard one, and can be endured only by those in the prime of life. Long days of very heavy exertion with much of the work done on piece rates or on contract basis, alternate with periods of enforced idleness when a new job is not immediately available, and migrants often have to try their luck in the next village. As one grows older there is an obvious reluctance to embark on this migratory existence. On the other hand it is striking how many young children accompany adults; I would estimate that they comprise a fifth of all migrants. When work teams are being made up, children under 14 are excluded as independent labourers, yet they do accompany adults from their households or families on these trips. Not all, but certainly most of them are directly or indirectly productive, otherwise they would constitute too great a burden. From the age of 10 or 12 children take part in agricultural work, although providing only half an adult's labour power. Children younger than this look after the youngest siblings and perform all kinds of odd tasks, thus freeing the adults for the heavier work. Talking about his recent stay in the plain, one informant remarked that anyone able to stand and walk, worked.

Where educational level is concerned, there is no difference between the migrants from Uchhal and those staying behind. The Vasavas who inhabit this area are still nearly all illiterate. In this respect the situation in Valod is different. Thanks to the efforts of the regional Gandhian organization, the literacy rate among Chaudharis and Gamits has clearly risen, but this does not apply to the households providing migrant labour. In other words the vast majority of migrants are illiterate, regardless of whether they come from close by or from the more distant parts of the tribal hinterland. Only a small proportion of them have gone through some of the lower school classes. Labour circulation does not combine easily with schooling. As a result of expanded educational provisions the level of literacy in the home area will gradually rise, but not among the migrants of the new generation. It follows from this that educational differentiation does not necessarily result from labour mobility but is in fact its inevitable consequence.

According to a widely held notion, the percentage of mobile women is disproportionately low. The general image of the migrant labourer is that of the young man who, alone or in a group, temporarily leaves the parental or marital home, leaving behind female dependents burdened with the care of children and the elderly as well as with other work. This widely held view finds support in various publications. On the basis of data concerning sixteen villages in northern India, Connell et al. calculated that, at most, one in every five migrants was a woman. On average their proportion was considerably lower (Connell et al. 1976: 42–5; see also Singh 1980: 332). According to this source, women comprised only 7 per cent of all working migrants. The proposition that intra-rural migration is especially male-selective can also be found in other reports. From research carried out in twelve villages in Mysore, Katti established that 70 per cent of the migrants were males (Katti 1966: 15–20). From a recent study in central Gujarat, involving a situation similar to the one I have described—seasonal migration by tribals from a backward hill area (Panch-Mahals District) to the highly developed agriculture of the plain (Kheda District)—there appears to be a higher female participation, 36 per cent of the mobile labour force (Gandhi and Shah 1978: 19–20). Nevertheless, women appear to be always much fewer in number than men. On the basis of my own research in south Gujarat I am convinced that the migration of women, also seasonal, has been grossly under-estimated.[2]

[2] I have not reached this conclusion only on the basis of the fieldwork reported on here. The earlier research in which I focussed on the seasonal migration of agricultural labourers from Valsad District to the brick fields in the vicinity of Bombay, produced the same picture. According to Singh there may even be a preponderance of women in rural labour migration (1980: 37).

There are different categories of women labour migrants. Firstly there are the married women who journey to the plain with their husbands and small children. During my fieldwork in Bardoli I have often encountered such a group, usually composed of several households from one *falia* or family. Next there are the girls and young women who form harvest teams together with boys and men of their own age group. In this case they usually work under the protection of a male member of the group—a brother, brother-in-law or husband—but this does not mean that they form a minority of the migrants. For some tasks such as transplanting rice or cutting grass, there is even a pronounced preponderance of women, and not only for agricultural work. I have already indicated earlier that women form the majority of seasonal workers employed by the ginning factories in Bardoli. Having examined all my data I conclude that 58 per cent of all migrant labourers are women; they are thus not only well represented in the workforce but sometimes even form a majority within it. My conclusion is supported by Kalpana Bardhan who shows that many women become mobile in the performance of agriculture labour:

> On closer look, it appears that the proportion of agricultural labourers was particularly high among the women migrating from other rural areas within the same district. Much of the short-distance' rural-to-rural migration of women workers thus consists of those in search of agricultural wage employment. The phenomenon of tribal and scheduled caste women in paddy areas migrating in the busy season to take up agricultural work like transplantation in prosperous villages seems not to be an isolated one, but rather of some general validity (Bardhan 1977: A45).

It still remains to be seen whether the proportion of women decreases with longer distances. Among seven gangs of Kathiawadis travelling round the plain, I found approximately the same male: female ratio as among the tribal labourers originating from the eastern part of Surat District.

Occasionally a work team is composed entirely of women. I was able to collect some information on a group of four young unmarried women from a village in the southern part of Valod Taluka who have been on trek together several times. The group comprised two sisters, their cousin and another girl from an unrelated household in the same *falia*. They provided the farmers not only with agricultural labour but with sexual services as well. Such semi-prostitution is not rare. I came to know of several cases where there was a regular traffic not only in tribal girls sent to the plain but also in the opposite direction, i.e., high caste farmers from the plain who visited their temporary women labourers in their own homes, buying the parents' consent with drink and money. In a more professional sense a similar sexual shuttle service has developed in which young tribal women are taken by procurers to Udhana or Surat for a few days. Socially inferior in the eyes of the *ujliparaj*, tribal women are reputed to be 'looser' and 'less prudish', not to mention attractive. They are 'black but beautiful', as several farmers told me meaningfully.

It should be obvious that the connection between this phenomenon and labour circulation is the result of a process of impoverishment. This brings me to the most important differential factor, economic status in the area of out-migration.

The extent of labour specialization cannot be used as a discriminatory datum, due to the almost total lack of occupations outside agriculture. Only in Valod do they exist to a modest extent. The conclusion I have drawn from material collected is that there is no labour migration, or very much less, in households in which members have secure and skilled jobs in their own home area. However, the limited number of households to which this applies almost all have relatively more land also. This then seems to be the factor to which the above-mentioned variables of age, education and sex are subordinated, or from which they derive.

As far as labourers are concerned, seasonal migration is the result of increasing pressure on resources for agrarian subsistence in an improverished milieu, and of the lopsided distribution of landownership which is inseparable from that pressure. The results of my survey in a village in Valod show that just under half of the migrant labourers belong to households with little or no land (less than one acre). Small-peasant households (1–5 acres) provide virtually the same proportion of this mobile labour force. The remaining 10 per cent or so come from middle- and large-peasant households. Given the distribution in the tribal hinterland as reported in the previous chapter, these figures point to: a slight over-representation of small-holding peasants, who constitute just over a third of the agrarian producers; a very marked over-representation, i.e. nearly twice the level of participation among the landless class to which about a quarter of the population belong; and finally a definite under-representation of the third of the households with more land.

This ratio also holds good for Uchhal. My findings in villages there are in agreement with the terse comment by one of my informants: nearly all of the landless go away, most of those with only a little land, and only a few of those with larger land-holdings. This sequence applies not only to the participation of households in migration but also, or even primarily, to their members. In other words the large proportion of landless households among migrant labourers is partly due to the fact that women and children as well as men migrate together. Among the landowning classes the percentage of those remaining behind rises in proportion to farm size. When I stated above that such factors as age, education and sex derived from economic status, I meant by this that the percentage of young children and older adults among the landowning migrant labourers is lower; that leaving children behind in order to attend school cannot be considered because of the lack of a sufficient basis for subsistence; and that the proportion of women taking part in migration is relatively the lowest in middle- and large-peasant households. Moreover the connection between land ownership and seasonal migration is not absolutely linear. To a certain extent household size is an independent variable in the sense that, with the increase in the number of household members, the temporary 'expulsion' of one or more members becomes both possible and necessary.

The fact that some members of small cultivators' households are obliged to stay behind derives not so much from the requirements of agriculture—labourers return temporarily in January/February for the harvesting of virtually the only winter crop, *jovar*—but is dictated by the daily care of livestock. However few in number—one or two oxen, sometimes a cow, a few goats or fowls—these together with some crude agricultural implements comprise their principal working capital. With these means of production it is also possible to sharecrop land or, as frequently happens in Uchhal, to work land clandestinely in the government-owned forest reserve. I have been able to establish repeatedly that in such cases the man stays behind while the woman leaves to find work elsewhere. The harvest yield supports those remaining at home even though the migrants take small shares of the harvest with them to tide them over their first days in the plain.

In so far as it occurs at all, seasonal migration among the larger landowners is not dictated by economic necessity. An informant from this category, the son of a village headman in Uchhal, told me that he had been away on trek several times out of curiosity. He was particularly interested in the agricultural methods used in the plain, and according to him he had profited a great deal from the experience. During his trek he had acted as spokesman for his work team. As a migrant he was able to behave differently from his fellow workers. He had been to the cinema in Bardoli with a farmer for whom he worked for a few weeks, had eaten and drunk with other employers, and thus gave the impression of having been treated more as a colleague than as a farm servant. Such cases are of course rather exceptional.

Although non-economic factors do play a role in the case of the large mass of landless and marginal cultivators the transition to dependent wage labour being easier to face at a distance than in their own village, yet their temporary or permanent departure from home is of a much more defensive kind. For these the home base offers inadequate year-round opportunities for survival. Wages for agricultural labour are very low, from Rs 2–2.50 in Valod to Re 1 with a little *nasto* (breakfast consisting of a piece of *rotla* in the morning) in Uchhal. In the latter district wages are still usually paid in kind and even then no more than 1 *atho* (a local measure of three-quarters of a kilo) of grain. It is obviously impossible to lay by a reserve for the slack period. Except in the short agrarian season the landowners can easily manage with the labour power available in their own households. For the landless who for one reason or another cannot leave the area, there are still a few odd jobs available in the Valod area but little or nothing in Uchhal. During this period they must somehow manage to survive by collecting edible forest roots and by illegal fishing, and by trying to obtain an advance of grain from households with a harvest surplus, in exchange for the promise of labour whenever this is needed. In a number of huts I visited there was such an acute food shortage as to suggest actual starvation. It is among this category especially that people reportedly still their hunger by eating leaves and earth in the months of scarcity before the monsoon.

The shortage of employment and the low wages paid results in a situation in which, compared with migrants from landowning households, not only do more numbers of landless households leave home but they also stay away longer and make more frequent trips. Occasionally however, the extremely low standard of living which permits no margin, acts as a brake on long-distance mobility even when people are aware of the road to employment outside the home area. An agricultural labourer I met in a village in Uchhal answered, in reply to my question about when he would leave, 'as soon as I have five rupees to rub together'. This amount is the minimum necessary for reaching Bardoli.[3] In addition, those who bind themselves to a year's labour for a tribal landowner in their home area, are also unable to participate in migration to the plain. However, this form of assured subsistence—which offers a cash sum of not quite Rs 100 in addition to food and lodging—remains limited to an extremely small category of workers.

Finally, when weighing the various factors stimulating or retarding mobility, we cannot take only the specific characteristics of individual migrants as our starting point. Labour migration is to a large extent a group event, which prompts a chain reaction and in which village, *falia* and family can be distinguished from each other within the participants' networks.

It goes without saying that the effects of migratory labour should be judged by what it yields for the home region. According to my calculations these external earnings provide from a third to approximately two-thirds of the annual income of the households involved. In general they account for an even higher percentage of wages paid in cash. For landless and marginal-landowner households it has undoubtedly become the most important source of income. I dare not venture

[3] By bus, at all events. Many migrant labourers from Uchhal go on foot or by bus to Navapur and from there take the train to Bardoli, a journey for which they often do not pay.

further than these broad statements, which indicate no more than the extent of the problem. Collection of information is a taxing and delicate undertaking in which informants' statements can only be checked through mutual comparison. For more quantified data, a longer period of research in the villages of out-migration would be necessary. Weber emphasized the economic motif underlying migratory labour as follows:

> The migrant would not accept at home the kind of living conditions (and diet is not the only or even principal factor here) that are offered to him by a distant place of work. Because of this lower standard and because of the lack of leisure and complacency that he enjoys at home he can work harder and is thus able to save significant amounts from his wages even when they are no higher than the local rates, something that would not have been possible had he not migrated. Moreover, once back he can afford to take it easy during the workless winter months (Weber 1924: 193).

Savings are dependent on the number of participants in migration from each household, the ratio of productive to non-productive members, the length of time away from home and the time of year in which migration takes place. During the harvest and other peak work periods, wages in the plain rise temporarily. An adult male worker who has only himself to consider, who does not drink heavily, and who finds work every day, is able to save about Rs 40 a month at most. However, given the variation among the migrants, it is impossible to use this as a standard amount. Even among landowning households in which a relatively larger number of non-productive members can remain at home, only a few reach the monthly sum mentioned. Moreover this is still not a net saving. When leaving home they take with them not only a little money for travelling expenses but also several kilos of *jovar* to eat during the first few days. During the stay in the plain new supplies are sent through team members returning to the home village for a few days. Landless or marginal-landowner migrants set out with even less—no provisions—and as a rule return with less. The total productivity of those accompanying the migrants is lower still. In their case, too, the amount of savings increases with longer absence, but the final sum bears no relation to the amount of energy expended. The agricultural labourer's household consisting of a man, his wife, three children and the wife's mother which returned home after eight months with Rs 192 is, in my view, more or less representative. This sum was saved out of service with one farmer who remunerated a working day for four people with a total of Rs 9.50: the man received Rs 3, his thirteen-year-old son Rs 2.50, the two women Rs 2 each. This meant that, of the total wages paid this group, about 15 per cent could be saved, i.e., less than Rs 50 per labourer for the entire period.

It will occasion no surprise that almost all the migrants' savings are spent almost exclusively on essential consumption when they return home (see also Gandhi and Shah 1978: 51–2). Many returning migrants buy a quantity of food grains, usually the cheap red *jovar*. It is evident from other expenditure on items such as clothing or pots and pans that the earnings from external work must be used to satisfy the most basic needs. Such durable goods are not brought back from the plain but are purchased in Valod or Navapur during the return journey. The migrant workers are justifiably afraid, as outsiders (they speak a different dialect or even a different language), of being cheated by shopkeepers in the Bardoli area.

Several cultivating households among my informants needed the income from migrant labour in order to repay (at 100 per cent interest) the seed grain they had borrowed from more prosperous landowners at the beginning of the rainy season. Those with farm holdings try to build up a small reserve from agricultural labour in the plain or to work off existing shortages and thus break even in the long run. It is expected of all able-bodied members of households which depend largely or entirely upon the sale of their labour that, in principle, they will provide for their own livelihoods. If they are unsuccessful in this in their own home area then there is little choice but to migrate. For the landless and the marginal landowner credit is very hard to obtain locally. They set out under difficult circumstances, they return with less to show for the same amount of time spent away, and because of this are only able to put by a small amount which they use up faster and therefore are forced to migrate again, sooner and more frequently than others.

Are the members of marginal households who go out or stay back, upwardly mobile? I have found no indications of such structural improvement, as suggested in the large part of literature on migration, in the hinterland of Surat District. The low income earned in the plain does not allow for the purchase of land or other capital assets after return. The majority of small owners are at best able to consolidate their holding with the savings they bring back home.

In conclusion, seasonal migration is a matter of survival or, at best, of consolidation, and hardly ever results in accumulation or re-investment in the home area.

Labour migration stems from a situation of inequality, but are existing socio-economic differences also increasing as a result of this? (Connell et al. 1975: 151). From my limited length of stay in the eastern part of Surat District, I am unable to answer this question in a definitive way. Yet it is certain that, however paradoxical this may sound, a growing percentage of landless and marginal-holding households can support themselves in the hinterland only by absenting themselves from the area for long periods. The small cultivators try to prevent a slide down the agrarian ladder or at all events to delay it, by taking part in migration.

The assumption of a natural solidarity which would prevail within the household sphere gave rise to the notion of a 'share family'[4]. The implicit line of reasoning is that the peasant household is an economic unit into which the yield of the efforts of members who have left flows back. Those who go out are, moreover, after some time replaced by those who have stayed back. This highly populistic view of the peasant order, however, does not acknowledge the inevitable process of atomization, aggravated by the seasonal migrations, which leads to conflicting interests, increasing the tension between household members.

Over the past few decades there has been little or no improvement in the quality of tribal life, certainly not for the large and growing underclass. Yet the cash income derived from labour outside the home area is not in itself enough for keeping one step ahead of the danger of social and economic deterioration. The origin of migration to the plain has also

[4] Jayaraman (1979) comes to the same conclusion for a tribal area in south Gujarat.

derived from the disappearançe of an economy in which money was insignificant in importance. Formerly labour performed outside one's own household was either recompensed in kind or was reciprocated, and articles of consumption and advances were provided by local merchants to be repaid with part of the harvest. The pattern of needs has not really been extended over the past few decades but it has certainly become monetarized; an increasingly large proportion of requirements, even the most basic, can now be fulfilled only with cash. Market mechanisms have come to predominate even at the level of a tribal household, although the development of agriculture has lagged behind, especially in the more remote *talukas*. A large proportion of the inhabitants must earn money by labour which has a very low local exchange value. Under these conditions seasonal migration has become necessary as a monetary supplement to a limited basis of production. Among the large category of small landowners especially, a new type of subsistence cultivator appears to have developed who grows only food crops intended for household use and who relies on household members' temporary migration to the plain for a cash income.[5] Once this process has begun it tends to harden into a cumulative segmentation. Is the future prospect, then, an economic dualism between plain and hinterland?

Circulation versus migration

The annual trek to the plain, as I have thus far described it, amounts to a periodic ebb and flow for which labour circulation would be a more suitable term than migration. At first sight this process appears to benefit all the parties involved. After all, this seasonal mobility equalizes the temporary glut of labour in the area of outmigration with a temporary labour shortage in the place of destination. In the functionalist interpretations which have long been current in the literature on migration, the advantages of this complementarity have been much enlarged.

In the interests of a more critical evaluation one should ask how such a labour surplus came to exist? A bleak environment

[5] See Epstein 1973: 207–11.

and the short agricultural season are features which had existed for a long time without leading to out-migration. Even increasing population density, which certainly is a noticeable tendency, does not automatically lead to migration. Finally, for a long while labour was a scarce commodity in the hinterland, the scarcity preventing better usage of available resources. More weight should be given to the transition to a mode of production which has evoked processes of differentiation and has allotted a price to labour which, although extremely low, cannot be matched locally. In other words pressure on resources has increased not primarily because of population size but because of the changed valuation of labour. As a result a proportion of the inhabitants are forced to seek at least a part of their livelihoods elsewhere although resources continue to be used as extensively as before. When growing inequality is indicated as the main cause of migration between two areas then we must still ask how this inequality came to exist. Samir Amin has observed in this connection that the division of factors of production is not established *a priori* but results from the kind of development policy put into practice (Amin 1974: 88–90).

In one of the 'theories' which seem to have dominated discussion in the relevant literature for some time, an economic explanation was recently given on the phenomenon of migration—one which the author himself recommended as the 'Todaro Model'[6]. His thesis is that the inclination to migrate is determined by differences in income at both ends combined with the chance of finding work on arrival. Todaro takes migration from countryside to city as his starting point, but his explanation is also relevant for intra-rural circulation as far as his opinions on the conditions for out-migration are concerned. However, as a number of critics have shown, his analysis is faulty in several respects.[7] Disparities in income and the lower level of wages in the home area, do not have the vital significance accorded them by Todaro, even in the large-scale displacement of labour in the tribal hinterland of south

[6] '. . . the theory assumes that members of the labor force, both actual and potential, compare their 'expected' incomes for a given time horizon in the urban sector (i.e. the difference between returns and costs of migration) with prevailing average rural income and migrate if the former exceeds the latter (Todaro 1981: 239).

[7] See for example Samin 1974: 90–3; Connell et al. 1976: 10, 30, 200.

Gujarat. In the first place not all work in the plain is better paid, not even industrial work. The migrants who find work in the cotton ginning factories in Bardoli earn a lower daily wage than the labourers remaining behind in Valod to work on roads or canals there. Even in the home area, work in the carpet factories in Valod town is lower paid than the already meagre earnings from agricultural labour in the nearby countryside. Secondly, rural migrants do not comprise a more or less homogeneous category of poor people, as Todaro seems to think.[8] He describes them as entrepreneurs who decide individually to migrate after weighing the possible costs and benefits. The element of free choice, assumed by Todaro to underlie the migrants' behaviour, is not attuned to the situation of extreme scarcity within which the majority of migrants exist in the home area. The rationality of their migration is not based upon a strategy of 'maximisation' as he argues, but upon a strategy of survival. The unit of analysis cannot be the individual (impermissably restricted by the author to youths and young men aged between fifteen and twenty-four) but must be the household from which available labour is distributed according to the principle of collective risk-spreading within the place of residence and outside it. One of the postulates in Todaro's reasoning is that in general there is little surplus labour in the countryside. An urban bias, which he otherwise rejects, appears to have blinded him to the home-area side of labour migration.

A similar naïveté, usually expressed in sociological jargon, presupposes a contrast between the traditional socio-economic order which the migrant is leaving behind and the modern environment to which he comes. Mobility itself is thus regarded as a yardstick for measuring the inclination for change, with the accompanying presumption that those who are mobile also act as agents in the dynamic of change in their own home milieu. This line of argument equates migration with urbanization and assumes that those who leave the village are less 'traditional' and that they introduce 'modernity' to the village on their return. Typical of this approach is a fairly recent

[8] 'In short migrants seem to come from all socio-economic strata with the vast majority being very poor only because most inhabitants are poor' (Todaro 1981: 238).

study by Saxena, who argues that migration ultimately results in progress. 'The overall inference therefore is rural emigration → urbanization → socio-economic development → rural development' (Saxena 1977: 8).

In publications like these the positive effects accruing to the home area are emphasized: a rise in living standards or even in productive capacity as a result of incoming earnings; a heightened level of awareness and the introduction of different norms and values by migrants as the most important agents of change, norms and values which spell the end of 'traditional' orientations. The 'attachment to agriculture' and the 'sense of belonging to the village' gradually give way to the desire for renewal, a broadening of horizons and the insight that migration comprehensively serves self-interest. The kind of questions which regularly reappear in many pieces of research, e.g., the National Sample Survey, concern people's *willingness* to leave the village or their *preference* for different kinds of work. Such questions in fact assume a passive, backward rural population who are difficult to move. Premises like these enable us to understand precisely why it is that modernization theories assess the phenomenon of migration so favourably.

Bardoli does not lend itself to such conventional views. Those who do leave, are not doing so in expectation of being able to 'better themselves'. They are driven, not by a higher level of aspiration than their non-migrating fellow villagers, but by economic necessity. Similarly the consideration that work elsewhere can perhaps produce savings which can be put to productive use on returning home, plays almost no role. Everything remaining over from the migrants' frugal life in the plain is taken home, but their absence from home serves primarily to lighten the burden on the household. To live according to standards of modern life demands a material level obviously beyond the reach of the overwhelming majority of migrants. For the same reason it is unwise to expect too much in the way of diffusion of innovation as a result of migration. Information acquired elsewhere is only to a limited degree relevant for the situation and problems in the tribal hinterland. It is only too easy to give the impression that the mobility of those involved is coupled with individual development and greater independence. This would mean a serious lack of understanding of the migrants' insecurity and dependence while in the plain. The costs of migration are high, not least for those remaining behind. From conversations I had in the home area I was struck by my informants' determination not to migrate that year (sometimes against their own better judgement) or at all events either to postpone departure or to return sooner. Small peasants hope to get land for sharecropping in order to justify staying on in the village. Agricultural labourers have little or no chance of escaping migration and the older people among them, especially, dread their trips to the plain. I can only conclude that labour circulation in south Gujarat has a starkly defensive character. Migratory behaviour is highly rational even though the choice underlying it has little or nothing to do with 'modernity'.

Conversely the majority of reluctant migrants do not succeed in establishing themselves permanently in the plain. Probably a greater variation among migrants than one presently finds in this unskilled, low paid and temporary labour-force is necessary for achieving an acceleration in socio-economic differentiation in the hinterland. There are certainly some indications of this, as for example in the case of marginal landowners who decide not to work their own land any more but to lease it out to bigger cultivators. However, there is still the question of how far this first step towards permanent alienation of land is a direct consequence of labour circulation. In the case I have described, a more plausible proposition is argued by Samir Amin among others, that labour migration from the home area results in a rigidification in the basic pattern and contributes to the reproduction of existing socio-economic inequality.[9] Available or potential resources remain underutilized. Small landowners, a dominant category in the eastern *taluka* also, are forced to neglect work on

[9] 'Emigration impoverishes the region, it also prevents the socio-economic structure from undergoing radical progressive change; also to defend themselves, to survive, these societies react by reinforcing those aspects of their traditional structure, which enable them to survive this impoverishment. But at the same time, this impoverishment reinforces the push effect on certain elements of the population, reproducing the conditions of emigration (Amin 1974: 104). For a critical analysis of the Ukai irrigation project and its impact on the life of the tribal population see Mankodi 1983.

their own holdings.[10] Cultivable land, already scarce, is less intensively worked than it might be, and efforts to bring more land into cultivation remain limited. New agricultural practices developed for 'dry' crops are rarely applied. In so far as development of the hinterland is influenced by seasonal migration the results seem to be more negative than positive.

In conclusion, we must consider the question of whether labour circulation is a continuing process. A fundamental change in both the area of out-migration and the plain could lead to a significant reduction or even a complete cessation of migration. Change in the former will take place when the causes for migration are removed, for instance by expansion of local opportunities for earning a livelihood. When I revisited Chikhligam in the more southerly-lying Valsad District, a village in which I had carried out fieldwork earlier, I could confirm that some of the small cultivators among the tribal Dhodhias had benefited from the arrival of canal irrigation. By intensifying agrarian production (especially cultivation of chillies) they had freed themselves from the annual trek to the brick fields (Breman 1974: 242, 247). By the same means Gamit and Chaudhari landowners will undoubtedly be able to make use of the opportunities for new cropping brought about by the extension of the irrigated area in the hinterland. For this part of the tribal population, seasonal migration has thus become a 'holding operation' which has enabled them by and large to maintain their relative position in the village and to avoid alienation of land as far as possible. Yet the larger part of the tribal milieu will remain excluded from this infrastructural improvement. Extrapolating from the situation in the immense hinterland, there is no reason for believing that the stream of labourers to the plain will dry up soon.

The possibility of change in the agrarian pattern of the plain

10 This tendency was already noticed in the first village monograph available for south Gujarat. 'Most of the Kaliparaj landholders and labourers who cultivate small rented plots go away to outside areas in search of work as soon as the rainy season is over and the crops are reaped. In the absence of the responsible man, the other members of the family grow negligent about the cattle' (Mukhtyar 1930: 135).

would require the emergence of a new labour regime involving no, or at least considerably less, seasonal migration. An example of this is mechanization of the harvest now being partially effected by the sugar factories in Bardoli and neighbourhood. This would mean a drastic reduction in the present mass importation of sugarcane cutters from Khandesh each year.[11] When such a labour market disappears and an alternative source of employment is not immediately available or accessible, then there may be an increased immobility. A precarious situation may also arise in the home regions if workers from other reservoirs of surplus labour come into the main arena of employment in search of work. There are indications that the recent opening up of the homogeneously tribal Dangs District in south Gujarat will bring with it a sizeable migration to the plain.

Seasonal migration can also result in permanent emigration, and in fact it may be regarded as a variant of step migration, i.e. the proposition that mobility follows a set sequence: from countryside to a small town and then to larger growth poles. In a similar manner rural circulation ultimately results in permanent settlement of hitherto mobile labour in the place of destination, so it is often claimed in the literature on migration. This premise is found not only in studies based on conventional modernization theories but also in more critical studies focussing on the sequence of modes of production. In both cases the experience of the industrialized countries appears to have been retained as a yardstick. Continuous back and forth migration on a large scale seems to conflict with economic logic. Viewed in historical perspective, circulation then becomes a transitional phenomenon between either 'tradition' and 'modernity' or feudalism and capitalism.

Migration takes place without earlier spells of circulation. The number of tribals from the hinterland who have gone

[11] The change from use of oxcart to use of tractors and lorries for bringing an increasingly larger part of the harvested cane to the factory is already an expression of this. Now the possibility of introducing machines into the harvesting of sugar is being explored. Not that this would be any cheaper—harvest wages are extremely low (Breman 1978–9)—but as productive capacity is raised, the wholesale use of human labour for cane cutting creates increasingly greater problems of a managerial and political nature.

elsewhere for sheer survival (after the floods in 1968 or continuous draught in the beginning of the seventies) is large but unknown. Many of them have settled down in the slums of Surat, where they are extremely difficult to trace. Seasonal mobility can be a stubborn process, as I have concluded from my earlier research. The trek from villages in Valsad District to the brickfields and saltpans in the vicinity of Bombay mentioned already half a century ago, still continues. In some families the third or even fourth successive generation takes part in this.[12] Temporary labour circulation appears to have become a concept nearly as elastic as that of the centre-periphery dichotomy as applied to the capitalist order within which it occurs.

[12] Mukhtyar, in his village study at the end of the 1920s, was already noting the seasonal migration of landless labourers from south Gujarat to the brick fields in the Bombay area (1930: 160). Three decades later this migration had increased greatly in extent, as I confirmed at the beginning of the 1960s (Breman 1974: 103–6). Even at the beginning of the 1980s there was still no change in this pattern.

8

SEASONAL LABOURERS IN THE AREA AROUND BARDOLI

The beginning and duration of the season

The influx of migrant labourers begins at the end of October, when the rainy season is virtually over. As we explained in the previous chapter, the shift to the plain is connected with the lack of available employment in the home regions during the dry winter months. It is at the tail end of the monsoon that the push and pull forces work most strongly against each other, since the harvesting of the staple foodstuffs—millet and other kinds of coarse grains—occurs during these weeks, while where possible the winter crop must also be sown. Herein lies, particularly for those who have land, a strong incentive for attempting to postpone their departure until these operations have been completed. Nevertheless, at the same time there is an urgent need for their presence in the south Gujarat plain, where the harvesting of rice and a few other crops represents one of the most important peaks in the agrarian cycle. The agricultural cycle of Bardoli and its environs places a premium on the early arrival of a large number of migrants, by offering a great deal of work and relatively high earnings for a short period. It cannot be taken for granted, however, that those involved have the luxury of weighing the relative advantages and disadvantages of either staying at home or leaving, since it is my impression that, with the increase of migrant labour in recent years, the time of departure has also been brought forward. The pool of outside labour has become subjected to the demands of the timetable of agrarian production in the central plain. Not only do higher wages play an important role during this period, but all kinds of other binding mechanisms as well, which will be dealt with later in this chapter.

The arrival of the mass of migrant labourers occurs shortly

after Divali. During the following weeks they stream in from all sides. They are present in the greatest numbers from the beginning of November to the end of January, and I would estimate that they constitute some 20 to 30 per cent of the working population of the central plain during that period. In some localities their proportion can rise to over half that of the normal number of inhabitants. Where the cropping system is most intensive, agricultural labourers number many hundreds more in this period than during the rest of the year. After that, their numbers gradually diminish, and most of them would have already left before Holi. However, the migration pattern varies with the distance from the home area. Those who come from close by and have to travel less than 100 km stay for a relatively shorter time, but make several journeys throughout the year. These visits last no longer than one or two weeks at a stretch, continuing nowadays through the hot summer months and the rainy season. A precondition for this cyclical mobility is the easy accessibility of the immediate hinterland, to which improved communications have contributed to a great extent.

In other words, the seasonality of migrant labour has diminished over the years. The concentration has, to be sure, remained highest in the early winter months, but these outsiders are not completely absent from the south Gujarat plain either before or after that. Furthermore, a proportion of them scarcely count as outsiders any longer. They came as migrant workers but did not leave again.

How migrants arrive and find work

Migrant labour occurs in both an organized form and a more unregulated form which I shall call spontaneous migration. I have published an account of the former in an article devoted to the organization of sugarcane cutting by the co-operative factories in south Gujarat (Breman 1978–9). In the nearby western part of Maharashtra, harvesting teams are contracted on a large scale for this seasonal work, by factory agents and jobbers. Labour is also recruited from other places for temporary service in other branches of rural activity. For example Surat District appears to be one of the main destinations for tribal gangs of road workers from Panch Mahals during the season (Jayaraman 1979: 1728; see also B.E.S., Gujarat State 1974: 6). Migrant labour in agriculture is comparatively much less regulated than in these rural industries. Organized recruitment, as in the case of sugarcane cutting for which a labour contract is made beforehand, does not fit in with the short-term employment on family farms in the plain. Many of these migrants must leave their homes with no warning and what is more, they have only an approximate idea of where they will be going, what they will be doing, and how long they will be away. In that sense their mobility is casual and unorganized.

The manner of travelling to the plain bears witness to the haphazard and undirected character of this labour circulation. Most of the migrants come by train or (S.T.) bus to Bardoli and other places. From there they go to the villages in the vicinity where some of them have been engaged before, in the expectation of being able to find work straightaway. Those who are not well known in the area prefer to remain on the bus station platform on arrival, until a farmer who has come to this assembly point takes them with him. The migrants behave like strangers. On 29 April 1977 I noted in my diary that:

> along the exit road from Bardoli a small group of transients have set up their bivouac. Altogether there are 10 men, women and children belonging to 3 households. It is evening and already nearly dark as I pass by. I have a chat beside one of the three small fires which have been kindled there. The group came by train from Navapur several hours ago. They are on their way to a village close to Navsari to harvest summer rice there. A young man has been there during the past season, and has persuaded the others to accompany him on the grounds of being able (so he claims) to earn Rs 4 a day. They have with them food for two days, enough until tomorrow evening. The women are now preparing some of this: broken rice with water. Why did the group not travel straight through to Navsari? Well, then they would have arrived in the dark and would not have known what to do. They are spending the night here, with an eye on the stop which the bus has to pass early tomorrow. My informant did the same thing on the previous occasion. From the Navsari bus station he knows how to reach the village on foot.

The difference between landowning and landless migrants becomes evident immediately on arrival. The former usually take with them a supply of food for a period ranging from one or two days to a week. Certainly this reduces reserves for those remaining at home, but on the other hand the departing members of the household have no need to settle immediately for the lowest offer made to them when they reach the plain. They can risk bargaining and even move further on if need be. Not so their landless companions in adversity: several informants from this category have had to get through the first days without food, or have been forced to be content with nothing more than a meal for a day's work. The landowners are in general exceptionally well informed over the weak position of the tramping labourers, and are totally unscrupulous about exploiting them to the utmost.

To talk of spontaneous migration is not to say that this periodic circulation of labour in the countryside takes place in an entirely haphazard and unstructured way. A foreman-jobber, in charge of the large gangs, consisting of 20 to 30 members at most, leave for the plain towards the end of the rainy season. Already some time before this, the jobber would have gone back to the farmers met on previous trips in order to offer his services for the new season. He undertakes to return at a specified date with the number of labourers required. This agreement is obviously based on a relation of trust. The only way in which farmers protect themselves against the risk of non-fulfillment of this understanding is by advancing money to a jobber with whom they have already had reason to be satisfied, and who is vulnerable to sanctions or their threat.

On his part the gang leader naturally tries to consolidate his reputation for trustworthiness, built up gradually. He is not always successful in fulfilling his promises. To begin with, there is no certainty of being able to recruit a sufficient number of labourers. The advance loans which he hands out are a means of establishing obligatory claims, but even then he has trouble in gathering together, on the advertised day of departure, all those whom he has recruited. Some let him down because they have accepted money from another jobber as well, others because they have given priority to work remaining unfinished at home. The gang leader tries, in such a case, to obtain another member of the household. The supplying of credit is necessary but is not sufficient to compel docility.

In order to set up as a jobber a man must first already carry some weight in the village, which implies that he does not belong to the poorest substratum, the landless. Moreover, he must have a reputation as a good gang leader, that is to say, as someone who provides sufficient work offering appropriate remuneration, and who knows how to guarantee decent treatment for his gang members during stay in the plain. If a jobber fulfills all these requirements this does not mean that he can take with him an unlimited number of labourers; an overlarge gang consisting of more than 20 to 30 members is difficult to manoeuvre, and also presents problems of management. During the stay in the plain the number of people gets gradually reduced. Some members return home unexpectedly, for a few days or for good. In the latter case others take their place, whether or not they come from the same household. These are the uncertainties with which a jobber has to reckon. Moreover, the work contracted for cannot always be completed according to schedule and in consequence a gang arrives at the next farm later than the arranged time—a source of conflict, because the availability of labour at exactly the right moment can be of crucial importance for successful agrarian production. In practice it boils down to a case of the jobber making only a limited number of arrangements, which bind him merely for the first few weeks after arrival. Only after that is he free to make further contacts. These are also ensured in advance if he obtains recommendations from landowners for whom he has already worked. A repeat visit takes place occasionally; sometimes there is regular communication and a farmer sends for a jobber by letter.

An even less planned and structured form of labour migration is that involving a more limited number of men and women with children, who usually originate from several related households. These small loosely-knit groups consisting of five to ten or at the most fifteen members, become more conspicuous as the season progresses and the main harvest tasks are over. With this form of migration one can also speak of a more or less fixed itinerary, over which short-term sorties are made on the basis of vague promises given on earlier visits. Only when too little is offered do people make for other old addresses, or leave to follow up information picked up en route. It is invariably the men who go round seeking work and making contact with the landowners. The women in these mixed groups stay in the background even where they form the majority of the members.

Finally, a number of seasonal workers have established themselves in the plain on a semi-permanent basis, taking up permanent service with farmers whom they first encountered as transients. These will be considered in the last section. I would just like to observe here that they also function as channels from a home reservoir along which their employers can draw the additional labour necessary for temporary work. When these workers return to their home areas for festivals, they are given the assignment of recruiting more labourers in their village, for definite tasks. Those who have already worked for some time as farm hands and who enjoy the trust of their boss, are even sent out on this errand with tractor and trailer. Away goes a load of stalks and other waste stuff intended as cattle feed for the tribal household; back come the required number of workers, carried on the trailer.

From the foregoing it is sufficiently clear that spontaneous migration of labour does not exclude a directed and regulated pattern of mobility. On the other hand this does not mean that this temporary movement of labour has in fact developed in a completely prestructured way. To begin with, presenting matters in this way detracts from the accidental, impulsive character of the departure. Whether large or small groups are involved, it often remains uncertain right up to the last moment when, with whom, to which place and for how long people are leaving. This is at any rate the case at the very beginning of the season, when there is an accumulation of agricultural work. If this first peak has passed, then the pattern of circulation becomes more capricious, i.e. after completing the work for which they were actually called, gangs which came to the plain for clearly defined assignments continue their stay afterwards on a much looser footing. The following case quoted from my diary of 1977 provides an illustration of this.

> 21 February: Along the roadside by the turn-off to Valod, I come across a group of migrant labourers from Saurashtra. The party consists of 5 men, 6 women, a few boys and girls of roughly fourteen years and the rest small children, the youngest among them running around completely naked, while the adults' clothing is scanty, old

and tattered. The camp consists of some scattered heaps of possessions, rags, store tins and pans. There are two tents improvized from wooden sticks over which a jute sack has been stretched with string. The children gather wood for the three fires set apart from each other. Around them the women are busy with the preparation of food for that evening: millet cakes with a little finely ground chillie. The camp gives an impression not only of utmost poverty, but even more of great haste, as if it has only just been set up and can at any moment be broken up again. As it turned out later the group spent five days in this place. The men, suspecting that I might be a government official, react in a reserved manner to my attempted approach. Only hours later, when it is already dark, are they prepared to tell me more. The group consists of relatives belonging to two households in Dhandhuka Taluka. It is a poverty-stricken border zone between Saurashtra and Gujarat. Only rough millet (*bajri*) grows on the little amount of land they have, as small cultivators. The out-turn this year was less than usual owing to heavy rainfall. The migration of both households was unavoidable, for survival. Only one old woman had stayed behind to look after a few head of cattle. It is not the first time that they have come to south Gujarat, except that when the harvest turns out well the old people and the women with really young children have no need to make the trek. For the last four or five years the men have worked for a contractor in Navsari. During the monsoon they received a letter from him telling them to go to Khergam and Chikhli Taluka after Divali for the excavation of an irrigation canal. Kathiawadis are renowned as hard workers and are particularly skilled as navvies. But this time the job was extremely difficult. The piece work rate was too low for the heavy ground that had to be dug. After ten weeks, earlier than intended, they left this work place. Somewhere en route they heard that irrigation work was being carried out close to Kosamba, and they are now on their way there. My reaction was one of surprise, because in that case they have really lost their way. But the men explained they did not have enough provisions to cover all the distance at once. They had just started to go in the direction of their new destination, but had to turn aside in order to obtain food. With references from farmers for whom they have worked as agricultural labourers, they walked to this place four days ago. They were unable to find work yesterday or today. If the same thing happens tomorrow morning too, they will trek further on. Will they reach Kosamba, and when? That is still the intention, but who can say? Two days later they had disappeared.

A number of unforeseen circumstances, arising rather frequently, can result in the trip failing to run according to plan. Quarrels with the jobber or mutual quarrels between gang members can lead to the precipitate return of some or all. Moreover, a lot depends on the way in which landowners treat the migrants. Discontent over fault-finding, or over wage levels leads to premature departure. The reconnoitring of new territory definitely has all the excitement of an adventure, particularly for young unmarried men and women, but a few days without work, and all too soon without food as well, are usually enough to dissipate the glamour of the wandering life.

The huge scale on which labour migration takes place today has increased the insecurity of life for those taking part, compared with earlier times. Before the transition to irrigated cultivation, the number of seasonal migrants coming into the area was limited, and moreover their presence coincided for the most part with the peak periods in the agricultural year, so that for the groups tramping through the villages there was always something to do. Now there is a much greater spread over the whole year, and the landowners can afford to withhold a job if the low pay they are prepared to give for it is not accepted—other applicants will soon present themselves. The time is also past when the landowners themselves made personal expeditions to the tribal hinterland of Surat District, to recruit extra labourers there for the post-monsoon harvest tasks. Nowadays the jobbers seek out potential employers in order to strike bargains for this dry period; for the rest the farmers rely on already existing channels, or wait calmly in the absolute certainty not only that the old gangs will turn up again at the right moment, but also that potential new teams coming to the village or the neighbourhood are ready to take their place.

The work

As we have observed, there is a constant stream of migrant labourers going down to the plain, continuing nearly the whole year with a considerable increase at the time of harvesting the most important agricultural crops. The sharpest fluctuation occurs at about the time of Divali, when these strangers are present in numbers which climb from a minimum to a maximum within a few weeks. Within a relatively short time, one after the other—in the months of Kartak (October-November) and Magshar (December-January)—the rice is harvested, grass on uncultivated land is cut, groundnuts are pulled from the soil and sugarcane slowly ripens. These are all operations demanding many pairs of hands from children as well as men and women. The winter crops follow: cotton, millet and wheat in the months of Posh (February-March) and Phagan (April-May); the cutting of sugarcane now reaches a peak, and as the season for this passes, there is the harvesting of summer rice. Bananas are picked in the rainy season, especially in August and at the beginning of September.

The harvesting of a crop is often given out to teams of seasonal workers on contract. This usually includes the performance of all sorts of extra tasks; for example, the rice is not only cut but threshed at the same time (often while still in the field), the left-over stalks are tied up, and the grain is poured into sacks, carried to the farmer's house and stored there. At the same time as sugarcane is cut, it is stripped of its leaves, chopped into pieces, bound into sheaves and carried away. More important than the actual picking of bananas is heaving the bunches away to the hard-surfaced road, where they are loaded onto a trailer or lorry. The variety of the tasks and the payment of piece-rates, makes it possible to put both men and women and even children to work.

The migrants carry out other agricultural work spread out between the harvest cycles—the planting of sugarcane in December, followed by weeding, maintenance work in the sugarcane fields and banana gardens, the removal of stubble or roots from ground in which crops have been growing, the preparation of land for monsoon crops, and in July the transplanting of rice and subsequent weeding. Finally there is soil improvement: the digging out, levelling and banking up of ground by means of which the high-lying *jarayat* which is rainfed, is converted into low-lying *kyari* which is easy to irrigate. Sometimes the different tasks are linked, in the sense that a work gang returns in order to complete the operations connected with cultivation of a crop—for example, the planting and some months later the harvesting of rice.

Whenever possible the landowners prefer to employ migrants from a particular area for the performance of a specific kind of agricultural work. As I have said, the Kathiawadi are well-known as navvies and for the hybridization of cotton, gangs from Chota Udaipur (central Gujarat) are called out. The special cattle men who have found their entrée into Bardoli and environs with the recent growth of the dairy industry, invariably originate from north Gujarat; sugarcane cutting is the monopoly of Khandeshi from Maharashtra. The existence of this regional specialization of work elsewhere in the state has been corroborated by other research findings.

> Migrants from different regions are associated with different types of work. Migrants from Panch Mahals, Surendranagar, Ahmedabad districts of Gujarat and adjoining districts of Madya Pradesh do the agricultural work as well as road and construction work. The gadawalas (the bullock cart owners) from Dhandhuka taluka of Ahmedabad district do the carting work only. Migrants from Banswara district of Rajasthan State do the agricultural work and migrants from Jalor district of Rajasthan State work as labourers in the rice mills (Bhatt n.d.: 16).

It is interesting to observe that what is said about the attributed skill can vary from place to place. To my mind this kind of reputation has little to do with real differences in training or specialization by area, but goes back to the accidentally established migration channel along which labour has since been recruited. If a category of migrants returns regularly to a region and stays there, diversification appears in the work they do. A group from Saurashtra which returned every year to a village in the plains, bought mangoes from the farmers in the season, which their wives hawked in the bazaars or villages surrounding their camp. Where this versatility is missing, the cause usually lies, not in the unwillingness of the migrants, but in their inability to gain access to other work. One example is the organization of sugarcane cutting by the sugar factories. Cane cutters are not allowed to stay in the area or to look around for other work, but are sent back immediately the campaign is over. The market for agricultural labour remains fragmented, although to a lesser extent than for urban and rural industries.

Todaro's model which begins with a linear linkage between differences in wage level and employment opportunities in the area of arrival and departure, does not take into account the particularistic character of labour migration. Bardhan here rightly observes: '. . . that the shape-ups of migrant labour tend to be group- or community-specific, that the markets for different types of even unskilled manual labour are not integrated and that the patterns of rural migration to other rural and urban areas are determined not just by differential wages and employment opportunities' (Bardhan 1977: A46).

It will be obvious that the migrants work for the large landowners, i.e. for the top 15 to 20 per cent in the villages. Besides Kanbi Patidars and members of the other high castes, tribals with more land are also to an increasing extent making use of these seasonal workers. Members of this agrarian class have the greatest amount of employment to give, and are moreover in a position to tie down the extra labour in advance. They have sufficient capital for providing credit, and the risk that a *mukadam* (jobber) to whom credit has been advanced will ultimately fail to turn up with his gang, is weighed against the need to be certain of finding sufficient labour at the right moment. With this credit they are not buying labour for a lower price during the peak season, but are certainly buying a preferential right to the use of that labour. Only when the harvest work is finished do the smaller cultivators have their turn. The larger the holding, the greater the number of labourers set to work on it, with greater frequency and for a longer duration of time. The jobbers have developed a finely tuned instinct for the varied standing of their employers. Even when they get the same rate for the work accomplished their behaviour towards smaller landowners is more casual, less deferential and less inhibited. The migrants who trek in smaller groups round the Bardoli area for any length of time, are less exclusively committed to the larger employers for their assignments; they find employment with all categories of landowners, although even in their case, the higher castes are disproportionately represented among their employers. The reasons for this are as much economic as social, for agricultural land is mostly concentrated in the hands of members of the higher social strata, while these try as far as possible to free themselves from manual labour.

How are the migrants' tasks supervised? The answer to this question requires a detailed examination of the functions of the *mukadam*, who fulfills a double role: besides being the jobber he also acts as foreman of his gang. The farmer assigns the work to him, and he is responsible for its performance. There is no direct communication between gang members and the employer. All instructions from the latter come through the *mukadam* as intermediary, who divides up the work, gives instructions, and corrects mistakes when necessary. He also takes charge of the earnings, and divides them among his gang according to the amounts of money advanced earlier as loans.

A number of attributes distinguishes the *mukadam* of a large gang from the rest of its members. As I have stated earlier, he is often already their superior, in a socio-economic sense, in the home locality. He is able to take with him a sufficient number of migrants, in good time, and is well known at their destination. He also knows how to bridge the gap between workers and farmers, how to get round the farmers in just the right way to obtain commissions, and how to hold his own in negotiations. Moreover he must of course be familiar with the work itself, as much to make his leadership acceptable as to ensure that he does not accept a job at too low a rate. An informant from this category summed up the typical *mukadam* as being able to pay in advance and think in advance. A gang leader from this level maintains some simple bookkeeping, i.e. he can read, write and reckon, however inadequately. He acts as confidant and spokesman for his people in what is for them, an unfamiliar environment. He uses this dependence to spur them on to an adequate work performance. In short, his role is that of an agent between two parties, when he has won the trust of both sides.

The role of the *mukadam* is not always really so formalized and prominent. The distinct occupational role of the middleman comes particularly to the fore with formally supervised labour such as one finds in the cutting of sugarcane (Breman 1978–9: 52–9). The jobber-foreman who makes contacts in the spontaneous seasonal migration is generally a person of more modest status who, in the home locality, lives the same life as the rest of his team, and is occupationally indistinguishable from them. He does not confine himself to supervisory functions, but usually works along with the others on the land. His continual presence is necessary and for that reason alone a *mukadam* seldom contracts more than one team or puts them out to work in different villages. Certainly from an outsider's view he gives the impression of being more a kind of informal leader than of one exercising authority over a team which is subordinate to him. Persuasion rather than discipline is more characteristic of his relationship with the workers.

For the rest, the distance maintained by landowners diminishes with the increasing attraction of paying migrants by the working day rather than by task. In this case they incline towards sharper personal supervision over the working of outside labour. The choice between alternative methods of payment varies according to the village, but before and after harvest time farmers generally prefer to pay day wages rather than piece rates, in which case the *mukadam* comes less to the fore, although even then he is still the recognized representative for the group. In the case of small teams without formal leaders, the employers' role is weightier. In other words, it is difficult to generalize about the manner in which relations between migrant labourers and landowners are shaped. Moreover, if the *mukadam* acts in the capacity of a middleman he can act as a buffer between the parties, but in the plain people more often regard him as no more than first among equals.

Working conditions

The manner of wage payment is fixed unilaterally by the farmers, and the migrants' preferences play no part. Piece rates are customary when a great deal of work must be carried out in a short space of time, as with harvest operations. The amount varies according to the crop: groundnuts, for example, are paid for by weight, and in 1977 the tariff for the first pulling averaged Rs 4 per *maund*. A rate of Rs 6–8 operated for the following round, in which the same amount of working time produced a lower yield; the yield from an eventual third pulling was shared equally between landowners and labourers. For grass, the price paid was expressed in terms of the amount cut: Rs 20–22 for every 1,000 bundles. The rice harvest was calculated on the basis of the unit of land: Rs 60–80 per *bigha* (about two-thirds of an acre). The rate for humping bananas from the gardens was 5–20 n.p. per head load, depending on the distance to the loading point. The amounts tell us little in themselves—the variation is too great for that. Among other influential factors are the condition of the ground and of the crop. If the rice fields are still wet at harvest time, the work is heavier and the wage rate rises. One can certainly always find specific circumstances to explain the lack of uniform conditions of wage payment, but differences arising between villages cannot always be reduced to this sort of circumstantial factor. They are also connected with established traditions in payment for labour. It is probably the increasing mobility of agricultural labour which has promoted the standardization of harvest tariffs. The landowners are well informed on practices existing elsewhere and conform to them, the lowest offer rapidly becoming the norm.

It has struck me that there is hardly any formal negotiation over the price of labour. The *mukadam* is just told what the landowner will give him for a particular operation. By accepting an advance the gang leader has made an agreement; thereafter he is no longer a free agent and has bound himself to give priority to this employer, and the time of arrival is too late for stipulating a better wage. It is not very different for smaller gangs trekking round without a *mukadam*. The farmer takes one or several of the men to the field, indicates what has to be done, and names his price. The migrants can react to this by trying to obtain a somewhat higher remuneration—saying that they have obtained more elsewhere, that living has become dearer, that they will make great efforts, etc.—but there is no question of real haggling and arguing. Occasionally labourers can extract a higher rate while actually on the job by complaining about the heavy nature of the work and all sorts of unforeseen difficulties. An appeal to the landowner's generosity and clemency is one possibility; when this produces no results, more negative tactics can be more successful—grumbling, quarrelling, going slow or wasting the crop. It is precisely in the case of piece work that both parties have rather limited room for manoeuvre in this respect. The migrants themselves are the losers by too much obstructionism, while on the other hand the farmers lose out by imposing working conditions that are too unfavourable.

How is the allotted labour divided among the members of a gang? Equally—at any rate, if there is little or no differentiation in the nature of the work performed. The *mukadam* sees to it that the load is spread more or less equally among his team. He tries to regulate the work tempo as evenly as possible, but he cannot always prevent a situation where, at the end of the morning and afternoon, some are still busy while others have already finished their allotted shares. In cases where—as with the groundnut harvest—the assessment of wages is based on the weight collected, it is possible to determine the team members' separate earnings. The members of a household working together in the gang are then paid according to the number of baskets they have filled each day: with such a division there is no need for the members of a team, as labour power, to be all approximately equal with each other. Even the labour of those who are not completely fit is useful here; various informants, landowners as well as migrants, assured me that women remain working in the fields up to the last moment of pregnancy, and sometimes give birth there, too. Moreover, tariff work puts a premium on child labour. The fact that small children of less than ten years of age contribute to the income of the migrant households to which they belong, as for example in the case of cotton picking or groundnut harvesting, does not mean that they are unproductive outside these operations. In the rice harvesting, for instance, they collect up the gleanings remaining behind in the field where the adults are at work. In order to forestall objections by the farmers (who are always quick to talk of theft) the migrants do not usually keep these heaps of grain for their own consumption; every day or so the children sell their finds in the village for a couple of annas, or exchange them for a few vegetables.

The intention behind piecework rates is to spur the labourers to maximum effort. By hard work they indeed manage to earn more than would be possible with the going daily wage. The differences are otherwise not so dramatic as they were once made out to be; in other words, the farmers are strongly cost-conscious and are not inclined to pay more than is absolutely necessary. The premium they put on piecework therefore remains on the modest side, especially outside the busy season. Payment by daily wage is current for less urgent work extending over a longer period, but locally the landowners give preference to this method in the harvest period as well, because they complain that the labourers work too carelessly on piecework rates, at the cost of the crop yield.

Closer supervision only partly obviates this, in their opinion. During my fieldwork the level of the daily wage differed as much between locations as between seasons. Naturally most of the farmers claimed to pay more than they actually did; men generally got Rs 3–4 a day, women Rs 2–3, and extras in kind were only very occasionally included with these amounts. The migrants' answers to my questions on this were nearly always in the negative, and even derisive, but the landowners nevertheless never omitted to mention that they provided free water and wood; cotton plant stalks and waste, such as sugarcane roots, removed from the ground. Several also claimed that they gave tea or some *bidis*. As far as the large gangs are concerned, this treatment remained mainly limited to the *mukadam*, who saw it as emphasizing his privileged position. In the other cases it only really materialized as recompense for extra work, in or around the farmer's house early in the morning or late in the evening.

The migrants also had to set their thumbprints in the wages book which landowners kept according to the government regulations of that period. Rs 5.50 was registered after their names, an amount very few actually received. One landowner alone, inspired by the Gandhian ethos, regarded it as his duty to treat his workers in a decent way. He followed government directives and paid the minimum prescribed wage for agricultural labourers. In similar exceptional cases a few farmers stand aloof from the methods current among the other landowners in the village for maintaining informal control of wages at a low level.

The migrants' working day is long, especially if they are working for piecework rates; then there are no fixed times for starting or finishing, and the gang works through until the job for that day is finished—until 7 or 8 o'clock in the evening or even later. The day-wage workers maintain a calmer tempo, usually beginning somewhat later in the morning—at 8 o'clock—and, with an hour's rest at midday, continuing until 6 o'clock in the evening. The field labour proper is finished then, but afterwards their temporary employer still sets all or some of the team members to work in his house. It is the same in the early mornings; the men are busy with the cattle or with small jobs in the farmyard, while the women wash clothes, clean pots and pans, and sweep the house.

Yet it would be incorrect to foster the impression that migrants do nothing but work continuously. Because tariff or piecework rate is paid exclusively on the basis of work completed, the landowners are not always so strict about allotting a sufficient quantity of work in good time. In contrast to hours of hard drudgery, it is a regular occurrence for part of the day to remain unutilized. If heavy rainfall during the monsoon makes it impossible to carry on working, the labourers are not paid for the idle period. When I asked about this they reacted with disbelief and began to laugh at the mere idea of payment for idle time. On the other hand, fixed rest days do not exist. The migrants work as extra labour power for a landowner as long as he has need of them, but periods of enforced rest occur between different employers. It gives the migrants an opportunity to recover their breath after the hectic exertion to which they have previously been driven. Their meagre reserves do not really allow them to spend too many days without work.

The settlement of wages takes place when the contracted work is finished. Naturally the farmer deducts from this the amount he has already paid the *mukadam* as earnest money, and the amount advanced to the gang on arrival for purchasing food. Travel expenses are reimbursed only if the gang had been contracted in advance. After a few days' work the deficit is already made up; nevertheless it is in the farmer's interest to withhold full payment at this point, for by doing so he tightens his grip on the migrant labourers. The labourers themselves often prefer not to take their earnings each day, for fear of theft. They make do with the amount they need for the purchase of their daily food, and for a few other expenses such as cigarettes and drink. If a team member goes home in between this time, he takes with him some of the savings of others who are kinfolk or who know him well. Most of the money stays in the farmer's safekeeping until the time of departure, and at that moment the migrants are entirely dependent on his good faith: they are given his calculation of what he still owes them and receive the balance. They have little choice but to be satisfied with it. On one occasion I saw how a group of migrants who considered that they had been cheated and who had the temerity to show that they were displeased about it, were thrown out of the village. It does not often pay to protest. Already vulnerable as temporary visitors in an alien environment, their illiteracy also hinders them from trying to correct the sometimes complicated reckoning on which the final total is based. Particularly when work is done according to piece work rates, the less scrupulous among the landowners are tempted to swindle their labourers. The fields occupy in reality more *bighas* than the labourers are paid for, and furthermore they receive even less than they expected according to the agreement. The members of a team easily lose sight of the total of their earnings, especially when members have carried out a diversity of work tasks over a number of days. Another possible way of cheating is to deduct more for the advance loan than the workers have actually received or have taken in the meantime.

Migrants who come with a *mukadam* seem at first sight to be less vulnerable. After all, it is his task to protect the team members against this kind of sharp practice. At paying-off time he can stand up to the landowner more easily because he is accustomed to this sort of situation—that is his special qualification—and it is in the farmer's interest not to earn too bad a name among these labour middlemen. But this representation of the situation already puts too much stress on the idea that the *mukadam* primarily serves the interests of his gang, without taking account of the fact that, at the same time, he is the landowner's trustee and operates as his agent. Pulled by these conflicting loyalties, the *mukadam* inclines towards conformity with the farmer's wishes, justifiably regarding him as the strongest party. An indication of how impossible it is for most gang leaders to behave autonomously is the fact that they are not paid separately for their services.

As I have already explained, there are different grades of *mukadam*. Only a few are so professional that they are occupied all year round with the recruitment and management of labour gangs, and only the fulltime agents charge a commission for acting as mediators and for supervising the work. The remaining *mukadams* heading smaller, more loosely knit teams also fulfill these functions but they work beside their gangs on the land. At best they are eligible for some preferential treatment—they are given tea, some cigarettes, now and then a meal—and at the end of their stay they receive a bonus as token of satisfaction. These smaller *mukadams* take a nominally equal share in the team's earnings, but payment is made through them, and all too frequently they appropriate an extra amount. The jobber also tries to pass the risks onto the labourers he recruits. For instance when a *mukadam* has received an advance sum for a greater number of labourers than he eventually brings along, the farmer includes the full sum in his reckoning, and the migrants are the losers. They are not paid for the full amount of work performed, and can only try to recover the loss from the gang leader. It often remains unclear to migrant labourers who has cheated them. Even if there is actually some question of collusion between the landowner and the *mukadam*, both are, naturally, inclined to accuse each other of dishonesty. It happens repeatedly that, upon completion of the job, dissension over wages and their division arises between farmer, gang leader and gang members in fluctuating coalitions, which do not exclude disagreement within the gang itself as well.

Nevertheless, if a good atmosphere is maintained to the end (which does not necessarily exclude cheating) it is the custom that the farmer will provide a festive meal before the departure of the gang at the end of a major job. This gesture is an expression of his satisfaction, but at the same time a way of demonstrating his interest in the group's return.

Daily life

The migrants lead a miserable existence. As we have seen in the preceding chapter, the frequent mobility to which they are compelled uproots them from the home locality, but they do not feel really at home in the working locality either. The temporary nature of their residence combined with their performance of the lowest paid, least status-conferring work, disqualifies them for integration as full members of the social order in Bardoli and neighbourhood. Migrants who, driven by economic need, move permanently to urban localities, are conspicuous. We know they arrive because we can actually see them, living in the slums. Compared with these, the proletariat circulating in the countryside is much less visible. Sometimes the only signs in the landscape of a gang of migrant labourers being present in the vicinity, are the small bundles hanging on a tree or one might meet them along the roads, walking in a line one behind the other, remarkable only for the *potalum*, belongings wrapped up in cloth or rags and carried on the head.

Naturally it is not altogether surprising that one only comes across these transients if they are travelling about the plain, but their marginality is also revealed in the way in which they live while in the plain. Many pass the nights in the fields outside the village centre; in particular, gangs working for only a short time in one place and then moving on again, do not even bother to set up a temporary camp. That term applies then only to the spot where each evening a number of people collect to prepare their food on a few fires and to sleep beside each other on the ground. In the mornings both they and their bivouac have disappeared.

However, there are migrants who set up quarters for a longer time, sometimes returning to the same place year after year. We can infer their presence from the obviously 'lived-in' state of the spot: a few improvised shelters offering some protection against rain or cold; some grass or straw for a more comfortable sleeping place; more possessions, including pots and pans; a regular place for preparation of food; a corner of the field used as a latrine. The landowners in the neighbourhood are familiar with these camping places and go there when they need labourers for a job. In the daytime there are always a few people present: an old woman, some small children, and some adults or adolescents on days when there is no work for them. I have recorded the following in my diary:

> I have repeatedly passed several days and nights in such a camp, to obtain an impression of the migrants' life style under these conditions. In an open field outside the village of P., five Kathiawadi families 'kept house': four married couples of differing ages with respectively four, one, three and three children, and one woman with two boys of around fifteen years. Only the members who could do little or no work any more stayed behind. They have to make ends meet with what reserves they have. Most of them have

been here often before; one woman is even here for the fifth year in succession. They are spending four or five months in this camp. Their main activity consists of digging field channels by order of the department of irrigation in this area. On arrival they reported to the local man who gives them work. He does not cheat them, but certainly cheats his superiors by declaring the shifting of more earth than they have in fact achieved. No, they do not share in this profit, but have to cover up for him at inspections; nothing is ever said about this, because they know that otherwise he would send them away. Earth shifting is paid by the brass; the men doing the actual digging while the children and women drag the earth away. A couple earns on average Rs 6 to 8 a day, but there is not enough work for the whole season, and they have to get work elsewhere. Nevertheless, when a new job is assigned by the department, they must be ready for it, immediately, even if at that moment they are busy with another job. Earth moving is heavy work and consequently they need good food. If there is work they eat twice a day, but when there is nothing to do they manage with one meal. During longer periods of unemployment there is sometimes absolutely nothing to eat, or else only the men and smallest children receive a piece of millet cake. The week before my stay, the group worked for only two days. Today the men are going off to look for work in the surrounding villages, and spirits are improving now that a farmer has sent for them to come for a few days' work. In exchange for the owner's permission to camp in this field, when they arrive they have to get rid of the stubble still lying in the ground, yet this agreement offers no effective security. A short time ago the village headman of P. gave them the job of repairing a country road at the *panchayat*'s expense. After three days' work he gave them only three rupees per head, without doubt noting a much higher amount in the books. When they protested, he threatened to make it impossible for them to stay longer. The farmer who owns a nearby well has forbidden them to make use of it, but they are still doing so in secret because the water in the adjoining field channel is unfit for drinking. It is badly polluted by agricultural chemicals, and the previous year, one of their children became seriously ill from it. For that matter, there are many complaints about bad health. It is already somewhat late in the season, in the middle of March, and the nights are no longer so cold as a few weeks ago. Apart from a few rags the migrants have absolutely no protection against the cold, and lying close to the smouldering fire only helps temporarily. Shivering and silent, the members of the group sit together, sometimes not even in a position to afford a cup of tea. At night I am bothered by mosquitos, like my camping partners, and

> I pull the sheet over my head, as is the custom. It was a discomfort that hardly disturbed me compared with the rainstorm, unexpected for the time of year, that once hit me in another camp. It was a particularly distressing experience because the migrant workers in fact wanted to keep me dry. They did this by placing a *khathelo* (a bed consisting of a wooden frame strung with rope) over me, and spreading old rags and cloths over it. Around me I heard the others getting wet, along with the few possessions they had.

Hard but badly paid work alternating with days of aimless hanging around, too little to eat and bad health, as well as all sorts of other lacks and deficiencies, characterize the life of every agricultural labourer in the vicinity of Bardoli, but the migrant labourers are exposed to the additional deprivation of living in the open fields.

The neglect of rural labourers, in research and policy, due to the migratory life that these people lead, also obscures our view of the life style accompanying such migration.[1]

Not all seasonal migrants camp in open fields outside the village. For reasons which will be considered more fully in a later chapter, an increasing number, particularly in recent years, have been seeking a lodging place in the village itself, mostly in the farmer's compound, or in the verandah against the house, and after that in the shadow of all kinds of public buildings—the verandah of a school, the porch of the village post office, the entrance to the water tower, beneath the covered bus stop, the overhanging roof of the temple, or a *dharmasala*—which offer any living space in which to sleep at night, and enable them to leave bundles behind in the day-time. Naturally, migrants never stay inside these public places, —always beside them or around them. Some larger landowners working with gangs of migrant labourers the whole year round have in various villages begun to set up separate sheds or

[1] It is exactly this lack of inside information that leads to bewilderingly superficial views, such as that in the following research report on seasonal workers from outside the area, who had set up their bivouac: '. . . under the shelter in the sky. They were enjoying open air and direct sunshine. This phenomenon is not very strange or unusual with farmworkers. They have to spend a large number of days and nights like that during the course of the year, particularly at the time of harvesting' (Khatti 1966: 95).

Such a distortion of reality can only arise if the researcher relies on information gathered from the landowners, and omits meeting with the migrants in their own surroundings.

to vacate old houses which provide lodging for about ten or twenty or even more people.

Especially in the busy months after Divali, there are too many migrants around in the village centre for them to remain unnoticed, but their status is definitely that of barely tolerated strangers, who have no right of access to any public facility whatsoever. They are needed for agricultural work and are, moreover, handy to have close to the house for all kinds of extra chores, but the village residents, including the landowners, regard them as a nuisance. Their behaviour must therefore be 'conspicuously inconspicuous'. To be there, but at the same time to keep out of the way—this is what others expect of them. In the open fields the migrants can lead their own lives, however unprotected—shut out, but at least together. There is no question of this in the village; the accommodation which they find there accentuates the incompleteness, the marginality of their existence to an extreme degree.

My notes run parallel with those of Bhatt, who has undertaken research on migrant labour in central Gujarat. I am borrowing from his report the following passage about their fate during several days of heavy rain:

> In the field their belongings were spoiled. Some of them tried to protect their luggage by covering it with grass. Those who had not gone to work and stayed in the open place near village school went under S.T. bus stand shed for shelter. As school was working they were not allowed to stay or even to keep their luggage in the verandah of the school. Only at night they were allowed to sleep in the school verandah. Most of those who were working in the field were brought back to their village in the tractor trailers by the farmers. A few of them were provided with the accommodation by the farmers. Others took shelter in the verandah of the market yard and under the ceilings of the shops at night. None of the two Dharmshalas was opened for the migrants during those three rainy days (Bhatt n.d.: 44).

The migrants' day begins very early, by five o'clock. The frugal breakfast consists of scraps of food left over from the previous day. Among the migrants staying in the village, some go to work immediately in the landowner's household. The preparation of food to be carried to the fields that day takes up a relatively large amount of time. Gangs coming to the plain for short trips bring their own grain from home: whenever a member returns to his village for a few days, he brings back a new supply of grain for himself, and sometimes for the others as well. Migrants staying in the plain for a longer time sometimes receive grain from the farmer as a portion of their wages, but usually they buy what they need in the village shops. Even weeks later they remember exactly what they had to pay—a great deal too much, to their minds. When they return to the place where they have been spending the night, by half past seven or eight o'clock, sometimes even later, the evening meal must first be prepared. The women especially are busy with this while the men rest. Those who stay close to the landowner's house perform quite a variety of small tasks for him in the early evening. In the village centres the migrants lead a retiring existence; they are spread around the various streets and buildings and do not stand out as a group. A freer atmosphere exists in the camps outside, and heavy drinking goes on there in the evenings, certainly among the tribal seasonal workers from the eastern part of the Surat District. As I established earlier, young people predominate among the migrant labourers. In this environment—strange for them—they can easily escape the social control to which they are subjected at home. Sexual contacts between the young men and women arouse tensions in and between the different groups finding themselves in proximity to each other, and coupled with drunkenness such tensions rather frequently degenerate into fights. These do not usually occur if one of the landowners is the instigator of the quarrel. Some of them have tribal concubines whom they maintain ostensibly as maids in the household. The whole village is nevertheless perfectly aware of the affair. There are many Kanbi landowners who have casual relations with women among the migrant labourers.

These observations all too easily create the impression that migrants form an undisciplined band, but such a conclusion would be an exaggeration; outside work they have little time left, and for the most part that also slips by in deadening routine, fatigue, insecurity and discomfort. When a *mukadam* heads a gang he also screens the members from the outside world. After all, he knows the area, he can find his way around, he is able to deal with outsiders, etc. Besides acting as contractor at home and foreman during the work in the plain, the *mukadam* also acts as camp boss. He makes sure that the daily schedule is adhered to, undertakes to purchase food and other necessities, and maintains order and harmony—but above all he functions as intermediary. His presence enables the landowners to remain at a distance from the labourers; possible complaints reach him first, and he is also answerable for their behaviour.

The inhabitants of the plain can perceive few or no differences between migrant labourers. For example, all those originating from the hinterland of Surat District are described collectively as Khandeshis, in spite of the fact that the term concerns the different tribal castes—notably Chaudharis and Vasavas—who moreover are very nearly all residents of Gujarat. The only thing they have in common is their status as migrant labourers, and this is not a sufficient basis on which to maintain contact with each other during their stay in the plain. In other words, the migrants lead very isolated lives even in relation to each other. Even within each gang cohesion is very weak—which is surprising, because in recruitment, proximity (habitation in the same *falia*) or kinship (membership of the same family) generally plays an important role. Most gangs, certainly the larger ones, nevertheless consist of a number of smaller nuclei which have relatively little to do with each other—not to the extent that working together is hampered, but certainly where further contact is concerned. The division into smaller units is most noticeable in the preparation and consumption of food, which is done separately according to kin groups. I have always taken the number of small fires burning in a camp as a useful way of learning the structure of a gang. The most frequent answer to my question as to whether it would not be easier to cook and eat communally, was that the needs of one were large while the needs of another were small, and this would cause disputes. The circle of equality and division is very narrow. Only once have I encountered a *mukadam*, migrating to the plain the whole year round, who took along two women to take care of meals for his team of nearly thirty members. He behaved as manager in other respects as well: in his own village (in Valod Taluka) he had a permanent stock of labourers who were bound to him by advance loans, and although he did not require all of them each time, they could not easily refuse if he called on them. For a number of them he had become the most important employer.

In comparision with his tight organization, the recruitment of most gangs of migrant labourers occurs in a very improvised manner. As I established earlier, departure is uncertain right up to the last moment, and the gangs which regularly go to and fro between the immediate hinterland and the plain, are characterized by a much greater fluctuation. With each trip of a few weeks the composition changes; there are usually some permanent members, but the remainder drop away, while still others take their place. The gangs which come from further away not only stay longer in the plain but also have a more stable structure. In their case the distance is too great to permit shorter visits home, and they maintain contact by exchanging letters, which are written by the teacher or some other local notable back in their own village, and read aloud by the landowner for whom they are working at that moment.

Migrant labourers are regarded as being extremely capricious. They are quite capable of walking out on a job without giving prior notice. According to the farmers at any rate, there is no clear motive for this unexpected departure—the migrants simply go away without anyone being able to stop them. This representation of affairs does not always correspond with the reality, for the capriciousness which marks migrants' behaviour is a reflection of the unregulated life they lead. They are badly informed about what is happening around them and often have no idea of what job they are to do the following day, how long it will last or what they will receive for it. The ignorance in which they live and are kept means that time is a factor they are not accustomed to managing in a controlled way. The impulsiveness in all this does not derive from an irrational mentality, as the landowners assume, but is bound up with the context of their work, i.e. it is caused by the migrants' inability to control the course of events even up to the following week. Next, tensions within the gang reaching a boiling point form another motive for a sudden break-up. I have already indicated the scant solidarity existing between the migrants of the same group. When a *mukadam* of authority and experience is lacking, all kinds of problems—not only over work and the payment for it—can arise between the different units comprising the gang, problems which in the end may render further association impossible; disintegration is surprising only to outsiders. The group returns home sooner or—less often—breaks up into smaller units which proceed independently.

Nevertheless, my impression is that the most important reason for premature departure is still the bad treatment which is the migrants' portion. When the employer does not abide by the agreement made, demands more work and pays less for it, there is little choice but to leave the village; this is particularly likely to happen to a gang without a *mukadam*, or with an inexperienced one. From fear of the farmer's anger and coercion, the departure takes place secretly, sometimes in the middle of the night. According to their employer the migrants do not even collect the balance of their wages—as if the farmers would pay it, even if the labourers asked for it! Landowners' complaints about the theft of tools, stores or household possessions by migrants appear upon enquiry to be made particularly under these circumstances; besides being an outlet for resentment, the complaints are also a way of trying to compensate themselves for the sudden loss of their servants.

Many landowners admit that they treat migrants with scant generosity. The latter are strangers in the region and those coming from the tribal eastern part of Surat District, especially, are less familiar with the strongly marked business-like character of the labour situation in Bardoli. The landowners themselves openly laugh at the naivety of these labourers. Nevertheless, upon longer contact with the migrants, it becomes clear that they are withdrawing from a situation which has become untenable for them. After all, they have come to the plain for the small amounts they can earn each day, and everything depends on that. In the last analysis, illiteracy and other traits of social immaturity make no difference to the feeling of whether or not one is being treated justly, or to knowing one's rights. There are scarcely any migrant labourers who cannot, from personal experience, give examples of unjust practices—of farmers who sent them away without any wages except for a little food, or those who start paying their workers only after a couple of days or a week, thereby prolonging their stay in the village needlessly without work. This kind of trickery and arbitrariness is, however, one of the risks of the migrants' existence. Through lack of any defence, there is little else to be done other than to make a new start based on the next employer's good faith. When this proves to be unfounded, they avoid that particular village in future.

The migrants are physically isolated and excluded from public facilities, but their exclusion goes much further. In social contacts they are ignored in a manner which smacks of systematic discrimination. The lack of hospitality is too striking to remain unnoticed by the migrants themselves, and it strikes them as all the more painful because their inequality in the home area is usually less pronounced. Moreover, many are cultivators themselves at home, while in the plain, dependent wage labour and the treatment accompanying it stigmatizes them as inferior in their own eyes. Under these circumstances it is not surprising that for the young people among the migrant labourers the glamour and excitement of being in a new environment quickly wears off. Certainly, they learn to be familiar with all kinds of modern facilities and comforts which are still lacking in their own territory, but they still have no share of these; on the contrary, they are denied access to them. Temporary residence in the plain is necessary but unpleasant, and this explains the tendency to put off the outward journey to the plain for as long as possible, and conversely to begin the return journey home as quickly as possible.

The duration of stay

Migrant labour cannot be reduced to a uniform pattern. In the foregoing sections I have distinguished between a number of variants:

a) harvest workers who come to the plain in large gangs under the leadership of a *mukadam*, mainly in the early winter months;
b) smaller teams which make relatively short but frequent sallies almost all year round;
c) comparatively loosely structured units which pass several months at a time in the area during the winter season,

either in one location or trekking around inside it;

d) semi-permanent residents.

A large number of factors other than distance influence the duration of stay, as for example the question of whether people who migrate are mainly of a younger age group, or whether they comprise more or less complete households of mobile people. In the case of the nearly or completely landless, the latter soon becomes inevitable. Still, it would be difficult to make more generalizations due to the element of uncertainty. Informants who, in the home area, assured me that they were on the point of departing, had still not left some considerable time later. Conversely, definite interviews which I had arranged with migrant labourers in the plain had to be cancelled because the migrants had disappeared unexpectedly and without trace.

When I began more systematically to collect data about these labourers coming from outside, it appeared that there were far more of them than I had originally suspected. Some of the newcomers have not been accepted into village society as full members but live, as it were, in the shadow of the farming activities with which they are linked. This makes them difficult to approach, particularly in the case of those living close to the farmers' houses—usually at the back, in the stable or the farm yard—whom I have seldom been able to meet freely. The proximity of the employer, and my position as guest in his household, precluded almost any casual contact. There was great success with those housed separately, nearly always in the pump house in one of the farmer's fields. Outside the village centre they also live inconspicuously, isolated from the other inhabitants, but at least free of the pressure under which they exist perpetually in the immediate vicinity of the landowner's household.

In the home area all these informants belong to households which are already landless, or which possess so little land that further partition between brothers is no longer feasible. Lack of employment opportunities at home, combined with low wage levels, were the principal motives for establishing themselves more definitely on the plain: as one of them put it, 'Here our children can at least be clothed and fed every day'. Many have already worked for five years or longer in the plain, sometimes still for the first employer whose path they crossed as harvest labourers.

Not all of those who are married have brought their families along. The claim to a tiny piece of land can be reason enough for a family separation continuing for year after year. The farmer usually has no objection to the rest of the family being present, because he can use all the members as labour.

> D. is a Vasava from Dhulia district, just over the border of Gujarat. He has been in the plain for six years already, the last two years in permanent service in this village. D.'s boss does not allow him to live in the pumphouse itself—besides the oil pump, there are some agricultural tools there—but D. has obtained permission to build a shelter up against it. From some stones and waste hides, plastic and old sacks he has made a home for himself and his wife and daughter. In the daytime he works on the land; before and after that he is busy in the farmer's house, and at night he is responsible for the irrigation, and guards the standing crops in the fields. When his wife has nothing to do in the farmer's household, she is given all kinds of other tasks to carry out. Together they earn Rs 150 a month Rs 90 and 60 respectively) for which they work every day. Their daughter of eleven or twelve years also helps a little in the household, cleaning pots and pans, etc., and receives only food for this. Naturally he knows that the minimum wage is Rs 5.50 but that is not given to anyone. He buys millet from his boss for Rs 30 a month. It is cheaper in the bazaar at Valod, but he then has to haul it and this is particularly difficult in the monsoon. For several days they have had a lodger: his brother's son, a boy of about ten years. He will be a cowherd for some other farmer in the village, and will then take up residence there.

It seems as if the landowners are increasingly choosing to entrust the more skilled tasks to these migrants, who drive a strikingly large proportion of the tractors which in recent years have become enormously popular in the villages round Bardoli. In village A. where I spent a month, of the total of 12 tractor drivers only 3 were local labourers and in M. only 5 out of 26. All the other drivers are new arrivals from the tribal hinterland, often trained by the farmers themselves or by their sons in the handling of these vehicles.

Semi-permanent is a somewhat metaphorical term for these intruders for an indefinite time. With a stay in the plain of longer than one or at the most two agrarian cycles, it becomes difficult to maintain that we are still dealing with migrants, but on the other hand they do not strike real roots in this new environment. The incomplete absorption of the outside labourers—certainly they are absorbed into the production process, but not into social life—is the sign of their marginality. Least of all do they feel 'at home'. Regularly, at least three or four times a year, they return to their home area, for visits which coincide with religious festivals or which are connected with important family events. In this way a regular migration channel is opened, along which come seasonal workers—summoned by the landowners—as well as more permanent labourers, sometimes really young ones. In village B. lying close to Valod, which was one of my research locations during earlier fieldwork in the region (Breman 1974, ch. 10), the farmers obtained almost all the local boy cowherds (*govalia*) through other adolescents of their own age group who came from the tribal hinterland.

Just as with seasonal workers, the number of farm servants coming from outside has also increased greatly over the past decade. This phenomenon has a clear connection with the cropping system, for wherever irrigation has been introduced rather late, there are still relatively few farm hands; on the other hand there are many scores of farm hands in the villages close to Bardoli. There, nearly every Patidar has at least one at work, while the larger households may even have several. Some larger landowners have decided to manage with these farm servants alone: for instance R. in the village A., has 15 of them in permanent service, all accommodated in a separate large shed. Even larger concentrations occur in other villages.

Tribals from the hinterland of Surat District are not the only outsiders who have come down into the plain as farm servants to the larger landowners. The Kanbi Patidars have been known from of old for their cattle keeping, as is appropriate to a peasant caste. The institution of the dairy co-operative SUMUL in Surat, has brought many of them there to buy more buffaloes. From a commercial point of view cattle rearing has become an attractive proposition, except that rather a large investment is necessary for this, and also the quality controls placed on milk production necessitate more specialized care of the animals. Several farmers who keep a fairly large stock of buffaloes (eight or more) have gone over to the employment of special cowmen, members of the cattle-keeping castes called

Rabari or Barwada, who originate from north Gujarat and Saurashtra.

> During my stay in A. I counted 12 of these cowmen for a total of c. 500 buffaloes in the village. The cowsheds are their working and sleeping place. Within this private domain they enjoy a great deal of independence as a rule. They are freed from other tasks in the field or in the household. As specialized workers they earn more than ordinary agricultural labourers: Rs 100 a month with keep.

Finally there is the labour coming from elsewhere for employment in the seasonal rural industries established in the plain. Those who are predominantly 'semi-permanent' are those who return anew every year to the cotton gins, brick kilns and stone quarries. At home they make their living in agriculture for some months of the year, as small cultivators or agricultural labourers, but after the rainy season they are engaged in industrial activities in the vicinity of Bardoli.

As I established earlier, this labour is likewise tied to distant reservoirs of recruitment. These channels—opened more or less accidentally—remain connected over a long span of years.

These annual migrants also lead an isolated existence while in the plain, finding or making shelters at their work site. The riverside camps of workers is the brick kilns and stone quarries especially, are difficult to reach. What should outsiders want there, anyway? Every week the labourers receive for their living expenses a sum far below the wages they earn. In this way they gradually build up a balance, with which the employers bind them until the end of the season.

What I want to demonstrate with these examples is that the distinct forms into which seasonal migration is split up are mutually exclusive. Between the different circuits there is little or no overlapping, i.e. the chance that those trekking temporarily to the plain for agricultural labour will come into contact with the equally seasonal labour force employed in the cotton gins or brick kilns is small enough, let alone the likelihood of changing over from one work sphere to the other. This marked fragmentation contributes to the impossibility of making an accurate survey of the phenomenon of migrant labour in quantitative terms, which contributes in turn to the underestimation of its extent and meaning.

Is seasonal migration a first step towards final settlement in the plain? I have given an affirmative answer to this question, for harvest workers who have stayed on as farm hands. Although not really absorbed into their new environment, at least they appear to have left their home area for an indefinite time.

To a much greater extent this can be said of those coming from outside but no longer having any home base to go back to. Usually the whole family is involved in the stay in the plain, which from the outset is meant to last longer than a season. In other words their departure is not temporary but permanent, and occurs in a manner which is reminiscent of expulsion.

> On the edge of Bardoli, on a piece of ground that the boys had been using as a cricket field, a score of huts have for several years been standing together in a slovenly huddle. For the most part these are inhabited by tribals from the hinterland of Surat District. I have talked extensively with 8 of them at least once. As reason for leaving, 6 named drastic events which made it impossible to continue their previous lives: the complete loss of possessions with the great flood of 1968, compulsory removal with the construction of the Ukhai reservoir, the death of the principal bread winner, a serious conflict within the household or family. They deny any familiarity with each others' affairs, maintain few or no links with the place of origin, and obtain their means of living with casual work. In contrast to the seasonal migrants they do not confine themselves to only one kind of work. Employers of very differing kinds know how to find them when necessary. It is not at all unusual to find that, on a given day within one household, the man is at work on the land in a neighbouring village, his wife is working as construction coolie in Bardoli town, and a son is riding as loader/unloader on a lorry. A week later this division of labour can be quite differently apportioned.

How have these newcomers won a permanent place for themselves? Not, by first shuttling back and forth as seasonal migrants for a number of years. Very nearly all have been forced by circumstances to make the final leap straight away, and have landed up in Bardoli more or less by accident, without having been in the plain before. Only one had spent a season here as cane cutter, but he denied any connection between that experience and his present stay.

The way back is closed for most of them, which certainly does not mean that their present living place becomes a new home. The future is too uncertain for that; for the huts stand on ground belonging to the municipality, which has already announced that a clearance will shortly be carried out. In the preceding months this has already happened elsewhere in the area where migrants live together semi-permanently—in an open field by Bardoli station, along the road to Surat.[2]

A further striking characteristic of such camps is the great variation among the inhabitants. Fluctuations in local employment opportunities, and the total labour capacity which the migrant household has at its disposal can tip the balance in this respect. Only a few have been able to begin a more regular life, finding permanent work, and in this way procuring admission to the social order around them. This applies for instance to the labourers who work in the paper factories, Khandeshis for the most part, and for the permanent personnel in the sugar factories, a large proportion of whom originate from Uttar Pradesh. The way in which the majority of the outsiders fit in is, however, of a temporary and volatile nature; these marginal households easily disintegrate, i.e. their members disperse in different directions—a mobility which shows a repetitive pattern. Since migrants are extra vulnerable in the event of sickness and other setbacks they cannot support themselves in the new environment and begin to drift again. A growing number of beggars go round the *bazars* of the larger places, or hang around bus or train stations in their attempts to survive. This is where circulation changes into pauperization.

> 30 March 1977: close to Bardoli station several beggars were sitting together under a tree. They were turned away from Unai and came here the day before yesterday. The company consists of a man with a completely putrified leg, his old mother who is senile, and a young blind man who has lost his previous guide, and tacked on to this pair several months ago. They are preparing a meal from refuse collected in the street and food leavings they have

[2] My fieldwork started in 1977 when the Emergency in India was still in force. Under the climate which then prevailed not only the urban poor but also the rural landless were regularly evicted from their homesteads. There is not much documentation on what happened to the underclasses in the countryside during this period. In Bardoli hutment colonies at the fringe of the town and along the highway to Surat were ruthlessly destroyed and migrants in particular were easy victims of these police operations.

begged. The man lived earlier in a village near Songadh, but lost his land there (it remains unclear why and to whom). For many years afterwards he worked here in the neighbourhood, in stone crushing, until an accident brought that to an end. He cannot return to his village. There is no one there to take care of him. He can manage well enough by begging, at least so long as he is able to move around.

Using the length of stay as yardstick, I have made a distinction in this last section between temporary and permanent migration to the central plain of Surat District. It appears that the last form of mobility does not necessarily result from the first.

Usually it has to do with the very different circuits along which labour comes flocking in. The great mass of migrants consists of agricultural labourers who only come temporarily, and who are expected to disappear again after the work ends. Those who are asked to stay on as farm servants are an exception to this. In the category of those coming to Bardoli and neighbourhood for an indefinite time, and who often cannot return again, only a small number have gained a really firm footing. The rest consist of transients staying in the area they have reached, or moving on again; they have left their familiar surroundings but never arrive anywhere definite. The present mode of production in this part of south Gujarat attracts a great deal of outside labour, but with no intention of keeping it on a permanent basis.

9

CHANGING PATTERNS OF EMPLOYMENT AND LABOUR RELATIONS

Transition to a new labour system

The large-scale presence of migrants in the plain indicates a fundamental change in the rural production system which has taken place in recent years. A relatively simple cropping scheme was replaced by a much more complex agrarian cycle after extension of the irrigated area. In the first instance the effect was an articulation of seasonal fluctuations in the employment pattern. According to a standard explanation, the available manpower fell short of requirements for work at harvest time and other peak periods, and it became necessary to attract temporary workers from outside. Once in existence, labour circulation gradually lost its seasonal character; many migrants stay in the area for a longer time, or return regularly, with the result that this imported labour has come to compose a substantial proportion of the labour force for much of the year. One could suggest that the increase in agrarian production has made it possible for migrants to extend the duration of their stay. To be sure, the greater intensity with which land is being worked at present has hastened the introduction of modern technology—motor pumps, tractors, sprayers, electric threshers—but this does not detract from the fact that the labour-intensive nature of the new agricultural cycle shows a significant net rise, compared with the earlier cropping system. In this way mechanization of production and modernization of cultivation methods have, generally speaking, influenced the nature of labour relations. Tractor driving, motor pump maintenance, the use of special work tools, the application of fertilizer and insecticide, more careful planting techniques, etc. require a certain skill. This means that work has become both more skilled and more specific.

However, the growth of new relations of production should not be ascribed only to the introduction of a much more intensive cropping scheme which, together with its accompanying technology, requires more agricultural labour and also places higher demands on that labour. In other words this transformation cannot be explained merely by drawing attention to the market orientation which has become supreme among producers. The manner in which the sale of an increasingly larger part of the harvest yield is organized, indicates a commercializing process in the agricultural economy which has had drastic consequences for relations between farmers and agricultural labourers. In many publications the changed attitude towards agricultural labour has been attributed to the effects of the Green Revolution. The importance of this strategy of change has been overestimated in the literature which emphasizes its negative effects. At best, one can talk of acceleration of a trend which had already begun much earlier. I have already indicated earlier the connection between the commercialization of agrarian production and the disintegration of the *hali* system in south Gujarat, and I even venture to suggest that the alteration in use of labour was not so much the consequence of the Green Revolution, but rather resulted in this. The process of social rationalization, which implies a more instrumental use of labour, took place over a period of many decades. This process facilitated the introduction of a new technology and modern farm management instead of being the end result of these innovative forces.

The transition to a new mode of agrarian production has led to a different pattern of employment which can only be partly explained by the difference in labour intensity between the earlier cropping scheme and that of today, and their division according to the agrarian calendar. The fact that the landowners free themselves and their families from manual work (particularly in the fields) whenever they are in a position to do so, also plays a part in establishing the total volume of work; a great many members of the dominant caste in the area have succeeded in fulfilling this new ideal. The need for the services of others cannot be quantified on the basis of mere farm management practices, but is partly dictated by the attitude towards agricultural labour. The revaluation which has come about in this respect—defining usage only in terms of a commodity has obvious consequences for the nature of the labour regime.

The total agrarian population is involved in the conversion to the new mode of production, but this process becomes most visible in the changed relations between big farmers on the one hand and agricultural labourers on the other. My research has been directed towards these two classes for reasons which I explained in chapter 3.

What is the nature of the relations between the local landless and the farmers? The first yardstick for assessing labour arrangements is the distinction between permanent farm servants and casual wage workers. Working conditions and other circumstances of employment will be considered in detail, through which it will become obvious that this distinction, based on the length of service, is in practice not so clear as it appears to be at first sight. I shall also pay attention to forms of labour such as work issued on contract, which enjoys a growing popularity. Although this chapter is devoted to agricultural labour, I shall touch on other sources of off-farm employment in a separate section. Subsistence for the great mass of landless can only be understood by taking non-agrarian sources of income into account, and the diversification which has arisen in the rural economy round Bardoli makes this theme more relevant than ever before. The interconnection between agrarian and non-agrarian employment opportunities—or lack of them—is also important for a good grasp of the way in which the regional labour market is structured.

To an increasing degree the government has interceded as a third party between farmers and labourers. The free play of market forces on which labour management has been based in the past, has given way to regulation aimed at improving the condition of the landless. I shall trace the course of this official intervention and its effects. Lastly I shall deal with the question to which recent government-commissioned research has also been directed, namely of whether certain forms of labour within (or outside) agriculture are in effect bonded labour. This question interests me less from the point of view of policy than from that of its importance to the discussion of the nature and dynamics of the rural mode of production, of which labour relations are a major indicator.

Farm servants

The disappearance of the *hali* system does not mean that the farmers do not keep permanent servants any more. The earlier trend towards replacement of attached workers by free labourers has not advanced further in recent decades, and the number of farm servants has probably even somewhat increased in proportion; I estimate that some 20–25 per cent of the total number of agricultural workers in Bardoli and its environs maintain a regular service relationship with one employer.[1] I shall elaborate further on this point later.

The need for one or more permanent labourers begins at the level of the middle farmers, i.e. those with holdings of 5 acres and above—a need dictated in the first place by the character of irrigation farming. In a farm of this size the diversity of the cropping system, involving intensity as much as continuity, renders it necessary to have the labour of others more or less permanently at their disposal. As I mentioned earlier, the new agrarian technology places higher demands on the skills of agricultural labour. Close supervision by the farmer does not detract from the fact that the use and maintenance of the new work tools, the greater care in working the soil which is a precondition for improved seed varieties, and the application of inputs such as fertilizers, not only at exactly the right moment but in exactly the right amounts, cannot possibly be left to casual labourers. Finally, the withdrawal of the farmer's labour power and that of his household, forces him to take on permanent labourers who, under supervision, carry out a wide variety of tasks both on the land and in the house. Certainly as far as members of the dominant caste are concerned, it is not exceptional for larger landowners to keep four or more servants. With regard to the farmers in village A, where I spent a full month in 1978, Patel had already established in 1961/62

[1] This figure, together with my estimates on the income per day and per year, are based on fieldwork data which I collected between 1978 and 1980.

that 'Working on farms is considered an "inferior activity". Women of these households, in particular, take very little interest in farming, and they look upon themselves as merely managers of the farms' (Patel 1964: 101). This trend has strengthened even more since then, resulting in an increased need for outside labour. Labourers in permanent service are also expected to be capable, in the busy season, of mobilizing the labour power of their family members for their master.

What is the present-day nature of this service bond, and how does it originate? As described in chapter 5, servitude was previously the end result of an enduring relationship which had already begun many years earlier, when the son of a *hali* went to work as cowherd for a landowner, usually his father's master. When he was somewhat older he then became a *chakar*, the name for a farm servant who worked for the farmer on the land and in the house. For this round-the-clock work he received a yearly payment as well as board and lodging; the farm servant took a little of this money now and then, for small outlays and for weathering unexpected difficulties. The remainder formed a balance which—supplemented by an advance loan from his master—enabled him to marry around his eighteenth year. Some time after that he tried to set up his own household, after which his master ceased to demand all his servant's time. From then on he was, as *hali*, primarily occupied with agricultural work, and could in any case return to his own hut at night.

The most fundamental difference between the earlier and the present situations, is that being a farm servant no longer involves a life-long commitment. Besides the fact that the service bond does not carry over from one generation to the next, means that there are only a few farm servants who began work as cowherds with the same landowners for whom they are working at present. Once established, the relationship can be much more easily broken after some time, on the initiative of one or both sides. It is characteristic of the unequal relationship that the farmer is able to put an abrupt end to the service bond, turning the farm servant away without notice, while the latter does not usually risk giving formal notice but, by absenting himself often and for an increasing number of days, lets it be known that he does not place much value on further employment with that farmer.

A difference still exists between the *chakar* who works in and around the house and the real field labourer in permanent service. The first forms a small minority—at the most, 5 per cent of all agricultural labourers—and the *chakars*' status still approximates most closely to that of the earlier *halis*. They are mostly young men and bachelors; those who spend the night in the farmer's house are on call at all times, the others coming early in the morning (between 5 and 6 o'clock) and staying until late evening (8 or 9 o'clock). With a markedly vague notion of time, one informant whom I questioned about this, said "I leave home when it is still not yet morning and I come back only when night has already fallen". The master (who is indeed still described as *dhaniyamo* by many of his servants) provides the *chakar* with his daily requirements, sometimes a set of clothes and shoes, and above that an annual sum of Rs 200–350, according to local standards, which is usually taken in small amounts at intervals. There is always something for the *chakar* to do, and in principle he therefore works every day. Expressed in cash, his total yearly income usually amounts, in my estimation, to no more than Rs 600–750. Although we cannot deny the possibility of a strong personal attachment in the relationship—as already observed, the *chakars* are house servants at the same time—the turnover among them seems to be high. Only a few remain bound to the same farmer's household for years on end. There appears to be no question of a fixed occupational career. *Chakars* do not seek permanent service more noticeably often than do other landless labourers. At the same time ex-*chakars* are not exactly under-represented among those making a living as day labourers or seeking work outside agriculture. On the other hand, the sons of casual labourers show a definite inclination to avoid beginning their working lives as farm servants. Nevertheless this is sometimes unavoidable because a period as *chakars* gives the landless one of their few opportunities of accumulating enough money (or—hopefully—of obtaining enough credit from the farmer) to be able to marry.

Involved in a much looser arrangement are those agricultural labourers who as a rule work for the same farmer, but who nevertheless manage to behave in a much more independent manner. These permanent labourers, called *kaim majur* or *rojio*, constitute 15–20 per cent of all agricultural labourers, and the differences between their situation and that of the *halis* of the past are much greater than the similarities. In the first place it is no longer taken for granted that they put in an appearance every day; they regularly stay away from work for one or more days at a time, without advance warning of their absence and of the reasons for it, naturally to the discontent of the farmers, who see this as confirmation of their subordinates' laziness and untrustworthiness. However, this behaviour is only apparently irrational as it is hardly sensible to request permission for absence beforehand when there is a good chance that the farmer will refuse it, if only to demonstrate his authority. Moreover the farmers, with their complaints about what they term wayward and irresponsible behaviour, find it convenient to gloss over the fact that they themselves no longer feel obliged to give continuous work to these permanent labourers. On days when there happens to be little to do, they send one or more farm servants away again, as soon as these turn up early in the morning. This means that even permanent agricultural labourers must from necessity maintain different work contacts in order to gain a measure of security. The strategy forced upon them can only lead to conflicting claims on their labour output; they try as far as possible to give satisfaction in this respect, but this 'trimming' always inevitably results in discontent on their principal employers' part.

The pattern is all the more complicated because the farmer, knowing that not all of his labourers turn up every morning, takes on more farm servants than he needs every day. He can do this easily because the risk attached to holding this reserve falls on the permanent labourers themselves, according to the simple principle 'no work, no wages'. As one employer explained to me, the farmer must certainly ensure a reasonable distribution of available work among his farm servants; if they remain too often or too long deprived of daily-paid jobs, then the disadvantages of the permanent-service relationship—in which the farmer has prior claim to his subordinate's labour—weigh too heavily on the agricultural labourers. It is in the employer's further interest to retain a labour reserve so that he can mobilize extra labour in the busy season, and members of the farm servant's household are likewise expected to make themselves available when the farmer needs them.

From the foregoing it is abundantly clear that the relationship is subject to constant strain from both sides, and it is thus not surprising that there is a high labour turnover among farm servants. This in turn is the reason why most farmers refuse credit to their permanent labourers, and herein lies a second important divergence from the *hali* system. Earlier, an agricultural labourer undertook to work for a farmer for an indefinite time, in exchange for an advance loan of several hundred rupees which he usually needed to defray the cost of his marriage. This source of finance has virtually dried up, resulting in enforced economies in the wedding ceremony and following feast, and the expenditure connected with a wedding can now only be financed through sale of a goat or other capital asset, supplemented by support from members of the household or family.

The farmers' unwillingness to accommodate their subordinates any longer in these matters has acquired extra impetus from the promulgation of the Debt Relief Act as one of the issues in the Twenty Point Programme in force during the Emergency period. According to this legal provision, not only did farmers lose the money they had advanced to their agricultural labourers, but in future it would be a punishable offence to extend a loan with the intention of demanding labour in return. In other respects one should not exaggerate the effects of this law; at most, it provides farmers with another justification for their negative feelings. They are apt to pay little attention to legal sanctions in any case. What deters them more is the knowledge that the labourers could not possibly repay their debts. The farmers scornfully reject requests for larger advances, demanding to know how their suppliants intend to repay them. One farmer who, a year before, had nevertheless helped his farm servant with wedding money, told me that he had brought in the police to give the man a thrashing in order to 'persuade' him not to leave his service. When I retraced this course of events, which took place in the village E, it became clear that the man's refusal to work resulted from the lowering of his daily wage from Rs 3 to 2, by way of enforcing the discharge of his debt. Certainly most permanent labourers still now and then receive consumption loans called *khavati*—literally, 'in order to eat'; they try to wheedle this in small amounts from their bosses on days when there is no work for them. Although it is given halfheartedly and stingily, it is still difficult for the farmers to refuse to give in to what they consider to be a constant harassment. Moreover, the farmers ensure a low price for the services of their subordinates in future. Actually, it is a form of advance wage payment, with the added advantage that there is no need to pay out more the moment there is a labour shortage. The pressure on labourers in permanent service to supplement the continuous deficit in their means of subsistence thus robs them of the profit they would otherwise gain from peak periods; there are seldom any extras left over for them. The extent of these consumption loans is in any case limited, involving an average of less than a hundred rupees. If the debt rises too high—which indeed seldom happens—then the farm servant's wages fall so short on working days that the idea of looking for another boss becomes attractive. Conversely, if the farmer gives too little, then in the same way he forces his subordinate to seek his fortune elsewhere. The labourer absents himself increasingly often, first in order to work as a casual labourer for a while, and subsequently to enter into a service contract with a new employer going through the same cycle again. The farmers unanimously emphasize their farm servants' lack of loyalty, but I am convinced however that the high turnover among these permanent labourers is not the cause but the consequence of the employers' refusal to supplement their subordinates' deficient subsistence means through loans and advances on wages, as in the past.

While debt held the *halis* in a state of dependence, present-day farm servants complain that they have lost their credit-worthiness. There is no one willing to help them; their ability to run up debts has diminished, while they have still not gained more autonomy. The material conditions for this are only partly satisfied. There is improvement to a limited extent in housing conditions. Increasingly farm servants live on land of their own, away from the shadow of their employer. Hutment colonies have arisen on the fringes of the villages where all Halpatis—farm servants, day-wage earners and other labourers—live together. This has resulted in the concentration of the landless in separate localities away from the farmers.

As described above, the working hours of labourers in permanent service are shorter than those of *chakars*, but longer than those of day-wage workers. They begin work between 7 and 8 o'clock in the morning and work through until after 6 o'clock in the evening, with a break of one to two hours in the afternoon. There are a number of variations on this rule, which are usually dictated by the season. For instance, in the hot season the working day is shorter: from 6 o'clock in the morning until half past one in the afternoon, with no rest. On the other hand, work during harvesting continues for a longer period of time while the rest period is shorter. Labourers report at the farmers' houses and perform all kinds of small jobs before leaving for the fields and on returning from them. It is not altogether unusual for farm servants to be assigned tasks in the evenings as well: guarding standing crops in fields, irrigating land, tending the motor pump, etc. Apart from such exceptions, present-day farm servants are distinguished from the earlier *halis* by the beginnings of standardization in working hours, and increasing specificity in labour performance.

With respect to both working hours and labour performance, the farmer can no longer freely dictate his permanent labourers' time and manner of working. The notion has gradually developed that work can occupy only a limited part of the day, and it is the farmers themselves who have stimulated this attitude in their drive towards a stricter discipline. Take, for example, the installation of a siren, wailing to signal the beginning of the work day; elsewhere labourers use other time signals such as the sound of a school bell, the whistle of a passing train, the arrival of a bus, etc. Certainly, farm servants are still busy in and around the farm, but they try as far as possible to avoid household chores. The most trusted labourer among them—not necessarily the one with the longest service record—has a rather higher position, putting the work tools in order, obtaining instructions for the division of the daily work, performing the most responsible work himself. He also acts as spokesman for the others and, after sometime, supervises the work of day labourers. As reward for his role as foreman and confidential agent, he can depend on somewhat kinder and more generous treatment from the farmer—without, however, the relationship attaining the intimacy and cordiality assumed to have characterized the *hali* system. Contractuality above all, on both sides!

Finally we come to the payment of labour, in which I shall distinguish between the composition of the wage and its size. While earlier generations of farm servants were already being paid a large part of their basic allowance in cash, this is even more so for present-day agricultural labourers in permanent service. This trend is not manifest to the same extent among all categories of labourers. Even now it is still the custom, especially in rather more remote villages, to provide *chakars* with a set of clothing, a shawl, etc., each year in addition to board and (sometimes) lodging, but those involved in a looser service arrangement have been deprived of this kind of emolument for some decades already. Only here and there do permanent labourers receive their daily basic allowance in the form of a grain ration (2.50 *seers* of millet). The situation which Patel encountered at the beginning of the sixties also applied to most of the other villages in the plain: 'Only casual labourers are paid preponderantly in cash. Perquisites constitute the main form of payment in the case of attached labourers. It is remarkable that payment in kind was not in vogue in a predominantly agricultural village like Afawa. Cash was paid to *attached* labourers only on special occasions such as marriages, births and deaths' (Patel 1964: 112). When Patel began his research, the Halpatis had just moved to their own village quarter. With their expulsion from the farmers' lands, those employed on a permanent basis found that they were no longer given bonuses above their daily wage, such as a small piece of arable land, the yield of which they were permitted to keep for themselves (*vavla*) or thatching material for the hut roof once a year. The present-day farm servants can no longer rely on obtaining assistance in times of sickness or other kinds of setback. The custom of tipping them at religious festival times with food and a little money has not completely disappeared, it is true, but the masters—according to their labourers—are not particularly openhanded even on these occasions. It is no longer taken for granted that firewood may be gathered from the farmer's land, although he finds no difficulty in providing gangs of seasonal migrants with such fuel.

The farmers are also no longer interested in what is literally called 'sharecropping of cattle'. Under this system a farm servant was entrusted with the temporary care of a buffalo cow in calf. The *hali*'s wife and children were permitted to cut grass in the owner's fields, for fodder, and after several years the young animal was returned to the farmer, at which time the *hali* was given, as compensation, half the beast's value as estimated by the farmer. Now that milk production is commercialized the farmers are interested in improving the quality, to the cost of the agricultural labourers, who are not in a position to provide appropriate feeding and stalling. Only a few still keep a cow or buffalo, and because of the opposition they encounter they often have to cut grass for the beast clandestinely, even along the public ways. Nothing has replaced all those extras which previously made attachment economically worthwhile.

Finally we come to the size of the money wage, which at the time of my fieldwork at the end of the seventies was most commonly Rs 3 a day. This was not however a standard amount applicable throughout the year and in every place. Slightly more was paid in villages where agriculture was most highly modernized and/or where conflict had arisen between farmers and labourers with the introduction of the minimum wage legislation. Sometimes more was paid only temporarily—for harvest tasks for example; as soon as the pressure was relaxed the wage dropped back again to its old level. These variations were present even within the same village. Exceptions to this were in the special cases of the few farmers who, under the influence of Gandhian ideas of social justice, adhered to the official minimum wage of Rs 5.50 a day against the pressures of their social environment. I can establish downward variations also, particularly in the somewhat backward villages. Here, as a consequence of the limited extent of the irrigated area, agriculture was still not practiced intensively, and no more than Rs 2 a day used to be paid. It was characteristic of the more traditional labour relations that the farm servants received a midday meal in addition to the money wage; in many villages where Rs 3 was paid, this was no longer the case, or still held good only on very busy days. Several farmers who I asked about this defended the refusal to provide a meal with the argument that the labourers, incited by Gandhian workers, were no longer willing to accept food—an incorrect presentation of affairs, because they tended to ignore the request for a rise in the money wage in place of the meal. The current situation is unclear. Many farmers no longer give their permanent labourers any meals while others still do so, but not every day. The same applies to smaller emoluments, which in practice are bonuses the farmer can give or withhold at his pleasure. The labourer who does some odd jobs before starting work in the mornings or after returning from the fields in the evenings, is paid with a cup of tea or a few *bidis* (country cigarettes). They are no longer standard constituents of a daily livelihood. Even taking these extras into account, wages for the majority do not rise above Rs 3.50 for a working day, i.e. two-thirds of the amount fixed by the government as the minimum. With a somewhat generous calculation based on the fact that, when there is no work for permanent labourers, they manage to obtain employment elsewhere for a number of the workless days, we arrive at an annual average income of Rs 850–1000 per annum for this category of agricultural labourer.

Finally I shall briefly discuss two other forms of a sustained master/servant relationship—those involving the maidservant working in the farmer's household, and the cowherd.

From my data it appears that roughly a quarter of all women from the landless caste still work as farmers' maidservants. The *vasiduvali*—literally, she-who-clears-out-the-stable-muck—was usually engaged in earlier days by the same patron for whom her husband worked as farm servant. As I established in chapter 5, the *halipratha* was a household arrangement, not restricted only to the persons of master and farm servant but one which also bound the wife and children of the *hali* in a set of rights and obligations. This system has definitely come to an end. It is no longer taken for granted (although it does happen) that the wife of a permanent labourer works as maidservant for the same farmer as her husband. Just as in other labour contracts, this service bond has become more impersonal and business-like. Finding employment in another household is more than ever before unconnected with the relations which the men—husbands, fathers, brothers or sons—maintain with their employers.

The number of farmers using the services of one or more maidservants has probably risen during recent decades. There is a connection here with the trend among members of the dominant caste to withdraw their own labour as far as possible. Where the women are concerned this is not confined to the cessation of agricultural work; they also try to free themselves from all kinds of household tasks, with a resulting increase in the distance between them and the women agricultural labourers. The latter no longer work with, but for, the farmers' wives—a change in position that finds expression in complaints about the arrogance and idleness of the mistress, and the bad treatment she hands out. The maidservant's most frequent tasks are cleaning out the byre, washing clothes, fetching water, cleaning eating utensils, and sometimes helping in the kitchen and sweeping the house. The working hours vary—depending on the number of cattle and the size of the household—from a couple of hours in the morning to a full day's work. This results in the variation of the wages, at the most, Rs 10 a month. In one village this rate was reduced from Rs 4 to Rs 3 after the water supply was laid on several years ago, 'because the maids' work has become much easier now.' The *vasiduvalis* who work for longer than a few hours in the morning also receive a meal over and above the money wage; they usually take the meal home with them. All sorts of other emoluments to which they were formerly entitled—such as a *sari* once a year—are now seldom or never given. Especially missed is the free *chhas* previously left over from the milk churning—an ingredient for the preparation of rice gruel (*rab*) and as such a welcome supplement to the meagre diet. Now that the milk goes to the factory much less *chhas* is made in the village, and what the farmers themselves do not use they sell to the agricultural labourers for 4 annas a potful. Early in the morning, women and children go from house to house asking if there is any *chhas* left over that day—often in vain.

With the increasingly contractual nature of the labour relationship, the maidservant has not only 'lost out' in terms of real wages. Previously she enjoyed the total protection of the patron and could occasionally lay claim to credit which in practice formed a bonus on her fixed remuneration. Now there is no longer any question of this either and a farm maidservant's income, reckoned on an annual basis, seldom amounts to more than Rs 200–300.

There are two types of cowherd (*govalia*). In some villages they are men, too old or disabled to be able to do a full day's work, who collect cattle every morning from several farmers, and graze them, at a rate of Re 1 to Rs 2 a month per head. Other farmers prefer to employ young boys between 8 and 12 years, whose help is at the same time used in and around the house. They are out of doors all day, and the youngest sometimes receive only board and lodging; those who are somewhat older get in addition a small amount of money, Rs 3 to Rs 5 a month. If they do not spend the night at the farm, they carry their evening meal to the parental home. When an agricultural labourer's household consists of a farm servant, a maidservant and a cowherd, they often do not share their food, each one eating the food brought home that day—a habit which evokes amusement, rather than compassion, among the farmers. It is however an unjust stereotype, because the youngest members of the family receive a portion of the food brought home by the older ones.

The annual earnings of the children who also work do not exceed Rs 200–250; the financial contribution of cowherds to their households is thus negligible. More important is the fact that, in bearing the cost of their own subsistence, they put no pressure on the household budget, and are independent in early life, as they still are in old age. After a few years the boys may become *chakar* but most boys try to avoid this type of attachment, which imposes too many limits on their personal freedom.

Casual labourers

Upwards of three-quarters of the agricultural labourers in the central plain are *chhuta majur*, i.e. they have no permanent employers. Other investigations carried out at approximately the same time in this area indicate a somewhat higher proportion still. Shah reckoned, on the basis of a survey of twenty-seven villages, that the ratio between casual and permanent labourers' households amounted to 84:16 (Shah 1978:10). Desai, in an investigation conducted some years earlier and limited to Bardoli and Palsana Talukas, also found a somewhat lower percentage of farm servants than I encountered in 1977/78 (Desai 1974: 3–4). Even retaining the higher figure, it must nevertheless be obvious that the proportion of day-wage earners has undergone a sharp increase during the previous decades, and this in itself is a clear indication of the transition to a labour system in which contractual, short-term relationships predominate. In view of the pronounced capitalist nature of the agricultural economy, it is hardly surprising that farmers tend to economize on labour. It is particularly attractive in a situation of abundantly available labour to engage labourers on a day-to-day basis.

Casual labourers differ in a number of respects from those involved in permanent service, but these differences are more relative than absolute. As we have already observed, the *rojio*—also paid by the day—do not work continually for the same farmer, while conversely casual labourers do not change employers every day. They work mainly for a restricted number of farmers who sometimes secure their labour in advance by providing them, or other members of their households, with small loans (*khavati*). The farmers compete with one another for available labcur through this sort of mechanism, not through payment of a higher wage. The casual labourers, in other words, are not always completely free to sell their services to the highest bidder; at the most favourable times for them—the months of greatest work pressure—some of them have no opportunity of obtaining the maximal price for their labour for these reasons. In the relatively quiet periods which still mark the agrarian cycle in spite of increasing intensity in the cropping system, they are the first to become redundant.

A relatively small landowner with 5 acres of irrigated land on which he cultivates mainly bananas, sugarcane and rice, told me that he keeps no permanent labourers but calls fairly regularly upon the services of two casual labourers. He expects them to come when he needs them, and even perhaps to free themselves from other obligations. In order to add force to his claim on them, he is prepared to furnish an advance loan from time to time. As anticipated, he showed bitterness over the labourers' lack of 'loyalty'; on the other hand, the latter hope to obtain regular work, even in the quiet time or—when this fails to materialize—at least some credit, with which the farmer is scarcely openhanded. The needs of both parties are thus incompatible, which places extra pressure on their already scarcely harmonious relationship.

There are only a few differences in the actual working conditions of the farm servant and the casual labourer. For the latter the usual working hours, outside the seasonal peaks—the days of greatest heat and the heaviest rainfall—are from 8 o'clock in the morning until 6 o'clock in the evening. If he starts work later, then the afternoon break is shorter. Employer and employee begin their relationship with the idea of an eight-hour working day, but there are mutual complaints that neither keeps to this; on the one hand that the employer makes excessive demands and, on the other, that the labourer achieves too little. The farmers who have reduced their own efforts to supervising the work of others believe that agricultural labourers should be hard at work from sunrise to sunset, and every hour in which they do not work is regarded as loafing by the farmers—hence their irritation. The notion is gradually growing, especially among day-wage labourers, that work can be tied to fixed hours and that outside these hours they are free to spend their time as they choose.

As far as the kind of work is concerned, there is also little difference except that the casual labourers avoid the extra little jobs performed by the farm servant in and around the farmer's house. It follows from this that the casual labourers work for a somewhat shorter time. One cannot determine from the nature of agricultural work itself whether it is being performed by casual or permanent labour. Even the farmer's attitude offers too few clues to this. To be sure, the farmer has less control over those he hires from day to day, but even from these he will tolerate only obedience and submissiveness, and permits no questioning of his own superiority.

There is little difference between the wages paid to farm servants and casual labourers. Keeping in mind the reservation made earlier, the latter profit slightly more from the labour shortage arising in the busiest work periods; instead of the customary Rs 3 they can count on a somewhat higher amount, Rs 3.50–4 per working day. Under exceptional circumstances this can even rise to the official minimum of Rs 5.50, but I hasten to add that this only applies for a short period or to a limited number of villages—that is, those in which the new irrigated crops occupy the largest portion of arable land; where labourers have wrested a higher wage from farmers after promulgation of the minimum wage law (I shall return to this in more detail); or where non-agricultural work is available to any extent. On the other hand the casual labourer does not obtain the extra emoluments still given to some farm servants precisely because they work longer hours and perform all sorts of small tasks. Only on days when work loads are particularly heavy are casual labourers also provided with a meal, which is eaten in the field at noon. The farmer no longer eats together with his employees, and eats different food, not prepared by the maidservant. Some labourers save a part of their meal to take home with them at the end of the day.

There is no connection between the burden of work and payment for it. This is according to the principle that it is not the actual performance which is the yardstick but the most minimal subsistence requirements of those who perform. According to this line of thinking women are supposed to have even fewer needs, i.e. they are able to survive on less than what a male worker requires. For instance, for the extremely strenuous weeding of rice fields during the monsoon, where a day more or less is of no consequence and labour is available in abundance, female workers receive the lowest current wage—even though they must stand bent over in water all day, with the rain falling in torrents. Indeed I found fairly consistently that women just as much as boys of up to seventeen years of age, earn a half to one rupee less, although the work they do is otherwise comparable with and sometimes even more strenuous than that performed by men. Only when there is a labour shortage do these differences disappear.

What has struck me is that wage settlement has taken on the character, not so much of a business transaction, as that of the granting of a favour. Payment usually takes place at the end of the work day. On returning from the land, the labourers hang around the farmyard for a while, and it is very common for the farmer to make them wait for sometime before coming outside. Depending on his mood, he passes either surly or jovial remarks, but even these often sound contemptuous. The kind of language used by the dominant farmers is particularly coarse and offensive, not least towards women labourers. The farmer deducts money given for loans without any explanation. When he does not have sufficient small cash (coins and rupee notes) available, he tells the labourers that he will settle the balance on the following evening—one of the many ways in which he is able to pressure them into staying to work for him. The act of payment itself possesses something of the nature of a ritual, over which the farmer takes his time, because it is a moment in which he demonstrates his power, handing over the money piece by piece to each labourer while the others look on with subdued excitment. When women as well as men from one household are present, the men invariably take charge of the women's wages along with their own.

Some forms of labour which were not prevalent (or which were less prevalent) in earlier times, have recently arisen in what is essentially the contracting out of agricultural work. This is usually done through the *mukadam*, who has already been discussed. The figure of the labour middleman is not confined to the employment of seasonal migrants alone; jobbers now operating in several villages originate from the ranks of marginal landowners or even of the landless, and it is the larger farmers who put out work on contract (*udhad*). A price is agreed in advance for a particular job—harvesting a crop, digging or making embankments, clearing roots from a plot of ground where bananas have been grown, planting sugarcane, constructing or repairing access roads and field channels, etc. The *mukadam* recruits his own labour gang and can increase or reduce its size at need, according to the nature of the assignment. Without exception he works only with casual labourers; among these are 'core' members—women as well as men—who the *mukadam* uses regularly, and who can obtain a small advance from him now and then. The area in which these labour gangs operate covers several villages, but through recommendations the jobber spreads his net for employers even outside his own *taluka*, from which follows labour migration into the region as a whole.

This extension in scale of agricultural work is typical of the open character which the rural economy has begun to assume. Still, the contracting-out of work is no more a completely new phenomenon than is migrant labour. According to one informant, some tasks—cutting grass, picking cotton—began to be carried out by piece work in his grandfather's time, and Patel, in his study of agricultural labour in the village Afwȧ in the years 1961–2, also mentioned the same practice (Patel 1964: 108). Everyone whom I questioned about this explained however, that this *udhad* system had gained greatly in popularity particularly in recent years.[2] Its application is greatest in villages with new irrigated crops—a clear indication that this labour practice is connected with the transition to a more capitalist mode of production.

Farmers prefer to use *udhad* when a great deal of work must be accomplished within a short time, i.e. when the tempo is faster than that paid for by a daily wage. Another factor tipping the balance in favour of contract work is that farmers can dodge the minimum wage legislation which stipulates payment on a daily basis in this way. The disadvantage they especially emphasize is that carelessness—with its resulting lower harvest yield or other loss of quality in labour output—is the price paid for the haste in which contract work is carried out. Their complaints are directed especially at local labour gangs, who work less hard and with less dedication than seasonal migrants and who also—according to the farmers—break the agreements made, by demanding a higher rate halfway through the job.

This does not alter the fact that the *udhad* system is till spreading. Neither party is guided exclusively by economic motives; social considerations also pay an important role, because farmers and labourers safeguard themselves against direct and personal interference from each other. The social climate is such that for farmers, the daily confrontation with the agricultural labourers is a trying experience. There is no need for them to engage in personal supervision of the required labourers, to maintain contact with them during the course of the work, or to pay them in person after completion of the work. By delegating these tasks to a middleman, the farmers can

[2] This was not so easy as the following quotation, referring to the same village, illustrates:

> At the time of our survey in the neighbouring village Isroli, one of the cultivators employed a group of Halpatis to finish the harvesting of paddy within short time. For doing the work expeditiously the Halpatis were to get some extra emoluments in the form of food and also some financial contribution for purchasing utensils for the use of their caste panchayat. The other cultivators opposed this move as this action was interpreted to encourage militant tendencies among the Halpatis. The matter went to such a critical point that other cultivators of the village threatened to beat the cultivator giving liberal conditions of work to the Halpatis. But the Halpatis of this liberal employer came together in a group and protected him from the wrath of his fellow cultivators (R. M. Patel 1966: 64).

withdraw from a situation in which they feel increasingly uncomfortable. Conversely, in this way the labourers are freed from the daily pressures inflicted by bosses who seldom express satisfaction, but always find reasons for complaints. The jobbers keep different working hours and also their control over the labourers is of a different nature to that of the farmers.

> Chhotubhai, about forty years old, is *mukadam* in village D (Valod Taluka). He began his working life as cowherd in the service of the largest farmer in the village, now a powerful man in the sugar factory situated close by. Ch. served loyally as a farm servant for many years. He enjoyed his master's trust and ultimately acted as a kind of foreman by regulating the agricultural work and supervising the other labourers. After a quarrel eight years ago he himself brought the service bond to an end. Because he was well-known and—as he put it—'knew how to take work', other farmers gave him assignments. So he established himself as *mukadam*. At first he was only asked now and then to undertake small jobs, and he worked for the rest of the year as a day labourer. But for several years now he has concentrated entirely on his jobber's activities. He commands a labour gang of 20 to 30 members, of which about a third consists of women, and two-thirds of men. Sometimes he has to extend his gang and split it up, in order to carry out jobs in two different places. He now goes to other *talukas*, usually for agricultural labour, but also digging and road work outside the busy period. His income varies daily between Rs 10 and Rs 30, but indeed it can also happen that he has no assignment for weeks at a time. He has learned to write his name and can reckon up to 3,000 in his head. He ascribes his success to the fact that he has always worked himself, and is not too lazy to lend a hand even now. Acceptance of a contract is risky. You have to know how much time a particular job requires and now and then to be able to make the best of a bad bargain. He has seen other *mukadams* trip up because they did not know how to calculate the exact charge for labour, could not earn or keep the farmers' trust, did not pay correct wages to the labourers punctually, were not able to maintain the right labour tempo, and so on.

The jobber cannot take the liberty of behaving towards his labourers as the master does towards his farm servants. In general the relation is much less hierarchical and is pronouncedly contractual, but the role of the *mukadam* is nevertheless still clearly in the process of development. In various villages I have met gangs numbering 6 to 9 members, in which no one acts as an acknowledged leader; at most, one can talk of a *primus inter pares* who maintains contact with the farmers and negotiates the assignments. Not everyone possesses the qualities necessary for this. The person concerned usually works alongside his labourers and receives no separate payment for his role as representative, although it can happen that the farmer slips him something extra. Furthermore these gangs have a very fluid composition, and function mainly in the busy periods, only to split up again after that. A number of other forms exist between this loosely structured and temporary group formation and the more institutionalized gangs headed by a fulltime *mukadam*.

The annual income of the *chhuta majur* is extremely difficult to establish. As already observed, they obtain a somewhat higher daily wage than the permanent labourers, especially in the busy seasons, but in contrast to this they are unemployed both more often and for longer periods at a time. From various agro-economic studies it appears that, while farm servants are kept busy the whole year round, casual labourers find work on only 200 days.[3] While this estimate is in agreement with my own findings and with other publications,[4] I am nevertheless of the opinion that the seasonal variation in employment opportunities really also applies to labourers in permanent service: earlier I indicated that the farmers do not feel obliged to keep the *rojio* working uninterruptedly, and in quiet periods they are all too often laid off. The difference between permanent and casual labourers in the number of days worked is therefore smaller than is usually assumed.

In my opinion there is insufficient empirical foundation for the often-heard assumption that among agricultural labourers, the farm servants—who in spite of a consistently low daily

[3] On the basis of a survey among 2,694 households of agricultural labourers Shah calculated that casual labourers (*chhuta majur*) worked for 186 days per year and attached labourers (*rojio*) for 351 days per year. In my opinion, the latter figure is too high. See also MWAC 1966: 40.

[4] Bardhan takes for granted all to easily that 'there is obviously little seasonal variation in the case of permanent labourers' (Bardhan 1977: 1108).

wage, still attain a higher annual income—are the better-off. This assumption too often stems from the protection which permanent service offered at an earlier time, but which no longer exists. On the basis of my own research material concerning agricultural labour in the plain of south Gujarat, I have acquired a more nuanced image. The landless—especially the younger and more vigorous ones—perceive a chance of securing a better living as day labourers inside and outside agriculture than as permanent agricultural labourers. They do not believe in the dubious advantages offered by a more permanent relationship and are inclined to permit the accompanying disadvantages of greater servitude to weigh more heavily. They try to make maximum use of the wage rises attached to different tasks in different seasons, and as far as possible avoid the advance sale of their labour. The risks they run drives them to greater occupational flexibility. For the labourers themselves the need to seek out work in regularly changing locations, instead of waiting at home for work to come to them, provides the attraction of a greater freedom and mobility. For some, agricultural labour provides a first step upwards—a final escape from attachment to a single farmstead. In conversations it is very clear that they disapprove of, or even feel contempt for the miserable existence led, in their view, by farm servants—particularly *chakars*.

In contrast to this category of casual labourers, who give the impression of being more articulate, there are those who do not possess enough courage, strength, skills or contacts to launch into independent labour. They are unable to cope with the uncertain freedom of the real day-labourer's existence, and it is not only personal qualities which play a role in this but factors such as the constitution of the household—i.e. the relationship between working and non-working members, setbacks such as long-lasting sickness, the existence and accessibility of non-agrarian employment opportunities, and so on. In unfavourable situations the preference goes to a more permanent service bond with one farmer, in an attempt to increase security. The worst-off in this respect are the agricultural labourers who, because of physical inadequacy, old age or other deficiencies, are not eligible for permanent service. While I would place the income of their more successful 'companions in adversity' at Rs 1,000–1,200 a year, earned in approximately 200 to 225 working days, most *chhuta majur* who lag behind attain at most two-thirds of this at Rs 600–700 —i.e. considerably more and respectively less than the average earnings of farm servants.

I would like to emphasize once again that these categories of labour do not form separate segments. Besides the fact that different types of labour are represented in one household, personal status is also liable to change: *chakars* may become casual labourers after some time, and entry into permanent service can sometimes be attractive, if the opportunity presents itself. On the other hand, *rojio*, on days when their bosses have no work for them, try to scrape up a living elsewhere as day labourers. These changes contribute to the income differences at the household level. The amounts mentioned above closely resemble the income pattern which Naik found in his investigations among 104 agricultural labourers' households in Navsari Taluka during 1977–8. Out of an average of 5.05 members per household, 3.10 were wage earners who together obtained an income as presented in table 8.1.

Table 9.1 *Annual income of agricultural labourers' households in Navsari Taluka, 1977–8.*

Annual income in Rupees	Member of household	Percentage
801–1400	15	14.42
1400–2000	37	35.56
2001–2400	21	20.18
2401–3000	16	15.29
3001–3600	7	6.73
3601 and above	8	7.69

Source: K. V. Naik, *Wage structure and economic condition of agricultural labourers in Navsari Taluka*. Surat 1979: 127.

The average monthly income of a household was not quite Rs. 200, which amounted to hardly Rs 2–3 per working member per day.

Employment opportunities outside agriculture

This study deals with labour relations in agriculture, but in order to understand rural dynamics I cannot limit my enquiry to this sector alone. Rural labour in the central plain of south Gujarat has become rather less agrarian in recent decades, a fact which is still inadequately brought out in socio-economic investigations and official censuses. The diversification of economic production which I indicated in chapter 2 has consequences for the overall labour regime. The size and composition of non-agrarian employment requires a separate study. I have not been able to collect data for this in a really systematic way during my fieldwork in the Bardoli area. It is possible, however, to appreciate its increasing significance. To what extent do the local landless manage to obtain entry to employment outside agriculture, and in what way do labour conditions in the agrarian and non-agrarian sectors influence each other?

What strikes one most immediately is that members of the agricultural labourer caste have so far captured only a few secure work positions in the new industries and activities which have arisen in the area. Although precise figures are lacking, it does not take much effort to establish that Halpatis are markedly under-represented in what are termed formal sector establishments. One seldom or never encounters them among the permanent personnel in the agro-industries (sugar and paper factories) and other industrial enterprises (textile factories, metal workshops). They lack the training for work positions demanding a higher technical skill; in so far as these are not appropriated by the dominant caste, only members of artisan and other intermediate castes are found eligible. In paper factories unskilled labour is paid Rs 120 a month for an eight-hour working day, and women Rs 100 a month. There is great competition for this type of factory employment, which does not pay high wages but certainly offers a secure income and standardized working conditions. Halpatis are few in number right down to the bottom levels of modern industry.

About two-thirds of factory employees in the area around Bardoli are imported from elsewhere, for the most part from

Khandesh in Maharashtra. When I questioned the owners or managers of these relatively large undertakings about the reasons for this, their answers could all be reduced to the idea that members of the local landless caste were not suitable for incorporation into an industrial production process. I was continually told about the laziness, drunkenness, lack of regularity, ignorance, and apathy which made Halpatis undesirable as labourers; thus preference is given to labourers coming from outside.

To a certain extent an exception to this rule is found in the employment of Halpati boys as diamond polishers in the small workshops which have opened in the villages surrounding Bardoli. Apart from members of several artisan castes (Soni, Mistry) the owners of these are principally Leva Patidars, who themselves had previously learned their professional skills as diamond workers in the cities of Surat and Navsari, where Vaniyas (the Palanpuri Jains) govern the trade. The arrival of this industry in the countryside followed on the heels of the enormous expansion in the diamond industry of south Gujarat which took place during the 1970s. A number of people who were polishers at that time cashed in on this expansion, buying some work benches (*ghanti*) with credit provided by a merchant or by the owner of the firm for which they worked, and setting up on their own. They returned to their villages, which already had electricity by this time, and installed themselves in empty houses or in sheds specially built for the work. Production capacity climbed so rapidly in this period that a great shortage of workers arose. Another reason has been even of greater importance. Since the introduction of the diamond industry in this region, wages have not been raised at all, with the consequence that the members of higher castes have gradually lost interest in becoming polishers. The workforce nowadays consists mainly of boys belonging to 'backward communities' for whom the wage offered, stagnant as it has been, still means an enormous leap forward. Even Halpatis are now considered for training in the profession, their entry being linked in most cases to payment of a lump sum for training in the business. The owner of the workshop charges Rs 500 for an apprenticeship of six months, during which time the apprentice is moreover obliged to provide for his own subsistence, and such a financial condition is far beyond the means of most landless households. Under another scheme the training is free, and the student also receives his board, lodging and a little pocket money, in exchange for which he pledges himself to work for the workshop owner without wages for two years after his training. On completion of this period, the polisher then has the right to a bonus, which depends upon the employer's satisfaction with his performance. As a result, in many villages scores of Halpati youths have now found work in diamond workshops run by young Patidar owners or managers, and the most fanciful stories circulate about their handsome earnings—an exaggeration which must be understood against the background of the miserable existence led by the overwhelming majority of agricultural labourers.

The diamond polishers work on piece rates, the tariff depending on the degree of difficulty in the polishing process. According to my data, they make on average Rs 10–15 a working day which usually lasts longer than eight hours, but on the other hand only a few owners obtain enough business to keep their work benches occupied the whole month through. Whenever they fail to secure enough assignments, work comes to a halt for days on end, and thus a polisher's monthly income in these rural workshops seldom amounts to more than Rs 300–350—still always a very respectable sum in an agricultural labourers' milieu. Compared with the majority of this generation who have remained farm servants or day labourers, the diamond polishers have really 'made it', and a different social behaviour results from the prestige derived from their work. In addition to higher incomes they have time for leisure, they dress in trousers and shirts, visit tea stalls and go to the cinema in the city. However, they feel rather insecure in this new status. The verdict returned on them remains outspokenly unfavourable—a condemnation clearly linked with the general negative image of the landless caste held by others. In contrast to members of artisan castes, Halpatis are not recognized as good polishers, and among workshop owners, Patidars in particular complain about their slovenliness and lack of diligence and work discipline.

The diamond industry is extremely sensitive to market fluctuations and shortly before my second period of fieldwork a recession started which continued into the beginning of the

1980s. The industry in rural areas, established later, suffered even more from this than did those in the city of Surat. A large number of village workshops were closed or remained idle for a long period. As one would expect, the Halpatis—who had penetrated into this new branch of industry at a relatively late stage—were among the first to be laid off. I was unable to pursue the repercussions of this, but I think it is unlikely that a workforce with this background will return cheerfully to agricultural labour. On the other hand, it does not look as though Halpatis will meet with any more success in gaining admittance to the so-called formal sector of non-agrarian industry. Even if we take into account the employment offered by the small diamond workshops in the countryside, we must still query whether Halpatis have captured a firm place for themselves in these. They are even more rarely encountered in other sectors of private industry that show less startling growth, and this also applies, to a somewhat lesser degree, to the public sector. In the less isolated villages especially, I have frequently met Halpatis who, in one way or another, were in permanent government service: a railway line worker, a watchman or peon in a government office, a field labourer in a state farm, and the like. One should keep in mind that this is only a small minority who are viewed jealously by the majority of their caste fellows because of the privileges they enjoy such as a fixed income, regular work and labour protection. Moreover, Halpatis disappear all too quickly from the scene as soon as the work becomes even slightly more skilled or better paid.

A second reservoir of non-agrarian employment lies in seasonal industries processing raw materials from the area itself.

In Bardoli town two cotton gins were still operating at the time of my fieldwork. One of these—called Patidar Gin—has historic associations, as the *satyagraha* of 1928 was planned there. In that period Gandhi, Sardar Patel and other leaders of the nationalist movement were frequent guests, and after independence great national leaders, from Nehru to Morarji Desai, were also welcomed. The two cotton gins combined employ 100 labourers, both men and women, the majority of whom belong to tribal castes—including Halpatis—originating from villages in the hinterland. For the duration of the season—a period of three to four months—they live in sheds on the factory grounds. When the pressure of work is great there is a switch to working in shifts. The daily wage amounts to Rs 4.50 and Rs 5 for an eight-hour working day. At the end of each week the labourers receive an advance (*khavati*) of Rs 10–15, after which the full settlement follows once a month.

A roof-tile factory close to Bardoli employs 80 labourers and operates for about seven months in the year, from Divali to the end of May. In spite of the unskilled nature of the work, all the labourers come from outside the area—principally from Songadh, Vyara and Dhangs. The labourers who return every year were already contracted during the monsoon, with an advance of Rs 200–300. The daily wage ranges from Rs 3.75 to Rs 6 per day, according to the type of work, and a bonus of 8 per cent is added to this at the end of the season. Each labourer draws a weekly allowance of Rs 15–20; the remainder is paid out every fortnight. Halpatis also used to work here previously, but the owner has replaced them with Khandeshis in the last few years, because he was dissatisfied with the quality of the Halpatis' work.

Along the river upstream from Valod lie several stone quarries. Some Halpatis working there are paid by piece rates (per brass, a measure of quantity) and they earn approximately Rs 7 per day. However an air compressor is necessary for making holes in the rocks, and they often have to wait days on end for this—earning nothing of course, while they wait. Each week they receive Rs 10 per person from the boss as *khavati*, but even this advance is paid irregularly. Halpati women work as loaders and unloaders on the lorries taking the stones away, making around eight runs a day with a group of six. For each run they get Rs 8 altogether, but here again we find that there is no work on some days. In two of the three quarries which I visited it turned out that the labourers come from outside. The advantage in this, so the licensee told me, is that the labourers are always on the site and can thus start and finish the work whenever he wants them to do so. He binds these outside labourers with an advance loan, given during the monsoon, and runs an account for them with a shopkeeper in the village, from whom they can buy their daily necessities.

Finally we come to the brickfields, which lie along the river just outside Bardoli, and which between them offer work to approximately 700 workers in the dry season. The work teams which make the bricks—the *patala* consisting of nine members each—all come from elsewhere, and are either Halpatis from the Valsad district or belong to tribal castes from Khandesh. They are contracted in the monsoon by a *mukadam* on the owner's commission, against payment of an advance to the head of the team, the *patavala*, who is responsible for the composition of his work gang. Each team makes between 2,500 and 3,000 bricks a day, and for this earns Rs 17 per 1,000 bricks; a team member's daily earnings varies between Rs 4 and Rs 5.50. Most work is carried out at night and in the morning, from midnight to 9 a.m. or from 4 a.m. to midday. The preparatory work for the following night—the mixing and kneading of the clay—which takes several hours, is done in the afternoon, after which the gangs go to sleep. Only the labourers who carry head loads of dried bricks to the oven (*bhata*) or who unload bricks from the oven onto lorries, come from the surrounding villages. They are usually Halpati girls who earn Rs 2.50–3 for every 1,000 bricks transported, which works out at a daily wage of about Rs 4 for this heavy and filthy work. When I asked the owners of these brickfields why outside labour was employed, I was told that the local landless were neither fit nor willing to work in the brickfields.

It appears from this survey that Halpatis are only considered for marginal employment in seasonal industries. Even where they have gained entry to it, there is clearly an inclination to replace them by outside labour, secured in advance by credit for the duration of the season. Further, although the wages in these rural industries are somewhat higher than those paid in agriculture, the differences are not very great. Those who do obtain employment are unable to detach themselves from agrarian life. Outside the season they remain confined to this, most of them as small landowners or agricultural labourers in another area.

Finally there are a wide variety of loosely structured activities which cannot be brought under one common denominator. We must count among these all kinds of half-skilled craftsmen, mainly self-employed and seeking their clientele among members of the lower social classes, who expect little in the way of technical perfection but who also pay less for the work done. These bricklayers, tailors, carpenters, etc. have picked up their trade skills by practical experience, or have been able to follow a short occupational training course through a social welfare organization such as the *Halpati Seva Sangh*. Their daily earnings reach Rs 10, but these are very dependent on assignments which are obtained only irregularly. I also include in the same category a number of semi-skilled or unskilled activities in the transport and service sphere, which yield less: tinker, station porter, bicycle repairer under a lean-to shelter somewhere along the road, vendor of snacks and soft drinks by the bus station. Also included are wage-dependents in small establishments: garage hand, shop assistant, tea-stall boy, and—the best paid of all—lorry driver. I have the impression that many Halpatis—comparatively speaking—are engaged in this rich variety of occupations, which form for those involved the only—or in any case the chief—source of their subsistence. In principle they are so engaged the whole year round, although in these occupations the rainy months are particularly difficult to live through. However, the term 'alternative employment opportunities' is especially applicable since these work activities are not as a rule combined with agricultural labour in the service of others. Even though their economic condition is far from satisfactory, at least they have escaped the even poorer existence of agricultural labourers.

This does not apply to the landless who are busy for much of the year on the farmers' lands, and only occasionally perform other work (but, as far as they are concerned, as often as possible!). The income obtained from this additional employment plays a particularly important role in the lives of casual labourers, to a degree which is a good indication of the diversification in the rural economy. This is accompanied by increased spatial mobility, by means of which young labourers in particular are engaged within a limited time period in a wide variety of jobs outside their own villages, although certainly in the close vicinity, as navvies laying roads or canals, as builders' mates or hod-carriers in construction work, as loaders and unloaders riding with lorries, and the like.

The work is irregular, is not tied to fixed hours, and is generally paid on a piece-rate basis; thus the amount received, for instance, by a gang of 'van boys' at the end of the day, depends on the number of runs made. This means that the labourers themselves shoulder the risks attached to the work—bad luck on the road, delays in loading and unloading, and so on.

It is difficult to determine the importance of these kinds of irregular jobs and the annual incomes obtained from them; for this it would be necessary to make a closer examination of the division of time and the composition of budgets than I have been able to achieve. Certainly these additional sources of support shed some light on a large category of Halpatis who remain committed to agricultural labour but who find insufficient employment within it.

For the rest, not all members of this landless caste succeed in gaining entry to these side lines; success in this depends upon a variety of particular circumstances. In the first place, the location of the village is important since, with too great a distance, the non-agrarian industry located for the most part in or close to the urban centres, or along the main roads, becomes inaccessible. Given the low wages, bridging the distance by bus is often too costly, and only those who have found secure work outside the village can afford bicycles. In Bardoli's *bazar* Rs 5 a day is paid for casual work, but the journey is not an economic proposition for those living further than walking distance from the *bazar*. A further role is played by the control exercised by the farmers over the activities of the landless. Where the Halpatis live less directly in the shadow of the Kanbi Patidars, the occupational differentiation among them is greater. Both these factors can be illustrated from my experiences in village A. When Patel undertook his research here in 1961–2, agricultural labour was the only, or principal, source of subsistence for 142 out of a total of 166 Halpati households. The 15 per cent, more or less, who were not dependent on agricultural labour—already a high percentage for that time—has slightly increased since then. Although during my short stay I made no survey of my own, it seemed to me very early on that in 1977–8 a relatively greater number of households had found their way to outside employment. The nearness of Bardoli has certainly made this easier since, at a distance of only 5 km, this town is accessible to the landless travelling on foot. For the same reason the sideline income of households of genuine agricultural labourers, which amounted to less than 10 per cent in 1961–2, have in my estimation risen to between 15 per cent and 20 per cent. This figure is certainly not representative of the situation in which the landless of the south Gujarat plain find themselves. In the absence of more aggregated data, I can only draw attention to research conducted by Desai in 1969–70 among 40 agricultural labourer households in Bardoli and Palsana Talukas. The results showed that, for male agricultural labourers at that time, non-agrarian activities formed 4.50 per cent of their daily work—an almost negligible proportion. (Desai 1974: 4). But even where—as in village A—a partial escape to the outside world has become possible, a repetitive theme in the conversations I had in the agricultural labourers' quarters was the days-long, sometimes weeks-long enforced idleness for men and women. The peaks and troughs of activity both in and out of agriculture are inclined to coincide, which means that lack of work in the village is never sufficiently counter-balanced by demand for labour outside it. Work outside the village reduces the pressure on available employment in agriculture, but not really much more than that.

The Halpatis' room for manoeuvre, and also their mobility, appears to increase when they can command something like a space of their own, dwelling (in a literal sense) outside the domain of the Kanbi Patidars. There was a striking contrast between the agricultural labourers in village A itself, and their caste fellows in the nearby settlement of K. Although even in this hamlet, which falls under the jurisdiction of A's *panchayat*, a large proportion of the arable land has in the course of time fallen into the hands of Patidar farmers, some Halpatis still have land here which they cultivate themselves. Besides this, a noticeably large number regularly work as bricklayers or carpenters in the neighbourhood at large, the income from this work being sufficient to permit them more independent behaviour, particularly in avoiding subordination to the Kanbi Patidars as agricultural labourers. They also maintain a social distance by avoiding the real centre of the village, where—according to them—there is no reason for them to go. The life style of this minority among the Halpatis reminds one of the more detached existence of other tribal castes in the central plain—Chaudharis, Gamits—for whom social progress has not yet been frustrated by an almost total subjection to the dominant caste in the area.

Lastly, there are the incomes obtained by Halpatis within the village itself but outside agricultural labour. To begin with, some households rear one or several goats, or perhaps a cow or a buffalo. The buffalo usually belongs to a farmer who has stabled the beast with a farm servant for some years in return for a maintenance grant—a practice which has become very rare, as I have already shown. The agricultural labourers do not have the facilities for cattle keeping, and only in exceptional cases is there any chance of building a separate shelter, so that cattle must usually be cared for in the already overcrowded hut. Moreover the farmers oppose the practice in several ways, for instance by refusing permission to cut grass for fodder, even along the public road. Sumul, the dairy co-operative in the district, encourages cattle keeping, but agricultural labourers are very seldom considered eligible for the various premiums and credit facilities provided.[5] Even the few Halpatis who dare to put themselves forward for membership are all too often refused admittance by the farmers who decide matters in the local branch of the co-operative.

In recent years, keeping chickens has become a lucrative business. Egg production is directed towards urban markets—Surat and Bombay—but the Kanbi Patidars have taken over this field also, as owners of the poultry farms with several thousand birds which have been established in several villages. Gandhian organizations are attempting to find a way of entering this chicken-breeding business for the tribal castes, on a commercial basis but on a more modest scale. Pithawala, a social worker in Palsana Taluka, persuaded Halpatis in a number of villages to set up chicken businesses on a co-operative basis, to the grave displeasure of the local farmers: over and

[5] In a study on three villages in the Surat district B. D. Desai observed that of a total of 358 landless households only 8 were members of the local co-operative society. One of the conditions for getting a loan from the society is to own a piece of land that can be mortgaged or to find a guarantor who owns land. This has resulted in keeping out a large section from this activity (1979: 15).

over again the chicken runs belonging to the landless went up in flames. Ultimately Pithawala himself was murdered in accordance with the very simple rule that those who set out to protect the labourers' economic rights invite the violence of those who regard themselves as the labourers' natural superiors.

The distilling or marketing of country alcohol is an illegal but very profitable source of income. From the proceeds, a form of hush money (*haphta*) must be handed over to the police, but for the Halpatis occupied in this business—often not agricultural labourers, but for the small shopkeepers in their neighbourhoods, for instance—quite enough remains over to provide a living. Besides members of their own caste, the customers also include the farmers who cannot always afford the 'English' liquor available in Bardoli—many Kanbi Patidars are heavy drinkers.

In drawing up the balance of alternative and supplementary employment opportunities, I have reached the following conclusions. To begin with, only a small number of members of the largest landless caste have succeeded as yet in capturing places for themselves in secure, skilled and protected employment in the expanding rural economy. Apart from lack of education they are also handicapped by lack of support and help on the way upwards, and they often meet direct opposition in their efforts to escape the agricultural labourers' life. The small vanguard who have succeeded in liberating themselves, keep their distance from the rest through a clearly different life style, living in better huts, having access to more consumption goods, and believing more in education for their children. They are successful in the eyes of the great majority left behind, but—stigmatized by their caste background—this group is more tolerated than respected in their new milieu. A far greater number are occupied alternately in agriculture and outside it, but also have to compete in the non-agrarian sphere with outside labour, to whom employers continue to give steady preference. As skilled labourers, they operate continually in the margins of rural industry and services, being drawn in according to temporary requirements, and subsequently being ejected again. The flexibility forced upon them gives an important impulse to the economic dynamic without the labourers themselves deriving very much profit from it, let alone lasting profit.

As far as labour earnings are concerned, rather than exerting an upward pressure on agricultural labour wages, these latter instead have a depressive effect on the composition of wages in the sphere of off-farm employment. In the report of the official commission which was assigned to calculate the minimum wages for agricultural labour in Gujarat, this factor was formulated as follows:

> . . . our assumption of the existence of an organised sector in agriculture in the form of the seed multiplication centres, demonstration farms, co-operative farms and even large organised individual farmers tending to give a lead in wage formation in agriculture seems not to have been confirmed. Similarly the public sector activities in the rural areas as giving a boost to the wage levels through the rates paid by them for non-farm work also seems to have not been confirmed. Instead of leading in wage fixation, they only follow the prevalent wage rates to decide on the payment to labourers whom they employ (Report MWAC 1966: 81).

Of more general application is the fact that, instead of acting as a positive model for labour relations within agriculture, non-agrarian employment is instead conditioned, in a negative sense, by the sweating of agricultural labour.

Regulation of working conditions

The restructuring of agrarian employment and labour relations does not derive solely from the demands of a modern agricultural economy; the change which has taken place in the whole social climate possesses its own autonomous importance. The idea has gradually grown that the government, acting in the common interest, has special responsibilities towards the weaker classes in the community, and is obliged to foster their interests. In the colonial past this attitude inspired a few half-hearted attempts to abolish the *hali* system—without much effect, as I have already described. After independence the central government took the initiative in providing a legal basis for the protection of agricultural labourers by establishing minimum wages. Little came of this in the first decade as a result of the unwillingness of most of the states to convert recommendations into concrete legislation. Apart from bureaucratic indifference, which was rooted in an urban bias, part of the blame must be attributed to the way in which more importance was given to the interests of the rural propertied classes (not yet strongly organized at this early point in time). The subjugation and social isolation in which the agricultural labourers live hindered them from taking collective action, and even the Gandhian movement, which remained the only one to be drawn by their situation, created no pressure for official intervention in the rural labour regime. Self-regulation in social life is basic to Gandhian ideology; the need for a direct and harmonious dialogue between concerned parties, which must produce a satisfactory compromise, and which the government invigilates from the background. In what was then the State of Bombay, of which Gujarat formed a part until 1956, the implementation of the minimum wage law, dating from 1948, came to little or nothing.

As more became known about the perpetually wretched condition of agricultural labourers—there was even reason for believing that, in some senses, a further deterioration had occurred[6]—interference on the part of officialdom became inevitable (although reluctant). In Gujarat a committee was set up in 1964 with the assignment of developing proposals for the introduction of minimum wages in agriculture. The spirit informing the report when it appeared two years later can best be conveyed by reproducing the passage in which the commission pressed the need for this regulation:

> The implication of a lack of policy for agrarian labour to the political and social stability would be easily appreciated. The developments in Asia and Africa are an eye-opener. The working class in general and the agrarian labour in particular in our country has retained their moorings to our basic philosophy of life and living. They might have grown restless and frustrated now and again, but by and large they have shown great patience in the otherwise discouraging situation around them. This is extremely healthy for the country and for all its citizens. This, however, should not make us complacent. It should be treated as a favourable factor to do something quickly to improve the lot of those on whose faces we

[6] For further elaboration see Breman 1974.

> read signs of discontent and disparagement. The forces of extremism are waiting to take over the situation once these indications intensify a little. Therefore, before developments suddenly take a turn and overwhelm us we should proceed to do our part of the duty. All concerned with the problem should wholeheartedly and enthusiastically join in this task to change the situation and to move towards a generally acceptable society and socio-economic relations (Report MWAC 1966: 78–9).

The committee allowed itself to be guided more by fear of social revolution than by genuine pressures arising from the objective necessity for effecting improvements in humanly degrading labour conditions. This attitude characterized the manner in which the panel set to work, coloured their analysis of the situation from the start, and excluded recommendations amounting to more than just marginal improvements.

One of the committee's findings was that fertile arable land and a relatively developed agriculture did not automatically result in high wages. The report attributed this phenomenon to the superabundant supply of agricultural labour from among the low castes, in combination with the socio-political dominance of supervisory farmers. With an average wage of Rs 1–1.25 (even less for women) the agricultural labourers in Bardoli and Palsana *talukas*, among other places, were found to be worse paid than in most other parts of Gujarat. The report recorded the disappearance of *halipratha* in south Gujarat and connected this with the farmers' reluctance to bind farm servants by means of advance loans on the occasion of their marriages. The committee adhered to the current opinion that what still remained of this system of bonded labour stemmed from the economically 'irrational' behaviour of the labourers.

> It is good that the system is dying. Whatever is left of it is due to ignorance of the Dubla and his apathy to search for an alternative. Maybe the alternative(s) themselves do not exist. In some measure the inertia and stiffened social sinews and the habit of indolent, indisciplined and disorganized village life to which the *hali* is accustomed inhibits a switch-over either in the same occupation elsewhere or in towns and cities in non-agricultural work (Report MWAC 1966: 48).

In this view a major obstacle to accomplishment of the desired changes was the deplorable work morality of the labourers themselves—thus the report reflected the farmers' constantly reiterated complaints about the agricultural labourers' failure to work hard enough and long enough; according to this viewpoint, improvement in work conditions could only be brought about when labour performance improved.

What were the concrete proposals? First and foremost that institution of a minimum wage should not negatively affect agrarian output, the level and profitability of which must remain intact. A further increase in productivity was considered to be of utmost importance. For this reason the committee dismissed the suggestion, presumably made by a Gandhian social worker in the panel, that the starting point for estimating a minimum wage should be the amount needed by an agricultural labourer for the basic necessities of life. The reasoning in the report was that this fell outside the scope of government action; only through the realization of a broadly based welfare programme—in which education, housing, rationing of food and clothing, and the creation of additional sources of income should take priority—would it be possible to raise the rural poor indirectly to a level of existence according with human dignity. Where the actual structure of wages was concerned, the committee investigated the rates current in the different zones of Gujarat in order subsequently (and in a very arbitrary manner) to push these up to a somewhat higher level—slowly and with moderation, because (according to the report) a too-hasty bridging of the growing discrepancy between rising agricultural prices and stagnating wages could easily create disturbance in the relations between employers and workers, and in the economy at large. In order to end abuses arising from payment of wages in kind, the committee finally recommended that labourers should be paid in cash only.

For Bardoli and Palsana Talukas, and for villages with irrigation facilities elsewhere in Surat District, this should work out at Rs 2 for men and Rs 1.50 for women, for each nine-hour working day. According to this proposal farm servants could count on an annual wage of Rs 550–Rs 450 on unirrigated farms. The old Gandhian social worker Jugatram Dave, who as a member of the committee was considered to have the agricultural labourers' interests at heart, pleaded—in vain—that this amount was not enough for subsistence, and that payment of a higher wage would be demonstrably feasible, certainly in the fertile plain in south Gujarat. In the end however, even he signed the report on the promise that a further increase would be made soon after introduction of the minimum wage. It is hardly necessary to mention that this promise has not been kept.

In order to ensure acceptance of the agreements, the committee finally recommended the institution of local panels—a council for each wage zone to be presided over by a government official and with equal representation for farmers and labourers. The related question of settlement of disputes and such matters was also to be entrusted to this tri-partite panel.

I lack information on the reaction in government circles to the findings and suggestions produced by the committee. There was no follow-up after the report was submitted. Only in August 1972 did a minimum wage law come into force in the whole of Gujarat, giving agricultural labourers the right to Rs 3 a day, and to Rs 120 calculated in an annual basis—too little and too late to be able to expect, as yet, a favourable effect on the condition of the Halpatis and other landless castes. The main rock on which the measure foundered, however, was the lack of machinery for implementing it. A new wage round which became effective during the Emergency period under the Congress party served equally little purpose. Because this official action took place a year before I began my fieldwork in 1977, I shall explain in greater detail the way in which it was introduced, and its results, in the area of my research. Firstly, let us examine the bare facts.

As part of the 20 Point Programme the minimum daily wage for agricultural labour was fixed, in January 1976, at a uniform amount of Rs 5.50 for men, women and children. According to the same instructions, a farm servant had the right to an annual wage of Rs 2,000—in other words, fully two to four times as much as he then received. The District Collector, who carried the entire responsibility for supervising the execution of this decree, would be obliged to present regular reports to the Labour Commissioner as well as to the district committees specially appointed for the purpose. (For the original wording see the appendix at the end of this chapter.) Each farmer was obliged to maintain a register of the labourers working for him and to make sure that they signed it every day for wages received.

The raising of the daily wage to Rs 5.50 created a good deal of disturbance among the farmers. It became the task of government officials to inform agricultural labourers of their new rights, and indeed locally a *mamlatdar* (the administrative head of a *taluka*) did come to talk to Halpatis in their locality. On the other hand, in various other villages the Patidar *sirpanches* convened meetings in order to dictate the conditions to which the agricultural labourers must adhere in the future: a nine-hour working day; stoppage of all allowances in kind including the right to gather firewood or to cut grass; sharp and continuous supervision over the performance of work, and wage cuts for harvest losses, damage to agricultural implements, and so on. Fully aware of the pressures their superiors can exert, the agricultural labourers have, as a rule, immediately abandoned all claims to the minimum wage. In some places farmers changed to paying the prescribed minimum wage at the beginning, but when it became evident after a short while that the government had not seriously considered affirmative action and continuous control, they soon reverted to the practices existing previously. The result was a lasting hardening of the labour-relations climate, in which there was no chance of securing the benefits of the new legislation.

The farmers have always known how to evade the working of the minimum wage laws in various ways, such as refusing to give tenure to farm servants, which would oblige them to pay a much higher annual wage, and by paying only Rs 3 daily to their labourers, who must nevertheless set their thumbprints in wage registers every evening for receipt of Rs 5.50. The labourers are naturally well aware of the fraud perpetrated by their bosses, but refuse to do anything about it for fear that they should be regarded as no longer willing to work. Lack of sufficient work is an excellent means of intimidating labourers. Several farmers boasted to me that their subordinates would claim to receive the prescribed amount, if any outsider cared to check this. A few went so far as to use my presence as a stranger to put the matter to the proof, thus providing the humiliating spectacle of a farm servant or maid servant giving the 'right' answers in a well trained manner.

Apart from all sorts of illegal evasions, the wage law itself is emasculated in a variety of legal ways—in the first place by reductions in the volume of work offered, farmers being less prompt in giving out tasks such as weeding or maintenance work. The labourers complain that, as a result of this economy, there is increasingly less for them to do, the women among them being worst affected. Equalization of wages has contributed to this, since women are now employed last of all except for operations regarded as being typically 'feminine' tasks. It was from women labourers particularly that I heard, in the landless labourers' quarters, the greatest number of complaints about the increase in unemployment. According to them, they hardly ever stayed at home, but now they often have to do so for days or even weeks at a time. Distribution of work on piece rates or by contract is another means of avoiding payment of the minimum daily wage rate, since these alternative methods of payment are not regulated by law—a lacuna of which the oldest and weakest among the agricultural labourers are victims. In addition to all this, there is the preference for migrant labourers, who allow themselves to be manipulated more easily than local labourers. The minimum wage law has certainly contributed to the replacement of these latter by migrants.

The Patidar farmers show absolutely no trace of bad conscience about the exceptionally low wages they continue to pay. If, during conversations with them, I tried to appeal to that kind of feeling, they reacted immediately with the argument that the Halpatis' meagre performance was not even worth the three rupees given. '*Kam chor*, *dam chor*', they said, shrugging their shoulders: they cheat us in work, we rob them of money. Another argument was that the labourers only converted their earnings into drink: 'they booze away at least one rupee in every three'—a variation on the theme that Halpatis have less needs than 'ordinary' people, and can thus make do with less. The harshness displayed by the farmers derives to a large extent from the loss of something to which they have always been accustomed and which they have always taken for granted—a total control over labour. Their discontent is directed against the government, but is actually vented on the agricultural labourers, to whom the farmers deny the right of social autonomy and the possibility of ever forming themselves into an opposing party with demands and rights of their own. The Patidars regard anything pointing in this direction as insolence, presumption, disloyalty—in a word, as a total collapse of earlier discipline. This is the inevitable effect of any attempt to redress the extremely inegalitarian labour relations. The advisory committee identified this problem in its report, but for all that still trusted the farmers' willingness to co-operate in the endeavour to accomplish greater justice and equality in the labour regime.

> There is a price attached to an attempt to subvert values that are being sought to be laid down either by the society or the State. There is no need to assume that the farmers-employers would adopt an anti-social attitude. There is no need even to single them out for a reactionary categorisation. Like all other strata, the large bulk of them would be socially enlightened (Report MWAC 1966: 78).

Such optimism has obviously been misplaced, since even the extremely modest reform proposals which the commission put forward evoked the fiercest and most reactionary resistance from the dominant landowners in Surat District, who regard every intervention from outside to improve the agricultural labourers' miserable plight as an unseemly and intolerable interference in their domain. The mentality underlying this attitude will be considered in more detail in a later chapter.

Which measures did the government take to overcome farmers' resistance? One can only conclude that remarkably little has been done by the state apparatus to tip the balance of labour relations in favour of the weakest party. The first excuse for this failure is always that there are too few personnel available for exercising effective control. At the time of my fieldwork at the beginning of 1977, seven labour officers were employed in the office of the Assistant Commissioner of Labour in Surat, and four of these were occupied with industrial labour, a section of the working population which was much more limited in size and which was moreover mainly concentrated in urban areas. The remaining three officers left free for the inspection of agricultural labour had to travel over the whole district, with the use of only one jeep between them. Yet the argument of insufficient manpower is not completely convincing, because instructions were in force by which government officers at sub-district level—among them, the *mamlatdar* himself—were also empowered to take action against contraventions of the law. With a few exceptions this action has seldom been taken, which in itself tells us something about the reluctance with which the government has gone to work in this matter.

Apart from the deficiency of adequate provisions in the material sphere, judicial possibilities for giving effect to the minimum wage legislation were also extremely limited. Farmers could only be summoned for failing to keep a wage register—a contravention which carried a relatively light penalty—while failure to pay the statutory daily wage of Rs 5.50 was not in itself a ground for legal proceedings. For these, it was necessary for the agricultural labourer to lodge a formal complaint, and even in the exceptional cases where Halpatis were able to follow this course, official action has usually hung fire, while most Halpatis have abandoned such ideas, believing that, in any case, access to the authorities is barred to them.

With that, we arrive at the last obstacle, namely the anti-labour stance among the majority of government officials entrusted with implementing the legislation. This negative opinion of labourers is especially striking in the lower echelons of the state apparatus, and the fact that a large proportion of the lower and middle cadre at district level originate from the same milieu as the farmers undoubtedly plays a role in this. However, another factor is probably of much greater importance, i.e. the propensity for deriving private advantage from the execution of public duties. Not all, but certainly too many of the officials entrusted with the implementation of rules and regulations manipulate them, using them as a kind of capital in order to acquire personal incomes from them. Instead of providing a counterbalance against the farmers, officials accept payment from the latter in return for neglecting to register complaints and track down infringements of the regulations. These state servants would not be averse to helping the a[illegible]icultural labourers but these, of course, cannot affo[illegible] f protection.

Taking into consideration all these unfa[illegible]

stances, the compelling question is whether promulgation of the minimum wage law has not in fact been counterproductive. Benefits for the agricultural labourers are small, while the damage inflicted seems obvious: less work for all, and replacement of local labour by outsiders; the termination of secure service bonds for farm servants; and for day-wage workers, the elimination of women's work and the transition to cheaper forms of labour. The Debt Relief Act, which came into operation at approximately the same time, has had a corresponding effect. While remission of debts was intended to put an end to the farmers' practice of ensuring a sufficient supply of cheap labour, the consequence has been that agricultural labourers remain deprived of the credit they need in order to survive.

On the ground that this kind of well-intentioned legal provision is inclined to produce the opposite effect to that intended, it has been argued that what is really needed is a more 'realistic' labour policy, which often means toning down the demands and settling for more modest grains considered to be really attainable. This was the attitude of the official *Study Group on Wages, Incomes and Prices*, which published its report in May 1978. This national working group concluded that the establishment of a wage law for agricultural labour was not practical, and recommended that, in its place, the aim should be a minimum income for an agricultural labourer's household to which all working members should contribute—an income set at a sum of Rs 1,800 a year. This was undoubtedly a much more conservative objective, which boils down to a per capita consumption level of roughly 50 per cent below the poverty line as defined by the Planning Commission—although the income of the average agricultural labourer's household in the south Gujarat plain still remained far below even that target by at least some 30–40 per cent, at that time. To what abysmal level of living must members of a class be reduced, before obtaining recognition of their right to exist? The editorial comment in *Economic and Political Weekly*, which provided the information cited here, rightly observes that the leading arguments against a minimum wage law are not valid.

> In fact, it is precisely because there is such a surplus of agricultural labour and because, on account of this as well as a variety of other economic and social factors, the agricultural labourer is in a hopelessly weak bargaining position *vis-a-vis* his employer that there is

need for government intervention on his behalf, including through the fixing and enforcing of statutory minimum wages (E.P.W. 1978: 973).

I would like to note further that all too easily we find a tendency to ascribe the deterioration in labour conditions to the introduction of protective legislation. This paradox can occur, but when it does, it mostly involves an incidental effect rather than the origin of the problem: even before the Debt Relief Act came into operation, farmers had shown reluctance to extend credit to their subordinates, and the trend towards replacement of local labour, which also means its elimination, did not begin only with the introduction of the minimum wage law. In fact the establishment of some basic provisions offering legal protection was a real attempt to halt the previous deterioration in labour conditions; the way in which farmers seize upon these prohibitions and injunctions as rationalizations for their own behaviour, does not alter this fact. When the regulations adopted appear to be ineffective this is, of itself, still no reason for simply abandoning further attempts. Rather, it is obvious that the legislation must be more precisely formulated in order to tackle the vulnerable situation in which the labourers find themselves. Also, by anticipating opposition in advance, it is easier to fight evasion and emasculation of the law, and the success or failure of such a fight depends upon the readiness of the government to compel a real observance of legal provisions.

I have been able to confirm that agricultural labourers in the central plain of south Gujarat are certainly well aware of the existence of the minimum wage law, and that wherever possible they use this knowledge to effect a compromise between the actual and the prescribed minimum. In the villages with advanced agriculture they pressure the farmers into paying Rs 4 a day in the busy season, which sometimes lasts for several weeks. Apart from strengthening their negotiating position *vis-a-vis* the farmers, the legal regulations function at the same time as a standard by which the agricultural labourers can measure their deprivation. The concept of government current among them is that of an apparatus which is not exclusively embodied in local functionaries, but which is rather, an anonymous power, the better disposed towards them the more distant it is. The possibility of support from above, however vague and distant, contributes to the growing consciousness of the agricultural labourers, and increases their militancy. Shortly after the proclamation of the Rs 5.50 measure, conflicts broke out in various villages around Bardoli over attempts to enforce payment of this sum. Nowhere have these been successful but, considering the unfavourable circumstances within which the Halpatis are operating, it is amazing that more or less organized attempts at improving their lot do occur. The form taken by these, and their chances of future success, will be a theme to which I shall return later. Meanwhile, a discouraging conclusion is that concerted action from below which is a precondition for giving effect to protective governmental legislation has not, as yet, attained a sufficiently organized form and intensity.

Bonded labour?

At the time of my fieldwork in 1977 a question of current interest was whether the farm servants of the central plain of south Gujarat were to be regarded as bonded labour. In various parts of India this still appears to be a frequently occurring practice. The National Labour Institute in Delhi, set up shortly before, played an important role in the collection of information by central government on the subject of bonded labour; a department of the Ministry of Labour was particularly active in this. Under the influence of the documentation which became available, a law was brought into force in 1976 for the abolition of bonded labour, but this phenomenon was only given wider notoriety when it was taken into the 20 Point Programme. Throughout the whole country, articles appeared in daily and weekly newspapers describing how farm servants were personally subjugated into remaining with the landowners for whom they worked throughout their lifetime—a subjugation which often embraced other members of their household as well. The roots of this servitude usually lay in indebtedness, which made it impossible for the labourer to break the service bond, and the law promulgated some years ago was intended to abolish precisely this labour bondage to a money lender. However, it is the conditions accompanying the debt, rather than the debt itself, which determine the coercive character of the service bond. The *hali* system in south Gujarat was a clear example of bonded labour, which I analysed in an earlier study. 'Attachment for an indefinite period, severance of the relationship only in exceptional cases and often its prolongation into following generations, work obligations for the servant's whole family and finally the nonspecific and exchangeable nature of the service were the chief elements of servitude in the past' (Breman 1974: 41). However, on the grounds of village research which was partly carried out in Valod Taluka, I established that farm servants were no longer bound for life, let alone hereditarily, and that the relation had become more contractual and specific and—barring certain exceptions—no longer extended to other members of the household. The concentration of the landless in separate neighbourhoods at the periphery of the village was as much cause as consequence of the dissolution of the labour relationship which had such a strongly personal character.

As I have already demonstrated in chapter 5, the change did not come about suddenly. The transition to a new labour regime has taken considerable time, and has still not reached a final form. Although the disappearance of *hali-pratha* was announced two generations ago, elements of the old order remain identifiable up to the present day. This explains why, even very recently, commentators have been suggesting that the continuance of the farm servant relationship is essentially a manifestation of bonded labour. Thus Patel (whose research, conducted during 1961–6 in village A to the south-east of Bardoli, nearly coincided with my first fieldwork in the area) concluded that this system displayed features which reminded him of serfdom, and following upon this, Vyas also spoke of coercion.[7] The report—appearing some years later—published by the government advisory com-

[7] 'The Hali labourer who was normally employed found it difficult to change his employer because of the tacit agreement among the latter for not 'pirating' one another's labourers. Even if the Hali labourer made himself bold enough to change his employer and found someone who was willing to accept him, the new contract had to be entered into before Holi. After that no one could find an employer other than one by whom the labourer was already employed' (Vyas 1964: 11).

mittee on the introduction of minimum wages, stated that the *hali* system was on the point of disappearing as a consequence of the farmers' reluctance to advance loans to the landless for their marriages, thus refusing to allow them to indebt themselves. The report attributed the remnants of this institution of bonded labour to the easy-going, economically irrational behaviour of the agricultural labourers; in this way, the commission reiterated the conventional view of the Halpatis, i.e. they themselves were held responsible for the continuance of their dependence.

How are we to judge the present conditions? Not only is this question relevant from the viewpoint of policy enactment, but the answer also sheds light on the nature of the economic order. Can the dominant traits of this be stamped as feudal, or has a capitalist mode of production already come into existence? In 1977 the government of Gujarat commissioned several studies, in order to examine whether bonded labour was still prevalent as maintained in a report published under the auspices of the Gandhian Peace Foundation.[8] In Surat District this research was guided by Ganshyam Shah for the Centre for Social Studies. The results, based on a sample survey of 2,694 agricultural labourers' households spread over twenty-seven villages, showed clearly that there is no longer any question of labour bondage (Shah 1978). This conclusion parallels that of another report, also sponsored by the government, for which material was collected during a briefer field visit to a number of villages in south Gujarat, some of them in Bardoli, Palsana and Valod Talukas: '. . . all the 250 informants gave the answer that they were free labourers not attached with (sic) any master on permanent basis' (Lal 1977: 14).

Before examining this finding in more detail, I should state at this point that I hold the same view. In some of the literature on this question, an erroneous impression is given that the farm servant—i.e. an agricultural labourer who works for the

[8] Edited by S. Marla and published under the title *Bonded Labour in India; National Survey on the Incidence of Bonded Labour* (1981). Although understandable as an indictment of on-going practices of bonded labour this book cannot be accepted as a reliable source on the subject. The well-known Gandhian social worker H. Parikh is the author of the rather superficial and highly misleading paragraph on bonded labour in Gujarat.

same farmer daily, or at least regularly—is by definition bonded. However, this is no longer the case, even when the indebtedness is a persistent feature of the labour relationship. The agricultural economy in the south Gujarat central plain, with its very intensive cropping pattern, dictates the maintenance of farm servants while, in addition, the style of living to which the farmers' households have become accustomed also requires the employment of maidservants. The exercise of supervision over the labour performed by others has a high place in the dominant landowner's scale of values. It appears from Patel's study that the labour costs per hectare increases with farm size (Patel 1964: 102), and the number of permanent labourers also rises gradually.

What strikes me is the inability of farmers and landless alike to give a modern-contractual content to their relationship. Economic need forces farm servants to maximize their material security by seeking protection in a service link from which they expect not only a daily wage but all kinds of allowances, and advance loans—in short, a guaranteed subsistence. At the same time they try to limit their responsibilities to the sphere of work, in order to avoid all personal subordination and the stigma of inferiority associated with it. Conversely the farmers have a need for continuous labour, without having succeeded in finding an acceptable contractual basis for this. They prove themselves to be hard and demanding masters, who are unwilling to offer their dependents even the minimal security necessary for an existence permitting some human dignity. For the farmers, labourers are a commodity to be bought at the lowest possible price and towards whom they have no responsibility. Even tractor drivers often receive no better treatment, and are hired only for the period during which their skill is required, from October/November to May/June. Labour costs have not kept pace with the growing capital-intensity of agriculture, labour costs per hectare being considerably lower than those of all other inputs taken together. This conclusion, based on M. B. Desai's farm-management research located in the Surat District is corroborated by Patel, who calculated in his micro-level study that labour costs were only one-third of all farm expenditure (Patel 1966: 136; 137). It would be oversimplistic to relate this figure only to the overwhelming numbers of landless labourers. The extreme under-payment of labour is also linked with the tendency of landowners to assess the usefulness of labourers not by the extent of their skill, sense of responsibility, or performance, but on the grounds of 'virtues'—now becoming rare—such as unconditional obedience, and obsequiousness.

Recalcitrant farm servants and selfish masters—so each party characterizes the other. Halpatis and Patidars have grown increasingly further apart, both emphasizing the distance that has come to exist, which makes the Patidars in particular inclined to idealize the past. Although it would seem that Halpatis have less reason to wax really enthusiastic about the past, even they give one to understand that the farm servant was relatively better off. It certainly still occurs, even now, that a farmer or farm servant more or less fulfills the expectations of the other party, in which case the contentment is usually mutual, but such examples of 'trusty servant' and 'good master' are actually very rare. Labour relations have become diseased; the landless feel cheated by being denied the right to a subsistence, while the farmers in turn are immeasurably irritated because their claim to superiority is no longer acknowledged. Quite justifiably they regard this as a challenge, an attempted escape from the relationship of inferiority which they had imposed upon their subordinates. The previous servitude provides too few points of similarity for a good understanding of the functioning of the present-day farm servant relationship.

In publications which take the continuity of bonded labour as their starting point, the emphasis falls too unequally on farm servants as a separate labour category. As I have shown, labourers in permanent service try to earn a daily wage elsewhere on days when there is nothing for them to do. Conversely the services of casual labourers are secured in advance by the provision of consumption loans via other members of their households. It is striking that, in the discussion over bondage, almost no attention has been paid to the maidservants, who—far more than the male farm servants—still live and work in the shadow of the farmer's household. Nonetheless I maintain that their situation does not constitute an unfree working relationship, either. Although there is a smaller labour turnover than among male farm servants, these women remain free to terminate their employment. Nowadays farmers do not have the power over their labourers' whole households which was a feature of *halipratha*, and man, wife and children do not usually work for the same farmer.

Finally the indebtedness regarded as the essence of bondage is not unique to the farmer/agricultural labourer relationship. The jobber who works in agriculture, or outside it, likewise avails himself of this mechanism, in order to enlist and retain workers for his gang. The wholesale recruitment of outside labour for the harvest season by the co-operative sugar factories is based on this principle.[9] To my mind it is unsound to deduce from this that unfree labour continues in either the same form or a new one. Extension of credit, in so far as this occurs, is a means whereby the employer and/or jobber is able to commandeer enough labour cheaply and in good time. Conversely, for the labourer indebtedness is an unavoidable result of the permanent insecurity of his life. The binding which accompanies this cannot, however, be equated with unfree labour. The pre-capitalist personal, or even familial bondage which the law of 1976 pretended to abolish had in any case already disappeared from the plain of south Gujarat, as also from various other parts of India. On the other hand the creation of sanctions against indebted labour—unjustly regarded as the only, or principal measure of servitude—has had hardly any effect. This has remained a striking feature of a variety of contractual labour relationships which mask the transition to a capitalist rural economy. I shall regard as unfree only that form of debt-labour which is rooted in non-economic coercion. Instances of physical violence or intimidation do occur but are on the whole quite exceptional in the situation I have described. I therefore agree entirely with Rudra who, among those following Thorner, defined bonded labour in terms of personal subjection and dominance; this relationship has nothing to do with the essence of present-day control over agricultural labour (Rudra 1978: 965–7; Omvedt 1981: A154).

[9] For the relationship between the jobber and his gang on the one hand and with the factory management on the other, see Breman 1978.

I want to make it clear that labourers are still threatened occasionally with physical violence if they do not behave 'correctly'—I have already mentioned the farmer who had his farm servant beaten up by the police when the servant was pressured to pay off his debt, and for this reason was expected to be content with an amount lower than the 'going' daily wage. Such occurrences have nevertheless become quite rare, and result moreover rather from rancour than from the supposition that it is still possible to force improvement of labour performance by this means. The unmistakeable fury shown by agricultural labourers over this kind of behaviour, and also over the farmers' sexual abuse of the women and girls among them, is likewise an indication that times are changing. In cases of clear intimidation the aggression evoked is vented in attacks on the employers which remain unpunished. I cannot escape the impression that many more elements of personal servitude are present in some other labour forms which have come into existence than in the farmer/farmservant relation. For instance, the relation between a jobber and the member of his gang is coloured by domination and subservience. Similarly, should sugarcane cutters contracted in Maharashtra for the harvest season in Bardoli take it into their heads not to appear on the day of departure or, once in the plain, to set out on a trip home against the will of the *mukadam*, they will be called to order in a rough way if necessary (Breman 1978–79:57). Seasonal migrants are also subject to extra economic coercion from their temporary employers. Nevertheless this sort of coercion is more an incidental phenomenon than an essential element of the labour relationship bearing a more capitalistic character. The transformation of labour into a commodity ('*Verdinglichug*') in a situation of boundless poverty and chronic unemployment, places limits on personal freedom without, however, turning into bondage.

To summarize: The dissolution of the previous relationship of dependence is the consequence of a transition to a capitalist mode of production. A greater problem than the farmers' appetite for subjecting one or more individuals, is that nowadays they pay little or no attention to the plight of agricultural labourers. On their part, the latter have become conscious of the stigma attached to bondage, and for that reason regard their increasing freedom of movement as a positive improvement. This does not alter the fact that they have lagged behind in a vulnerable position, and have even become socially isolated. In spite of assertions to the contrary, the government fails to protect the landless labourers and to provide them with a minimal security of living. One can indeed attribute such an intention to the law on abolition of forced labour, but it is also possible to explain this legislation as an attempt to hasten the transition to capitalist relations of production, by clearing away the last remains of traditional forms of labour control, where this still existed. In so far as incidental legal provisions promoting the real interest of the agrarian proletariat are promulgated—for instance, the wage law—the government has lacked the genuine will to begin enforcing these, with the result that the landless have fallen victim to the freedom that has come to exist in the labour sphere. This theme will occupy a central place in subsequent chapters.

APPENDIX TO CHAPTER 9

Implementation of the minimum wages fixed for agricultural labourers under the Minimum Wages Act, 1948.

Government of Gujarat
Education and Labour Department
Circular No. MWA-2967/30132-T
Sachivalaya, Gandhinagar,
Dated the 29th April, 1976.

CIRCULAR

1. Government of Gujarat has revised minimum rates of wages for the employees employed in Agricultural vide Government Notification, Education and Labour Department, No. KH-SH-11-MWA-4275/105322-T, dated the 5th January, 1976. As per this notification, the minimum rate for casual labourers is fixed at Rs 5.50 per day and for permanent labourers Rs. 2,000/- per year. These rates are applicable in all the area of the State for men and women workers uniformally. For detailed information a copy of the aforesaid Government Notification is enclosed herewith.

2. For implementation of the above statutory wages rates and the provisions of the Minimum Wages Act, 1948 and the rules made thereunder, Government has appointed officers of the Labour Department, Revenue Department and Taluka Development Officers as Inspectors under Section 19 of the Minimum Wages Act, 1948. Besides officers of Labour Department, Revenue Officers who are notified as Inspectors under the Act are all Deputy Collectors, Mamlatdars, Mahalkaries, Aval Karkuns, Circle Officers vide Government Notification, Education and Labour Department No. MWA-2961-53606-T, dated 16-11-1961 (copy enclosed). Similarly Taluka Development Officers are notified as Inspectors vide Government Notification Education & Labour Department No. KH-SH-432/MWA-1069/55654-T, dated 10th April 1973 (copy enclosed).

3. Implementation of minimum wages for agricultural labour is one of the points in 20 point economic programme of the Prime Minister. Government attaches a great deal of importance to the effective implementation of the Minimum Wages Act. As the Revenue Officers and Panchayat Officers are widely in contact with the people of the district, it is expected that by their effective application to the enforcement of the Minimum Wages Act, the purpose of the Act will be successfully served. In view of these positions, Government has issued instruction—vide Government Circular, Education and Labour Department No. LAVADHA-1072/107036-T, dated 4-7-1973 and also addressed two D. O. Letters No. MWA-1075/68822-T dated 5-9-1975 and No. MWA-1075/28020-T dated 1-4-1976 to all Collectors and District Development Officers. They are also requested to take monthly review of the inspections carried out, the cases detected and prosecutions launched and send this information to Government every month in the prescribed proforma.

4. Government has recently reviewed the position and gives the following further instructions for the effective implementation of the minimum wages for agricultural labour:

(1) While the Labour Commissioner continued to be responsible at the state level to ensure effective implementation of the minimum wages, so far as the agricultural labour is concerned, at the district level Collector shall be the over all co-ordinating authority and shall be responsible for the effective implementation of minimum wages for agricultural labour.

(2) For this purpose all officers notified as Inspectors under the Minimum Wages Act, 1948 shall be answerable to the Collector.

(3) The Collectors along with the District Development Officers shall review the progress of the enforcement of the minimum wage provisions in the monthly meetings of the Revenue and Panchayat Officers and report to the Labour Commissioner every month, the number of inspections carried out and the number of cases filed.

(4) The District Development Officers shall ensure that the Special Justice Committees, where operational, play an effective role in the implementation of minimum wage provision for agricultural labour.

(5) The Collectors shall undertake a comprehensive review of the work done in the district at the periodical meetings of the

District Committee for the 20 point programme, so as to take stock of the situation and to discuss ways and means of strengthening the enforcement process and also to create the proper climate of understanding and acceptance of revised minimum wages on the part of the cultivators on the one hand and the agricultural labourers on the other hand.

5. All Collectors, District Development Officers and the Commissioner of Labourers are requested to follow the above instructions of Government scrupulously and instruct suitably the officers under them so that the specially and economically weaker persons of the society i.e. agricultural labourers who are unorganised and un-protected can avail of the benefit of the revised minimum wages notified by the government.

sd/-
Deputy Secretary to the Govt. of Gujarat
Education and Labour Department.

10
INTRUSION INTO AND EXPULSION FROM THE RURAL ECONOMY

Rural migration: the inadequacy of some standard explanations

The emphasis in this study lies on the presence of migrant labourers in the central plain of south Gujarat. In Chapter 5 I outlined the circumstances under which the tribal hinterland of Surat District has become a recruitment area for temporary labour over the last few decades. Seasonal migration is certainly not a new phenomenon in Gujarat or, for that matter, in India. However, the magnitude of rural labour circulation is of recent origin, and is a direct consequence of structural changes which have taken place in the destination area. The statement that 'pull' rather than 'push' factors are primarily responsible for the large-scale movement of labour does not mean an absence of change in the home area. A demand for labour elsewhere will only be followed up when prescribed by local conditions. In other words, leaving home must be either attractive or unavoidable. In connection with this I have drawn attention to increasing population pressure within an unfavourable ecological environment, and progressive social differentiation linked with a gradual penetration of the market economy.

Besides these factors there is the accelerated effect of more accidental occurrences such as the construction of the Ukhai Dam, and of natural disasters such as the great flood of 1968 or the long-lasting drought in some later years. Thus an un- or under-utilized pool of labour came into existence ready to be released through improvements in communications. Increasing land scarcity or even acute subsistence crises are nevertheless not a sufficient condition for the drain of manpower. Also in these circumstances mobilization of the created labour surplus is determined primarily by the need for labour (whether on a temporary or semi-permanent basis) arising in other places. The capitalist development of the agricultural economy has become the mechanism which regulates the annual movement over great distances. What are the determinants of the demand for outside agricultural labour in Bardoli and neighbourhood? Conventional explanations are the sharply increased labour-intensity of the new cropping pattern; the absorption of the already present landless labour force into the rapidly expanding non-agricultural employment; and lastly the unsatisfactory labour performance of indigenous agricultural labourers. I shall test the value of each of these arguments in turn.

To begin with, it seems to be a natural inclination to deduce the existence of local labour shortages from the fact of in-migration itself—after all, why otherwise should there be an influx of labour? Especially where there are clear seasonal differences in the pattern of economic activities, migration is regarded as being so obviously necessary that this phenomenon hardly appears to require explanation.[1]

Since the introduction of irrigated cultivation in Bardoli, greater fluctuations have appeared in the deployment of labour each season. When I questioned the farmers about the outsiders' arrival, they repeatedly indicated the increased need for temporary labourers for the cultivation of irrigated crops. The intensity of the agrarian cycle requires the completion of the various operations within a short time, and during the main peaks particularly this presupposes command of the services of a maximum number of labourers—far more than are available locally, according to these informants. Yet this argument carries little conviction. The previous cropping pattern—the combination of millet, cotton and rice—also involved an extremely uneven distribution of agricultural work over the year. Seasonality had already been a feature of the agricultural economy in the central plain for a long time, without leading to extensive migration.

There remains the increased intensity of the cropping system, which also demands faster dispatch of the successive work tasks. As I showed earlier, total employment opportunities

[1] Indicative is the following observation in a report on labour migration in a district of Karnataka. 'It is a well known fact that there is a greater demand for labour in these seasons as local labour would be insufficient. Hence, we find the seasonal in-migrants coming to these areas in these two seasons in large numbers' (Katti 1966: 11).

in agriculture have definitely increased in spite of the labour saving created by the gradual spread of modern technology. The net result of the new cultivation pattern is nevertheless not of the kind which can justify the massive and continual influx of temporary labour. On the contrary, one could argue that the surplus of agricultural labour already existing at that moment would be more than sufficient to satisfy the fluctuating demands of the new production cycle. The calculation of the cost of cultivation (table 10.1) shows that the labour

Table 10.1 *Average labour cost of cultivation per acre in the Bardoli area, 1971-2–1976-7*

		sugarcane		bananas		paddy	
		1971–2	1976–7	1971–2	1976–7	1971–2	1976–7
relative share of	in Rs	160	240	460	680	255	355
labour	in %	10.4	8.1	19.2	17.4	29.6	31.8
total	in Rs	1535	2961	2397	3898	863	1118
increase	in %	100	193	100	163	100	130

Source: compiled from Parmar 1978: 57.

component in rice growing is always high, but that it is both absolutely and relatively the lowest for the new and most important crop, sugarcane, and has, moreover, decreased even further during the course of time. It is true that farmers—especially if they do no manual work themselves—have always been inclined to complain of a shortage of labourers, but as far as the situation in the central plain of south Gujarat is concerned, such statements are extremely misleading. The report of the commission set up nearly two decades ago to make the investigation necessary for framing a minimum wage law, paid scant attention to this kind of complaint and, on the contrary, wrote of an excess supply of labour (Report MWAC 1966: 56 and 84). Similarly, in a recent study commissioned by the government this conclusion is again repeated with specific reference to Surat District.

> Set against this background is the supervisory cultivation pursued by a minority of farmers belonging to the upper castes who in consideration of social status or dignity shun physical work and, therefore, draw the entire labour requirement in their agriculture from these tribal and backward people. The preponderance of these backward classes with their large population both absolutely and relatively offer such a massive employable potential in relation to the limited employment opportunities that the phenomenon has a highly deleterious effect on wage levels (Report Gujarat State Land Commission 1979: 204).

The changes which have taken place do not remain limited to the demand side, the elasticity of which has brought with it insufficient economic relief, partly as a result of the continual increase in numbers within the landless class. The caste from which the bulk of the agricultural labourers comes displays an increase which is nearly in line with total population growth, while as a result of intensifying pressure on agrarian sources of subsistence and the likelihood of even further subdivision of holdings, members of small and marginal farmers' households in the plain in particular are going to be excluded from land ownership. This combination of demographic and economic factors has led to an accelerating increase in the supply of labour, with the extension of agrarian employment opportunities falling behind, relatively speaking. The proportion of the total agrarian population in Bardoli and its neighbourhood formed by the landless class, large and still growing steadily, therefore makes it unlikely that the influx of large numbers of seasonal workers to this area can be explained by a periodic shortage of local labourers. For them the new irrigation facilities have not resulted in more but in less employment, as the complaints of a group of young Halpatis make abundantly clear:

> . . . the canal waters have given us a mortal blow. Earlier, we had enough days of employment and the wages were though lesser than now, but sufficient to live through the day. We were able to buy vegetables as they were grown around here and there and were cheap. But today (due to the availability of Ukai canal water) no one grows them. Same is the case with cereals too. Jowar, our staple food, has become more and more dear. We cannot afford it. Earlier we could afford to have a few guests at home, but now if they come, we just do not know how to feed them a square meal.

Wages are also not paid according to the declarations. We are paid Rs 3 or Rs 4 a day with constant fear whether the same will be available to us the next day or not (Patel 1982: 8).

An entirely different situation should arise when the present labour force succeeds, in course of time, in withdrawing from employment in agriculture. This appears to have been the case in the Punjab, where landless labourers have also profited to a modest extent from the growth of urban and rural industries. There seems to be a direct connection between the exodus to these new sources of subsistence and the arrival of migrants from outside the state for the performance of harvest tasks.[2] At first sight a similar displacement of labour could also be postulated for south Gujarat, since a remarkable industrial expansion has taken place in the principal urban centres—Surat, Navsari and Bardoli. The district headquarters in particular, with the industrial enclave of Udhna, has become an important growth pole where in recent years a number of new and modern enterprises have come into existence to which labour has been drawn from far and wide. Besides this, even in the countryside itself there has been diversification in the pattern of economic activities; apart from the factories processing agrarian raw materials, one is also struck by the expansion in the construction industry as well as by the markedly increased importance of transport and the service sector.

The impression that this growth and diversification of the economy in the western part of Surat District has resulted in a considerable restructuring of the total pattern of employment, must however be reconciled with the observation that the local landless, particularly, have great difficulty in obtaining access to this new work arena. Supervision and management remain, as a matter of course, the preserve of the younger generation of the rural upper stratum, who are in a position to obtain a suitable training for this. Members of the lower castes—artisans and smaller landowners but also migrants coming from other places—for the most part already make great demands on all types of occupations outside agriculture which are permanent and relatively protected. Only the

[2] For an account of a study on labour migration into and out of rural areas, see Oberoi and Singh 1980. See also 'Punjab: Plight of Migrant Labour' in: EPW, vol. 14 (17), 28 April 1979: 755.

least skilled and lowest paid jobs are left for the landless in their own district—jobs which because of their irregular nature offer scant security in an existence which is thus scarcely any more comfortable than the agricultural labourer's life of abject poverty.

Does the solution to their problems lie in an escape to the city? After all, urban centres such as Navsari, Surat and other expanding industrial and commercial concentrations along the Bombay-Ahmedabad railway line are easily accessible from the western-lying *talukas* of south Gujarat. They are indeed not very distant geographically speaking, but it is the socio-economic distance which forms a great barrier for these rural lower strata. As I mentioned earlier, Halpatis—the principal agricultural labourer caste—are markedly under-represented in the urban locations. A recent study among members of this caste in Surat City showed that only 3 per cent of all households investigated had established themselves there during the past decade (Desai 1979: 3). This slow rate of urbanization is undoubtedly due to the miserable life most urban Halpatis lead. Nearly half of them had a working day of more than eleven hours. Nevertheless the average income of a household member was only Rs 2.25 per day, not sufficient for two square meals, clothing and housing. A quarter of the households covered by the survey even had to maintain themselves on less than a rupee per head. Child labour was an absolute necessity in order to survive. Only one-fifth of all the children attended school. These and other data from the study mentioned above make it clear that the somewhat attractive and secure positions in the urban labour hierarchy are beyond the reach of the landless class in the rural hinterland. The youngest household members do not succeed in gaining access to urban employment. According to a recent study devoted to child labour in Surat City, children of agricultural labourers are heavily under-represented in the junior ranks of the urban work force. Most children do have a rural background but they belong to petty landowning, artisan and service castes. This means that the rural proletariat is excluded even from the most unskilled and lowliest paid of all jobs (Sahoo 1981). In spite of the economic dynamic which one can notice—a remarkable growth and diversification of production—the landless remain imprisoned inside a rural order within which opportunities for earning a living have for many of them decreased rather than increased. In various studies it is stated, correctly, that the present generation of the poor lack contacts with influential people who could help them to obtain a foothold in the economic sectors outside agriculture. The social isolation in which they are trapped ensures that they are left behind in the competition—becoming ever fiercer—for the new permanent labour places which nowadays have become available. Lack of specific skills, in so far as these are required in the lower echelons of the non-agrarian economy, is not the principal obstacle, because many of those who actually penetrate this sphere of labour are similarly handicapped.

Does this mean that the landless are immobile? My informants from the higher social strata immediately agree with this notion: it is not the Halpatis' ability to leave their present homes which is called in question, but their will to do so. Farmers as much as local civil servants attribute all kinds of negative character traits to the rural underclass—inertia, limitless improvidence, and so on—with a resulting lack of any economic drive to leave the village and find work elsewhere. Besides being an inaccurate estimate of the chances open to the landless outside their own environment, this widely held view amounts to a distortion of reality. Even if relatively few members of the main landless caste surface in an urban environment, this still does not mean that they are immobile in the countryside. Repeated research in the plain of south Gujarat has taught me that there are many migrants among the Halpatis: a high percentage of the members of this agricultural labourer caste—a quarter to a third of the heads of households surveyed—appear to have come originally from a different village to that in which I encountered them during my fieldwork. This mobility is of a geographical, not socio-economic nature, however,—i.e. the movement remains necessarily limited to circulation within the rural structure without much occupational change. Nevertheless, opportunities arising outside this circuit—scarce though they may be—are eagerly seized. As already stated, imposed backwardness and subordination are responsible for the fact that this does not happen more often. The causes are structural and are not due to a behaviour pattern of the Halpatis (and of the landless in general) reminiscent of a culture of poverty. In the following sections I shall deal in greater detail with the mechanisms which block the absorption of landless labourers into the non-agrarian economy. I will be content here with the conclusion that the seasonal trek to the central plain is not due to the propulsion of indigenous agricultural labour into the new industry in or around the district. Neither is the opposite true, i.e. that an accelerated exodus of local landless occurs as a result of the arrival of a vast body of outsiders. Pauperization of a main segment is the inevitable consequence.

Ultimately, defence of the use of migrant labour rests on the conviction that labourers from the area itself are unfit for satisfactory execution of the work assigned to them. Whenever a plentiful and constant supply of experienced outside labourers is assured, the indigenous labourers' lack of familiarity with the cultivation of new crops, or with other forms of employment which have come into existence recently, is all too often manipulated in order to pass them over. In any event, it is a justification for the preference for (among others) sugarcane cutters, cattle men, road builders, factory workers and canal diggers, coming to the plain from other parts of Gujarat or even from far outside it. Why call on the local landless, who are unaccustomed to this work, when there are enough efficient labourers from other places who are prepared to stay and establish themselves, or to return for a few months every year, according to how much their presence is required?

This line of argument is unconvincing for several reasons. The work performed by most migrants is scarcely specialized, and it would cost the local labourers little effort to learn it. In this respect they are no different from migrants making the journey for the first time, who on arrival have no prior command over the routine alloted to them in advance. For that matter the demonstrable fact that the services of the local landless were certainly used earlier for the same type of work, completely destroys the credibility of the argument of the migrants having a relatively better work experience. As I mentioned in an earlier publication, this applies for instance to the cultivation of sugarcane, which a number of decades ago was carried out on a small scale in this area; Halpatis performed all of this work, including the harvesting (Breman 1974:42, 74–5). It is only since the beginning of large-scale sugarcane cultivation that the army of harvest workers has been imported from other places. A more recent example is that of the replacement of local brick makers and stone-quarry labourers by seasonal migrants.

Lastly, many migrants do precisely the same work as the local landless; this applies to (among others) the gangs of harvest workers who come to the plain from the tribal hinterland after the rainy season. From these examples it must be apparent that for a long time now the preference for outside labourers has not always been tenable on the grounds of their greater skill or experience.

Specific skills are indeed attributed to migrants—a sort of regional specific work knowledge or proficiency—but on further questioning it appears that this is not what employers mean when they complain about the lack of aptitude of the local labourers. Migrant workers, according to the unanimous verdict, work harder and longer and are moreover said to be more malleable and obedient. In these respects the local landless distinguish themselves only in a strictly negative sense in the eyes of their superiors, the worthlessness of their work being self-evident. The question of why agricultural labourers should exert themselves for a daily wage which does not even allow them to satisfy their most elementary needs falls beyond the interests of their employers. However, as Kalathil rightly comments: 'I was able to observe that labourers had some very clear ideas on the amount of work they owed an employer for the wage they were getting. As this did not amount to much in their own estimation, they at times took pain not to do much work' (1979: 28).

There are two variants of the view why Halpatis, in particular, are not highly esteemed as labourers. According to the first reading, the Halpatis lack a work ethos, and a number of illustrations and anecdotes suggest that they have never had any inclination for work. There is the tale—already venerable—that when the farm servant awakes in the morning, he feels with his toe to discover whether there is any rice gruel left in the cooking pot, and only goes to his master if the amount left is insufficient for that day. Similar old saws, very popular among the farmers, make a direct connection between the boundless laziness imputed to the agricultural labourer caste, and the degraded nature of their eating and other habits. The implicit suggestion then is that modern agriculture has become much more demanding, and that present-day landowners cannot be satisfied with labourers who are not up to their tasks. One could start from the somewhat different assumption that the Halpatis lost (still only a relatively short while ago) their working energy and stamina as a result of their growing poverty and even outright pauperization. This is basically, what the farmers want to believe and they accept no personal responsibility for this state of affairs. Acknowledging that wages are too low to permit a dignified human existence, they always add the remark that the Halpatis' labour output simply does not permit a better payment. 'We give what is due to them, and if that is too little, the cause of it lies in the local labourers' inability to hold their own by working hard enough'—so the farmers claim.

An argument in line with this is that raising wages will not result in improved labour quality, as the Halpatis would still only spend this higher income on alcohol instead of buying more and better food in order to recover their physical strength. It is the classic indictment, according to which the poor are to be blamed for their own misery, which is further perpetuated through their irrational behaviour. The remedy lies in self-discipline and abandonment of wrong or harmful needs. The farmers consider a change in the mentality of their inferiors to be a precondition for payment of the statutory wage, which will only then be socially justifiable as well as economically acceptable. Some informants among the farmers pointed out to me that the government has also contributed to the pauperization of the landless. With the establishment of a minimum wage payable and its compulsory payment in cash, the practice of providing all sorts of extra allowances in kind has increasingly fallen into disuse, lowering the living standard as a result. In particular, the meals and other foodstuffs which labourers in permanent service took home with them, were an essential part of their daily consumption. More than ever the Halpatis are earning the reputation of being weaklings, and considering this it is no wonder that outsiders' zest and energy for work are held up as an example to the Halpatis:

> '. . . by their efficiency and capacity to put in hard work, Saurashtra labour secured preference over local labour both for farm and non-farm work. The Kakrapar before and the Ukai now (N.B. both

> reservoir projects which were completed in the sixties) employs labour which is mostly from Saurashtra and partly from Andhra. Even in progressive agricultural regions of Surat the farmers prefer Saurashtra labour. The labour from Saurashtra working in Gujarat turns out to be cheaper as they are efficient, responsible and do not need constant supervision while at work. (Report MWAC 1966: 43).

This favourable judgement on the early flow of migrants applies just as much to seasonal workers who since then have been coming to Bardoli from other areas in increasingly large numbers.

I have dismissed the insufficient quantity of local labour as a possible explanation for the mass influx of migrants into the central plain of the Surat District. The alleged lack of quality among local landless labourers in official reports provides, to my mind, evidence of poor understanding of the real sources of the strikingly positive valuation accorded in principle to all labour from other places. Before going further into this, I shall first elaborate on the significance of labour mobility for the structure of the regional labour market.

The creation of a labour surplus

The extensive labour mobility which has come to exist in Surat District as the result of the transformation to a modern capitalist agriculture, leads us very easily to the notion that rural society there is in a state of flux, and that a part of the population is—temporarily or permanently—drifting around the countryside. Earlier I myself evoked the image of a stream of migrants which like a locust swarm descends on the plain every year, yet this does not mean that labour circulation takes place in an undirected, uncontrolled manner. Structural changes in the home area compel land-hungry peasants to migrate, but they do not wander aimlessly about. Their coming to the plain is systematically encouraged, and is moreover often well planned.

This is clearly apparent from the through manner in which sugar factories in the vicinity of Bardoli must set to work in order to ensure the services of tens of thousands of cane cutters each year. Mass seasonal migration has become an important aspect of the functioning of the regional market for agricultural labour, but this also applies in principle to the coming and going of gangs of harvest workers from the tribal hinterland, who report for work with the farmers in the plain at the peak periods of the agrarian cycle. Their presence suggests a much greater degree of spontaneity and casualness compared with the tight organization with which labour is imported for cutting sugarcane. The impression of a lack of planning is linked with the character of this pattern of migration, of which the following elements are essential:

> the separation into a great number of small, self-constituted groups (gangs) which are not firmly integrated and which also vary in size;
> the lack of standardised and uniform labour conditions;
> the short duration of stay, and therewith the need to move on at frequent intervals;
> the fleeting, impersonal contact with a multitude of employers.

Are these features characteristic of a structureless labour market? Fisher reaches this conclusion in his analysis of the deployment of Mexican migrant labourers in the harvesting of agricultural products in California (1951: 463–91). In contrast I want to argue that the recruitment and employment of migrants is in fact structured and is moreover consistent with the functioning of the labour market. I am alluding here especially to the particularistic orientation and fragmented character of this ciculation for work—two aspects which typify, to a great extent, the organization of the overall labour regime.

The whole migration process has a decidedly particularistic colouring. Regarding the questions posed earlier—who goes away, in what manner, to what destination, for how long, etc.—can only be answered by taking personal ties as a starting point; these exert a strongly regulating influence. What at first sight appears to be a kind of tidal movement—a capricious pattern of wholesale influx, a haphazard swarming over the villages in the plain to be followed in time by a gradual dispersal—is in reality a movement of labour which is prestructured by highly personalized control mechanisms, that bridge the distance between home area and destination. A key figure in this is the jobber who, in providing the link between supply and demand, is on the one hand bound to the employers with whom he maintains regular contacts and via whom he enlarges his territory, while on the other hand striving to secure labourers in numbers which match his current needs. The *mukadam* does not operate as an independent agent in a free labour market, but depends instead on a limited number of employers who have subordinated him to their needs by extending credit. In his turn the jobber maintains a clientele in his own home territory, on whom he likewise imposes the obligation to supply the required labour power at a given moment, by provision of advances. For the composition of his gang he makes use of primary loyalties—selection on the basis of kinship or neighbourhood (*falia*)—which enable him to make demands on his clients. The farmers of the plain also make use of this kind of personal control mechanism, for instance by recruiting additional labour from the hinterland through migrants already employed as farm servants.

The periodic migration of small and more loosely structured groups consisting of members of one or more families, as well as of neighbouring households, usually takes place on the basis of already existing contacts.[3] The preference is for a familiar route—one or more villages which several of the migrants have already visited on a previous trip, and where tentative arrangements have been made with farmers (and perhaps confirmed through written or verbal communication) for a subsequent visit. Naturally seasonal workers sometimes leave their homes without having a definite aim, beyond that of trying their luck in trekking around at random. I have already given examples of this in earlier chapters. Nevertheless it is my opinion that such a lack of structuring applies only to a small proportion of the total stream of migrants. Whenever the movement of labour over great distances lacks a formal framework, other, more personal channels for regulating this traffic take its place. Mechanisms of a particularistic nature ensure a very effective linkage between supply and demand in the hinterland and in the plain respectively. For the rest, these arrangements based on primordial ties are also recognizable

[3] 'The seasonally migrating labourers usually move in groups. It would thus be reasonable to think that often the inflow, and by implication, also the outflow of rural labour for seasonal agricultural operations is more or less pre-structured rather than a completely unorganized convergence of independently moving labourers' (Bardhan 1977: A 48).

in the organization of cane cutting by the sugar factories around Bardoli. The *mukadam* is the connecting link here, between factory management and the work force attracted anew every year for the duration of the harvesting campaign. The informal setting within which the *mukadam* operates merges with a more formal sphere of management in which he functions as the entry point (Breman 1979: 80).

Isolation is another basic trait of labour circulation. The migrant's mobility has mainly to do with the changing environment in which he finds himself, and much less with the type of work he performs. The majority of those going to the plain remain involved in agricultural work and see no chance of penetrating into another sphere of labour. At best, seasonal workers may remain behind with farmers who take them on as farm servants. Sometimes formal barriers are raised which prevent a longer duration of stay, or transfer to another segment of the labour market (see also Fisher 1951: 484–5). Thus the *mukadams* who lead the cane cutters are contractually obliged to return home with their gangs after the campaign is over. The temporary nature of their stay in the plain, and their confinement to agricultural labour alone, automatically follows from the isolation within which seasonal migrants operate. Even unskilled employment outside agriculture is mostly unattainable for them; in my opinion this is more because they lack contacts than because they are unfit for such labour. Their temporary residence in the plain is organized in such a way that they remain screened off from other employment opportunities. Conversely, non-agrarian seasonal migrants are bound to a large extent in the same way to the specific work for which they were recruited. Thus canal diggers, road workers, brickfield coolies, etc. are confined to mutually exclusive work sites, passing their time in the plain segregated from local labourers and from each other. The group character of the migration and the fragmentation of the labour market tend to reinforce each other.

Confinement to a separate arena is not characteristic of the life led by seasonal migrants only, since the same phenomenon is found among those who have established themselves more permanently in the plain. A large proportion of the labour in the paper mills, for instance, is imported from other places.

workers were brought here by those who were foremen and fellow villagers at the same time. Although working here for years they remain strangers who live in the shadow of the factory and who make themselves invisible, as it were, to the local population. From these enclaves links are maintained with the home area, forming a recruitment channel by means of which (it goes without saying) vacant work places are filled. The trouble it costs to gain entry to another sphere of employment is a result of the inclination to keep the already occupied work places free from interlopers.

Those migrants who do not come to the plain as members of groups appear to be more flexible and are not confined to contacts existing previously. Departure from home is often enforced by a situation of acute need arising for instance, from a natural catastrophe or a crisis in the family household. This is the type of migrant encountered in improvised camps or shelters set apart on the borders of Bardoli town and in various places along the main road to Surat. Although they have not entirely lost contact with the home milieu, nevertheless the way back is cut off for most of them. Conversely they do not succeed—even after a sojourn of many years—in capturing a recognizeably permanent place for themselves in the labour structure of the plain. One day they work on the land, the next day in construction work, the day after that as navvies; thus this category corresponds most closely to the image of a free and mobile rural proletariat. The continual changing of the work situation is not based on personal choice but is, rather, a necessity imposed from without, and indicates the greatest possible insecurity of livelihood.

On the other hand this does not mean that the migrants who—for the length of their residence in the plain—remain confined to one and the same type of activity (through all kinds of binding mechanisms of a particularistic nature) lead a more secure existence. The fragmented way in which most migrants are recruited and employed prevents them from making a common stand and hinders the spontaneous transition to better-paid work. This fragmentation is, as already stated, a distinguishing feature of the whole labour regime. The barriers thrown up within and between the agrarian and non-agrarian reservoirs of employment in the south Gujarat countryside, result in the enclosure of labour in separate compartments, as far as possible.

Having drawn attention to the sharply compartmentalized structure, I would like to stress further the relative autonomy of the urban labour order compared with the rural. In contrast to the suggestion, in much of the literature, of a comparatively simple town-country duality, further mitigated by the mobility of labour, I am inclined to emphasize the internal heterogeneity of each of these networks as much as the lack of a direct linkage between them. My interpretation runs parallel to that of Bardhan:

> . . . the process of migration from rural to urban areas is structured connecting specific groups of rural migrants (from specific regions and for specific groups and communities) to particular types of urban work. The mechanism of such structuring is a combination of factors: specific needs (like the need for seasonal jobs) and skills of the migrants, personalized or community based systems of contacts and information, and the use of gang leaders and other intermediaries for labour recruitment in industry and civil construction works (Bardhan 1977: A 46).

I have particular doubts about the validity of the theory which says that displacement of labour follows a phased pattern, with rural migrants passing through and remaining briefly in one or more intermediate work situations, en route for the big city. This model of step migration presumes personal choice and freedom of movement, an assumption which conflicts with the manner in which labour relations are structured in south Gujarat. It is already clear from my previous argument that migrants arriving in the rural areas of Surat District are indeed seldom encountered in the city. The limited data which I collected on the phenomenon of urbanization lead me to the opposite conclusion that those who have found employment in the cities have come directly from their villages. By way of illustration, witness the following diary fragment noted in Udhna, the industrial headquarters of Surat.

> *15 April.* On a building site I encounter a group of 32 labourers, nearly all from Khandesh. They are usually split up in work units usually consisting of man and wife, with or without working children. Next come a number of single people, women as well as men. Only a few are older than the late twenties or early thirties.

The group has been assembled by a *mukadam*, who received his instructions from a contractor. Today he has sent for 12 people from his native place in Jalgaon. The rest were recruited in the *bazars* of Udhna and Surat, either personally or with the help of some trusted labourers in the gang who regularly work for him. Those who have already spent a long time in Surat—a period of two to three years is not exceptional—also came straight here from their villages, in the same way as newcomers today. For the landless among them there is really no way back. They enter a life of circulation within the urban economy without a fixed residence. As long as work is in progress they have the use of a temporary shelter made from building materials or the waste from these. After a job is finished the group breaks up and the camp disappears. The labourers hang around the *bazar* and other meeting places in the hope of a new assignment. Do they use this time to make a return trip to their home villages? Contact is not entirely lost, but those who stay longer in the city and have their wives and children with them, seldom seem to return. The answer given by one informant was repeated by others in various tones: 'if there's work there's no time—if there's no work, there's no money'.

The *mukadam* is a key figure in the urban market for unskilled labour. He does not operate independently, but maintains a permanent relationship with one employer, or sometimes with several. The jobber at this building site has already worked for years for the same contractor. When there is no work his boss still gives him an allowance by way of compensation and advance wages on services still to be rendered. The work begun today is paid by piece rate. The men receive Rs 6, the women—for somewhat lighter work—Rs 4 per brass. The mukadam's remuneration consists of a commission of Re 1 a day on every labourer working under him, while in addition he passes on to his workers a lower rate per brass than the contractor gives him. When a husband and wife work together they earn no more than Rs 10 daily, Rs 70 per week. This evening the contractor has come, to provide an advance that will enable the labourers to buy food for the coming week. He provides a total of Rs 600 which the jobber divides out among the couples of labourers in portions of Rs 30–40. Those who are known as hardworking and trustworthy receive a higher amount, while newcomers have to be content with less. Once a week the settlement of accounts takes place, but the jobber does not pay out everything to the labourers, so that they are tied to him for the duration of the job.

It should be clear from this example that the structure

and dynamics of the urban market for unskilled labour do not differ fundamentally from the rural market, which is not to say that the two are linked with each other in a direct way. The organization of work is directed towards maintaining labour in separate compartments, not only between city and countryside but also within these. What appears at first sight to be a loose, amorphous structure is in fact a systematic breaking up of the lower echelons of the whole labour regime, with the result that migrants are also mobile along a great number of separate channels (Joshi and Joshi 1975, ch. V).

Further study of the trek to the city falls outside the scope of the present study. I content myself here with the conclusion that there is no reason for accepting the idea that those circulating in the countryside view the city as their ultimate destination. There is a great diversity of migration routes and the subdivision of these into a rural and an urban component does not, in itself, do justice to the much more complex reality. Particularism and fragmentation are the regulatory mechanisms for the supply of labour to the south Gujarat plain. The effect is an enormous extension of supply, far more than is required inside and outside agriculture. In the previous section I have rejected standard explanations for labour migration which assume local shortage of manpower either in a quantitive or in a qualitative sense. On the basis of my outline of the structure of the labour market, I can now be clearer about this. Labour from elsewhere is rendered mobile not in order to satisfy a shortage in the area of destination but in order to create a surplus. The advent of migrants enables farmers and other employers in Bardoli and its neighbourhood to make less use of the local landless. Why this preference for outsiders? This question is the starting point for my argument in the following section.

Preference for outside labour

The first motive to be considered is of a strictly material nature. There is no difficulty in finding acceptance for the idea that migrants are cheaper than local labourers. When the going wage rate amounted to Rs 3, the outsiders were prepared to accept only Rs 2, as I have repeatedly been able to confirm. The underpayment of outsiders is greater in all kinds of tasks; for instance, the wives of migrant labourers who now and then do household work receive only food for this, with no extra money. The farmers themselves maintain that they operate a uniform rate, and instruct even their temporary labourers to deny, if questioned, any difference in wage payment. I gained the impression that this difference in payment diminished or even disappeared entirely with increasing pressure of work, yet the migrants still remain cheaper because, for the same daily amount, they work two to three hours longer than the local landless. Besides this, the strangers are much easier to cheat, being forced to accept their ultimate dismissal with even less than the sum agreed upon.

Apart from this direct profit—a lower price for the same effort or the same price for a better output—there is yet another economic advantage for the farmers in employing outsiders. The massive supply of migrant labourers results in cost cutting because of its depressive effect on local wages, and thus the bargaining position of the local landless is weakened. Does this mean that the extra labour supply is a deliberate attempt to keep the wage level low for agricultural labour, by the creation of a surplus? In his analysis of the migration of Mexican harvest workers to California, Fisher rejects this proposition, which according to him is much too simple. 'The lowering of wage rates where it occurs is as much an effect as it is an objective of oversupply . . . the demand of farmers for more labor than an outside observer would think they require is a rational response to the peculiar circumstances of the harvest, and is largely independent of the effect that the supply of labour may have upon its price' (1951 : 471). This conclusion is also applicable to the situation I have been discussing. Migrant labourers are cheaper, but this is an incidental advantage and not the principal reason why they are preferred.

A second motive is the farmers far greater control over migrants, who are in a strange environment and are not familiar with local usages against which they might be able to judge the treatment meted out to them. I have already indicated that the migrants worked much longer hours than the local landless. The demands imposed on their time and working strength are not specific or subject to fixed agreements. Those who have been allocated accommodation in or close to the farmers' house, are continually available for all kinds of tasks, from early morning until late evening. It is no wonder that the farmers praise their diligence, conscientiousness, uprightness and docility. This high degree of versatility and pliability makes the migrants greatly valued as labourers. At the same time this is an implicit judgement upon the shortcomings of the local landless, for they are perceived as lacking in all these desirable qualities. In contrast to the Halpatis, the seasonal workers cannot retreat to a milieu of their own in order to make a stand against the farmers' dominance. To be sure this resistance among the local landless is mainly of a passive nature—a counter point culture in a situation of oppression which finds expression in escape, sabotage, and the like, more than in organized action. Underlying this is a common stand, a community of interests of which farmers as much as agricultural labourers are becoming conscious to an increasing degree, and which is also becoming clearly articulated. The migrants are excluded from this, the isolation which characterizes their life in the plain preventing them from forming a common front against their employers. They are split up into small groups and the particularistic links accompanying these, keep them separated from the local landless and from each other. In this respect also, the fragmentation of the labour force is clearly to the advantage of the farmers.

Finally, a third motive is that contacts with migrant labourers in the plain need to be only fleeting and of short duration. Farmers can limit the relationship with the strangers to the actual sphere of work alone, much more easily than they can in the case of the local landless. The relationship concerns—literally—a work arrangement, i.e. a commitment embracing nothing more than the performance of labour and the payment for it. The reduction of labour to a commodity means that it is deprived of all social significance. The farmer is not interested in the agricultural labourer's personal qualities and prefers to ignore his background and the burden of dependent family members. It is obvious that the employment of outsiders suits to perfection this desire for a contractual relationship. While in the plain, the migrant labourers maintain no social life which can create claims conflicting with the demands made by the farmers on them. The kind of circumstances which sometimes keep Halpatis from their daily work (to the great discontent of their bosses) such as sickness in the home, a family celebration, religious ceremonies, etc. do not affect the migrants.

The local landless still expect a wage that enables them to survive, and are prepared to work in exchange for this. When there happens to be nothing for them to do, they depend on the kind of relief which will enable them to keep their households intact. As I demonstrated earlier, the farmers are increasingly less willing to respect this claim to survival, and the advent of seasonal workers provides them with an alternative. After all, these migrants are paid on the basis of actual performance and expect nothing more. It becomes obvious that it is the home area which bears the cost of their reproduction.

While reporting on his research into rural labour relations in eastern Germany at the end of the nineteenth century, Weber drew attention to the importance of this factor:

> The migrant worker, torn from his family and usual environment, is regarded as simple labour power both by the landlords and by himself. The barracks of the migrant workers are the money-economy equivalents of the slave barracks of antiquity. The estate owner saves on workers' housing, since accommodation for the migrants costs little or nothing. He has also no need to allocate plots of land, but above all he is not regulated by laws governing conditions of work and pay. Thus while the seasonal wage rates are higher, taken over the year the employer lays out no more, usually less, than he used to for a resident worker throughout the year[4].

[4] Weber (English translation 1979: 193). In the original German version published in 1893, Weber examines more extensively the question of preference for outside labour.

'Durchaus nicht immer deshalb, weil diese Wanderarbeiter einen niedrigen Lohn bekämen, sondern in erster Linie, weil man keine verwaltungsrechtlichen Pflichten, keine Armenlasten u.s.w. für sie übernimmt—man schiebt sie eben nach Ausnützung ihrer Arbeitskräfte wieder ab. Und ferner: der Russe muss sich auch etwas anderes bieten lassen als der einheimische Arbeiter; er ist prekärer gestellt und ein Wink an den benachbarten Amtsvorsteher genügt, um ihn schleunigst über die Grenze zurück zu spedieren, falls er sich an den Wünschen des Grossgrundbesitzers nicht überall fügt. *Deshalb* müssen—das ergeben die Berichte der Enquete—die selbstbewussten Arbeiter West-Preussens, die alten deutschen Instleute der Weichselniederungen, weichen zu gunsten der pölnischen Wanderarbeiter' (Weber 1893: 71).

Besides being compartmentalized the migrants in the plain are also reduced to a commodity. The farmers making use of their services do not see them as individuals and they also remain hidden as a collective entity in the social environment at large. This underlines their isolation.

Besides the motives already stated, which argue directly in favour of migrants, there is yet another consideration among the landowning class of the plain—namely the inclination to make as little use as possible of the services of the local landless. Although employers inside and outside agriculture usually deny that this is a conscious policy, yet this seems to be the only possible conclusion one can make. In the previous chapter I regarded as untenable the argument that labourers from the area lack the experience necessary for undertaking the new production tasks. This unskilled work, demanding hardly any experience, does not justify the importation of outsiders. It is also untrue that the latter only occupy work places which have been recently created. On the contrary, they have ousted the Halpatis even from their own territory of employment. The only possible conclusion therefore is that the intrusion of migrants into the labour process of the plain has to an increasing extent resulted in the expulsion of the local landless. The threat to the latter's basic means of livelihood is a direct result of the change which has occurred in their attitude towards the upper farming class—a change in the social climate to which I have already drawn attention. Also, Weber assumed that the import of seasonal labour from Poland in the latter part of the nineteenth century was actually a weapon in the rural class struggle in the Eastern regions of Germany: 'The introduction of Poles is here a weapon in the anticipated class struggle which is directed against the growing consciousness of the worker, and it is obvious that in this connection it is a very effective weapon' (1979: 199).

Growing consciousness among the landless has aroused the farmers' wrath. In the past the local landless were simply there, all the time at the beck and call of the Patidars, in exchange for which they had the right to a guaranteed subsistence. Labour had to be maintained at the behest of the employer, but was not something that had to be paid for. The dependent workforce, which was once not much more than an extension of the landowners' households, now emphasizes its independence and tries as far as possible to behave in an appropriate manner. This indicates a fundamental change in the interpretation of labour value. The farmers are reluctant to accept this change, which they themselves have created by ushering in a capitalist mode of production, because they rightly perceive this as an undermining of their own social dominance. They refuse to accept the new rules of the game, but conceal this refusal behind the complaint that the Halpatis want too large a wage for too little work. Apathy, incompetence, laziness and untrustworthiness are the most notable failings imputed to their former subordinates. The Halpatis' attempts to free themselves from docility and servility are all too eagerly explained by their superiors as an inability to meet work obligations. They speak in terms of the unprecedented inefficiency of the present generation of labourers, a failing which betrays 'their' dissatisfaction in all sorts of ways, instead of awaiting the chance to make demands in a decent way.

29 May. Bikhu P. is a big farmer in village M. He cultivates sugarcane almost exclusively because, according to him, this crop has solved a labour problem for him. He never grows tired of talking about the earlier times when the Halpatis knew their proper place, were loyal to their master and showed gratitude that he filled their daily needs. There is no question of that now. According to his own claim, he was the first to bring labourers into the village from outside, because the uselessness of the local landless stood in the way of agricultural progress. The farmers could no longer rely on them. The Halpatis had only themselves to blame for the poverty in which they live. Every effort to help them is futile, and one would even think that they did not actually want to be helped. Only the previous week he had been compelled to send away a farm servant who had worked for him for years. The man held Bikhu responsible for the sickness of his wife and daughter who, while working on Bikhu's land, had drunk water out of a field channel that was polluted by fertilizer. Well, they should not have done so, and in any case, who said the poison came from there? Perhaps they had really become sick from home-made liquor. Bikhu had given the farm servant to understand that he did not intend to pay the cost of medical treatment, or even provide an advance for it. The man had refused to accept this, had become very emotional, and had even threatened to take what he had not been given, i.e. to steal standing crops from the fields—an unforgivable insolence to which instant dismissal was the only possible reaction. Bikhu did not let himself go in front of me, adopting rather the pose of being a temperate and a reasonable person. He wants to produce the impression of someone whose trust in his inferiors is invariably betrayed, but who nevertheless continues to have the best of intentions towards them. The tone adopted by his son is much more aggressive and vindictive. Vinod is the archetypal young, businesslike farm manager who has picked up his modern outlook in the Bardoli college. He is even more open than his father to new agricultural methods, mechanization, calculation and planning. He gives unreserved evidence of his distaste and contempt for the Halpatis, who indulge to excess in all kinds of bad practices. To prevent theft, he has to remove the starting motor from the pump house every evening, and even then fixed parts and wiring are wrenched out on occasion—not only to provide the means for satisfying their craving for drink but also out of a spirit of sheer vandalism, so he told me indignantly. Sacks of fertilizer or work tools are regularly thrown into the wells. He has made a firm decision not to allow this malicious and rebellious behaviour to go unpunished. While we are discussing this he points out a field lying fallow. It should have been possible to cultivate summer rice here, yielding some Rs. 800–1,000 per acre profit. Not a great deal as compared with sugarcane but still quite attractive. Because there are not enough migrant labourers during these months he would have to call on the Halpatis' labour for this, and he refused point blank to do so. In order to spare himself anxiety, trouble and annoyance, he was gladly giving up the extra income. The idea that he is dependent upon those who sour his life, is unbearable.

Perhaps a rather extreme example of the conscious sacrifice of economic profit for the desire to withhold an attendant advantage—the income deriving from agricultural labour—from one's opponents? To suggest that this kind of behaviour only occurs occasionally would show misapprehension of the 'irrationality' of the farmers, who are potentially prepared to sacrifice their material self interest for their yearning to teach the local landless a lesson. In the words of a highly placed district official 'The Patidars rejoice in the actual starvation of the Halpatis'. Their animosity is not lessened by the fact that the attempt to subdue others no longer always succeeds.

For the bigger landowners the plain, economic profit has

without doubt become the most important driving force for the rapid transition to cultivation of sugarcane and bananas in the last two decades, but as I have already observed, the popularity which these crops enjoy is definitely connected with the low labour intensity they require on an annual basis, and as far as sugarcane is concerned, with an escape from labour management in the most important operation.

The distribution of less work than is possible, or even than is optimally required, has become a weapon in the local dominant caste's battle against the landless caste. I was assured, from different sides, that weeding for example is only done occasionally, to the cost of the yield. Halpatis see in this the Patidars' reluctance to permit them a livelihood, and some of the latter acknowledge the justice of this accusaction. Predatory capitalism extends not only to maximal exploitation but is further characterized by the striving to do as much damage as possible to the underclasses, even when the antagonism produced in this way is counter-productive economically and ultimately threatens the established order. This point appears to be rapidly approaching in Bardoli and surrounding *talukas*. Only now and then did I meet a landowner from the dominant class who behaved as a modern capitalist entrepreneur in his dealing with labourers.

14 June. Ashok has finished his studies at the agricultural college. He is a member of a farmer's union and has been given the opportunity to make a study trip to the United States with a number of other younger farmers from all over Gujarat. He has returned in a very enthusiastic frame of mind—full of ideas, convinced of the need for further expansion of the capital intensity of his efficiently run farm, and deeply interested in all kinds of new initiatives which expand agrarian productivity as well as the political power of the leading farming class.

He employs a permanent core of labourers whose wages nearly reach the daily minimum of Rs 5.50 or Rs 150 a month. The casual labourers obtain Rs 4 a day without food or other allowances in kind. In exchange for this all those mentioned must work a nine-hour-day, from 07.30 to 12.00 and from 13.00 to 17.30. A foreman maintains strict supervision. There is a fine for late arrival but extra is paid for overtime work. Ashok devotes great attention to the cost factor. In earlier days his father had to keep more labourers than were required for daily needs, in order to be able to tie other members of their households as temporary labourers during the

> peak period. This is no longer necessary now that gangs of harvest workers come in from outside. Ashok's reasoning is that the minimum wage works to the farmers' advantage—in other words, he can demand a maximum amount and quality of work, and those who do not fulfill this can take themselves off! There are always enough interested people to fill the places falling vacant. His style of labour management is business-like rather than paternalistic. Everyone knows his own task and negligence is punished, as for instance when an agricultural work implement is lost or broken, and Ashok recovers the cost from the labourer. He no longer gives his workforce credit or loans—they bind the farmer as much as the labourers, who then have to be kept on even if their work is bad, so that the credit money is not lost. Too low a wage leads to the labourers' indebtedness. The amount lent is never seen again, which only stirs up even more trouble. Ashok criticizes the short-sightedness shown by the other farmers, who have a good deal of money to spare for fertilizers, for instance—in fact, they use them far more than is either necessary or good—but who deprive labour of all dignity through underpayment.

However great their dislike of the landless from their own area, the farmers cannot afford to operate exclusively with migrant labour. The agricultural work to be carried out the whole year round is too extensive for that, and secondly the arrival of seasonal workers in sufficient numbers is erratic and remains uncertain right up to the last moment. When the harvest in their own home area turns out well, fewer make the journey away from home. It is also never entirely certain which route the strangers will follow, or whether they will keep the tentative appointments they have made, as well as the definite ones. Further, there is no certainty about the length of time the migrants will stay; many depart again just as unexpectedly as they came, for reasons which remain unclear to the farmers. The migrants leave without having completed the work, and attempts to restrain them are of no avail. When Halpatis are subsequently approached they may very well refuse their services out of sheer spite. The fact that Patidars must continue to rely on the local landless explains why farmers try to conceal their general rule about using migrant labour as much as possible behind the less hostile formula of using migrants as far as possible to supplement local labour.

A small minority of Patidars show genuine concern over the hard way in which their caste fellows treat the Halpatis, and it is from this corner in particular that voices are heard urging the social importance of improvement in mutual understanding. After all, both parties have to live together: This is a plea which leaves no impression on most farmers, who are not keen on making concessions to local agricultural labourers by guaranteeing something like a right to work, or even by merely giving preference to these above strangers. It looks as though they have chosen the opposite course—the elimination of the landless caste from the rural production process dominated by the farmers.

> . . . the Dublas are destined to remain poor and backward. The processes of civilization are strenuous and requires hard labour and skill. We, Charotarias (Patidars) have created wealth wherever we have gone. Why? Because we are hardworking and our style of living is cultured. Whereas, these Dublas have none of these traits. They are the laziest in the world. They do not educate themselves. Their habits are bad and they live immoral living. They drink limitlessly and cause strife in their families. A (code of conduct) similar to our concept of life and living does not exist among them. Gandhiji and his innumerable workers tried to improve their lot but they will simply not change. Civilization requires thinking about future and these Dublas, sometimes do not even think of the next meal, if they secure one for the present. No government, howsoever, well intending can improve a Dubla's lot (Patel 1982: 9).

Pauperization of the local landless

The combination of too little work with too low a wage determines the life of poverty led by agricultural labourers in the south Gujarat plain. Over the last two decades agriculture has become a dynamic industry which in addition has created a number of new economic activities in the countryside itself. Together these ensure great pressure of work nearly the whole year round. But it is precisely in Surat District, where intensification and diversification of production has been most rapid, that this development has led to growing unemployment among the local landless; in the villages where I carried out my research, it was never difficult to find agricultural labourers at home during the daytime. From answers to my repeated question about the number of days worked during the week just passed, I could form an impression of the work schedule of the informants. Outside the busy seasons, this usually fluctuates between 12 and 20 days a month for the men. For the women (apart from those who worked in the morning hours as *vasiduvali*) I calculated a much lower number of work-days still—no more than 6 to 10 on average. Only at the peak points of the agrarian cycle did I encounter mainly old people and children at the hutments. I tried to verify the picture emerging from this by daily visiting a limited number of agricultural labourers' households (thirteen in all) in three different villages during the course of one week. The outcome of this confirmed the information mentioned above, but I am aware that this random sample has been too small and the spread over the seasons has been too haphazard to be able to draw more definite conclusions. More thorough and detailed quantification is required than that provided by the more qualitative research method I have followed. An investigation of 250 households in south Gujarat, dating from the end of 1976, i.e. shortly before my first period of fieldwork, provides confirmation of the situation I have sketched above.

> There was only a small number out of the total 250 households who reported that they could manage to get regular employment during the entire agricultural season. But for the majority of farm labourers, times have become extremely hard so far as finding work was concerned. Majority of them reported that for more than a fortnight in a month they had to remain idle for want of employment. In the villages of Surat District, the situation appeared to be really quite grave . . . During our field-trip in the villages of Surat District, more than 75 per cent of the informants were sitting idle. [My note: information of this nature is not very illuminating if the time of visit is not mentioned.] Many of them lamented that there was some sort of security in the past but now no landowner of the non-tribal community was keen in employing the Halpatis for their farmwork (Lal 1977: 11).

As I have already stated, the migrants coming to the central part of Surat District are involved in a process of proletarianization, and labour circulation is for the majority of them in essence, a holding operation. With the help of earnings from outside, these small and marginal farmers manage to maintain themselves as landowners in their home areas and to continue producing enough food for their own needs. Thus temporary absence can indeed help to prevent the alienation of land, but where very small holdings are concerned, it is migration itself which accelerates the transition to landlessness. A temporary transfer of land rights in exchange for part of the yield ultimately changes into a final alienation from all rights within and without the household of origin. This proletarianization is not only the result of seasonal migration, but can also open the door to permanent departure. Downward mobility is easier to accept away from home, and those who stay on in the plain as farm servants mask their descent down the social ladder.

The Halpatis' starting position is different. Their opportunities for moving to another environment are extremely limited, and they can find no lower pockets in the stratification of work. These landless have always formed the bottom layer in the rural order of which they are a part, and for this reason the fast economic growth in the area they inhabit has for the most part passed them by. Only a small minority has had the chance to penetrate the more skilled and better paid employment which has come into existence. Indicative of this is the situation in S., a village which lies at a small distance from Navsari town, which is rapidly getting industrialized. Although employment in agriculture provides a meagre income, only a minority of the earning members of Halpati households have succeeded in finding other jobs. At the same time not less than 43 'foreign' households, coming from all parts of India, were staying in the village and commuting to Navasari where they had found work in industrial enterprises (Kalathil 1979: 57). Urban employment nearby—insofar as this is even within the reach of the local landless—offers them no security of living, and as unskilled workers they pass directly into the lowest echelons of the labour hierarchy. Thus there are few openings and not much prospect of improvement.

The bulk of the Halpatis remain tied to the traditional work of this caste—agricultural labour—but even in their own home territory they have to compete with and often are defeated by the stream of migrants coming temporarily to the plain, or staying behind at the end of the season to establish themselves there. While the latter undergo the transition to a landless proletarianism many of the Halpatis (whom the migrants are in the process of displacing) find themselves entrapped in a process of acute pauperization. By this I mean a drop in living standards to a level lying substantially below the officially designated poverty line. This is a remarkable fact precisely because this trend towards deterioration exists in an area characterized not by economic stagnation but by accelerated economic growth. The picture may be worse than in the north west of India, for which Bardhan established that: '. . . even in the prime "green revolution" area of Punjab/Haryana the proportion of people below a bare minimum of living increased, and . . . even though the average level of living of agricultural labourers got a little better, the degree of inequality among them increased, leaving many more of them below the bare minimum' (1977: 1114). In the case of south Gujarat it cannot even be said that the agricultural labourers have made some progress or at least consolidated their relative position. From my research it would appear that the share of labour cost has not risen but has actually dropped. My findings show that labour constituted a negligible proportion of the total production costs. In a village close to Bardoli even at the beginning of the sixties—i.e. still before there was any mention of a green revolution—the farmers spent more on fertilizer than on labour (Patel 1966: 137). The last item amounted to one-third of all farming costs—a percentage which since then has declined even further. The rise in agrarian production has worked one-sidedly to the farmers' benefit, while labour's share in the total yield has neither risen nor remained the same even on a relatively low level, but has dropped still further. I shall elucidate this conclusion with data for the wage trend for agricultural labour over nearly half a century.

In the past farmers were obliged to provide their farm servants with a subsistence livelihood. In exchange for their claim to the labour of their inferiors, the latter received a daily allowance in grain (*bhata*), in some places also a plot of land (*vavla*), periodically supplemented with all kinds of other emoluments—footwear, roofing material, etc. When sickness or other setbacks occurred in the household, the *hali* could depend on help from his master. Thus the reverse side of the indebtedness and bondage inherent in the farmer servant relationship was that the permanent labourer's right to a living was acknowledged[5]. It is interesting that the commission

[5] Insistence on the contrast with the present trend towards pauperization can

which advised on the abolition of the *hali* system shortly after independence, suggested that wages for agricultural labour should be linked to what was traditionally regarded as a minimum subsistence. In accordance with the price levels of the time this amounted to Re 1 a day, the equivalent of 8 *seers* of food grain. The government would need to dictate the compulsory payment of this amount—adjusted to rising living costs—through promulgation of a minimum wage law.

Two elements in this advice are of fundamental importance. In the first place there is the consideration that government intervention would not be permitted to extend further than guaranteeing the agricultural labourers the absolute minimum necessary. According to the report, notice could only be taken of pressure for the passing of a 'fair wage' law after a sufficient rise in agricultural productivity (Report HLEC 1950). Since then this standpoint has never been abandoned as the official guiding principle. A subsequent investigatory commission in 1966 explicitly rejected the suggestion that remuneration for labour should be adjusted to the daily needs of the worker and his family. Apart from arguing that this would cause endless discussion about basic needs, the report insisted that the carrying capacity of agriculture and of the farmer must remain the point of departure (Report MWAC 1966: 81). Although since then growth in productivity has brought increasing prosperity to the farmers, the agricultural labourers have had no share in the raised profits, and neither have they ever received the living wage which was definitely granted to them on paper at that time. This is connected with a second recommendation appearing in the original advice (as also in the later), i.e. the replacement of a wage in kind by a sum of money. Otherwise this conversion did not result from direct governmental interference. Rather, the suggestions made by the official investigators in 1947 and 1966 followed a trend which had already developed under the influence of the transition towards capitalism. The allowance proposed was based on the principle that an average agricultural labourer's household required 6 *seers* of food daily, and that the equivalent

---

easily lead to a rose-tinted representation of the past situation. Scott in particular seems not to have entirely escaped this danger (1976: 32–4). Also in previous generations not all agricultural labourers could claim a subsistence, but only those who were farm servants. For the most pointed critique of Scott's argument, see Popkin 1979.

of a further 2 *seers* of grain was necessary for the fulfilment of other basic needs. This package indeed approximates to the payment the *halis* were accustomed to receiving in earlier times. In the villages where I did my first fieldwork in 1961–2 a farm servant could traditionally claim 5 *seers* of millet daily (c. 2½ kg), two meals and tea, regularly supplemented with all kinds of perquisites (Breman 1974). Together with the extras obtained by his wife as maidservant and by his working children, this worked out at the 8 *seers* which the commission of enquiry judged to be the essential minimum.

Considering that this minimum was already fixed at the lowest possible level, the tendency to convert this living allowance into a sum of money has resulted in an even further lowering of the labourers' living standard. The principal cause is definitely that the prices of daily necessities, particularly food, have risen far faster than wages[6]. This acceleration is manifested in the discrepancy between the wages proposed and determined, as against the amounts actually paid.

I add the following notes to table 10.2. In the first place I would like to repeat the observation that the recommended wages were intended as a basic rate in order to ensure at least the survival of the agricultural labourers. As the *Land Commission Report* from 1979 established with reference to the original attempts at official intervention: 'The minimum wage lays down the lowest reward payable. Any payment below it would be exploitative and unsocial' (*Report of the Gujarat State Land Commission* 1979: 208).

There is every good reason for taking good note of this judgement. The amount with which the farmers have fobbed off their labourers remains (fairly consistent over the years) only a third to a half of the minimal level regarded as being minimally necessary. Or, to put it another way, at the moment moment that a concerted effort from the official side to push up wages could no longer be evaded, the real daily payment

[6] Bardhan points out that this is a common phenomenon which can be documented on the basis of evidence from other parts of the country as well: 'Studies on trends of agricultural wages and food prices . . . all tend to indicate that the real wage rate for agricultural labour declines with rising food prices. During the mid sixties, it dropped in almost all the states. Studies on differential price increases also show that food price had gone up at a higher rate for the poorest deciles of rural households than for the higher ones' (1977: 1104).

Table 10.2 *Rise in daily wages for male labourers in Bardoli area during the past decades*

Year	Proposed/ fixed wage	Going wage rate	Source*
1938–9	Rs 0.28	in kind	Dave: 36
1947	Rs 1	in kind	HLEC: 38
1962–3		in kind or Rs 1	Breman: 237
		Rs 0.62 plus two meals & tea or Rs 0.95	Patel: 107; Vyas: 14
1965–6	Rs 2	Rs 1–1.25	Report M.W.A.C.: 94 and 97
1969–70		Rs 1.90	Desai: 6
1970–1		Rs 2	Naik: 122
1972	Rs 3		officially determined minimum wage
1973		Rs 1–2	Kalathil: 52
1974		Rs 1.50–2	own fieldwork data
1976	Rs 5.50		revised minimum wage
1977		Rs 3	own fieldwork data
		Rs 3	Lal: 12
		Rs 3.50	Shah: 39
1977–8		Rs 3.14	Naik: 122
1979		Rs 3–4	L.C. Report: 205
1980–1		Rs 3–4	own fieldwork data
1982	Rs 9.50		revised minimum wage
1983		Rs 4–6	own fieldwork data

*J. Breman, *Patronage and exploitation.* 1974

J. Dave, *Halpati mukit.* 1946

M. D. Desai, *Employment, income and levels of living of agricultural labourers; a study in the Surat district, Gujarat 1969–70.* 1974

M. Kalathil, *The sociological implications of industrialisation in a locality in Gujarat.* Ph.D. thesis University of Delhi 1979

R. B. Lal, *Bonded labour in Gujarat.* 1977

——, *Report Gujarat State Land Commission.* 1979

K. V. Naik, *Wage structure and economic condition of agricultural labourers in Navsari taluka.* M.Phil. thesis South Gujarat University. Surat 1979.

J. M. Patel, *Agricultural labour in a South Gujarat village.* 1964

——, *Report of the Hali labour enquiry committee.* 1950

——, *Report of the minimum wages advisory committee for employment in agriculture,* Government of Gujarat. 1966

G. Shah, *Agricultural labourers: are they bonded?* 1978

V. S. Vyas, *Agricultural labour in a South Gujarat village.* 1964 received by the labourers was approaching the level which had been regarded as the absolute minimum many years earlier.

In the second place I would like to point to the agricultural labourers' growing inability to purchase, with their daily income, the amount of grain necessary for their subsistence needs. In order to be able to buy 8 *seers* of grain—the point of departure for the 1947 commission of enquiry—the wage for an agricultural labourer in 1980 should have amounted to at least Rs 8 for which he would have got grain of the most inferior quality (*lal jovar*). In reality he collected at best only half of this amount, which moreover remained far below the official rate of Rs 5.50. I conclude from this that with the rapidly progressing monetization of the agricultural economy, the correlation formerly existing between wages and living allowance has been lost. A further contribution to the deterioration in the agricultural labourers' dietary conditions resulting from this, was the gradual diminishing or even disappearance of all sorts of supplementary payments in kind, which included an evening or midday meal and tea. According to the farmers, this happened because these perquisites have been incorporated into wages payable in cash.

Repeatedly, and genuinely uncomprehendingly, agricultural labourers calculated for me that the food they needed each day cost more than the money they were in a position to earn. In their reasoning they still continue to believe in the right to a subsistence, but instead of receiving support they meet with actual obstruction in their daily struggle for existence. The farmers no longer have any concern for what was formerly an inviolable right. They chase away agricultural labourers who cut grass or gather firewood on the farmers' land or even on public property so that the poor are forced into cannibalizing the trees along the roadside through lack of sufficient firewood. The right to graze one's livestock on the village pasture is nowadays sold to herdsmen who come every year with their flocks of sheep and goats from north Gujarat. Further, the waste left over from agrarian production which formerly fell to the agricultural labourers' share is now destined for other purposes: the straw once used as roofing for their huts now goes to the paper mill, the *chhas* does not return to the village from the dairy co-operative in Surat City. Credit formed an important part of the agricultural labourers' subsistence allowance. Several decades ago when the cropping pattern was less intensive, the agricultural labourer could depend on *khavati* in slack times. The labour-intensity of agriculture has increased sharply since then, but so also has unemployment among the local landless in the slack periods. Increasingly fewer farmers are demonstrably prepared to alleviate the starvation which then occurs in many households by providing consumption loans. As a rule they resolutely refuse requests for larger advances. Present-day agricultural labourers are less burdened with debt; they have become free, but in a way which smacks of redundancy. Their state of pauperization has become an additional excuse for the farmers to pass them by and to give preferential treatment to outside labour.

While some of the migrants in their movement to the plain are becoming alienated from the means of production at home—and are thus caught up in a process of proletarianization—the class of landless labourers which belongs to Badoli region is increasingly alienated from the means of consumption. To be sure, the Halpatis have always been poor, but the only term which adequately describes their present retrogression is pauperization.

The farmers' increased prosperity accentuates even more glaringly the agricultural labourers' impoverishment. The Patidars are accustomed to displaying their leisure and opulence in a very conspicuous manner.

> A wedding in the household of a large farmer required some Rs 50,000 in 1980: 'There's quite some capital sitting there' said my host in A., pointing with a sigh but also with pride to his young daughter and some of her friends on the *hitchko* (swing) on the porch. As a real *nouveau riche* he sometimes indulged in exorbitant expenditure—for instance, having his *mama* (mother's brother) brought up in a taxi from the Bombay airport, a gesture which cost him hundreds of rupees. In the same way we went on a family visit to Kaira District, a trip lasting a couple of days, which has remained only as a hazy memory for me, thanks to the bottles of whisky we drank on the road.

According to the previous generation of landowners, in the past, they differed little from the landless in their outward behaviour, but such stories must not be taken too literally, since they mainly express satisfaction with the present state of affairs. But then again, the agricultural labourers still remember the time when the farmers worked side by side with them in the fields and ate rice only when they had guests. An old farm servant assured me bitterly that he had helped to defray the costs of college education for his master's children while his own have had to remain illiterate. The often opulent houses built by the Patidars in recent years are a sharp reminder to the local landless of how poor their own accommodation is. Granted, in many villages they now live on their own land, and an increasing number of huts are being roofed with tiles in place of straw, but the bad siting of the land, the rough access roads and the great distance to the village centre hardly make these colonies attractive places in which to live. Conditions of life described by the Commission of Enquiry into Agricultural Labour in the mid-sixties exist even to this day.

> Visits to *Halpati* colonies presented a picture of unhealthy and unhygienic conditions of accommodation with meagre household effects for less than a bare living. The surroundings were filthy and neglected. Vices, particularly if illicit drinking were the rule. The *halis* and their families were under-nourished and in poor health. Large families with many children doing nothing or little and living in purposeless or directionless life were other tragic features (Report MWAC 1966: 39).

I have previously devoted attention to the emergence of a small top layer among the Halpatis who have gained entry to more regular, more skilled and better-paid work in the countryside or cities. Their better clothing and housing makes them easily recognizeable in the agricultural labourers' quarters. Does the presence of this minority act as an example—as a success story stimulating emulation? Just as tenable is the reverse assumption that their relative security of living excites the wrath of the majority left lagging behind in poverty. The uniformity in payment existing earlier has given way to differences which are not justified by the nature of the work itself. It remains a matter of incomprehension for the Halpatis why they can only earn Rs 3–4 by agricultural labour while unskilled labour outside agriculture offers Rs 5–6. Those who drop further behind perceive these variations as in some way arbitrary and unjust. Now and then the casual labourers among them also profit from employment opportunities outside agriculture, but most have no illusions about the possibility of a better existence for themselves by their own hard work and energy alone. Instead of migrating on their own initiative, most of the landless stay by their huts, sitting and waiting until someone comes along to call them out. Farmers, officials and other social superiors label this behaviour as symptomatic of the inertia and apathy of the landless underclass. I prefer the term 'realism'. It is all too easy for the reproach of passivity to turn into the suggestion that the Halpatis are also resigned to their misery. As we shall see shortly, this is not the case. The limited range and view conditioned by their isolation does however prevent them from distinguishing, soon enough, the openings in the economy which do occur even at their level, while on the other hand they meet with opposition in their attempts to hack a path to a wider work territory, The Report of the first Commission of Enquiry provides penetrating image of their material deprivation.

> The information collected indicates that out of 285 families, 94 families had absolutely no valuables. Of the remaining 191, 129 families possessed tiny gold and silver ornaments whose value would not normally exceed Rs 5 on an average. . . . Further, of 285 families, 124 possessed the indigenous grinding stone. Some of them purchased it when they began their family life, but most of them inherited it from their ancestors. The grinding stone is an article of every day necessity with the Halis, but on account of extreme poverty not all could possess it. The practice ordinarily appears to be a sharing the service of the mill among a number of families closely related to each other. On a very rough estimate the property of the Hali families examined may be valued at Rs 32547. Thus on an average the property of all the families investigated comes to Rs 11–6–0, while for those in actual possession of it, it is Rs 17–5–1 (Report HLEC 1950: 39–40).

For a large majority there has been hardly any change in this sparseness of property. Patel during his village research in Bardoli Taluka in 1961–2, saw in agricultural labourers' households little more in the way of expensive consumption goods than a few cups and dishes, a *khathelo* (a wooden bed frame) and a couple of lamps. Furthermore, in the year of his research they lost more possessions than they acquired. The degree of undernutrition, for which his study provides accurate figures, was already alarmingly high at that time, in spite of the fact that food purchase constituted 86 per cent of all expenditure (Patel 1964: 113). Their condition remains invariably sad as is apparent from the study made in 1977–8 by Naik based on a survey among 104 agricultural labourers' households in Navsari, a *taluka* which is adjacent and in many respects similar to Bardoli. He calculated that out of an average annual income of Rs 468, about 83 per cent was spent on food, two thirds of which consisted of millet or rice. This, as well as all other expenditure, remained far below basic requirements. From all those investigated 56 per cent had only one set of clothes, while most small children went around naked (Naik 1979). Consequently, there should be no cause for surprise in the fact that the percentage of people among the agricultural labourers who are older than sixty, does not amount to half the proportion of the whole population formed by this age group (Shah 1978: 19; Naik 1979: 85).

Can we actually maintain the proposition of *increasing* poverty—even pauperization—against the background provided by these findings? I certainly think so. The service relation into which agricultural labourers were previously driven excluded any possibility of accumulation, but it at least ensured a daily subsistence in which food from the farmer's house was an essential component. When there was insufficient work they still received their grain ration, even if only in the form of a consumption loan. A *hali* could also claim the right to help in fulfilling the extraordinary needs of his master's household such as those connected with sickness, marriage, etc. for which he received an advance, largely in kind. In those times the landless already received less for their labour than was necessary for a minimum subsistence, but they received the deficit in the form of extra allowances and credit, on the basis of which they remained bound in debt.

From the account books of several farmers in two villages in Bardoli Taluka it appears that in 1946 and 1947 the average number of days worked by a *hali* amounted to 158 and 204 respectively (Report HLEC 1950: 46). It was not the wage payment on a daily basis but a guaranteed subsistence on a yearly basis which made the farm servant a relatively expensive labourer. It is no wonder that with the rapid progress in monetization of agrarian production, an increasing number of farmers began to complain about the inefficiency of the *hali-pratha*. The decision resulting from this was the refusal to act any longer as guarantor for the reproduction costs of their inferiors. The slide from poverty into pauperization was revealed not in the agricultural labourers' increasing lack of property—they really could not have ended up with less than they already had—but in the landowners' reluctance to acknowledge the principle that the landless had a right to a subsistence. Release from indebtedness is not really a release, but a sign of their redundancy, their labour power having lost all value.

For the rest, material deprivation is not the only yardstick of pauperization. Erosion of the protection offered by the farmer farm servant relationship, with all its disadvantages, has led to the social marginalization of the landless. While the *hali* could even depend on his master's intercession with, or protection against third parties, the present-day agricultural labourers meet with indifference, if not actual opposition in the protection of their interests. What certainly needs correction is the suggestion that as a consequence of the erosion of vertical ties of patronage with their superiors, the landless poor have remained behind as a fragmented, amorphous mass. To start with, all kinds of new relationships of dependency have emerged, with a variety of new 'bosses' such as the jobbers, petty shopkeepers, social workers and henchmen of party politicians, and who bind the agricultural labourers by providing access to work, credit and government facilities. Contrary to the earlier relationship of patronage these new ties are more specific and should be defined in terms of brokerage. If only for that reason it would be wrong, in my opinion at least, to talk about neo-patronage. Still, in a situation of extreme scarcity these relationships of dependency can act as a barrier to the emergence of solidarity along horizontal lines. The assumption that farm servants in particular try to capitalize on the rather insecure protection provided by their employers is in my opinion rather one-sided[7]. The complaints of large farmers about the secretiveness of their permanent workers, their professed lack of a relationship

[7] See for instance Bardhan: '. . . in villages where some form of group bargaining took place, most of our tied labor respondents reported non-participation in the movements, and the majority of them cited their ties with the landlord as the primary reason for non-participation' (Bardhan 1982: 89).

of intimacy with servants who have been with them for years, point in another direction. Moreover, typically client-like behaviour may be continued in a variety of new attachments, more contractual than personal in nature, which however remain restricted to the milieu in which the labourers themselves live. The concomitant loyalties have a rather narrow basis, i.e. the urge for survival, and will disappear once the transition to a class consciousness and class action gains momentum. The structural changes which are a first manifestation of this process take a long time before they reach maturation.

Participation in education is a first requisite if they are to be able to defend themselves more effectively. The arrears they have accumulated in this respect mark the social isolation in which the majority of Halpatis operate. The rise in the percentage of literacy among them—from 9 per cent shortly after independence to 11.6 per cent in 1961 and 13.7 per cent in 1971 (Report HLEC 1950: 22; Shah 1977: 105) is very slow and clearly lags behind that of other tribal castes in the region. More Halpatis remain lilliterate than ever, and this while the demands for skill, even on the lowest employment level, have increased rapidly. In the short term one cannot look for improvement in this situation. In the village which Patel researched at the beginning of the sixties, only 7 per cent of Halpati children went to school—a telling figure when one considers that the lower school in this village had already existed since 1867, i.e. for nearly a century (Patel 1964: 94). Those among the younger generation of landless actually being educated often do not attend school together with higher caste children, but depend on schools set up specially for them. These are the *ashram* institutions operated in the region by the Halpati Seva Sangh or other Gandhian organizations. Further segregation appears in the more recent tendency to open small schools in the Halpati quarter, limited to the first two classes of the lower school; by such means the attendance of the Halpati children at the more centrally situated village school is avoided, since the majority of them rapidly drop out during the first few years.

Lastly, the pauperization of the agricultural labourers is not counter-balanced by a government really concerned with the fate of this poorest of all classes. The official programmes for socio-economic development include little that can be viewed as a serious attempt to check the deteriorating condition of the landless. This is even less visible in the actual conduct of bureaucrats and other state personnel at the district level and below. On the contrary, their actions are guided—whether consciously or unconsciously — by preconceived notions about the link which is always supposed to exist between criminality and a pauperized existence. In the officials' eyes the Halpatis in particular indulge to excess in strong drink. Home brewing of illicit alcohol is the commonest ground for the prosecution of the Halpatis, but one also often hears accusations of theft, mostly brought against them by landowners. Next come charges of gathering wood or cutting grass along the public road or of selling the roof tiles provided by the government. Last but not least, the resistance of agricultural labourers to the injustices done to them, counts as a criminal offence. When the trouble is not settled by farmers' vigilante parties, the local police (called 'brown dogs' by their victims) only too gladly allow themselves to be used—and paid—to intimidate those who do not know their proper place. Stigmatization of the Halpatis must demonstrate that they are socially dangerous. As I remember one of the few government measures taken under the Emergency which satisfied the Patidars and even inspired enthusiasm in them, was the sterilization programme which was implemented quite forcefully. Without saying this in so many words it became clear for all concerned that the landless underclass was the main target group of this 'public health' policy.

Alienated from the means of production, increasingly also from the means of consumption and expelled to the periphery of the village (or even thrown outside it), the agricultural labourers are penned up within their own milieu. The class of new rich have called into being an opposing class of new untouchables.

Part IV

DYNAMICS OF RURAL CASTES AND CLASSES

11

FROM CASTE TO CLASS

'Caste for itself' type of mobilization

The transition from a caste to a class society is a recurring theme in recent social science literature. In the more dogmatic type of argumentation, caste and class are principles of social stratification which cannot exist at the same time, being mutually exclusive. The concepts thus refer to the successive phases of development by which caste, as a traditional or feudal formation, disappears and gives way to class as the social format of a modern or capitalistic society. The notion that the main principle on which inequality is based changes in the process of transformation has been refuted from opposing sides for more or less the same schematic reasons. On the one hand we have the extreme view that caste has never been more than an ideological screen behind which the reality of a class structure remains hidden.[1] On the other hand there is the cultural-anthropological argument of those who, right up to the present day, regard the caste system as being fundamental to the social order in India and who prefer to ignore class articulation.

The common element in all these theories is that they assume a social order characterized by an unequivocal standard of

[1] In this sense Meillassoux especially has expressed the opinion that: '. . . caste is seen to be no more than an ideological screen which hid social reality by scattering social divisions along the whole length of a formal hierarchy, and submerging exploitative relations among them. This conservative and repressive ideology, reinforced by physical violence and religious terrorism, was one of the factors that prevented the classes from recognizing themselves as such, maintained the subject and exploited sections in a state of alienation, and unaware of suppressed critical and conflictual relationships beneath the cloak of divine harmony. The so-called 'caste system' thus represents the perpetuation and adaption of the status relationships and status ideology within a class society which was continuously changing under the effect of its own contradictions and the import of outside forces, as a means of domination in the interests of the dominant classes which were themselves transformed' (1973: 108).

inequality, regardless of whether this basic principle has changed in the course of time or has remained the same. A more subtly shaded interpretation, which appears to do more justice to the complexity as well as to the dynamics of social organization, suggests the existence of two patterns of stratification which were interlocked in the past but which have gradually begun to diverge. Beteille in particular has used his original village study to develop this view, giving it a more general applicability in a later publication (1974). In a theme number of the *Economic and Political Weekly* on this subject some years ago, Joshi discussed a number of empirical studies at the local level, with a similar drift (1979: 155–66). There is an unmistakeable trend towards economic differentiation in each separate caste, as I too have established in the foregoing chapters. The incongruity between caste and class position resulting from this differentiation lends an indeterminate, disintegrated character to social organization. Still, we must ask how far our view of reality, rather than the reality itself, has changed as a result of other accents and fashions in sociological research. Saberwal, in his contribution to the theme number just mentioned, criticizes the preoccupation with the caste hierarachy in most social science publications of the 60s (1979: 243–54). With Daniel Thorner as an early and outstanding forerunner (apart from the work of the previous Marxist authors), interest in rural class configurations is still of recent date. It is precisely the blending of anthropological concepts based on local fieldwork with a politico-economic vision inspired more by analysis on the macro-level, which produces the image of an amorphous social framework not permitting of classification according to one single criterion (see also Mukherji 1981 and Omvedt 1982). My departure point is that agrarian relations, past and present, can only be understood by beginning with the complementarity of caste and class. In itself that is still saying very little. This proposition must be made more specific by establishing the importance of both structuring principles according to place and to direction of change over a period of time. Therefore, as a preliminary discussion of the present-day situation, I shall first place in perspective the process of change that has taken place in the area of Bardoli in the course of the twentieth century.

First of all I would like to observe that organization based on caste precedes that based on class. This is evident from the manner in which the Kanbis, still a barely respectable middle caste of cultivators at the end of the previous century, have since then succeeded in attaining rural dominance as Patidars in south Gujarat. As outlined in chapter 4 their mobilization had begun early with the formation in 1908 of the Patidar Yuvak Mandal, which aimed at the total uplift of the Kanbis. 'The Yuvak Mandal has been formed for spreading education among the Patidars, for social reforms, for abolishing harmful customs and traditions in the caste, for mobilizing and cultivating public opinion and for protecting the interest of the farmers' (Bhatt 1970: 302). The fulfilment of this programme of activities, which reflected the aspirations of a typical upwardly mobile caste, was accomplished through caste gatherings, the institution of an *ashram* for students in Surat, and the publication of the Mandal's own magazine. Until the First World War the emphasis lay on social reform: raising ritual status through sanskritization of behaviour, and breaking through the lines dividing this low-middle-caste into different segments. Only after this did economic objectives come to occupy a more central place. In Bhatt's words:

> . . . from organising the Patidars as a caste group the Mandal sought to organise farmers as an occupational group. The parochial basis of organisation began to broaden out into a more secular identity' (1970: 310) and: '. . . for the first time the symbol of *khedut* (peasant) to indicate the occupational identity of the Patidars was used in the 1917 conference. It was argued that all Patidars were peasants by occupation and the well-being of the peasants was therefore the well-being of the Patidars (1970: 308).

The consciousness necessary for the formation of an agrarian class nevertheless existed earlier, as can be gathered from the objectives of the reform movement cited above, and it has made positive contributions to organize the Patidars as a class in a caste setting. The consolidation of the Kanbis into a caste 'for itself' coincided with their incorporation into the world market as producers of cotton, the paramount commercial crop in south Gujarat, even before the end of the nineteenth century. If the class motif lay in the emancipation from the economic oppression of Vaniya and Parsi merchants, the caste motif lies in the emancipation from the ideological supremacy of the Brahmins, who wished to confine the Kanbis to Shudra status.

The fiction accompanying this type of social mobilization is that caste interests and class interests are synonymous. Thus the reform movement appealed to all group members, regardless of the varying sizes of their property, while on the other hand all others, even those occupying a comparable position in the hierarchy of land distribution, remained shut out. Hardiman argues forcefully on this: 'These middle peasant movements were class movements. The natural class organisation of the middle peasant was the local caste body'[2]. He adds that these agricultural producers did not remain a passive force in the struggle for national independence, allowing themselves at most to be organized from outside.[3] On the contrary, according to Hardiman this class came, through self-mobilization, into opposition against the colonial regime in reaction to the economic deterioration in the first decades of this century, pressurizing the nationalist movement from beneath into adopting a more radical stance. This position contradicts the thesis that the background of the political dynamic in the countryside was composed of peasants who were economically upwardly mobile. Stokes (1978) has professed scepticism about the leading role ascribed to the middle peasants by Hardiman and others, a variant for colonial India of a more universal model posited, for instance, by Wolf and Alavi. Further to this critique, Charlesworth has investigated and denied the validity of the middle-peasant thesis for the rural agitation occurring half a century ago in Bardoli (1980: 259–80). Hardiman has reacted to this in another publication, in which he indicates that he has abandoned, or at least amended, his earlier standpoint (1981: 367–80). Considering the importance of this discussion for the subject of my study, I shall deal with it in somewhat more detail, except that I shall restrict myself to the situation in

[2] Hardiman 1976: 369. The ideas he works out in this article are based on a case study of peasant agitations in central Gujarat during the late colonial period. For a concise report on these see Hardiman 1977: 47–75.

[3] Guha gives a powerful elaboration on this standpoint in his introduction 'On some aspects of the historiography of colonial India'. In *Subaltern Studies* Vol. I, 1982: 1–8.

Bardoli, while touching on the more general tenor of the argument.

The first thing we encounter is a lack of clarity in what we are to understand by 'middle peasant'. In the classic definition, he is a subsistence-oriented cultivator with sufficient land for his own labour power. Charlesworth rightly points out that the average Kanbi farmer from the period in question is difficult to recognize in this category. Although the alienation of land from the Adivasi owners was still taking place, the modal holding for a Kanbi household was even then probably more than the approximate 5–15 acres generally maintained as the criterion for identifying the middle-peasant in that period. Further, it is true that Kanbis at that time were then still working in the fields themselves, but many employed one or more farm servants in addition, a fact which does not tally with the image of a middle peasant. Finally, in contrast to this strereotyped image the Kanbis had already become more market producers than subsistence cultivators, from the last quarter of the nineteenth century. Their somewhat obscure origin as a middle caste still does not automatically identify them as middle peasants.

In view of these objections, Charlesworth thinks it is impossible to show that one particular class in Bardoli acted as the spearhead of peasant militancy in the late colonial period. His conclusion underestimates the central role most certainly played by the Kanbis in that momentous struggle, and there is a rich documentation to show this. They were neither middle peasants in the meaning which Wolf attached to the term, nor an elite already prosperous, an assumption with which Brown, for instance, begins her analysis of the Patidar agitation in central Gujarat at the start of the 1920s (Brown 1972: 11; see also Stokes 1978: 277–8). But they were certainly a middle caste coming to dominance. By the beginning of this century the already considerable landownership among the Kanbis of Bardoli began to form a source of greater prosperity for the farmers themselves only to the extent to which they succeeded in freeing themselves from the imprisoning clutches of the controllers of the agrarian product. This liberation from economic dependence on money-lenders-cum absentee landlords formed the backdrop to their social advance.

When the Kanbis began the *satyagraha* of 1928, they were

taking the offensive rather than acting on the defensive. To be sure, the direct cause of this protest movement was the sharp rise in land tax imposed at a moment when the fall in prices for cotton—the principal commercial crop—had not yet started. Temporary recessions of this nature which directly affected the farmers had occurred earlier as well. Yet it would be incorrect to attach too much weight to these setbacks due to varying market conditions. In the light of the Kanbis' material progress over a long period the slide backwards occurring in some years must not be given undue emphasis. My opinion thus differs from Hardiman's initial interpretation and also from Charlesworth's, in the sense that I ascribe the readiness of the peasant castes to engage in action, not to their economic deterioration but rather to their progress. The Kanbis wanted to capitalize on their growing economic and social importance by entering the political arena as well, and the national movement offered them the opportunity for doing so. The Kanbis were ready and they were in a hurry; in 1921 they insisted on mounting a campaign which Gandhi had to call off at the last moment. In rejecting his own earlier view and reacting to Charlesworth's argument, Hardiman also establishes, rightly, that:

> For the Patidars of Bardoli, the no-revenue campaign of 1928 was a direct continuation of the 1921–2 movement. Thus, although the slump in the cotton prices hit their pockets, it hardly increased their militancy, for they had already been extremely militant in 1921–2 when cotton prices had been high. Patidar discontent was in other words long-term and political, rather than short-term and narrowly economic (1981: 375).

The emancipation of the Kanbis along caste lines was confirmed in the *satyagraha* of 1928. With a caste member from central Gujarat as leader and with a cadre composed for the most part of local notables, the caste found acknowledgment of its claim to dominance. During the campaign, in which the Kanbis functioned as the vanguard, the rest of the population was also mobilized in a jargon which was appropriate to their own caste. One *satyagrahi* complained about this in the following terms:

> One can easily see that but for the organization of the subcastes and castes we would have never won the battle of Bardoli. But it

> is immoral and improper. When philosophers of the world consider even nationalism as narrow, has not the Sardar of Bardoli given new life to communalism? Have we not commited immorality in defeating the enemy by throwing at them the mud of casteism? (quoted in Bhatt 1970: 333).

The agitation in south Gujarat was not a movement of petty cultivators driven into a tight corner; the initiative stemmed from substantial landowners, and primordial loyalties (kinship and locality, apart from caste), played an important role in the organization of the protest. It is a mistaken idea to conclude from this that, as Charlesworth suggests (1980:274), the movement must have lacked radicalism. Neither do I share Hardiman's view, even though a harking-back to a better past permeated the *satyagraha* (1976:369). Certainly this arcadian nostalgia was encapsulated within the Gandhian ideology, but this was not the reason why the Kanbis took action; this peasant caste did not have the kind of past which they would like to yearn after—on the contrary they were absolutely determined to part company with it.

The strengthened alliance of Kanbis from a position of middle caste, brought them to rural dominance and helped them to form a class of rich farmers. By attaching themselves in a militant way to the nationalist movement, they signalled their desire to move outside their own domain. Moreover, the striving for power as a new agrarian elite was not restricted to their own region, but extended in scale. Class motivation played the principal role in the formation of a Patidar front, but a caste-based articulation accompanied this horizontal expansion. In the light of an observation made by Sartre on class, one could argue that castes also do not simply exist but are constructed.

Mobilization of the landless in the Bardoli area has remained far behind that of the landowners. In their case also, caste loyalties played an important role in the various attempts made to prove their social identity, internally and externally. That is, organizational effort has been directed more towards their common lot as Halpatis than as agricultural labourers. Implicitly this leads to an improvement in terms of the traditional order.

This trend was manifested as early as 1911, in a petition to the government made by several students belonging to this caste, staying at a boarding school, seeking permission to return themselves as Hindus in the census of that year. The designation 'scheduled tribe' which was to remain in use for decades more, kept alive the memory of the stigmatized past the Halpatis shared with other Adivasi groups in the south Gujarat plain. At the beginning of the 1920s members of these tribal castes, in search of respectability within the Hindu society, fell in with the Devi Movement, which dictated the purification of social behaviour.

> The programme of the movement included giving up non-vegetarian food habits and abstaining from liquor and toddy. The social consequences of this programme were that the Adivasis could claim equality of status with the higher caste groups of the non-Adivasi society. It was a sort of sanskritisation process which endeavoured to bring the Adivasis into the pale of the surrounding non-Adivasi society (Desai 1977: 77).

As I established in chapter 5, accommodation with the caste hierarchy according to values regarded as dominant, did not preclude the fact that this reform movement originated in the protest made by the tribals against discrimination and exploitation by the *ujliparaj*, the high-caste money lenders and landlords. The Gandhian doctrine which had earlier obtained a footing in the tribal area, prevented the indigenous population from adopting a more violent form of resistance against social and economic subordination. Harmony and reconciliation by adapting a model imposed from above also characterized the way in which Gandhian workers tried to promote the upliftment of the Halpatis. Under pressure from the fiercely resistant farmers they abandoned their initial attempts to release the agricultural labourers from bondage to their masters. In chapter 5, I had already reached the conclusion that a real emancipation of the landless has remained subordinated to the preservation of the existing order. By narrowing their programme of activities to a fight against the lack of hygiene, to a propagation of teetotallism, etc. the Gandhian do-gooders (almost all members of higher castes) strengthen the impression that the Halpatis stand in the way of their own progress by clinging to their bad habits. In this way it is instilled into them from above that they deserve no other place than the inferior one allotted to them in the caste system.

This still does not explain why the landless labourers opposing their social superiors have not succeeded in mobilizing themselves on their own terms. In this respect they have, in the course of time, been outstripped by other tribal groups from the eastern part of the plain. How has this come about? A first important difference is that the Halpatis do not have a territory which they can call their own and within which they are predominant, even if only by force of numbers. Other tribals such as the Chaudharis and the Gamits have also been rendered dependent upon the *ujliparaj*, but these form only a small minority within the hinterland of Surat District. The difficulty of access to that region in the past has, moreover, placed the local tribals in a better position to preserve their original identity, which has furthered their self-mobilization on a caste basis. A second point of difference, from which it appears that autonomy and capacity for self defence reinforce each other, is that the so-called Adivasis have until recently remained to a great extent cultivators—to be sure, as sharecroppers and as leaseholders on their own land—but the indebtedness characterizing their relations with the *ujliparaj*, the intruders who came to dominate them, was still less than the dependence of Halpatis in the more fertile part of the plain, who did not even own the land on which their huts stood.

In spite of all the critical footnotes one could add, land reform legislation before and after independence was instrumental in rehabilitating the Adivasis to their former position of independent landowners (Baks 1969). The Gandhian workers who recoiled from confronting the substantial farmers in the western part of the plain, thereby sacrificing the emancipation of the Halpatis to the interests of the Kanbis as an up-and-coming elite, were less reluctant to support the tribal peasants in the eastern part in their struggle against the Vaniyas and the Parsis. This was easier also because the merchant-capitalist elements formed only a fraction of the local population and served, moreover, as the supporting pillars of the colonial bureaucracy. The objectives of the nationalist movement were temporarily consonant with the emancipation of these Adivasis, even though Gandhian ideology did not permit too radical a stance against their exploiters. The landless Halpatis were exceptional primarily in their personal bondage to the households of higher-caste masters. This relationship of dependence—institutionalized in the *halipratha*—inhibited the consciousness of sharing a collective fate, let alone action based on such consciousness. There is no better illustration of the passivity of the agricultural labourers than the custom of allowing mutual disagreements to be settled by their social superiors. According to Jugatram Dave, the leader of the Gandhian movement in the region, the *hali* even prided himself on his subordination: 'As a woman without having married a husband has no prestige, similarly a Halpati without a *dhaniyamo* (master) has no prestige in his community' (Dave 1946: 18). The picture emerging from this is one of a complete internalization of dependence.

Could the behaviour of the landless really be reduced to this image, or was it a caricature of reality, a representation of matters to which the farmers all too readily attached their own prejudices? I suspect that the latter was the case, for whenever an opportunity for turning against their masters presented itself the Halpatis did not fail to make use of it. Their behaviour in such a situation testified more to resentment and antagonism than to unconditional fidelity to their masters. This was evident during the Bardoli *satyagraha* among other events. Instead of following their caste *dharma*—prescribing obedience to superiors—to which the campaign leaders urged them, the agricultural labourers willingly allowed themselves to be used by the colonial authorities:

> During the struggle the government officials and other vested interests have used the Halpatis as an instrument to break the unity of the landowners. On the occasion of confiscation of the property of landowners, no one from this class was available to the government to carry away their belongings. But at this time it was very easy to use Halpatis as instruments by instigating their bitterness towards landowners (Dave 1946: 35–6).

This is not the only example demonstrating that the agricultural labourers' tractability fell behind expectations. However, due to the emphasis on the uplift of the Halpatis, through the peaceful road of the Gandhian movement, the more authentic forms of protest which have arisen in the recent past and in which the Halpatis have also taken an active part, have to a large extent remained hidden—principally because of the lack of written sources. Thus little is known about the Kisan Sabha which, between the 1930s and 1950s, was active in the tribal area (Desai 1977: 75). This left-radical organization, which strove for mobilization on a class basis, directed itself primarily towards the tribal peasants who lost their land and/or the yield thereof to the invading *ujliparaj*. The initiative in this case also began with outsiders, but almost immediately the cadre came to be composed largely of the members of the target group itself, including the Halpatis among them.

During a last spell of fieldwork in the summer of 1980 I met several of these activists, who retained vivid memories of their earlier fighting spirit. During local research at the beginning of the 1960s, I ran up against the aftermath of the Sati-Pati Movement, a tribal revolt which took place in the eastern part of Surat District. The form adopted for this protest showed clear affinities with the Mata Movement at the beginning of the 1920s, and this time also it resisted economic and political oppression which—as one already suspects from the name of the movement—had acquired a religious tone. The followers had to promise to lead a pure life which implied marital fidelity as well as abstention from meat and alcohol, but more fundamental even than these cultural reforms was the rejection of the social order in which they were embedded. A repetitive theme at secret gatherings was the future expulsion of all *ujliparaj* (regardless of whether these were landlords or money lenders, or even Gandhian workers) whose land and other possessions would be divided up among the Adivasis. There were supporters of this movement among the Halpatis from village B. in Valod Taluka, where I spent some time in 1962. They gave me to understand that a small core had made very precise advance arrangements about who would receive which house and land after the day of reckoning. So far that day has not yet arrived. During a march in Valod in 1956 the police opened fire and some of the tribals—who had believed that bullets would change into flowers—were killed. The violent character of the protest provided the government with a ready-made excuse for arresting the leaders and banning the movement.

The underground continuation of this movement came to the surface again some years later in a more political form.

This Adim Jati Rashtriya Sabha cut itself off from the Hindu order instead of trying to win a better position for the Adivasis within the caste hierarchy. It aimed instead at awakening a separate ethnic identity, coloured by severe economic grievances (Desai 1971: 1–20 and Shah n.d.). It is interesting to note that the landless Halpatis, with no consciousness of a past as landowning peasants, appear to be sensitive to appeals to free themselves from the yoke of higher castes, along with other tribal groups. Nevertheless I still doubt whether these will form the framework for joint action by the rural underclass. Anyone studying the social history of south Gujarat must come to the unavoidable conclusion that to speak of a tribal identity is a mystification (see also Bose 1981). Although not necessarily revivalist, this form of particularism has a strongly populistic undertone, like the call for caste unity. The social dynamic points to another direction, namely a co-ordinated streamlining of interests and attitudes along horizontal lines of division.

Social change has become most visible where modernization of the agrarian economy has been pushed through most rapidly. It is true that caste as a normative principle of collectivity has not disappeared, but it has certainly acquired a different meaning. In connection with this, Beteille talks of the change from hierarchy to stratification (1974:94). Particularly at the top and bottom of the rural order, large farmers and landless labourers respectively have, even in their own estimation, solidified more than ever into social classes. The acute opposition between those at the extremities have led some to argue that the entire social structure has been reduced to this simple dichotomy. According to this reasoning, which cannot be sustained, about half the agrarian population—the mass of small and middle cultivators—is stamped as a residue. The difficulties of ranking those who belong to the intermediate classes should never be a reason for abandoning attempts at a more complex classification.

The nature of my research dictates that I should restrict myself to the polar classes, but I am convinced that exclusive attention to what happens at the top and bottom of the rural regime means missing the complexity and dynamic which exists in the middle of the spectrum. Beteille's statement that the social order has become diffuse (1974: 94) derives, in my view, from the fluidity governing the intermediate levels. The convergence of caste and class positions decreases towards the centre of the social spectrum, resulting in increasing diffuseness. The process of economic differentiation which is coupled with ascents and descents on the agrarian ladder, can only very partially be understood in terms of the principles of collectivity borrowed from a very different schema of social hierarchy.

An example of this is the development of a relatively small upper stratum within the landowning tribal castes of south Gujarat, disposing of more than the average holding on the one hand, and a landless underclass rapidly growing in size, on the other. Some of those occupying the still-surviving middle positions (small and middle landowners as well as artisan and service castes) have made attempts to consolidate the traditional way of life as a means of resisting the trend towards polarization as far as possible. Certainly, rich as well as poor make the most of loyalty mechanisms still existing, in order to promote their separate and conflicting interests—the poor by way of compensating themselves for their loss of dignity and in the usually vain hope that their claim to protection and help will be eventually honoured, the rich in order to make their increased weight felt internally and externally. 'The better-off strata take not only advantage of the docility of the poor, but also tranquillize them further in the name of 'tribal culture', and instill in them 'we-ness' on an ethnic ground. This enables them to maintain and advance their interest as against similar strata within and outside the tribal society' (Shah 1977: 197). The mutual play on primordial sentiments does not mean that these will necessarily work. For instance, it happens with increasing frequency that Adivasis divide their votes at elections according to their economic position. The economically most 'progressive', voting for the most 'conservative' parties and vice versa. Their political behaviour bears witness to a much more realistic assessment of the social dynamic than politicians (who continue to see the tribals as a solid block) are inclined to believe.[4]

[4] I was able to observe this personally in the elections that followed close upon the

There are indications that similar centrifugal forces are at work among the non-tribal intermediate strata in the south Gujarat countryside. For the socially mobile elements of these, irrespective of whether they are rising or falling in status, there is often such an increasing incompatability with the milieu from which they originate that their caste identity becomes overshadowed by their class position. Indicative of this are the complaints of a middle-class landowner that:

> the farmers are unnecessarily blaming the government for their problems of irrigation, fertilizers, electricity or labour: Actually, the big farmers themselves are to be blamed. They accumulate and aggrandise like an insatiable hungry giant. Big farmers are like big fish, they simply disregard the small varieties. And when they want support for this or that issue, they come to us in the name of farmers' fraternity, solidarity and unity. For instance, the issue of electricity for pumping the water into fields. It is said that the richer, big and more powerful farmers of Bardoli are influential in changing the course of power distribution. They go and bribe the power-grid people. Similarly, about the irrigation waters too. Stronger the lobbying is, greater are the rewards. In such a situation, who really cares or bothers for the small farmers. Their plight is soon going to be as worse as that of the Dublas.

The more well-to-do seek connections with the rich farmers from higher castes and strive as far as possible to match their life style. Those who remain behind try to escape from merging with the rural proletariat by becoming geographically mobile. Economic and social motives—respectively, lack of employment and the need to avoid a decline in status, or at any rate to mask it—leave them with little choice but to leave, and seek a temporary living in the plain as seasonal labourers or even settle there for an uncertain period of time.

---

ending of the Emergency at the beginning of 1977, in a constituency in south Gujarat. While the candidates' platform and the subsequent campaign strategy still relied entirely on tribal docility, economic interests played a definite role in voting behaviour. G. Shah observed that: 'The votes of the Adivasis belonging to the poor and the middle strata were divided between the Congress and the Janata Morcha, though the former identified themselves more with the Congress than with the latter. Thus, politically—in terms of participation, ideology, party functioning—tribal society is not distinctly different from the surrounding non-tribal society. Differences arising out of economic differentiation are increasingly reflected in the political preferences and attitudes of different groups of Adivasis. So far, no elections have been fought on distinctly "tribal" issues' (Shah n.d.: 11).

Does economic differentiation lead, then, to the disintegration of caste together and simultaneously with the formation of polarized classes? There is no one answer to this. The polarization does not lead the multi-layered agrarian structure to break apart into a dichotomy. Instead of disappearing, the intermediate strata of middle and small landowners survive, although not without difficulty. The strategy they follow is directed towards economic stability and consolidation of their social position. They try to attain the first by making use of the opportunities offered by the diversification of the rural production structure in order to supplement the yield from land ownership with additional incomes. In order to gain a foothold in the new avenues of employment, they appeal to ties of caste, ethnicity, locality and kinship. This strategy often develops strongly populist tendencies in an otherwise vain attempt to neutralize or even deny the operation of the class dynamic.

At the top and bottom of the agrarian order however, where class formation has come more to the fore as a result of mutual antagonism, caste and other particularistic principles of social organization continue to play an important role. The situation in Bardoli illustrates this. Once the substantial landowners became dominant as farmer castes they concentrated on bringing together, in class organizations, their social interests as agrarian producers. Agitation against government schemes for implementing land reform was the basis for forming the Khedut Sangh in 1952 and the Khedut Samaj in 1972. In the following section the nature and the background of the farmers' movement will be considered, but here I shall be content with the observation that a deliberate use has been made of caste cohesion in order to create an acceptance for the idea of a 'class for itself'. The verdict by Beteille which follows fits this situation very well:

> Thus, the top of the emerging agrarian hierarchy consists of a set of individuals having certain common social economic properties linked together in loose-knit networks and becoming increasingly aware of their common economic and political interests. Those at the top have advantages of both resources and skills. Sociologically the most distinctive feature of the 'progressive farmers' is that they combine ownership of land and capital with skills in manipulating both 'traditional' and 'modern' institutions (1974: 112).

It goes without saying that in Gujarat the Patidars take the initiative in setting up a common front as rich farmers. Srinivas uses the term 'horizontal stretch' to describe the association of these related castes of substantial farmers in different areas of the country (1979: 241). Under the label of Patidars they came to prominence in Gujarat during the struggle for national independence, but their power has been considerably strengthened since then by the shifting of their political influence to the district level. The Patidars take the lead in the mobilization of larger farmers, setting the tone for their agitations. Others may join in, not as equals but in a clearly subordinate role, and thus a loosely integrated class alliance of various landowning castes has come into being. The Patidars' supremacy within this alliance is uncontested, deriving partly from the obscuring of internal differentiation and the possible divisions resulting from it, by maintaining the fiction that all caste members have the same interests, served by caste solidarity.

How does the caste/class nexus operate in the case of the landless masses? As stated in chapter 5, mobilization has up to now been achieved mainly on the basis of caste affinity. The Halpati Seva Sangh has received generous government subsidies over the years. From its inception the Gandhian leadership has been set on making better 'Hindus' of the members of this tribal community, through a programme of social activities in which the emphasis lies on instructing them to adopt a more acceptable form of social behaviour. While intent on removing the sharp edges of the social discrimination suffered by the Halpatis the main stress is still on their adaptation to the rural environment in which they live and work, rather than on the principle of combatting the inequality inherent within it. This could be described as accommodation in place of emancipation (Breman 1974b). It was the continuation of a policy which expressed itself in a community-oriented jargon but which had as its main objective the subjugation of the lower by the higher castes (see also Spodek 1975 and Dhanagare 1980). Paternalistic leadership from above rather than self-organization is characteristic of the mobilization of the Halpatis. The image of a passive, docile mass dominates not only the viewpoints of the outsiders, since even the Gandhian social workers express negative opinions about their clients. Given this line of thinking it is obviously easy to seek the origins of the Halpatis' continuing poverty and social inferiority in their own lack of willpower, discipline, sense of responsibility and intelligence, and in other mental or behavioural deficiencies.

Nothing can be expected from the Halpati Seva Sangh in terms of raising the Halpatis' consciousness of their exploitation and oppression, or of the reversal of these through class solidarity. Invariably, whenever the growing militancy of agricultural labourers threatens an explosion, the leadership of this organization opts for immediate pacification and tries to settle the dispute in an attempt to ward off unrest and to reconcile the opposing parties. Although its non-antagonistic ideology stands in the way of the real promotion of Halpati interests, it would on the other hand be unjust to show the Halpati Seva Sangh as the only, or even the principal obstacle to the organization of solidarity on a horizontal basis. To begin with, the rich farmers are opposed to the mobilization of the agricultural labourers as a collectivity, regardless of whether this is based on caste or class. Quite justifiably they regard every attempt in that direction as potentially disruptive of their own sphere of power. Also, after the severance of the vertical relationship between them and their *halis* characterized by strongly personalized dependence, the farmers have a vested interest in maintaining the divisions within the mass of landless who, imprisoned in their hutment colonies, remain deprived of mutual contact. The rural elite, united in farmers' unions and other pressure groups, systematically try to prevent the organization of the underclass.

The economic differentiation existing among the Halpatis further hinders the articulation of loyalties accompanying caste solidarity. A minority who have succeeded in finding employment outside agriculture aim at adopting the life style of the higher castes. Most Halpatis however are unable to do so, and sanskritization—the purification of behaviour according to Hindu values regarded as respectable—is incompatible with the poverty-stricken existence led by agricultural labourers. In order to make themselves more acceptable, members of the upwardly mobile group join in the expression of harshly prejudiced views against their more backward caste fellows. This growing economic disparity produces social differentiation that ends the identity derived from the membership of the same caste, but it has been replaced by common solidarity based on the identity of a common class that transcends caste boundaries. Taking as our starting point the antagonism between the indigenous labourers and the migrants brought in from outside, there is every reason to doubt this supposition. The time for caste unity is definitely past, while the time for class solidarity does not appear to have arrived as yet.

This is a somewhat meagre conclusion, which does not do justice to the situation I have described, in which the triangular relationship between the landowners, the migrant labourers and local landless occupies a central position. In the subsequent part of this chapter I shall maintain that this relationship is a dynamic one. After discussing the social hegemony of the large farmers I shall investigate the divisiveness existing at the base of the agrarian order, which will allow me to conclude with what is, in my opinion, the principal opposition— namely, that which exists between the mass of agricultural labourers and the dominant landowners in the plain of south Gujarat. By way of conclusion to this first part however, I shall summarize some important findings which will act as a starting point in the further analysis of the rural transformation.

Exclusive attention to the extremities of the agrarian order produces an inadequate picture of its social complexity. Processes of change taking place at the intermediate levels determine what happens above and below them. I am thinking here of the phenomenon of migrant labour, among others. My point is that rural transformation is encompassing the total structure of production, i.e. it permeates every level in society. In my research I have been unable to find confirmation of the thesis of a new socio-economic dualism posed by Djurfeldt and Lindberg (1976). In their representation, the village is embedded in a capitalist macro-structure through the market and the state, but at the same time has endured as a pre-capitalist formation. It would be wrong to connect caste and class *exclusively* with social formations belonging to either a feudal or a capitalist mode of production, respectively. A view I share with several other authors is that different principles of inequality mutually exclusive are involved, but occuring side by side, although in oscillating relationship varying according to time, place and level. In this connection it is interesting to note Hardiman's remark that the Patidars of central Gujarat formed a class even before they crystallized out as a caste.[5] Instead of constructing a direct and linear transition from a caste to a class society I have tried in agreement with Hardiman's viewpoint, to suggest that the social ranking of both landless labourers and substantial farmers, as well as the change that has taken place in their mutual relationship, is determined by these dual components of the social order. The rise of the substantial farmers to rural dominance is the consequence of the combination of primordial loyalties centering around caste, and horizontal solidarity derived from class. Both types of linkages arise also among the landless labourers, but they are much weaker and are moreover opposed from above. Supremacy at the top and fragmentation at the bottom are thus characteristic of the rural order in the Bardoli region.

The hegemony of the large farmers

The political supremacy of the Kanbi Patidars is both an expression of their position of economic power and a means of maintaining it. This cultivator class has achieved rural dominance in the past half-century by establishing many kinds of interconnected social, economic and political organizations. The articulation of primary sentiments has played a decisive role here, as I have established earlier. After the *satyagraha* of 1928, caste remained an important basis for the presentation and realization of the dominant farmers' collective aspira-

[5] 'The original meaning of the term 'Patidar' (a meaning dating back at least to the seventeenth century) was that of a man who possessed a share in the village land. In medieval times the Patidars were, in other words, a *class* of substantial peasant proprietors. During the nineteenth century this *class* turned itself gradually into a caste based on kinship links. Thus, although by the twentieth century the Patidars were strictly a caste rather than a class, a strong element of their original class nature survived' (Hardiman 1981 : 372). Without investigating this matter further, I think it is quite possible that in south Gujarat as well, the Anavil Brahmins transformed themselves into an elite *caste* after having first ensured their rights to the agrarian yield as landlords-cum-tax farmers.

tions. One example is the Shri Leva Patidar Samaj in Surat District, still functioning, which takes the social development of this community as its object, but attempts particularly 'to undertake activities aimed at spreading education and culture, to encourage female education and to publish necessary news-letters for that purpose and literature on education for attaining these aims and objectives'.[6] This caste association is split into nine circles, the delegates of which meet at least once a year. The Pratinidhi Sabha is concerned with constructing a code of social behaviour governing everyday life, mainly related to marriage ceremonies and other *rites de passage*. Sobriety and simplicity are the key notes here, but it would be a mistake to think that it has been fully effective. Thus the caste leaders determined at their meeting in 1977 that weddings must be conducted without display—i.e. with little ceremony, few guests and modest presents—but the extremely detailed instructions were hardly meant to be followed. In the same year the association secretary—the same man who had laid these instructions before a prominent selection of notables for approval—appeared as the host at the marriage of his niece (come over from the U.S.A.) with the son of the manager of a nearby sugar factory. It was an enormous feast with hundreds of guests, lasting several days, during which extremely costly presents were exchanged.

To deduce from this only a discrepancy between norm and practice does not do justice to the Patidars' need to express what outsiders are inclined to explain as contradictory or even hypocritical behaviour. On the one hand they have an overriding wish to reinforce their claim to higher status in the traditional hierarchy by formulating stringent caste rules binding for all members, and on the other hand they (or at least some of them) desire to win prestige by an ostentatious demonstration of their newly acquired power and wealth.

A caste association probably produces the impression of a formal organization for which members are proposed, with an elected governing body, financial means, procedures for meeting, and the like, all statutorily regulated. What actually happens is very different from this formalized stereotype. A small, self-selected vanguard among the Patidars put

[6] The constitution of the Shri Leva Patidar Samaj (in Gujarati).

themselves forward as leaders of their caste, and act on behalf of a following whose approval is at best tacitly given. These notables decide between them the tasks to be performed, even if they pretend to be acting under orders from their caste fellows by referring to the rules of the alliance. Entry to this limited company remains restricted to those already holding key positions in the social life of Surat District. For instance, it was no accident that the annual meeting of the managing committee of the Shri Leva Patidar Society in 1977 was held in the Astan Gin building—another Patidar stronghold in Bardoli.

What I wish to demonstrate here is that a regional network of notables has come into being, who co-opt each other into leading positions in a number of organizations. The same names continually crop up in the managements of the various co-operatives, political party branches, school boards and other social and cultural establishments. Thus an effective platform of Patidar power has been built up, from which the promotion of collective interests is achieved in an institutionalized manner, while accountability to those beneath runs principally along personal channels.

Finally I would like to point out that, even though the Patidars are linked by all kinds of bonds at the regional level, the earlier dividing lines within this caste have been preserved. The Levas have not only strengthened themselves by forming their own association, but have also set the tone outside it; the influence of members of this sub-caste is disproportionately great, particularly in the co-operatives. That which presents itself to the outside world as a closed Patidar front appears on closer scrutiny to disintegrate into various factions and sections. Nonetheless the unity of and the community of interests among all Patidars is emphasized in the presence of others and in the face of conflicting interests.

Organization is the device by which the Patidars have converted their local importance as principal landowners into that of regional dominance. The supra-local institutions which they dominate have branched into small-scale organizations at the village level, also run for the most part—or even exclusively—by members of this caste. Already by the beginning of the

1960s, various types of organizations, all loosely structured, existed for example in village A.: Gram Vikas Samiti, a committee for village development set up in 1947; Yuvak Mandal, a youth league that came into being in 1955, and—of more recent date—Mahila Mandal, a women's club. As in the case of the school, village council and library, all these are run by and for the local Patidars exclusively. '. . . all these activities are concentrated on and dominated by the so called high caste Hindus, and the agricultural labourers, who belong mainly to low castes such as the Halis and the Harijans, do not have their share in these activities nor are they much benefited by these institutions' (Patel 1964: 94). This is from the report of an investigation in this locality conducted at the beginning of the 1960s. I found no change when I did fieldwork in the same village in the autumn of 1979. Moreover, it struck me that only households belonging to the dominant caste have joined the agricultural co-operatives active in the region. They have taken part in the various production co-operatives for the processing and/or purchase of sugarcane, bananas, cotton and rice, and are the members of the Shri Sardar Bardoli Taluka Farmers' Cooperative Selling and Purchasing Union which, among other activities, distributes fertilizer, petrol and cement. The Patidars govern the economic traffic in the countryside through these organizations, the board members of which, as one can see from their annual reports, are once again related to each other through cross-connections. This monopoly is carried through right down to the village level, as in A., where a co-operative rice husking plant has been set up, as well as a local branch of the Sumul Dairy Produce Cooperative of Surat. Membership is reflected in the local composition of the leadership: all fifteen management members are Patidars with the exception of one (an obligatory Harijan), and the same applies for all board members of this village branch.[7]

The large farmers are becoming increasingly accustomed to functioning in organizations—dealing with administration, taking part in meetings, notifying their approval or disapproval of current policy-matters affecting them. Yet one should not make too much of this sort of formal communication and the

[7] Annual report 1978–9, A. *Vikas khetipakna rupantas ane vechan karnari sahakari mandali Ltd.* and annual report 1978–9, Shri A. *dudh utpadak sahakari mandali Ltd.*

transactions accompanying it. The leading figures who look after organizational matters can operate with the tacit support of their caste fellows, as long as they do their work with propriety and do not engage in rivalry. The non-economic associations in particular lead a drowsy existence. Sundry respondents were generally speaking, unconscious of the existence of either a youth association or a women's club, and most of the other organizations were unable to name a single activity. These institutions are tenuous and passive, but can be activated immediately when the need arises. The Yuvak Mandal came into force in A. with the farmers' agitation of 1973–4, in which youths played a prominent role. During a similar action an appeal was also made to Patidar women members of the Mahila Mandal to take part in a protest march which took place in Delhi at the instigation of the farmers' union.

More important than the organization itself are the people who operate at its apex. What is the background of these leaders? In the first place, those who aspire to such positions must be prepared to offer their services over a long stretch of years. There can be no better departure point than one's own village for gaining a reputation in wider circles. In order to begin such a career willing candidates must have prior involvement in 'social work'. Only those with adequate financial means can be sure of having a sufficient amount of free time and energy, and only these are in a position to extract obedience and respect. Local leadership also demands a proper schooling, at least upto the intermediate level, and there is much more to the rules of the game of social-intercourse than the mere ability to read and write: one must know how to associate with government officials on an equal footing, speak in public, and conduct an administration, which includes being able to handle the telephone.

Only if sufficient experience has been gained locally is it possible to take the plunge into posts at higher levels with a reasonable chance of success. The village atmosphere is a good training ground for learning how to hold one's own against rivals, how to win the confidence of others, and how to command a heterogeneous following which should be as large as possible, flowing outside one's own caste. The leader must foster the impression of not being too parochial, in order to act as arbiter between differing interests and to be able, as a broker, to introduce some of his clientele to benefits and facilities without alienating others. He must, moreover, always be on the lookout for what is happening at the higher levels, and spend time in visiting government offices, the principal co-operative institutions and the residences of the more prominent leaders. This is very time-consuming because a great deal of the communication is verbal. In the regional power centres there is a continual coming and going of visitors, who generally hold very fleeting conversations over a broad spectrum of subjects. During my own visits to these places and awaiting my turn, I made the acquaintance of a number of up-and-coming leaders who I subsequently sought out in their own home areas. I succeeded only very laboriously in obtaining an insight into the pyramidal configurations formed by the really big patrons and the small-scale leaders. These patterns became manifest more explicitly during the election campaigns, but the greatest fluctuations also occur then, with unexpected and sometimes dramatic side changing. Transfer of loyalty is not free from individual aspirations for winning personal influence by changing party or patron at a convenient moment. The qualities which in combination are necessary for forcing one's way through to the regional centre of power are seniority, political instinct, success in business, organizational ability, and a reputation for political virtue. Let me give a brief characterization of the style of leadership at this level. The style *vis-à-vis* outsiders is assertive. A very interesting phenomenon is the change in attitude towards the state apparatus. Bureaucratic rules and regulations are no longer sacrosanct. Peasant submissiveness towards authorities which became a byword in colonial times—the *ma-bap* syndrome—has been replaced by a self consciousness which has grown naturally along with the growing importance of the Patidars as rural producers. Illustrative of this new behaviour is a statement made by some leading members of the sugarcane co-operatives in Maharashtra and which can equally well apply to the Bardoli scene.

> The changed relationship with government officials was dramatically revealed at a meeting of sugar cooperatives in Maharashtra where the Joint Registrar for cooperative sugar factories—a senior IAS officer—was present. The leaders were contemplating a cer-

tain action when the Joint Registrar observed that it was against the provisions of the Cooperative Societies Act. One of the leaders got up and said, 'Saheb (sic), please do not tell us about the legal difficulties. We shall get the law amended. After all we are the lawmakers' (Baviskar 1980: 228–9).

The attitudes of the leading men of the old guard, still clearly inspired by Gandhian principles, contrast with those of the new generation who are eager to be seen as modern managers. In their behaviour the older leaders radiate simplicity and sobriety. They are clothed in spotless white *khadi*, although only the veterans among them remain attached to the *dhoti* with a long shirt. However, even those who prefer trousers and a bush shirt often maintain a reverence for the Gandhi cap. Their presentation is that of social workers who have spent their lives in public service. The room where they have their office is hung with photographs showing them in the company of ministers and other dignitaries from Ahmedabad and Delhi. In order to hold their own as successful intermediaries with their clients' interests at heart, their connections with those higher up must, with an alteration of power—a change of state government, another regime for the country—be adapted as quickly as possible to the new situation. The veterans pride themselves on the visits made to Bardoli, before and after independence, by the most prominent figures within the nationalist movement.

> *20 April.* From the *hitchko* in the gallery of the Patidar Gin, the elderly manager points out to me the spot where, according to this informant, Rajagopalachari gave his first political speech after the setting up of the Swatantra Party, which was expected to enjoy great popularity among members of the dominant caste. Inside the office there is the dais, still in use, on which Gandhi, Nehru and more recently still, Morarji Desai among others, conversed with local leaders, but it was still Sardar Patel of whom the manager spoke with most respect.

Many business houses and institutions bear the name of the Lion of Bardoli. Plaster busts or photographs hung with garlands show how enduring Patel's memory is among his admirers. More than that, by honouring so emphatically the memory of this protagonist of the farmers' interest, the Kanbi Patidars give expression to their longing for a strong man, one of their own, destined to lead the country and the people. Patel's behaviour was marked by a great deal of forcefulness and decisiveness. Accustomed to speaking his mind bluntly and to getting his own way, inclined to use the language and dress of his own milieu as a means for clearing more polished opposition out of the way, he embodied authoritarian qualities which are regarded as typical of his caste. Such qualities can produce behaviour of a negative kind—excessive bluntness, uncontrolled aggressiveness, an unwillingness to listen to what others have to say, and a clearly demonstrated contempt for every view different from one's own.

> *8 May.* D.K. is the very successful managing director of a co-operative sugar enterprise in south Gujarat. Under his expert management (he gained a degree in agronomy at a mid-western university in the USA) the factory has grown to be one of the largest in India. On the strength of this reputation he has become the acknowledged champion (dreaded for his rage) of the sugar lobby which, together with those promoting the interests of groundnut producers in Saurashtra, exercises a decided influence on the politics in the state of Gujarat. In addition, he has won his spurs as an organizer in the mobilization of farmers in the Khedut Samaj, which played an important role in the rural agitations of 1974. In the conversations I had with him, my role was restricted to that of a very polite listener—he is not accustomed to being interrupted, let alone contradicted. His long monologues were bitter diatribes against the government, which instead of supporting the landowners opposed them as far as possible, and against the landless who no longer knew their place and had lost their value as labour. But it was exactly this fierceness and lack of flexibility which made him the champion of his caste fellows: 'at least K. dares to say what's what'. Yet, apart from the fact that my Gujarati was no match for his verbal flow, it would have been impossible to have made myself heard above his noise. The Patidars are so accustomed to commanding that this hampers conversation even among themselves, since such conversation consists of forceful, unsubtle pronouncements with which they assail each other loudly and in an almost quarrelsome tone.

It would be a mistake to suppose that leaders of this stature allow themselves to be guided principally by caste interests. On the contrary, several of them have none of the parochialism of their following. They give you to understand very emphatically that their ideas are appropriate for all the landowners in the area, and they advocate a common front for all *kisans*. This term does not refer to a particular agrarian class, but has a more wide-ranging meaning, which implicitly suggests 'we country folk against the state'. K.M. is one example of such a populist leader.

At the time of my fieldwork in 1979 this eighty-four-year-old had just retired from public life. I sought out this unique personality in his country house, situated in a large mango orchard in Bardoli.

It was about 10 o'clock in the morning when I was admitted to his presence, on the balcony of the upper story. A young man (a distant family member who acted as a secretary of sorts) read the newspaper to him while a servant was busy shaving him. He signed to both to continue, and only when the last had finished did he ask me why I had come. He would only talk about his life as a 'social worker' if he was able to find out more about me. The secretary started telephoning and also went out in the car. When this produced no immediate result I was asked in a curt fashion to wait in another room for his return. It was one of the few occasions on which I have had my identity so thoroughly checked. In the conversation that followed, what impressed me most was the sharp memory and the cool understanding of this old man whose health by then was declining. In imitation of some other Matia Kanbis from his home village, his father had ventured to cross to South Africa in 1904, by ship. K. followed in 1911. There he met Gandhi and already by 1913 he had landed in jail for several days while pursuing the registration issue. Shortly after his return to India in 1919 he took up residence at the Swaraj Ashram in Bardoli. He belonged to a small group which Gandhi persuaded to hold a *satyagraha* in Bardoli in 1921. He was greatly disappointed when Gandhi decided to cancel the movement at the last moment. He was also active in the 1928 campaign under Sardar Patel's leadership. In 1937 he departed for Bombay to start a factory, from which he retired in 1958, leaving his sons to carry on the business. K. had firmly decided to devote himself to public affairs in Bardoli again. He had retained his contact with Bardoli even while staying in Bombay because his business did not occupy all his time. When the Bardoli farmers were in a difficulty during a period of drought in 1948, he took the initiative in setting up a production and consumption co-operative, of which he was the chairman until last year. In a few weeks' time there was to be a very grand farewell reception for him, an occasion on which the most important guest speaker would be H.M. Patel, minister of finance in the Janata government at Delhi—and like him, an erstwhile member of the Swatantra Party. This man succeeded K. as the chairman of the Khedut Sangh, an alliance of landowners which K. helped to set up in 1952, in order to co-ordinate the resistance of the farmers against the proposed land reform. With the same object he provided the stimulus for the inception of the Khedut Mandal, a combined platform for the large farmers from the Congress and the Swatantra parties in Gujarat. It was the Khedut Samaj however, which became a forum for the rural agitation of 1973–4, in which K.M. (like D.K.) was very closely involved.

K. patiently explained that he did not represent the interests of any one group, whether it was the Patidars or all the other farmers in the area. Rather—his war was with the government interference in the lives of people. The state had no business to meddle with property rights. Everyone must be free, not only the farmers but also the Adivasis in the jungle and the landless in the villages. It is not therefore acceptable that the government should prescribe an obligatory minimum agricultural labourer's wage. That is the concern of those who are directly involved, those who are dependent upon each other. Unfortunately even in the villages, there is little understanding of the nature of the problem among the landless labourers. It is because of this that they accuse the farmers of not accepting any responsibility towards them. Charan Singh's ideas are good, but are not put into practice. Of all the parties Janata (Morarji Desai) is still the least of all the evils. There will be some improvement in the situation only when the *kisans*, who constitute the majority of the population, get their own way. There is a slow development but in the right direction, although not right across the board, and not constantly. Still, the tide is changing. Take for example the Sumul Dairy Produce Cooperative. This undertaking was created and set up at Surat in the interests of the urban consumers, but the centre of gravity is gradually shifting to the producers in the village. Has not the school teacher in A., (the village where I was living at the time) been elected its vice-chairman?

I cannot avoid the conclusion that with the leadership just portrayed, a class rather than a caste interest is being served. One must immediately add that in practice this distinction is not so simple to make. At all events a fundamental change has occurred over time in the rural order of south Gujarat in the transition of peasants to farmers. The penetration of the capitalist mode of production goes back to the development of cotton cultivation in the last quarter of the nineteenth century.

Although this transformation has undoubtedly affected rural life directly, in the beginning its effect was reduced because the market was linked through traders and money lenders whose interests lay in maintaining precapitalist formations, while the large landholdings existing at that time stood in the way of a more intensive exploitation of the agrarian resources. This situation began to change in the first half of the twentieth century, especially with the establishment of the co-operative cotton societies in the first decades which took over the marketing of this main agricultural commodity from private traders. Gradually rent capitalism became obsolete under the influence of tenancy reforms and similar legislations, shortly before or after independence. Extension of the irrigated area and the modernization of agrarian technology in recent decades have accelerated the penetration of the capitalist mode of production into farm management.

This has resulted in a different life style from that of previous generations, especially within the class of large farmers. While earlier they wanted to pass as Kshatriyas and emulated the Rajput model (like their more illustrious caste fellows in central Gujarat), more recently it is the Baniyas who have become their reference group (Pocock 1972: 32, 62 & 158). However, in my opinion the Patidars' present-day life-style cannot be understood simply by pointing to the behavioural model they choose to follow. That would be a misinterpretation of the self-esteem and the self-consciousness that has come to characterize this now dominant caste. It was no accident that Sardar Patel called them the 'sons of the soil' (Shah 1974: 102). Looking outwards from this *bhumiputra* ideology, they take their landed interests for granted while denying the claims of other, lower castes to the right of first land clearance. The identity derived from their social prominence allows them to find resemblances in position with similar groups elsewhere and they claim kinship with the Jats of north India.[8]

However materialistic in orientation, the Patidars' capitalistic spirit has retained a strongly religious tinge. Pocock has discussed this in his excellent study *Mind, Body and Wealth* (1973). Within the Vaishnavite tradition to which they adhere,

[8] According to several informants the Patidars and Jats originated from central Asia. See also Pocock 1972: 102.

members of this caste show decided preference for virtues which emphasize capital accumulation. During my research in Surat District I met several large farmers and local leaders who considered themselves to be the followers of Kabir Panth, a sect with a doctrine in which worldly asceticism (*innerweltliche Askese*) takes precedence. There is a widespread abhorrence of the lack of religiosity, a charge made against Halpatis in particular. The sharp rejection of secular ideologies particularly is the consequence of a caste morality that has a religious base. However, pragmatism guides everyday life. The majority of the Patidars in Bardoli have scant interest in the discussions about the meaning of existence or about their personal background. It is also striking how little they know about the differences between their own subcastes, and the whys and wherefores of these. Is the past remembered only sketchily because, in most cases, there was little glory in it? I do not think so. It is more a case of great involvement with the here and now; what counts is acquired, and not discarded status.

The term *kulak* seems tailored for the Patidar farmers in Surat District, as distinct from the landowning Anavil Brahmins who mainly inhabit Valsad District in the extreme southern part of Gujarat State and who can without doubt be seen as *junker* (Breman 1974). Behaviour linked with the *kulak* image is not restricted to those obtaining their living from agriculture. In seeking extra-agricultural sources of income the Patidars strive to set up their own businesses or industries. The Anavil Brahmins, by contrast, show preference for the 'services'; a wide range of official and administrative callings which imply leadership or at least the exercise of supervision. In the words of one Anavil Brahmin 'we are better able to deal with subordinates than with clients—we are too short-tempered for those'. He gave this piece of information not to convince me of his self-importance, but to demonstrate his contempt for the business-like attitude of the Patidars. The latter are in their turn justly proud of their reputation as successful enterpreneurs.

The transformation to a capitalist order is not yet complete in the south Gujarat countryside—this applies above all to a vanguard of large farmers—and has moreover (as I showed earlier) not implied an erosion of primordial relations, which have acquired a more instrumental significance. The following comment by Beteille is relevant to this situation.

> There are in rural India two interpenetrating systems, one based on personal ties and loyalties and the other on impersonal rules and standards. There is also a small but powerful (and growing) minority of people—progressive farmers, capitalist farmers, rural entrepreneurs—who are successfully using both those systems apparently without being deeply committed to the values on which either is based (1974: 109).

The type of rationality accompanying a capitalist behaviour pattern has not yet fully developed. In the production sphere this is obvious in, for instance, the use of many more (and much too expensive) inputs, such as the application of high dosages of fertilizer or the purchase of tractors which remain underutilized, than is acceptable from the viewpoint of optimal farm management. Another example is the decision not to cultivate a particular crop, merely out of spite in order to prevent a relatively modest proportion of the profit from reaching the local labourers. Much more easily visible is the wasteful conspicuous consumption, such as the building of absurdly big and pretentious bungalows or the giving of exorbitantly high dowries. There is a great distance between the Gandhian purity and rigour of some of the leaders and the affluence and comfort in which a large part of their following are eager to indulge themselves. I see a rather pedestrian materialism as opposed to a feudal life-style, in the behaviour of the new rich. There is however, a feudal lust for personal dominance, the urge to reduce others to a state of inferiority but without assuming any obligations towards them. After storming at a migrant worker, a Patidar said to me by way of explanation: 'we need inferiors around us in order to be able to bully them'. In a more restrained tone, Pocock sums up this attitude as follows: 'For the Patidar the idea of the good life implies immediate superiority, superiority over someone else' (1973: 23).

The Patidars' power lies in their ability to carry through community action. It is almost taken for granted that the agitation of the farmers is connected with the protests of those who oppose vested interests, but I would like to point out that it is often precisely the socially strong in the countryside who are the first to organize themselves, both to exert pressure on the government and to forestall or defuse claims from those beneath. One example of such an alliance of substantial farmers is unquestionably the Khedut Samaj, which has been active in Bardoli and its environs for sometime.

At the end of 1973 the Khedut Samaj began a campaign directed against the plans of the Gujarat government of that time to implement a new land reform, and against the levy of a part of the rice production by the government for a fixed price. Not without cause, the large farmers in particular felt threatened by this legislation. The preceding land reform, directed primarily against land tenancy arrangements made by large, often absentee owners, had worked to the advantage of the main farming caste. However, Patidar dominance was jeopardized by the enforcement of the resolution to assign to the marginal landowners and landless labourers the surplus land that would be freed by lowering the ceiling on landholding still further. Again, the legislation intended to withdraw some rice from sale on the free market did not hit the small producers so much as the substantial farmers. The landowners in the irrigated zone of Surat District in particular, refused to observe this regulation. A mass meeting in the state capital of Ahmedabad in which many tens of thousands from the whole of Gujarat took part, demonstrated that this vanguard of agrarian capitalism commanded an extensive following (including middle farmers) and was able to mobilize them effectively.[9] Also, the roughly one thousand women and children from Bardoli who joined a procession to the official residence of Indira Gandhi, were applauded in their own circle.

In the next stage resistance gradually took on a grimmer character. Through *morchas* and *gheraos*, members of parliament from the Congress Party were pressured into tendering their resignations and local civil disobedience actions led to the closure of the government offices. Significantly, Sardar Patel's

[9] In a recent study G. Shah commented on the organization as follows: 'In terms of caste, the Khedut Samaj is dominated by the Patidars. It secured support against land ceiling and paddy levy from the Koli, the Rajput, the Bareeya and the Adivasi middle and rich cultivators. At the same time, however, the Samaj was backed by the poor Patidar cultivators who were not adversely affected by the land legislations. Of course, they were not directly benefitted by them either' (1982: 146).

daughter Maniben won an election victory as member of the opposition (Congress O). At public meetings the farmers, egged on by their leaders, solemnly pledged never to return surplus land to the government for distribution among the landless. For that matter, this last was not seriously expected to materialize because, as a spokesman for the Khedut Samaj explained to his audience, it was the custom of the Congress politicians to do precisely the opposite of what they promised. Indeed, the government had already allowed the suggestion to filter through that it would not be in any great haste to implement this particular land reform. Under pressure of what was termed public opinion most of the government party's representatives now voted for raising, instead of lowering, the ceiling for landownership. These concessions however were not enough for the farmers. In Surat District they organized themselves into vigilante patrol groups, with a commandant at the head of every ten villages, and the Samaj instituted Sardar-Senas—an unambigious reference to the patrols which Sardar Patel set up in the days of the *satyagraha*—for the protection of the crops.

Incidents were inevitable. When farmers' sons wanted to put an end to a meeting of agricultural labourers in Bardoli, held to discuss the situation that had arisen, a fight followed in which some were injured, and the tension continued. The Khedut Samaj mounted a *satyagraha* in Bardoli, Kamrej and Palsana Talukas against the levy on rice. In order to reinforce their demands and to demonstrate their strength, the farmers stopped the delivery of milk and vegetables to the urban centres. The government reacted half-heartedly, the agricultural labourers much more fiercely. The latter, realizing that the farmers' campaigns against the land reform and the levy on rice were not only directed against the government but struck at them just as much, offered their support in collecting the rice quota and to lead officials to the places where the farmers hid their stocks.

> Anger over this and over the arrest of two leaders of the Khedut Samaj in Surat District caused rioting to break out in Bardoli on one of the first days of 1974. Young Patidars, for the most part students at the local college, held a protest demonstration during which they called at the house of A.D., leader of the Halpati Seva Sangh. They burned his belongings, dragged him

outside, tore off his clothes and forced him to walk naked down the street, after which they beat him senseless. He told me later that they had left him for dead. The news of this surprise attack spread like a wild fire among the agricultural labourers in the area. That same afternoon groups of Halpatis made their way to the nearby sugar factory with the intention of setting fire to it. Rushing to the scene, Gandhian social workers managed only with difficulty to deter them from doing this. In several villages the Halpatis destroyed crops, working equipment, tractors and other farmers' property. Here and there fierce fights broke out in which a Patidar lost his life. More arrests were made following which a general strike (*bandh*) was called several days later in the principal market places of south Gujarat, with the added threat that if the leaders were not set free, the whole of Gujarat would go up in flames. Yet the peak of the action was now past. The clandestine accord concluded with the government at the beginning of January meant—so the chairman of the Khedut Samaj explained—an acknowledgement of the organization and of the farmers' demands. On the same occasion a religious leader pointed out that the first Minister of Gujarat was himself a *khedut putra*—a farmer's son. Agrarian interests would not be served by his fall.

The above account is taken from a study made by Ganshyam Shah on the course of events during this agitation in south Gujarat at the end of 1973 and the beginning of 1974 (Shah 1977). The following commentary (which remains anonymous) is also illuminating:

> The opposition to the levy on paddy was not an economic issue, but a political one. The levy did not even bruise the farmers who, organised under the banner of the newly started Khedut Samaj, actually promised to give more paddy than required under the government order, provided the levy was abolished and it was made voluntary. Their demand was that the government should have arrived at a 'samjuti', or understanding, with them as it had done with the groundnut and oil magnates. The issue was, who had the power—the government or the kheduts (Anon. 1974: 131).

A second consideration in ending the action was anxiety over the rapidly growing militance of the landless labourers, whose demobilization was a major concern as much for the farmers' leaders as for the Gandhian leaders of the landless themselves. The anonymous commentator reports on this as follows:

> The Khedut leaders at the reception of the released *satyagrahis* mentioned in no unmistakable terms that they cannot have any animosity against the Halpatis and that they must see that they do not suffer. At the meeting of the workers of the Halpati Seva Sangh the Gandhians have advised the Halpatis not to be impatient with their starvation and to go by the Gandhian path.[10]

The alliance linking the farmers is not a standing organization with clearly outlined objectives, a fixed membership and a programme of activities. The Khedut Samaj is much more of a social movement with a committee of leaders who have accepted the mandate to appear in public as a pressure group, and who mobilize a diffuse following in shortlived campaigns when the need arises. A relatively long period of peace can suddenly erupt into an activism that makes a rather spurious impression on outsiders, but which is in line with the mood of the clientèle. I had the opportunity of testing this in the course of my fieldwork, beginning while the Emergency was still in force. The Khedut Samaj was hostile to Indira Gandhi's regime because her political intentions conflicted with the farmers' interests. In the state power as represented by Indira Gandhi they perceived a threat to their regional dominance and the consolidation of this in the political arenas of Gujarat. The emphatic way in which the leaders of the farmers' alliance (who were at the same time local notables) testified to their belief in the free play of social forces, meant an almost absolute rejection of governmental interference in what they regarded as their own personal domain. Erosion of private property was the least of their reproaches against the government. The anti-governmental stance of the farmers was encouraged still further by the support which, in their opinion, the landless received from officialdom. In this anti-government and anti-labour attitude the farmers are continuing a tradition which began half a century ago.

The Khedut Samaj was one of the organizations which was banned during the Emergency, but contact with supporters was ensured through the distribution of a bi-monthly paper,

[10] Anon. 'The role of landed interests in the current agitation in Gujarat' (manuscript n.d.): 8–9. Eric Stokes, who made the comparison with earlier actions, came to a similar conclusion (1978: 281).

Khedut Vani (Farmers' Voice). This organ, which circulated underground, had a very attentive reading public, as I could deduce from the surprisingly similar answers in a large number of villages to my questions about labour relations. Time after time I was forced to listen to the view (once again, always put in a wholly stereotyped way, as if it was a well-learned lesson) that, in counting all kinds of emoluments—which only a few farmers in fact give—the agricultural labourers definitely received a daily wage of Rs 5.50; that their inferior labour performance was not worth even half this amount; that equal pay for men, women and children alike was senseless; that it was unfair to make the farmers keep a labour register, etc. What sort of benefit could be expected from a government which involved itself in the fate of what was, after all, a stupid, ignorant and irresponsible mass, but which paid no heed to those able to raise productivity necessary for development? In contrast to the Congress Party, 'preparing the way for communism', the farmers typified their kind of democracy as 'being master in their own home'. 'Why a ceiling?' was a recurring question. 'Is there also a ceiling in industrial production?' The populist rhetoric is unequivocally anti-state in its appeal and directed against a pretended preferential treatment of 'urban interests'.

Immediately after the Emergency was lifted, the revived Khedut Samaj demanded the repeal of the ordinance regulating the enforcement of the minimum wage law. Nevertheless, when the election campaign came up, the *Khedut Vani* adopted a friendly tone towards the agricultural labourers. They were told to put their trust in the farmers with whom they lived and worked in the villages, instead of relying on the loose promises of Indira Gandhi and her Congress Party. In gatherings held expressly for a combined audience of landowners and the landless, D. K. called for harmony, saying that the farmers would gladly pay the labourers Rs 10 a day but could only begin to do so when the government drastically raised agricultural prices.[11] All this was an attempt to win the vote of the agricultural labourers for the Janata coalition—an attractive idea, considering the size of the landless proletariat. This expectation, that the agricultural labourers would be prepared to

[11] *Khedut Vani*, 10 and 17 March 1977.

vote for the party of Charan Singh and Morarji Desai did not show much understanding of the prevailing mood among the landless. However sceptical labourers might have been about the Congress Government, above all else their vote would definitely never have been given to the farmers' candidate. Calls from the Swaraj Ashram (in 1928 the action centre, and now the Janata headquarters for the Bardoli region) to the landless to join with those who wished to live in freedom, had no effect. The farmers had tried earlier to buy the vote of their subordinates' I heard from various Patidars that they were prepared to give money or a *maund* of *jovar* (20 kg of millet) in exchange for the labourers' promises not to vote. Once again the usual stories about fraud went around. For example, the management of the sugar factory had the Khandeshi sugarcane cutters (who as migrant labourers were not enrolled in the voting registers) carried in lorries to the voting centres, where they received precise instructions on how to fill in voting slips —a rumour not worth taking seriously, but characteristic of the atmosphere.

There was great joy over the Janata election victory, shadowed only by the fact that Morarji Desai, who was to be designated as the prime minister in Delhi and who stood as a candidate for Surat City, won with only a relatively small margin of votes in his own constituency. By contrast the district seat went unchallenged to the Congress Party—an inevitable result which the farmers' jubilation could not really mar, as one can see from the note I made in my journal on the evening after the election result:

> In the agricultural labourers' quarter of village S., a weary mood prevails when I return there after my previous visit of some weeks before. The Patidars had kicked up a racket the previous night, when the overthrow of Indira and her regime was confirmed. The conversation I now have concerns a conflict which the local Halpatis had some time ago with seasonal workers from outside. Because farmers' children are standing some distance away and are trying to follow what we are talking about, not all those present are prepared to talk freely. They are derided by the other Halpatis for their reticence—'Are you afraid?' While we are sitting together in a small group, girl comes to tell us that the Patidars are on their way to the Halpati area with their tractors. This procession passes by a little later—half a dozen tractors with

> trailers, in which migrant labourers hired for this purpose from a neighbouring village, have taken their places beside the farmers' sons. They chant pro-Janata slogans as they ride between the huts of the quarter, and call out to the Halpatis: 'Now your Mataji is through you will get only *lal juvar* (red millet, imported from the U.S. as cattle feed, but which has become a permanent element in the agricultural labourers' diet) and will have to start work before sunrise and return to your huts only when it is already dark'. The aggressiveness behind the swagger is unmistakeable, and has the intended effect. The Halpati men are visibly intimidated, the women are less so. As usual they are much more adamant.

The farmers however made it clear that they would be critical of Janata politicians. Only a few weeks after the change of government D.K. demanded, in *Khedut Vani*, the withdrawal of the regulations for enforcing the minimum wage legislation, and raising of the ceiling on landownership.[12] The farmers' lobby in the state assembly, consisting of the delegates of various parties, superintended concession to these demands.[13] In order to keep their clientèle up to date with current events and to build up a wider political platform, communication is, naturally, of prime importance. I was therefore not at all surprised to hear that the Patidar leaders and businessmen plan to bring out a weekly which will eventually be converted into a daily.

In the past decades the dominant landowners have tried, without much success, to take shelter within different political parties. They turned away from the Congress Party when it became obvious that the party could not ignore the mass of the rural poor in its agrarian programme. The Patidars have been ideologically drawn to the Swatantra, Congress-O., KIMLOP (a strongly rightist populist coalition in Gujarat) and Janata Parties successively. Moreover, in the last few years interest in the Jan Sangh has been growing fast, especially among the younger generation, who are not inhibited by Gandhian sentiments like their elders. College students from the higher castes are active in spreading the ideas of this party over the countryside. How-

[12] *Khedut Vani*, 21 April 1977. One of the arguments he put forward in justification of this demand was equality in the trials of women, including of course women landowners.

[13] *Gujarat Mitr*, May 1977.

ever, so long as the Jan Sangh does not have an agrarian ideology, it will continue to have a rather limited reach.

In spite of the continuous change of course evidenced by the above, political capriciousness is the last thing with which one can charge the Patidars; on the contrary, their social attitude displays a striking consistency. It is only to be expected that they turn away from parties which, in the last analysis, are unwilling to (or lack the power to) put farmers' interests first. In their struggle against the government and the labour, which has lost none of its fierceness over the years, the farmers feel cheated in politics. In their view, politicians are the entrepreneurs of an urban limited company in which interests other than the rural-agrarian are dominant. With great self-confidence however, they give one to understand that the end of this state of affairs is in sight—'then it's our turn' say these champions, of a future rural bias in politics. Continued agitation is inherent in this scenario, and certainly in latter years protest has not been lacking. Collaboration between the farmers' organizations active in the various parts of Gujarat has acquired a more institutional basis with the inception of the Krishi Rakshaka Sangha late in 1980. In this comprehensive alliance, priorities include not only a crop insurance scheme and the introduction of an agricultural prices commission, but also the institution of a corps of village guards to ensure maintenance of peace and order, and an appeal to forbid propaganda for 'the ideology of class conflict' (Sanghavi 1980: 2127).

Elsewhere in the countryside of western India at about the same time, larger farmers initiated the action for obtaining higher prices for their produce and for generally altering the terms of trade in favour of agriculture.

> I heard confirmation of my impression that it indeed tended towards this when I made a short visit to village A., in the spring of 1981 after having stayed there for two months earlier. My host, previously a Janata supporter, declared contentedly that "Indira is our man". She would see to the restoration of labour discipline which had been lost under Janata—incomprehensible, he said laughingly, when you consider how the landless have supported her.

The struggle between high and low castes which flared up in Gujarat at the beginning of 1981 over the *anamat* issue (protective discrimination in favour of the deprived castes) led to a further strengthening of class polarization (Desai 1981: 819–24; Yagnik 1981: 977–8). Even though the backwardness of the tribal castes in the south Gujarat countryside is so great in every respect that they can offer no real threat to the Patidars and other *ujliparaj*, the latter are nevertheless increasingly set against the conferring of extra facilities, such as job reservations, on the weak in society. Bardoli college remained shut as a mark of support to the resistance against the reservations policy; and in high caste households this was a hotly debated topic of conversation. Several Patidars pointed out to me that what was happening now in the more northerly part of the state—the higher castes pushing back the Harijans—would in the next stage be repeated in south Gujarat, but this time it would be directed against the Adivasis.

What strikes me each time I return to the area is the unqualified social-Darwinist outlook of the prosperous farmers. This is illustrated by the harshness of their behaviour as individuals towards the landless and the shocking judgements they delight in making in public. Naturally, as members of the dominant caste they permit no doubts regarding their personal superiority, and added to this, they react with condemnation and bitterness to what they perceive as the untrustworthiness of their subordinates, and their reluctance to work. These feelings have acquired a collective basis in relation to labour of briefer duration. In other words their anger is directed against the landless group as a whole, rather than against individual labourers. The Patidars react very aggressively to signs of discontent and resistance from beneath, and anxiety as well as fear, is evidenced in the landowners' spoken views.

> *10 August.* The village headman of A. spoke in respectful terms of the toughness and physical strength of specifically-named agricultural labourers of the previous generation. Their masters occasionally made use of these qualities to settle their mutual differences, but the work people of today are worth nothing any more, in this respect. The farmers' sons can manage them without difficulty. Nevertheless, however weakened through drink and complete wretchedness, the number of the landless is so great that the farmers are forced to fear for their possessions. Material progress has made the Patidars vulnerable to attack from a mob. In several villages riots have erupted in recent years, in which the

> landless have marched *en masse* to the farmers' quarter, where the farmers have had to barricade their houses in great haste. The possession of firearms has sharply increased among the members of high castes, in the light of these events. It is illegal, but certainly understandable, said my informant.

Further escalation—increasingly violent—seems impossible to avoid. At a higher level of social action the leaders of the substantial farmers present their demands with a rigidity and shortsightedness concerning the needs of the agrarian underclass, which can only be understood by those who know the intransigence of their following in the villages. However, the more the dominant landowners assert themselves in a militant way towards the outside world, the more their local power basis trembles under the pressure from beneath—a pressure that is becoming increasingly obvious. I will devote further attention to this in a later chapter.

In order not to oversimplify this dynamic by confining it to the struggle between the landless and the landowners, I shall first clarify the oppositions between the migrant labourers and the local landless, so that I may subsequently examine the visible confrontation along vertical lines.

12
SEGMENTATION AND CONFRONTATION

A triangle of tensions: relations between migrants, local landless and landowners

Circulation and the final departure of labour from the hinterland of Surat District is dictated by a survival strategy, as I made clear in Chapter 8. There is no reason for presuming that migration is a first step towards improving the position of those directly involved, mostly landless and small peasants. The shift to the plain is more of an attempt to avoid socio-economic decline, or at least to mask it, than a prelude to upward mobility. Existence in Bardoli Vibagh is precarious because inclusion in the rural labour order is almost without exception at the very lowest level. Apart from the fact that the work carries low prestige, it is also very badly paid. This means that even with a longer duration of stay, savings remain too small to be employed productively by the migrants on their return, or by those staying behind in the village of origin. Under these circumstances, the most that people can expect from a temporary absence is not an improvement of their position but its maintenance. Seasonal workers help to prevent continuing deterioration (through indebtedness, sale of lands, etc.) of the households to which they belong and they use what is left over from their earnings to tide over difficult times, and use it purely for the purposes of consumption.

Immigrants into the plain are exceedingly vulnerable. The farmers require them only for a limited part of the year to perform tasks which require little or no skill, and even those who stay on longer, and become more familiar with their new environment, never entirely lose their status as strangers. For rural employers the migrants form an easily exploited labour category. They have to be content with exceptionally low wages and long, irregular working hours, easy to employ at short notice and at the same time immediately replaceable.

What I want to make clear is that labour migration works as much against the local landless as against the migrants. Max Weber in his research on agrarian labour relations at the end of the nineteenth century in what is now East Germany, reached the conclusion that landowners responded to the growing consciousness of the landless proletariat by bringing in outside labour, but saw the departure of indigenous labour to work elsewhere as a disguised strike.[1] In order to find out whether (and in what way) the migrant labour is a weapon in the struggle now taking place in south Gujarat between the rural classes of haves and have-nots, an assessment of the relationship between the local and the mobile proletariat is of prime importance. As one would expect, the strong opposition of interest between these two proletariat segments is further aggravated by those above them. However, besides the mechanisms by which divisions are created we should also give consideration to the emergence of the underclass solidarity, even though this has not yet been structurally consolidated. The reasons for this will be examined at the end of this section.

Usually, whenever the farmers complain of a labour problem, they do not mean a shortage of labourers at crucial times in the agrarian cycle. They are rather exasperated beyond measure by the altered behaviour of the local landless, who no longer conform to the stereotype of the obedient, anxious-to-please farm servants of earlier times, and who make plain their resistance to the existing order in an increasingly emphatic (although still hardly organized) fashion. In reaction to this, but also partly in anticipation of it, the farmers prefer to adopt a cropping pattern and a style of farm management which enables them to reduce to a minimum both the frequency and the intensity of their contact with labour. As I have stated elsewhere, the admission of temporary workers from outside also plays a part in this anti-labour strategy.

Against this background it is no wonder that the Halpatis are

[1] 'The argument over whether domestic migration has given rise to emigrant workers, or vice versa, will never end; but in any case the result is the same in both cases, since both increase in relation to each other being as they are weapon in a struggle between property and labour. Migration is a tacit strike, and the inflow of Poles a means of combating it' (Weber 1979: 199).

irritated by the presence of the strangers in the plain. Without restraint they can vent their anger on the migrants, with an aggressiveness they dare not show too openly to the farmers. Not unjustifiably, they are inclined to interpret the employment of the outsiders as an insufferable attack on their territory. This impression is all the more stronger because the Halpatis see a connection between the promulgation of the minimum wage law and the advent of the Khandeshis. To their way of thinking, the decisive factor was not, as the farmers told me, the construction of the system of canal irrigation, but the attempts by the Halpatis to bring about compliance with the legal provisions.

> *13 February.* Inhabitants of an agricultural labourers' locality in V., close to Bardoli, told me that they went on strike when the farmers refused to pay the minimum wage of Rs 3 which became legally operative that year. They kept up this action for several months by seeking work in nearby villages, but had to give up in the end because the farmers were importing increasingly larger numbers of labourers from the eastern *talukas.* I came to hear a similar story in U., but this time over the misfired attempt to force the acceptance of the legal minimum of Rs 5.50 some years ago. In this village also, the Halpatis refused to work in order to put pressure on the farmers into keeping to this new regulation. To break through this blocade, the farmers called on the landowners in the neighbourhood not to offer work to the landless labourers from U., and conversely to send as many migrants as possible to the village. To put an end to this inflow, the Halpatis went to the *mamlatdar* in Bardoli. He called a meeting in the village, during which he impressed upon the Patidars that they had a moral duty to give precedence to their own agricultural labourers, and only if there were not enough should they employ migrant labourers. If they kept to the nine-hour working day, the Halpatis would probably be content to accept a somewhat lower rate than Rs 5.50. All this was agreed to, but before even a month had passed, the Halpatis were obtaining increasingly less work, and so things have remained since then.

In several villages migrants have been brought in as strike breakers and, naturally enough, this has not made them any more popular with the local landless who are, nevertheless, realistic enough to recognize that they will not easily be rid of these uninvited guests. What they ask from the migrants, persistantly and emphatically, is that they should at least refuse to work for wages below the local 'going' rate, and that they should leave the village if farmers refuse to pay this. In practice, even this appeal for fair play evokes little response since the farmers resist the pressure towards standardization of wages by preferring to issue contract (*udhad*) work to the migrants. The Halpatis showed great discontent over this, especially in the first years. Gangs of Khandeshis camping in the open fields were attacked at night, robbed of their belongings and the women raped. Incidents of this nature also cropped up during the period of my fieldwork, and were flashed in local newspapers.

> *20 April.* Close to the village where I was staying at that time, a road workers' camp was smashed up. According to the *mukadam's* statement the following day, the members of his gang had been unable to do anything in the face of the attackers armed with sticks and mattocks. The gang members were robbed of all their possessions. The suspects, as it appeared some days later from the list of those arrested, were mostly Halpatis from two nearby villages. See also *Gujerat Mitr*, 31-3-1977.

In order to protect themselves against this intimidation, the farmers have turned more and more to bring the migrants closer to their own houses or onto their own lands, or at least to give them permission to seek temporary shelter in the village centres. Even then in some places it has been necessary to take the Khandeshis to the fields each day by tractor, escorted by farmers' sons, and to pick them up again at the end of the day. Further, the animosity that has developed between local and outside labourers makes it necessary for the farmers to keep them apart, as far as possible, while they are working on the land. Whenever they must work side by side, which is sometimes unavoidable, the farmers themselves exercise supervision. Migrants who have entered into permanent service cannot as a rule act as the foremen of their bosses, as the local day labourers would obey the instructions of these farm servants only with the greatest reluctance.

From the attitude of the Khandeshis it appears that they are well aware of the irritation they arouse in the local landless. They behave as unobtrusively as possible, scared that otherwise they will be driven away, and while in the vicinity of the indigenous labourers usually gave vague, evasive answers to my questions about their earnings. They claimed to have little or no contact with the village Halpatis, and did not know what the farmers gave them, but at the same time they denied being content with less—a different representation of affairs from that which they gave me on their return to the home area. They talked then with greater freedom about the machinations of the farmers, who played them off against the Halpatis, and also with understanding for the unfriendliness with which the Halpatis treated them—an insight sometimes accompanied by a shoulder-shrugging commentary in the nature of: 'but what can one do—we have to live, too.'

Migrants who have stayed behind in the plain as farm servants have to behave even more cautiously than the seasonal workers.

> *18 April.* While I sit talking to some agricultural labourers in S., B.N.—a Khandeshi who has already lived several years in this village—comes by up the road running in front of the hutment colony. When the Halpatis nod invitingly to him, he comes shyly up to us, and sits on the ground at a distance of a couple of yards.
>
> The tone they use towards him is arrogant and sneering; there is much aggressiveness towards the 'blacklegs' in their area. B. concedes that many seasonal workers receive no more than Rs 2, but denies that this applies to him too. Is he not, after all, the one who comes to tell the Halpatis about migrants in the village working for less than Rs 3? He demonstrates the behaviour of a 'good' Khandeshi, complaining along with the Halpatis about the callousness of the farmers and the advent of so many 'strangers'. He grins sheepishly as the Halpatis relate how the Khandeshi women work only for food in the farmers' households. His policy is obviously to avoid giving offence, to show approval and to appear meek. By behaving in such a way he does not make himself really accepted, but can at least survive.

The seasonal workers and also the migrants who have established themselves more permanently live separately from the landless. The Khandeshi farm servants either lodge with the farmers or in the pump houses outside in the fields allotted to them as living quarters, and seldom or never come into the Halpati locality. This lack of contact prevents the growth of a common identity, and ill-will against the interlopers is kept alive by their aloofness from action undertaken by the local landless to bring improvement into labour conditions. The Halpatis very seldom succeed in getting the Khandeshis on their side,[2] while on the other hand the presence of the Khandeshis allows the farmers to recruit more labour quickly in the hinterland, in the event of a strike.

By extending my research to several villages where conflicts had arisen between local and outside labourers shortly before the beginning of my fieldwork, I was able to form a more precise idea of the immediate cause of these conflicts and their later course. In S., the situation remains disturbed. When the Halpatis here asked for a wage rise after the introduction of the Rs 5.50 law, the farmers used only the labourers from nearby villages. Because these were fellow castemen the Halpatis went to talk to them, and 'requested' (it is clear that some vigorous pressure was exerted) them to stay away. The outsiders renounced further employment in S., even when the Patidars offered them more than what the local labourers had previously earned. The farmers then brought in Chaudharis from the eastern *talukas* who, up to then, had only been used as seasonal workers. The Halpatis tried to talk them round as well, but without success. After a good deal of intimidation including some physical force, the Chaudharis left, after which the Halpatis went in a body to the village to protest to the farmers. The Patidar streets were deserted; the inhabitants had withdrawn into their houses.

Initially, matters were confined to a little shouting back and forth, until a young Patidar began shooting from a window at the Halpatis with a small-bore rifle. Angered by this, the Halpatis forced an entrance into the house, dragged out the owner and beat him up. Afraid of further escalation, a leader managed to persuade the Halpatis to return to their own quarter. Several farmers then went by car to Bardoli to register a complaint, whereupon the police arrived and immediately took the Patidars' side, carrying several agricultural labourers away to Bardoli and locking them up there. Through a social worker the Halpatis informed an MLA, himself an Adivasi from the area. Only when he put pressure on the District Superintendent of Police to intervene in person were the Halpatis allowed to present their own version of the events, on

[2] Singh reports that during a strike in the Punjab agricultural labourers from surrounding villages were successfully prevailed upon to remain neutral but that the boycott of the big farmers eventually failed because migrant labourers continued to work for them (1979: 1754).

the basis of which two Patidars were arrested. The affair is still under investigation, but the agricultural labourers who tell me all this already know that they will get the rough end of the stick. Fourteen of them have already been summoned eight times to the law court in Bardoli, to answer all kinds of questions. They cannot work on these days and even have to pay their own bus fares there and back. A social worker-cum-lawyer has offered to act as their pleader, but is asking for Rs 100 per head as a fee!

A similar incident occurred in U. As further illustration, I have reproduced here the complete indictment, clearly drawn up at the farmers' instigation.

THE HONOURABLE JUDICIAL
FIRST CLASS MAGISTRATE,
BARDOLI COURT.

Complainant: Chaudhari Shiva Panchiya,
Age: about 40 years.
Occupation: labourer.
Permanent address: Umrakh.
Present address: Sarbhon, Taluka Bardoli, dist. Surat.

Accused:

1. Gopal Amaidas Halpati, age about 35, labourer, of U., tal. Bardoli, dist. Surat.
2. Keshav Sojat Halpati, age about 40, labourer, of U., tal. Bardoli, dist. Surat.
3. Mohan Morara Halpati, age 40, labourer, of U., Tal. Bardoli, dist. Surat.
4. Nathu Nagar Halpati, age 50, labourer, of U., tal. Bardoli, dist. Surat.
5. Chhitu Thakor Halpati, age about 22, labourer, of U., tal. Bardoli, dist. Surat.
6. Ramesh Dhula Halpati, age about 25, labourer, of U., tal. Bardoli, dist. Surat.
7. Raman Keshav Vankar, social worker, of Bardoli, dist. Surat.

Complaint made under I.P. Code, clause 153A, 143, 586(2), 114.

Following are the complaints made by the complainant:-

I, Chaudhari Shiva Panchiya, the complainant, live at U. and

I have been working for Patel Chhaganbhai Rambhai for 14 days as a labourer.

I am making a complaint against these seven people. The first six are Halpatis from U., and the other, Aman Keshav Vankar, is a social worker from Bardoli.

On the twentieth of May 1976 in the morning at nine o'clock, I and Sahed Isharia Raya and other family members were working in the field of Chhaganbhai Rambhai Patel. At that time the accused, numbered 1 to 6, arrived armed with sharp weapons, viz: axe, sticks, etc., and they started to abuse us in a loud and rough manner.

Number 1, namely Gopal Amaidas, said that we Chaudharis should not be working there, and told us to leave immediately otherwise they would kill us.

Then I asked: 'What have we done wrong?' The accused number 2, Keshav Sojat replied that Ramanbhai had told them that we had no rights to work there because we were Chaudhari, and that we should therefore leave that place.

Afterwards, I made enquiries in U. and came to know that the accused number 7, Raman Keshav Vankar, had been agitating and leading his henchmen to drive the Chaudhari caste people away from U.

The accused and their followers had assembled a large crowd and they were in a barbarous mood. We were threatened with murder, and in addition to this they started to act violently. That is why I left U. and came to Sarbhon.

In this way, they caused so much fear among the Chaudharis that all decided to leave U. and settle in Sarbhon.

Thus the accused number 7, Raman Keshave Vankar, created conflict between Halpatis and Chaudharis, and the accused numbered 1 to 6 aided and abetted him.

I hereby request you to start legal proceedings against them according to the rule of I.P.Code, Clause 153A, 153, 143, 506 (2), 114.

Following are my witnesses:

1. Chaudhari Isaria Raya, of Sarbhon.
2. Chhaganbhai Rambhai Patel, of U.
3. Thakorbhai Dahyabhai, of U.
4. Chhitubhai Haranjibhai Patel, of U.

Dated: 20th. May 1977.

In this case, too, the farmers will undoubtedly succeed in victimizing the Halpatis for their resistance to the migrants, thanks to their familiarity with the ways of the law and to the co-operation they receive, especially from the lower authorities. The Halpatis' action appears to have achieved nothing, because when I came to the village (in the same month in which the charge was brought) nearly every Patidar household was once more employing one or more outsiders, and a great many of the Halpatis were unemployed. Yet I would like to caution against too great a pessimism. The remarkable feature of the situation is not that the local landless are so often the obvious losers, but that in spite of this they return to the fight again and again. Moreover the farmers clearly show themselves to be in awe of the militancy of the Halpatis, who by participating in conflict have become accustomed to acting collectively.

Ultimately their activism appears to result in a certain amount of localized success, perhaps precisely in places where escalation has gone the furthest, as in P. for instance, where several years ago matters came to an armed encounter between the farmers and the landless in which one person was killed. Since then no more Khandeshis have been employed, except as seasonal workers, because (so the Patidars told me euphemistically) after what had happened they could no longer afford the Khandeshis' labour. Sometimes even this ultimate violence is unnecessary.

> At Bamni village of Bardoli taluka, the Halpatis staged demonstrations in October-November 1975 against the landowers for importing labourers from Uchhal and Nizar regions. The Halpatis could manage to drive out those labourers from the village and in the scuffle between the Halpatis and the outside labourers some of the labourers were beaten up by the farmers. A couple of leaders of the Khet Mazdoor Parishad (mg note: this organization will be discussed in the next chapter) intervened to settle the issue but the landowners refused to negotiate with them. The landowners, meanwhile, arranged to bring police force in the village and brought back the labourers to do the farm work. However, the leaders managed to remove the police force from the scene. Soon after the police force went back, the Halpatis once again assaulted the outside labourers who left the place finally. Thereafter, the landowners agreed to negotiate with the leaders and ultimately succumbed to the demand of paying the fixed wages of Rs 5.50 per day (Lal 1977: 20–1).

I must immediately add that in the long run success has turned into failure. During a visit I paid to this village a full year later, I learned that the migrants had returned, while after the Janata Party came to power, shortly after the state of Emergency was lifted in India, the wages of the Halpatis fell again to the old level. I cannot escape the impression that resistance by the local landless to outside labour has in latter years lost some of its power. Without there being any question of resignation, the Halpatis give one to understand that even concrete action produces no results. They are afraid that the farmers will carry out their threats not to employ them at all any more, and—as of old—find no hearing among the local government officials regarding their complaints about being excluded from employment. Would they not be much better off cultivating solidarity with the migrants, rather than clashing with the farmers? That would be a long road to tread, beset with disappointments. The local landless know full well that the Khandeshis come to the plain because of poverty.

The Halpatis argue that, in contrast to themselves, a great many migrants are landowning cultivators. In referring to the seasonal workers who often bring with them their own grain supplies for their short sojourns in the plain, the Halpatis tersely point out the difference: 'they come to earn *money*, while we are still unable to buy enough *food* with our labour!' Moreover, say the Halpatis,: 'if things don't work out well for them, they can always go back home. Where can *we* go?' It is an understandable reaction, and I therefore do not much value their short-term chances of being able to form a common front with migrants against the farmers.

Not that the relationship between the migrants and the farmers is so companionable! Although the Patidars' behaviour towards the outsiders is less motivated by rancour, the treatment to which the latter are exposed is hardly better than that which the local landless are forced to endure. I witnessed a shocking incident of the administration of instant 'justice' when, during my leave in A., an 'impertinent' migrant was called to order.

11 May. In front of the house where I was lodging, a great cabal gathered early one evening. Several farmers had brought in a Chaudhari labourer whom they had seized just before, while he was involved in a fight with the farmer for whom he worked. The latter did not show up because, as I heard later, he was too drunk. His absence was no insuperable obstacle to the procedure, because the *sirpanch* was not concerned with finding out what precisely had happened. Rather, the sole object of the hearing was to establish that the seasonal worker had used his fists, knocking his adversary to the ground and hitting him—an unforgiveable sin because his opponent was a Patidar. It made no difference that the Chaudhari had gone for the farmer first because he objected to the latter importuning his wife. The aim of the sitting was not the ascertainment of the facts—it seemed as though all those involved had agreed to remain silent about these—but to carry out the sentence, which was a pubiic display, one in which only members of the dominant caste were involved. From the *hitchko* (swing) on the raised porch of his house, the *sirpanch* spoke harshly to the arrested man and swore at him, repeatedly calling him a *bhencod*. The Chaudhari stood below in front of us, and with bowed head accepted the reproaches and curses. The by-standers all Patidars, for their part answered the rhetorical questions put to the Chaudhari, whose wife had also come. She was less crudely attacked but was nevertheless scared. She bravely tried to stand up for her husband, her voice shrill and sometimes cracking, intimidated as she was by the hostile crowd surrounding her. The *police patel* standing next to the Chaudhari took up the *sirpanch's* reprimands, underlining his harangue with physical violence. Amidst demonstrations of approval from the bystanders, he took off his sandal and gave the Chaudhari many blows with it, left and right in the face. It was a shameful spectacle, this view of the village notables meting out their punishments with great emotion and satisfaction. The *sirpanch* wound up his tirade with the remark that the Chaudhari had probably been drunk and that for this reason alone he was being let off lightly. Never again must such a thing happen. With a couple of well-aimed blows the Chaudhari was driven into the outer darkness, his wife walking behind him, crying and protesting at the top of her voice.

Several Halpatis with whom I talked on the following day refused to show excitement about this incident. To begin with it was not their business, and in addition, well—that was how things were. This viewpoint is not accepted lightly by migrant labourers. The farmers may be accustomed to behaving in this way towards the Halpatis but this still does not mean that the Adivasis have to submit to this humiliating treatment. The numerical dominance of tribal castes (such as the Chaudharis) in the hinterland of Surat District and their identity as self-cultivating peasants gives the Adivasis a much greater feeling of independence and dignity than is permitted to the landless proletariat in the plain. As was to be expected, the Patidars' disciplinary action in A. ensured that the gang of harvest workers of which the Chaudhari in question was a member, left the village only a few days later before the work was finished.

The farmers however were not greatly disturbed by the incident. Those with work still to be completed had to arrange quickly for replacement labour, but given the presence of large groups of labourers in the immediate neighbourhood this was not so difficult. The massive extent of the seasonal migration enabled the Patidars to make their dominance felt. Being subjected to the same rules and sanctions as the indigenous labourers does not make the migrants stay away for good, but at most leads to an accelerated circulation. Even this is only an inconvenience rather than a real hindrance to their employers.

Defenceless as they are, they seem to be less vulnerable than the strangers who have remained behind as farm servants. The isolation of the latter irrevocably binds them to the farmers for whom they work. In contrast, the seasonal workers are (precisely because of their mobility) much less affected by the extra-economic pressures to which the local landless are exposed. Lack of a permanent footing in the plain, which at first sight appears to be only a disadvantage, can under certain conditions markedly increase the chance of real resistance.

An example of this is the action taken by the Khandeshi sugarcane cutters at the end of the harvest campaign in 1981. In an earlier publication I wrote about the exploitation of these migrants by the co-operative sugar factories in the south Gujarat plain (Breman 1978–9). Although this account (which appeared in a Gujarati translation at the time of the elections in the state assembly at the beginning of 1980) provided the immediate excuse for an official investigation, little or no improvement has been made in labour conditions since then. During a later stay in the spring of 1981 I paid visits to two of the three factories in which I had conducted my original research. The management swore to me that the rates paid for the cutting and carrying of the sugarcane had been raised much higher, amounting (according to their reckoning) to a total payment of Rs. 15–16 per ton. Even if one accepts this figure, my calculation based on the factory's working capacity clearly shows that the daily wage per labourer still remains some 20–30 per cent below the officially established minimum wage. Furthermore the amount quoted to me is not, by a long stretch, actually attained.

In the Khandeshi camps I visited the general mood was sombre. The basic rates the Khandeshis obtained were much lower than that they had been tricked into believing before their departure from home at the beginning of the season. The few rupees they obtained from the *mukadam* on paydays once a fortnight was too little with which to buy all their daily necessities, and they had no choice but to exchange a portion of the subsidized monthly ration of rough millet (*bajri*) allowed them by the factory, with buyers coming to the camp—not because they could do without the millet, but in order to be able to obtain additional daily necessities. They had already protested several times and hoped that the shortage they now suffered would be made good at the final wage settlement two months hence.

Alas, that hope was not to be fulfilled. On the last payday the balance for the whole campaign was made up and it was customary for all the harvest gangs to come to the factory at that time, to receive the remainder of their earnings so that they could begin the journey home immediately after. The arrangement was the same this time. At the end of the first week in May, several thousand Khandeshis assembled in the grounds of the Chalthan factory to receive the amount still due to them. They had reckoned on a payment of Rs 15 per ton of cut cane, and felt they had been cheated when the sum appeared to amount to only Rs 9.50 per ton. The factory management's argument that, with the allowances in kind and the advances, the labourers had more or less reached the amount first mentioned, made no impression on the Khandeshis—and with reason. The harvest workers demanded that the difference should be made up in cash, while the management did not want to go further than an increase of Rs 0.50 per ton.

As a concession it was too little and too late. The migrants, gheraoed the office personnel in order to add force to their demands, subsequently molested the managing director and embarked on a course of destruction (with the interesting incidental feature that the stalls along the road to the factory, whose only clients were cane cutters, were also set alight). As the local newspapers did not forbear to mention, the factory founder's statue in front of the main office was also desecrated. For that matter, throughout the reportage on the incident, only the factory management's viewpoint was presented, with no attempt to foster an understanding of the workers' points of view. According to the local dailies a reign of terror was let loose which was entirely unexpected and for which no rational explanation could be found. The impression created was that the factory management became suddenly confronted by demands with which it found impossible to meet.[3]

This incident made it clear that seasonal migrants working in gangs are certainly capable of being mobilized; i.e. they are prepared to engage in direct action in pursuit of better working conditions. Whenever the success of a harvest operation depends upon the employment of large numbers of migrants, their organization can lead to collective agreements difficult to achieve individually.[4] However, there are no indications in south Gujarat that whenever the outside army of cane cutters prepares for action, they can count on the support of local labourers. The two categories of labour do not form a common front, but arrive at resistance along different paths. What do the landless from the plain itself achieve in this respect, and what are the opportunities and limitations for making a stand against the class of dominant landowners?

The incitement to rural class struggle

The situation within which the landless labourers operate illustrates the well-known thesis of Marxist origin that conditions of poverty and immiseration are not necessarily translated into social consciousness. Moreover, this discrepancy between objective conditions and subjective experience applies not only to the members within a class but also between those belonging to different social classes. While the agricultural labourers in

[3] *Gujarat Samachar* and *Gujarat Mitr*, both 14 May 1981.

[4] McEwen Scott reports on this in her interesting study of the organization of migrant labour in Argentina (1973: 56–64). For quite recent actions among sugarcane cutters in Maharashtra see Abraham in EPW, 1979 and 1980.

the region of Bardoli have hardly passed the stage of being a a class-in-itself, the large farmers of the region have reached the point where they can be seen as forming a class-for-itself. For these farmers membership of co-operatives and the farmers' union (among other institutions) forms respectively the economic and the political counterparts of the joint pursuit of common interests along class lines. Within rural dynamics the organization of the agrarian underclass has clearly lagged behind. Their mobilization (in so far as one can talk in such terms) is still directed primarily towards strengthening their common identity as members of the same caste. I am alluding here to the Halpati Seva Sangh, with its headquarters in Bardoli. Following on my observation in chapter 5 concerning this organization, I would like to dwell now in more detail on its ideological orientation and programme of activities, discussing the recent developments in particular.

Despite the intensification of social polarization in recent decades, the Halpati Seva Sangh remains firmly committed to harmony, reconciliation and non-violence as basic principles taken from Gandhian teachings, with the accent on the 'uplift' of the Halpatis through the diffusion of Hindu values. Without beating around the bush, the annual reports express the belief of persuading the Halpatis to adopt 'civilized' habits of behaviour in order to enable them to join the mainstream of the society. This aim forms an essential contribution to the internalization of the inferior position of the Halpatis in the social order, because a cultural ideal is being held up to the members of this tribal caste which is based on demands they cannot possibly fulfill by reason of their poverty. The Halpatis are thus being shown how to assist in their own subordination. The Gandhian leaders are guided by an outspokenly *ujliparaj* bias deriving from the milieu into which most of them are born, and it is against this background that one must understand their patronizing behaviour and the moral tone they use in relation to their clients[5].

In my opinion one of the most important functions of the Halpati Seva Sangh has been the fostering of a caste con-

[5] In the Gandhian view tribal resistance is unexpected and results from the cunning and doctrinaire fanaticism of left-radical, godless agitators for whom the simple and naive tribals are no match. Raghavaiah's study of tribal revolts is characteristic of this representation of affairs.

sciousness, a totality of norms and values that, serves to make the inequality of the Halpatis both comprehensible and acceptable. The fact that things have not in fact worked out this way is connected with, among other factors, the frustration of a different postulate from the Gandhian hierarchical world view, namely the right of the weak in society to exist and survive. Claims for support and protection, made by the leaders of the organization on behalf of their clientele, have always been resolutely rejected by the high caste landowners. Evasion of this responsibility has compelled the Halpati Seva Sangh, by way of compensation, to carry out a broad and complex programme of welfare activities for which the government has provided the fund. Included in this fight towards increasing the Halpatis' capacity for social self-defence is the building of huts on their own land, school and occupational training centres. Available employment is extended to the Halpatis through the encouragement of *khadi* and other handicraft industries and (in latter years) by laying the foundation of a large number of local labour co-operatives, to which the execution of small-scale infrastructural works can be assigned.

Finally, there are all sorts of activities in the social-cultural sphere, including the formation of womens' and boys' clubs intended to combat such evils as drunkenness, indebtedness and other 'anti-social' habits, and to reinforce public spiritedness. However, this extensive programme appears more imposing on paper than it does in reality. Intensification of the programme under the *antyodhaya* scheme, a neo-Gandhian development strategy surrounded by a great deal of propaganda at the end of the 1970s, which purported to reach the poorest of the rural poor, in fact achieved little or nothing. Although well intentioned, the efforts of these non-government agencies up to now have probably increased rather than diminished the social vulnerability of the groups towards which they are directed.

Thanks to these relief programmes, the isolation in which the Halpatis exist has been institutionalized. The new huts built for them stand on land usually lying far outside the village centre. The deficient facilities in these colonies and the difficulty of access to them epitomize the marginal existence led by their inhabitants. The seperate education given to Halpati children contributes further to this new untouchability, as I called it earlier. Working on the diagnosis that the Halpati children seldom frequent the main village school (and not, as a result of opposition from higher castes) the Halpati Seva Sangh has concluded that they are best served by small schools in their own neighbourhood. Lessons do not progress beyond the primary level, and are given by teachers often belonging to the Halpati caste themselves. There is barely any question of providing literacy and education in general; the function of these schools does not go much further than that of keeping the children away from the huts while their parents are at work. This can certainly not be said of the *ashram* lower and middle schools created especially for the Halpatis, but which are accessible to other Adivasi children as well. These are located throughout the whole of south Gujarat, with hostels attached to a number of them. However, this type of education has a strongly Gandhian thread running through it, with the disadvantage that after graduation, students arriving in the labour market find that they have already dropped behind their counterparts from the high castes.

The special provisions made for the Halpatis have not produced the desired results, even when measured by the subjective standards of the Halpati Seva Sangh, and this is partly due to the modest extent of the resources available. By entrusting the execution of this broadly diverse but always inadequate programme to a voluntary agency, the government has failed to take responsibility for the emancipation of the Halpatis. As a result attempts made from within the Gandhian camp over the past half century to improve the conditions of the rural poor, have to a large extent failed. To be sure, in recent decades an Adivasi cadre (trained in the institutions set up by the Gandhian movement) has gradually taken the place of social workers originating from the *ujliparaj* castes. Understandably these Adivasi cadre members have learned to be severely critical of the social milieu from which they themselves have sprung, and the indoctrination of high-caste values has led to the adoption of the current stereotypes about the Halpatis and their lack of discipline, intelligence and sense of responsibility. It was always shameful to hear staff members of the organization passing negative judgement on their own caste.

14 March. An example of this is M.P., a young matriculate who has been entrusted by his organization with the day-to-day management of a small brickyard which came into existence as an employment project. While we cycle there, he allows it to be understood that he regards himself as being too good for this work. The labourers are lazy, following orders carelessly or not at all, and 'big-mouthing' him if he corrects them. 'They are not really worth our trouble—they cannot be helped and do not want to be helped'—so he talks in imitation of his superiors. I have encountered this type of 'social worker' many times who, as a kind of extension worker for the Halpati Seva Sangh, try (more as a routine than with any genuine inspiration) to arouse interest among the Halpatis for the work of the organization. Dressed in terylene trousers, shoes, socks, and shirt with fountain pen in the breast pocket and with a plastic briefcase under his arms from which he pulls papers containing the newest plans and activities, he demonstrates own self-importance, but does not make much impression. At the meetings in the colonies of the landless such a social worker addresses his drummed-up clientele (sitting, poorly dressed, in front of him on the ground) using schoolmasterish tones, as if the Halpatis were a class of none-too-bright children who have to be forced to attend to the lesson by a simple question-and-answer game. The audience, listening in boredom, join in listlessly at appropriate moments. The whole affair gives the impression of an obligatory performance in which neither the actor nor the audience believe.

And yet, radical voices are not completely lacking within the Gandhian movement. Social workers regularly come to the fore who show a greater degree of social engagement, and who do not seek the cause of the organization's poor results in the mental inferiority of its clientele, but rather in the opposition coming from the rural elite, and its reluctance to make concessions. However, they hardly ever obtain the chance to put forward their notions, let alone put them into practice. With their arguments for a more militant and antagonistic attitude towards the large farmers these critics are of course offending the ideology which denies the existence of a class opposition. Ultimately there is no room within the Gandhian movement for those who hold a different opinion, and therefore whenever attempts to bring these opponents of the official line to their senses fail, they are expelled.

The hierarchical constitution of the movement leaves no room for misunderstanding: the leaders decide, the cadre executes, and the clients follow.

Sometimes, however, the latter do not keep to this tacit agreement and show rebelliousness, for example by initiating conflicts with the farmers. When incidents of this nature occur, the farmers often call the social workers to come between the two sides, which the latter hasten to do, exerting themselves to quell the disturbances as quickly as possible, even when this results in a straight defeat for those they claim to represent. The social workers are compelled to attempt de-escalation not so much through anxiety about provocation, as through the sacrosanct principle of arbitration. In a situation of extreme and still increasing inequality, restoration of harmony, or at least the reconciliation of opponents, usually occurs at the cost of the weaker party. Consequently there is no reason to revoke what I said earlier about the Halpati Seva Sangh:

> The Halpatis have not much cause to regard the HSS as an organisation that fights for *their* interests. For them, it is an obscure body, affiliated with the government and representing external interests. It is therefore doubtful whether the HSS may be called an emancipation movement at all. Its aims and methods rather seem to prevent mobilisation (Breman 1974: 495).

Even so every organization, however moderate, aiming at the welfare of the agricultural labourers, is suspect in the eyes of the dominant landowners. They are convinced that the Halpati Seva Sangh instigates the agricultural labourers to resist the farmers, and has created the present-day climate of unrest and discontent. Does the drive for a minimum wage not come from this corner, and did not the social workers, several decades ago, incite the Halpatis to ask for land on which to build their huts and money wages in place of wages in kind? According to the farmers, the interference of these outsiders is to blame for the estrangement between the landowners and the landless. For them, the destructive role of the Gandhian workers is an established fact, and this attitude is in no way modified by the fact that they call on these same social workers to help pacify the Halpatis in the localized and short-lived explosions which continue to occur with increasing frequency. On the contrary, it strengthens their resentment about their loss of social control over the caste which has always been subservient to them.

The rural agitation of Patidars in Bardoli at the beginning of 1977, which culminated in the attack on the leaders of the Halpati Seva Sangh already described, was directed against the Adivasis in general and the landless labourers in particular. Thus was the commentary of Jugatram Dave from the *ashram* where he spent the last years of his life. (Desai 1977: 145). The difference in the style of leadership marks the changing times, for by contrast to this Gandhian veteran, regarded as almost holy by his disciples, his successor behaves much more like a politician. The new links maintained by the Halpati Seva Sangh with the Congress movement made it obvious that the cadre would call upon the Halpatis to vote for this party at election time. However, when A.D.'s aspirations for a seat in the state assembly remained unfulfilled, he set a new course by going over to the opposition party which promised him a seat, and tried to move his clientele to vote for it. This brought him into the farmers' camp, and the same people who, a short time ago, had beaten him up because of his sympathy for the cause of the landless labourers, now became his allies. He was able to put pressure on the cadre of his organization into following him in this opportunistic change of course, but certainly not the Halpatis. In vain he has campaigned, in the second half of the 1970s and the beginning of the 1980s (successively) for KIMLOP and Janata, combinations of parties which were subjected to the control and interests of the principal landowning castes. The Halpatis remained the steady followers of Indira Gandhi's Congress Party, although they did not have many illusions about this either.

> At an election meeting which I attended in 1977 in a Halpati colony, one of those present asked, in an ostensibly naive way; 'how is it that we get no further? Morarji himself told us here that the Janata lot have the best of intentions because they are followers of Gandhi. And Congress has already governed a long time in the name of the poor, but we are still as poor as ever. Does the cause still lie with us ourselves, then?' (Loud laughter).

The Halpatis realize very well that they are being manipulated as a vote bank, but their political behaviour is not based on this realization. In their voting behaviour they do not allow themselves to be led by the promises politicians hold out to them: they choose, not for a party or a programme, but against the farmers. In this they give the appearance of possessing more insight into what is the most fundamental opposition than do those who set themselves up as their spokesmen.

The popularity of the Halpati Seva Sangh has never been very great, but after the political escapades of its current leader the organization has completely gambled away its credibility among the Halpatis. Thanks to government subsidies the work of 'uplift' continues as usual, but only in an extremely routine kind of way.

> A.D. has withdrawn into his office and from there manages a number of projects for which he obtains financial support from an international organization. The last time I met him, in the spring of 1981, he had lost his earlier *élan*. He has no political ambitions any more, but no ideals either, he gave me to understand. Under his leadership the organization has acquired a markedly bureaucratic character. The management of many projects and activities demands an extensive administrative staff, accommodated in the headquarters lying opposite the *Swaraj ashram* in Bardoli. In the autumn of 1980 a great office building was completed for which, significantly enough, Morarji Desai carried out the opening ceremony.

If the Halpatis have a good reason for scepticism over the intentions of the outsiders about emancipating them, why then do they not engage in action on their own initiative and with their own leaders? A first obstacle to mobilization is the poverty in which the majority live; the low level of material existence simply does not permit the Halpatis enough free time and energy for such action. Moreover, those who value the chance of work must be especially careful not to behave too boldly. Although real submissiveness as a token of dependence has become very rare, only a few risk arousing the farmers' ire by calling upon their fellow-sufferers to close ranks. The climate is anything but favourable to the achievement of horizontal solidarity and thus the landless class does not form a unity but, rather, separates out into different labour categories with divided interests. The low level of literacy hampers both the development of a cadre and the communication within the rank and file.

> Research in village A. at the beginning of the 1960s showed that an agricultural labourer's household spent on average only

Rs 0.95 (0.15% of the available budget) per year on education, an amount which contrasts glaringly with the Rs 79.74 in the same time period which the farmers' households spent on this. The Halpatis' more meagre investment is predictably blamed, in the accompanying commentary, on their 'social backwardness and apathy' towards education (Patel 1964: 115–16).

The front rank which has nevertheless crystallized among the Halpatis—consisting of primary school teachers, petty shopkeepers in landless labourers' colonies, jobbers and artisans who have found employment outside agriculture and outside the village—lay claim to positions of leadership, but have neither understanding for, nor interest in the majority of their caste fellows who remain dependent on agricultural labour. They do however stay in the same living areas and thus continue to be in contact with, and inevitably involved in, what happens there.

Viewed from outside these factors, to which I also drew attention in earlier chapters, appear to create almost insuperable obstacles to a confrontation between the landless and the rural elite. Yet confrontation does repeatedly occur, in which landless as a class is involved and which goes beyond the mere quarrels between individual farmers and agricultural labourers. What stands out is not the sum total of cases of personal resistance, but rather the Halpatis' readiness to call strikes, perhaps against their better judgement, or to give vent to collective discontent in some other way. The fact that this resistance usually remains limited to a particular locality and is of a short duration does not make it any less imposing. While conflicts with migrant labourers almost by definition remain hidden from view, action by the local landless is not so easily forgotten. Certainly, such action is never mentioned anywhere, but it lives on in the collective consciousness. In most of the villages I visited the Halpatis could tell me in the minutest detail when, why, how and with what result they had turned against the farmers.

The militance of the landless is undoubtedly growing, but there is nevertheless the question of how far a recording of the number of 'incidents' provides a good yardstick for measuring such resistance. At the least such a tally prevents the illumination of the tensions of the past. Agricultural labourers as much as farmers are rather inclined to give an all-too-rosy representation of their mutual relations as they used to be, in reaction to the polarization which has come to exist. In illustration of the purportedly narrow and intimate bonds existing in the previous generation, the Patidars in A. talked very wistfully about the devotion with which the faithful farm servants stood guard over their possessions and even brought the harvest produce to them, while the latter had escaped to nearby villages, to escape the colonial British government during the Satyagraha in the early 1930s, so the story goes. This was told to me especially in order to emphasize the contrast with the insolent, rebellious stance of the present generation of landless labourers. This image of the harmonious relationship supposed to have existed earlier—an image to which even the Halpatis adhere, for that matter—becomes open to doubt on reading government reports written at the time of the *satyagraha*, which mention the bad labour climate and the outbreak of strikes around harvest time, in village A. and others (Broomfield and Maxwell 1929: 15).

Nevertheless, the extremes of the agrarian order—the principal landowning and landless classes—are at present confronting each other more fiercely than ever before. A preliminary climax was reached in the middle of the 1970s, when the farmers began to hire small private armies of field guards in order both to protect their possessions and to intimidate the agricultural labourers. In a number of villages around Bardoli in particular, the landowners made contracts with gangs originating from northern India, known locally as Sindhi or Khanamia. Sums of money were raised from obligatory contributions made by the farmers at rates which accorded with the extent of one's landholdings and which varied between Rs 28,000 and Rs 30,000 for one village, or several villages together. The leaders of these bands of ten to fifteen 'Sindhi' took it upon themselves to act as the strong-arm men. They were quartered in the village, obtaining their daily food from the farmers. There is an interesting correspondence between these *zim rakha*—literally, guardians of the village boundaries—and the Pathans transported from the north half a century earlier by the colonial government to force the farmers to end their *satyagraha*. In illustration of this, see the following passage from the biography of Sardar Patel:

> In desperation, the Government employed Pathans hoping that

> their presence would terrorise the villagers and make them pay. These men from the North-West Frontier, tall, hefty and fierce, make good soldiers. But they are also known for their furious temper and are difficult to restrain if let loose on normally peaceful people. Arrival of these desperadoes made even Vallabhbhai anxious lest they provoked violence—they were, indeed, *agents provocateurs* (Tahmankar 1970: 103).

This was precisely the reason why the farmers were now employing these mercenaries, and the Halpatis were no more prepared than the Patidars fifty years before to allow themselves to be disciplined by these private armies. More or less immediately after the coming of the *zim rakha* riots broke out in various villages, the immediate cause being, without exception, the violence used by these guards against members of the landless caste.[6] Among the details I noted was the thrashing of a small boy who was cutting grass along the roadside, and the mishandling of a labourer accused of theft from a sack of groundnuts while he was carrying it from the field to the farmer's house, and finally some cases of rape of Halpati women or girls in the open fields. In reaction to such incidents the Halpatis marched *en masse* to the village centre to demand the dismissal of the hirelings.

> On 25 August 1975 a band of ten men installed themselves in village P. Within a few days their misdeeds had so roused the fury of the landless that the latter took action. After first closing off the entry roads to the village, many hundreds prepared to storm the water tower into which members of the band had withdrawn. These shot into the crowd of Halpatis, killing one of them. The band escaped in the confusion which followed.

There were many repetitions of this kind of skirmish in which farmers also made use of firearms, as a result of which several Halpatis died, but the Patidars paid for the escalation of violence which they had initiated. Protest actions are certainly not a new phenomena in the rural areas of south Gujarat. However, what had to be tolerated in highly personalized relationships in the feudal past—as the arbitrary behaviour of a superior to whom the servant is bound completely and unconditionally—may well change its character

[6] See also annual report of the *Halpati Seva Sangh* 1975–6: 41–2.

during the transition to a capitalist mode of production and lead thereafter to collective resistance. It is hardly a coincidence that riots are much more frequent in the region dominated by the Patidars—*kulak* pesants who are upwardly mobile—than in the area inhabited by the Anavil Brahmins with their *junker* tradition as a landlord aristocracy. Collective resistance among the agricultural labourers is no longer limited to the calling of strikes. Nowadays they are not averse to using violence. In reaction to the shooting affrays they began in their turn to take the offensive, for instance by marching to the village centre and attacking the shut doors of farmers' houses with iron staves. Although armed, their opponents were no match for these numerically superior forces. Where the Halpatis have been successful in driving away the *zim rakha*, the Patidars have had to promise not to make new contracts with hired guards. Further, I observed that in these villages there were fewer migrant labourers, and more farmers who kept to the payment of the higher wage agreed upon as a part of the compromise reached at the end of the confrontation with the Halpatis.

Disturbed by an incident occurring a year later in Bardoli, the Governor of Gujarat—making use of his unconditional powers under the Emergency—ordered an investigation into the background of the rural violence. The findings of this investigation have never been made public, but the first official statement made it clear as to the kind of interpretation that would be given. Reassuringly, it was claimed that there was no question of a class conflict. It all boiled down to a collision between different factions of 'agriculturalists', a term under which dominant landowners and landless labourers were brought together into one uniform category. (EPW 1976: 1415) However, the incident had given the government the excuse for prohibiting the use of armed guards by private parties. The local authorities in Surat District took any notice of this regulation only when a conflict arose somewhere. Since the abolition of the Emergency the Khedut Samaj has continued to devote itself to the institution of a village corps guard, and in anticipation of this the *zim rakha* have returned to several villages.

In village M., for example, in which some ten Halpatis were wounded in a shooting affray at the beginning of February 1980, the Halpatis mounted a counter-attack in which they succeeded in killing one of the mercenaries and in driving out the rest. After this incident the agricultural labourers mounted a strike, which was only ended fourteen days later through the intervention of the Collector of Surat. The Patidars promised to refrain from further provocation and consented to a somewhat higher daily wage than is customary in the surrounding villages.

The picture emerging from the foregoing confirms my earlier conclusion that the class action towards which the farmers have shifted, forces the landless to meet their opponents on the same ground. It was not only the pessimists among the farmers who prophesied to me the outbreak of a *varga vigraha*—a class war. Naturally they deny that this is their own objective; only a few landowners are capable of comprehending the standpoint that the growing consciousness and solidarity of the local landless is a reaction to the farmers' own attitude and alliance. They are sooner inclined to ascribe the militance of the Halpatis to the mischief of the politicians—agitators who have disguised themselves as Gandhian workers.

The model for this is Jinabhai Darji himself, originating from Surat District, who began his political career as a typical *ashram* worker in the Gandhian tradition, but who has gradually turned out to be a more radical champion of the rural underclasses within the Congress Party of Gujarat. (See also Shah 1977: 26–7 and Sanghavi 1980: 2127) Loaded with the same qualities as Sardar Patel—coarseness, obstinacy, fierceness and directness, and all this in a rather peasant style—he has incurred the special hatred of the Patidars. On the grounds of his unrefined use of language they liken him to a 'Dubro' (i.e. Dubla, the earlier caste name which has now become derogatory), a creature who lies close to his heart, according to the sneers of his enemies. In this they forget that their own champion Dhayaram K. Patel, leader of the Khedut Samaj, was accustomed to expressing himself in a possibly even cruder manner. Various murder attempts have already been made against Jinabhai, which have only enhanced his fame among those to whom he directs his message. The main reproach levelled at him is that he preaches the ideology of class struggle, an imputation that stamps him as a great sinner in conservative Gujarat. Without wishing to damage the credibility of this politician, who conveys the impression of a genuine radicalism, I would still like to point out that Jinabhai Darji would put his leadership at risk if he chose to become a moderate in the Gandhian fashion, by calling on the landless and Adivasis to be patient. Rather, he has no choice but to fall in with the radicalism of his rank and file, a reversal that says a good deal about the nature and direction of the social dynamic. Complaining about this regrettable turn of events, one old Patidar landowner stated:

> It was Gandhi's instigations that has made the Dublas braver and defiant now, otherwise in Gaekwadi, if the Dublas tried to disobey even a little, 'we used to cut them into pieces and bury them in ground'. Dublas were under our foot, but this Gandhi pulled them in the Independence struggle and made them fight first against us, the benevolent care-takers of ignorant Dublas. Now, today they are stuck into worst economic conditions. Jhinia's (Jhinabhai Darji, a well founded spokesmen of Adivasis) instigations abolished Halipratha and today they are rotting on daily wage system. They are getting twenty times less than what they got as a Hali to a farmer like me. Today they are without employment. Now, they are waiting for our land to be distributed to them as Jhinia has promised them in return of their votes (Patel 1982: 10).

Although this is scarcely a popular topic of conversation, the farmers are definitely apprehensive of the increasing assertiveness of the landless proletariat. To be sure, they still choose to represent the Halpatis' behaviour in terms of a culture of poverty—of people who want nothing, know nothing, can do nothing, and who moreover allow each other nothing—but there is a new undertone of disturbance over the fierceness of the agricultural labourers and their readiness to fight back. The Patidars realize that they have lost their grip over their underlings, and thus feel unsure of themselves. This disturbance finds expression in complaints about the craftiness and secretiveness of the Halpatis, in the litany (sung in many different keys) that they are, individually and collectively, no longer to be trusted.

Approaching the end of this chapter, my conclusion is that the objective and subjective conditions for organized action among the rural proletariat of south Gujarat, are fulfilled. The reason why this point has not yet been reached has something to do with the failure, as yet, to bring about political mobilization, the causes for which I have sought mainly in circumstances external to the lives of the agricultural labourers. The role of the government in this will be considered in the final chapter. The Halpatis' apparent readiness to engage in action must be characterized as being sporadic, spontaneous and localized, and there is room for doubt about whether, in the short term, this situation will change. I am inclined to attach a good deal of significance to initiatives taken from outside; without this assistance the landless will be unable to attain very much, but it is precisely this organization of the counterforce that leaves much to be desired. Little can be expected from such captive organizations as the Halpati Seva Sangh. Beyond these there are several weak attempts discernible, not altogether directed towards accommodation and conformism.

The Khet Vikas Parishad springs immediately to mind, but it hardly appears to be an alternative. This union-like organization was set up at state level by several Congress Party leaders (among them Jinabhai Darji) in 1977, but so far has struck few roots in Surat District. Although there is no firmly outlined working plan, the principal starting points are moderation and arbitration. The tense situation in Bardoli gave the Khet Vikas Parishad cause for anxiety, as one of the progress reports makes clear: 'Those who believe in the struggle for social justice by violence will find fertile ground here. Khet Vikas Parishad, which believes in creating social justice by Gandhian means, will have a difficult time here to pass the test'.[7] In this organization the landless are not the members but the clients who can claim assistance. Communication is achieved through a network of contacts ending with the local leaders of the landless in the hamlets. Some workers are appointed whose principal task is to provide help in difficult situations. They told me that the police sometimes warns them of incidents arising elsewhere, not from a sense of fair play but from the desire to put pressure on the farmers in this way into paying more for the settlement of disputes in accordance with their wishes. During election campaigns the network is mobilized in favour of the Congress, from which I gather that the Khet Vikas Parishad have made it their task to secure the votes of the landless for this party.

The same can be said of the Halpati Union led by Jaswant

[7] Khet Vikas Parishad Administrative Report. Ahmedabad 1 February 1978: 42

Chauhan, who operates from the district capital, Surat. He is the classic example of a political entrepreneur with a wide experience gained from very different parties. At the moment he belongs to the Congress Party, for which he stood as a candidate in the 1977 election against Morarji Desai, whom he knew how to corner very well. Chauhan is seen as an opportunist who periodically mobilizes his following, mainly urban (he draws a large audience and, as a real populist, is a first-rate orator), as a measure of his local strength against the political world in general, and the government in Ahmedabad in particular. Finally there is the Lal Vavta, a left-wing union under the leadership of S., who has his base among the municipal workers in the city of Surat.

> In 1977 I met him up in his untidy office-cum-lodgings. When I went there again in 1981 Lenin, Stalin and Mao were still next to each other hanging on the wall in fraternal fashion, as if to suggest that the division within the communist movement elsewhere in India has little relevance for someone who derives his inspiration more from what he sees around every day than from the ideological differences penetrating down to him from above. In the long conversations I had with him, S. revealed himself to be a disillusioned man. The harsh industrial climate of Surat is truly a jungle particularly for the unskilled casual labourers, in which they hold their own only with great difficulty. According to S., trying to bring about changes in this is a waste of labour, for he sees a new type of capitalism emerging that, harshly and more ruthlessly than ever before, uses the enormous labour surplus that is available—a reserve army that is still growing every day as a result of the influx from the hinterland. He had difficulty in holding back his tears as he told me of the repeated arrests, even after the coming of independence (the last occasion being his imprisonment at the declaration of the Emergency) and of his failure to bring much improvement into the existence of those for whom he has fought all his life. He came originally from Maharashtra, and although he has lived for many decades in Surat, he still feels himself to be an outsider.

When the legal minimum wage of Rs 5.50 was carried through, S. rented a small office in the chief town of each *taluka*, including those of Palsana and Bardoli, where he held consultation sessions twice a week. It was his platform for organizing the agricultural labourers in the district and for registering their complaints against farmers who adamantly refused to pay the legal wage. After only a few weeks he had to abandon this attempt to extend his union work to the countryside. The explanations he gave for his failure were: lack of money for the office rent (involving only some Rs 30–40 per month); opposition from vested interests and the local government; and mistrust of his intentions among the Halpatis themselves. I think that, in addition, lack of an entrée and of access to a cadre which is already operative in the rural slums also played an important role. Since then S. has been more successful in his action among the semi-permanent workers of the sugar co-operatives, who come from outside Surat, mostly from Maharashtra. In recent years there have been several strikes, and the negotiations he conducted on behalf of the factory workers for wage rises have come to nothing.

There is a probable connection between the increasing unrest among the cane cutters, which led to an outburst in the Chalthan factory in the spring of 1981, and the union work in this industry with which S. has made a beginning in south Gujarat. As a result he can hardly be said to be popular with either the farmers or the government. Using an anti-agitation regulation from colonial times, the Collector of Surat banned S. from the *talukas* in which the sugar factories were established. This prohibition indicates an acceleration in the polarization of the agrarian classes that has come to exist in the countryside. I once again draw attention to the fact that migrant labour has become the soil in which such organized action is taking root. This seems to confirm a statement made by Weber that '. . . "the oft lamented" mobilization of the rural labourers at the same time sets in motion the beginnings of class struggle' (1924: 493).

The term 'proletarianization' is inadequate for understanding the changes taking place within the agrarian order in the south Gujarat plain. The indigenous proletariat in this area has always been landless as far back as memory goes, yet (as I established earlier) it would be incorrect to conclude from this that alienation from the possession of land no longer occurs on a large scale. For a large number of migrants their steady trek to the plains is the direct result of alienation from land in the home area. On the other hand, the dynamic of the already landless underclass in Surat District itself, is better defined by the concept of immiserization ('*Verelendung*'). Thus pauperization occurs, but not in a manner leading to the development of an amorphous mass of lethargic people. In the countryside, social fabric is maintained for the greater part along caste lines, which increasingly acquires a class emphasis. It is of crucial importance that economic interests and political loyalties do not run parallel anymore but are articulated along different lines which are moreover, mutually contradictory. There is no reason for me to close with the same discouraging conclusion reached by Djurfeldt and Lindberg at the end of their monograph about a village in Tamilnadu.

> It is obvious that, despite all poverty and suffering, Thaiyur is a coherent and even harmonious formation. There are few dissidents, and few conflicting world-views. This conclusion tallies well with our spontaneous and most frustrating experience in the field: There is so little which augurs revolt, or even a protest (Djurfeldt and Lindberg 1976: 316).

As I have made clear in this chapter and the previous one, consciousness of exploitation and oppression is growing, not the least as a result of the dominant landowners' horizontal linkage. What Pocock established for the Untouchables in central Gujarat also applies to the Halpatis, who have a heartfelt hatred of the Patidars (Pocock 1973: 23), which is increasingly made manifest in their behaviour and action. For an answer to the question of why organized opposition on the part of the landless still remains so hesitant and tardy, I direct attention in the final instance to the character of the state as it operates in rural south Gujarat.

13

STATE AND RURAL LABOUR: CONTAINMENT OR UPHEAVAL?

Privileged and criminal classes

According to a view which is still widely held, stagnation, forms the crux of the agrarian problem in India. The foregoing will have made it clear than such an interpretation does not conform to the situation I have encountered in the countryside of south Gujarat. My choice of the Bardoli region in which to undertake research was prompted by the supposition that the dynamic occurring here represents a much more general trend manifested in various parts of India, and for which one can predict an acceleration in the near future. What I have developed as a case study can in fact claim to be a representation (in the ideal-type sense) of a drastic shift which has had radical consequences for the nature of the rural order. I am alluding here to a combination of infrastructural and institutional changes leading both to a substantial rise in the agrarian production and to a diversification in the rural economy.

The advance of a capitalist mode of agricultural production has in essence been pushed through by a class of large and middle farmers, originating from intermediate castes who have gradually gained dominance in recent decades, with the support of the nationalist movement before the coming of independence, and of the coalitions of leading parties since then. The working classes have derived much less profit from the extension of employment which has accompanied this transformation. Playing on the growing differentiation among the agrarian population in the poor hinterland, landowners in the irrigated zone of south Gujarat have been making large-scale use of migrant labourers who stream into the central plain after the rains and who are beginning to stay on there in increasingly larger numbers.

Those who come in as proletarians occupy a large proportion of the new employment which has come into existence, ousting the indigenous landless from the work they have always performed. This expulsion forms part of a much wider process of marginalization following on the disintegration of vertical relations of dependence such as were once institutionalized in the *halipratha*. In contrast to the advances made at the top of the rural social stratification in terms of living standards and the augmentation of power, the dynamic at the bottom-most level appears to be expressed far more in terms of proletarianization and pauperization. Mutual antagonism, initiated aggressively from above and answered defensively from beneath, leads to a polarization which discharges itself into violent social conflicts.

After what has been established in the foregoing chapters, I can be brief about the manner in which the state intervenes in rural labour relations. The inequality of the parties involved in agrarian production is not the accidental result of autonomous processes of change beyond the control of public policies. This does not mean that there has been a conscious and systematic effort on the part of the government to construct a social regimentation such as that which I have described for the south Gujarat plain, although such an order has been inevitable given the manner in which the government has helped to promote the development of the forces of production. Agrarian policies have been tuned to the interests of the principal landowners, to which the interests of the landless proletariat (if the government bothers to look at these at all) have very obviously been subordinated.

Has the state, then, had no concern for the fate of the agrarian underclass, when the substantial farmers made it plain that they no longer regarded themselves as being bound by the traditional right to help and protect their subordinates in exchange for all kinds of services, whether economic or otherwise?

Labour utility has been reinterpreted in such a way that a surplus has come into being which cannot be attributed to demographic growth or agrarian regression alone. The disappearance of the mututal involvement which had typified a 'moral economy' certainly did not lead immediately to public provisions intended to compensate the landless for the loss of their guaranteed survival. According to Beteille the explanation for this was the economic and organizational incapacity of the government to provide the rural poor with protection for their livelihoods when the legitimacy of the old order disappeared and the landowners abandoned their clients.

> If landowners are today disinclined to meet their customary obligation towards the tenants and labourers, what about the legal and administrative machinery? We have first of all to realize that nowhere can such machinery take over the entire range of obligations customarily fulfilled within the context of a more or less organic community. Certainly a country like India and Pakistan has neither the material resources nor the organization to enable individuals to meet their lifecycle crises through an impersonal administrative machinery.[1]

A typical response by public agencies to indications that there is reason to suspect a real deterioration in the conditions of the rural poor, has been to react very slowly indeed. A standard attitude has been not to interfere in the relationship between the parties immediately concerned, with at most an appeal to the landowners to show generosity and to the landless to continue to exercise restraint. The reluctance of the authorities to become involved directly in labour relations is obvious, for instance, in the repeated vain attempts to prohibit *halipratha* as a system of bonded labour in south Gujarat. It was only a few years ago—in fact, only when this institution had already died out—that legal regulations came into force. The government did not intervene when, as a consequence of the gradual transition from payment in kind to payment in cash, wages lagged behind the rise in the cost of living. Only when the situation threatened to become untenable did the state government proclaim a minimum wage for agricultural labour. Even then this was done with obvious reluctance and a determination not to put this law into effect, but to impress it on the concerned parties as a kind of norm for indicating both the area in which one party fell unreasonably short, and rights to which the other party could reasonably lay claim—and all this with the tacit acceptance that ultimate compromise is a matter of the free play of social forces.

[1] (Beteille 1974: 114). Although Beteille emphasizes that one should not overestimate the state's capacity, in his view, there has been a particularly marked lack of will among those in power to intervene in favour of the landless.

The weak bargaining position from which the landless operate means that they derive little or no profit from the regular facilities offered to the population at large out of the government apparatus. Access to education and health care, for example, seem destined by tacit consent to be highly differentiated. The quality and the quantity of these and other services lying within the public sphere and financed from public resources, are such that the lowest social classes are practically excluded from it. Diagnosis of this inequality of access to services has led—particularly in recent decades—to the floating of a number of so-called target group programmes, in order to diminish the backwardness of those living in poverty, by instituting special provisions for them and also commissioning the execution of such provisions by separate agencies.

This policy has not produced the desired results, due to lack of adequate effort. Moreover attention has been mainly devoted to that part of the working population which could be regarded as somehow economically viable. Small farmers for instance are expected to be able to produce a marketable surplus on the basis of concentrated effort such as cheap credit, intensive training. For the landless there remains little or nothing left over; as before, their material progress remains dependent upon economic growth ultimately producing more employment and income for everyone. The little that has been done specifically for the landless—such as providing subsidies for the construction of huts for the Halpatis on their own land outside the village—has not so much diminished their backwardness as increased their isolation.

Neither has the State shown much concern for increasing the ability of the landless to defend themselves by encouraging initiatives towards organization, or at least by creating a favourable climate for this, in the plausible assumption that horizontal alliance is a necessary condition for collective improvement of their lot. Official support for attempts to form a counterweight against the strong in society goes no further than the sanctioning of organizations which have the interests of the landless at heart in a manner which assumes, first and foremost, their adjustment to, and further dependence upon, the existing social order. The authorities therefore set a premium on class collaboration, conciliation and compromise, i.e. on strategies contributing to what is regarded as the restoration of harmonious relationships while rejecting radical demands that speak of impatience and that lead to direct, militant action. Perhaps the kindest judgement one can pass on this official aloofness is that it is half-hearted. The gross inequality and the tensions it summons up can only be redressed by resolute and effective intervention on behalf of the lower classes in society. The reluctance to embrace such a course appears to confirm the thesis of the weak state, as expounded by Myrdal[2]. However, is this really the manner in which government behaves at the local level towards the parties immediately concerned, i.e. the dominant landowners and the landless poor?

The Patidars very obviously cash in on the many advantages of the modernization and diversification of the agrarian economy, financed by the state. The land reform carried through after independence has strengthened their grip on the means of production, which have gained in value thanks to governmental investment in infrastructural works. The raised yields attained with the help of subsidized inputs indicate a substantial surplus formation from which few or no taxes are extracted. In the full realization of their importance as the principal agrarian producers the Patidars can, with no trouble at all, lay the first (if not the sole) claim to all kinds of provisions for the welfare and well-being distributed in the countryside by the government. 'Outsiders' occupy second place when it comes to benefitting from these public facilities, and then often only by paying an extra price for them.

Does it appear from this that the state is an instrument for the use of the principal landowning class? This is certainly not the attitude adopted by the farmers, who for various reasons do not regard themselves as owners or employers of the official agencies and their power holders. In the first place the Patidars came to dominance to a large extent by their own efforts and in opposition to the colonial government. Mistrust of the government has endured since those times, under the influence of what Lipton has called an urban bias in government policy (1977). With this he has put into words the ideas that continue to be held, stubbornly, by the dominant castes in India's country-

2 (Myrdal 1968: part II, para. 13 & 14). For a more detailed description of the phenomenon of the soft state, see Myrdal 1969: 5–24).

side. A recent expression of this in south Gujarat was the fierce opposition towards the grain levies which the authorities tried to impose, in an attempt to ensure the provision of foodstuffs at a reasonable price for the urban population. Grimly, the large farmers gave their opinion on the 'high-ups' in Ahmedabad and Delhi—an unwholesome coalition of bureaucrats and politicians whom they perceived as being their opponents rather than their allies. What had been permitted them as favours they now demand as rights. The state will remain soft in their eyes as long as they do not occupy the '*khursi*' themselves, their rural hegemony having become the basis for claims to the exercise of central power. Territorial hegemony has become so strongly developed among the dominant caste that any effort to challenge their power, however weak and inadequate the attempt, immediately arouses the greatest possible ire. The notion of a public interest guarded by the state is lacking. From the Patidars' perspective any official political intervention directed towards the correction of the lopsided balance—for instance, lowering the land ceiling in favour of the small-farmer castes or the promulgation of a minimum wage for agricultural labour—is intolerable because it attacks their freedom of action and casts doubt on their supremacy. They censure in great detail, as 'pro-labour', the most elementary laws the government tries to promulgate, even those meant only to preserve the existing relationships. At the base of this attitude lies a social-Darwinist ethos in which the principal landowners appear as the mainstay of agricultural production, and in a more general sense, as the social pivot upon which the rural order and, in fact, the society at large revolves. The reverse image applies to the landless underclass: an inferior, ignorant and largely useless mass which can have no claim to equal rights—general suffrage has given its members much too great an influence, according to a widely spread elite notion—and which must be kept under control by sharp discipline. In this scenario the strong state is not an arbiter between parties, but a state of the strong.

In their turn the agricultural labourers also appear inclined to act on the assumption that the state is soft, in so far as it has not succeeded in giving effect to the legislation intended to put an end to their exploitation and oppression. In contrast to the very complaisant view that the landless are not up to date with all kinds of legal regulations and provisions which concern them—a stereotype suggesting naiveté and ignorance—local leaders in the Halpati colonies showed themselves to be consistently well informed about these. The best-known provisions were the injunctions and prohibitions in the sphere of labour (establishment of a minimum wage, sanctions against indenture) but the leaders were also aware of other facilities to which they ought to be able to claim a right within the context of the target-group programmes.

How do they themselves explain why so little good comes of all these benefits and good intentions? There is a general complaint that the landowning class arranges the work in such a way as to frustrate the realization of the objective of these special regulations and provisions. That they succeed so well in doing so is partly due to the indisputable fact that the members of the middle and higher castes fill the executive positions in the regional governmental apparatus, and, for that matter, in the whole of social life. Even if there is no question of favouring the milieu from which this cadre originates, there is still often a lack of impetus to comply with the wishes of a clientele from the lowest social classes. The belief is not wholly lacking among the landless that this mingling of interests in the higher spheres is decreasing. The expression '*sarkari ma bap chhe*' (the government is our mother and father) speaks not only of resignation but also of an appeal to feelings of fair play which are presumed to exist outside and above the sphere in which they encounter their immediate superiors and opponents.

Against this assumption that the more distant the authorities the better disposed they are towards the landless, stands a completely different maxim, based on long experience, that teaches one to put no trust in what one is led to expect from authorities. The landless are sceptical about the words and the deeds of the politicians and their agents. They are conscious of their numerical superiority, but realize that on that basis alone they will get no hearing from the power holders. Without daring to question the legitimacy of the state, they have no reason for accepting it as benign. As we have said, they remain shut out from all sorts of facilities being distributed in the welfare field. In describing the relations between the government and the landless, terms such as 'neglect' or 'discrimination' fall short of the reality. The landless frequently have to deal with functionaries to whom the maintenance of order and peace have been entrusted. There are few officials who have any reason to go into the agricultural labourers' colonies, apart from the police and (for instance) the functionaries who go there in order to track down candidates for family planning.

Supervision and discipline sums up the character of the state's intervention in this milieu, and as a rule it is carried out in an intimidating way. The manner of dealing with people demonstrates the prevailing attitude towards this public: every conversation all too soon turns into an interrogation in which condescending affability alternates with snapped orders. Small wonder that the landless prefer if possible to withdraw from these sanctioning institutions by limiting contact with them to the absolute minimum, and that when encounters are unavoidable they affect an air of ignorance, vagueness, submissiveness and helplessness. The behaviour of the police in particular gives the lie to the supposition that the poor have nothing that can be stolen from them. In the first place, affirmation of petty authority is a very sensitive matter for those invested with it, and in interchanges with those who count for the least in social terms, even the lower functionaries obtain maximum satisfaction from exercising that authority. While members of this executive arm of the government must behave with restraint towards the landowning class, or must even be eager to oblige, the lowliest of power holders make themselves felt as almost absolute rulers in the hutment colonies of the landless. There they encounter a clientèle who are scarcely in a position to resist or even contradict them. The lower authorities find easy victims in the landless for the successful execution of all kinds of unpopular government programmes, such as sterilization during the Emergency.

While Patidars are seldom or never pursued for transgressing the laws on the prohibition of alcohol, this is an offence for which the Halpatis are fined out of all proportion. In their case it is not even necessary to commit an offence to be convicted of it. It seems to be no exaggeration to suggest that those who live in poverty are suspected of breaking the law purely because of their degraded condition. Once classified as criminal castes under colonial rule, the rural poor nowadays seem to be stigmatized as criminal classes. However, it is not the poor man who gathers wood who is a criminal but the landowner who does not want to recognize this customary law any longer; thus commented Marx on the newly introduced law on the theft of wood in the middle of the nineteenth century (Marx-Engels Werke Band, 1956). In the area around Bardoli, gathering wood, collecting herbs or cutting grass for the calf is nowadays quite sufficient to incur the charge of theft, even when these activities take place on waste lands or along the public road. A bounty from the farmers provides the incentive for the police to adopt this form of persecution, which in the last resort is waived if the landless are likewise prepared to pay the right amount in cash. Failure to bring a case against the landowners, and even the application of physical coercion at the instigation of local notables is not exceptional, reinforcing the idea that the government apparatus is an instrument in the hands of the propertied class, in the eyes of those undergoing such treatment. Under such conditions any insistence on the compliance with legal provisions can be seen as an act of resistance. A farmer who does not pay the minimum wage is only prosecuted if the labourer lodges a complaint against him. But when, after the elections in the spring of 1977 that brought the Janata Party to power, I suggested to several militant Halpatis that they might take this course of action, none of them was prepared to do so. In their judgement the only possible result would be to arouse the antagonism of the authorities in Bardoli towards the Halpatis rather than towards the farmers, and who in his right mind would risk that? A thorough thrashing was the least they could expect.

Nevertheless, it would be unfair to judge state intervention in rural labour relations by the behaviour of individual officials who are given a great deal of discretion in the handling of rules and procedures at the lower end of the society. Much more important is the institutional working of the administrative machinery. The inescapable conclusion is that the accelerated transition to a capitalist mode of production in agriculture has led to only a slight adjustment of the growing socio-economic imbalance resulting from that transition. The state apparatus which is so reticent and tolerant when implementing legislation which runs counter to the interest of the rural strong, acts with firmness and brutality when the rural poor are making efforts to force a better treatment. The restoration of 'order and peace' when this is given highest priority actually means continuation of injustice and exploitation. It would seem that the power holders have accepted the trend towards polarization as being inevitable, and are more concerned with controlling the tensions emerging from this than with solving the contradictions themselves. To facilitate and to encourage on the one hand and to appropriate and to impose on the other hand, are two functions of the governmental apparatus with differential social results. The first works primarily to the advantage of those who are already better off; the last hits the most vulnerable in a disproportionately heavy way. Too little, too late—and even that undertaken with reluctance—is the only way to describe official attempts to effect a different distribution of costs and benefits in the process of capitalist expansion.

There is a remarkable lack of information in the offices of the authorities about the presence of seasonal labourers and other migrants. No one registers the numbers of the proletariat streaming in, and they are strangers who remain invisible, as it were, in the south Gujarat plain. There is no official assigned to deal with them, let alone any, who on his own initiative, takes some interest in their existence. At higher levels in the bureaucracy there is some understanding of the problem provoking such a wholesale influx of labour, but still no acknowledgement of all the dimensions of the problem. Policy makers I met in Ahmedabad however, declared themselves to be powerless to intervene because—they said—freedom of movement is guaranteed in the constitution. Naturally this basic tenet need not conflict with laws protecting outside and local labour alike, but readiness to apply such protection appears nevertheless to be lacking, as is shown by the course of events during the sugarcane harvest in Bardoli and environs. I demonstrated earlier that it would be very simple to apply the minimum wage-law to this operation and to enforce strict observance of it. But instead of doing so the government, by tolerating the practices of the co-operative sugar factories in employing jobbers to recruit and supervise the necessary work force (by tens of thousands during each harvest campaign) in the hinterland, and thereby shifting all the burden of risk onto this army of cane cutters, is tacitly assenting to the exploitation of the labourers. The authorities only step in when the tensions arising from this exploitation reach the point of explosion, and even then official interest hardly goes further than the immediate restoration of public order and the ending of spontaneous strikes, deemed to be unlawful and not in the 'national interest'. All too readily union action is labelled subversive and it then encounters great difficulties.

I am aware of the fact that fine distinctions in judging official attitudes and actions are necessary—nuances which allow for differences in circumstance according to time, place, and level of operation. However, the situation in south Gujarat does not exist independently of the political changes occurring at the national level. Under a Congress government the climate is relatively favourable for rural labour, but this is primarily a reflection of local power relations—brought about by the growing antagonism between the farmers and the agricultural labourers—and has very little to do with any sincere determination to improve the lot of the landless masses. Consequently such improvement has not been forthcoming. It gives cause for thought that the excessive powers enjoyed by the government at the time of the Emergency were not used to implement necessary changes in favour of the working class, but were instead directed against those who were pressing for these changes. I share Frankel's interpretation.

> On the whole the emergency was perhaps less remarkable for official 'excess' against individuals, which followed the familiar dynamic of corruption and abuse of authority associated with unrestricted power, than for the limitations on government's ability to use such absolute powers in bringing about basic social changes . . . At most, it could suppress the disruptive consequences in popular discontent and disorder of the Congress party's inability to devise a peaceful substitute for a frontal assault on the strategic position of the dominant minority of propertied castes and classes (Frankel 1978: 566)

How does this statement tally with the prohibition on bonded labour and the annulment of debt relations taken up in the Twenty Point Programme? Ignoring the rhetoric behind these policy slogans—which all the parties involved see through, as a result of what is for the most part a lack of concrete action—these laws highlighted the logical end result of the transition from a traditional agrarian economy to a free labour market in the countryside. In other words it was not the protection of labour that was the paramount consideration but the acceleration of a capitalist mode of production in agriculture.

Conditions in the south Gujarat plain demonstrate that the breaking down of vertical dependence mechanisms does not in itself lead to a better existence for those being freed from them. The structural change necessary for this involves a strengthening of horizontal solidarity among the landless, as well as the economic and political organizations based on this. The larger landowners try in a number of ways, to block such solidarity and organization. The co-operation, both active and passive, they receive from the official side (whether individuals or institutions) creates doubt about the thesis of the relative autonomy of the state. Approaching the end of my argument, I can draw no other conclusion than that the landless in the south Gujarat plain encounter more opposition than support from the bureaucracy in their struggle for emancipation. There is still hardly any room for them within the state system.

Prospects

It is easier to analyse the situation as it exists and the factors creating it, than to trace the line from the present to the near future; there is no scenario for things to come. The changes now taking place are the result of a configuration of forces which do not all point in the same direction, and which to a great extent have their own uncontrolled momentum. Any conjecture—however speculative—about the further course of events in the Bardoli region, must take as its point of departure the maturing of an extremely virulent rural capitalism, driven forward by the dominant class of agrarian entrepreneurs. The economic dynamic they create is purely locally based, though facilitated by outside forces. In contrast to the image presented in some of the literature, in which emphasis falls on dependent development if not on stagnation—the countryside as the periphery of a national or international market system—I am inclined to seek the explanation for the process of transformation primarily from within, that is to say in the particular milieu of Bardoli and neighbourhood which has become a growth pool.

This dynamic does not remain limited to agriculture but has also opened the way to economic interests outside it and, as I have been able to confirm, part of the surplus thus created has an urban destination. Patidars from the district are increasingly moving, as owners or partners, into commercial enterprises and industries in Surat City. The transfer of capital generated by agrarian production, and the gradual rise of the Patidars as a new industrial elite, presents a totally different image of the rural connection than that drawn by Lipton. Further study is necessary for establishing more precisely the nature and direction of this dynamic. In my opinion the development in the south Gujarat plain is not unique, but strikes one forcibly as a trend which is also discernible elsewhere in India. Only comparative regional research can establish the configuration of this more general pattern, consisting of several variants.

The transition to a capitalist mode of production began early, but has been pushed through more rapidly, in the last two decades. The effect of this on rural labour relations has been the central theme of my research in the area around Bardoli. To begin with, this transformation has led to a considerable expansion of employment, within agriculture as much as outside it. However, for the work force already present the profit derived from this has to a large extent been nullified by demographic growth and especially by the greatly intensified mobility of labour occurring at the same time. The large-scale circulation of labour is indicative of the harsh climate that has emerged in Surat District. Differentiation among the agrarian population in the tribai hinterland leads to the expulsion (temporary or lasting) of marginal and landless peasants, whose arrival as circulators and migrants in the central plain is harmful to the very large agricultural-labourer class already existing there. These outsiders monopolize a large proportion of the new employment that has come into being, and moreover oust the indigenous population from the jobs the latter have always occupied.

The end of this dual process of proletarianization and pauperization is not yet in sight. New reservoirs of labour in the hinterland are being opened up even now. As I predicted in an earlier publication (Breman 1978–9), the co-operative sugar factories have begun in the last few years to obtain part of their enormous army of cane cutters from the isolated Dangs District. This strategy of recruitment over a spread-out region is partly dictated by the fear of this seasonal proletariat forming a united front during the harvest campaign. The labour regime is such that disturbances cannot be avoided; the violent outburst at the close of the 1980–1 season in the Chalthan factory was a writing on the wall for all the agro-industries in the area. The managements bargain on being able to obviate this risk by mechanizing the various tasks as rapidly as possible, as I confirmed on my last visit in the summer of 1982. Credit lent by the co-operatives on a huge scale enables the farmers to procure tractors with which the cane is carried from the fields to the sugar factory. The pressure to take to labour-saving harvesting methods and equipment is likewise increasing: the agro-industries set the example for mechanizing production and the dominant landowners follow. The reduction of dependence on labour plays a considerable role in their farm management, and in the calculation of costs.

Application of modern technology is no longer possible without having at one's disposal a core of permanent and more skilled labourers. Gradually an upper stratum has crystallized from among the agricultural labourers, who receive better payment and treatment and obtain work more regularly. In contrast to their relative security there is the continuing pauperization of a much greater percentage of the landless households. Can one expect any change in this situation, in the short run? By no means. Neither am I optimistic about the chances and success of collective resistance. To begin with, this is frustrated by internal segmentation. The livelihoods of the seasonal labourers, particularly those migrating in small groups and working for individual farmers, are too vulnerable to embark upon resistance against their exploitation. The same applies to the migrants who have come to the plain with the intention of settling there more permanently. Their status as strangers—barely tolerated—compels them to keep a low profile. The local landless being squeezed out of the labour process certainly do not suffer their presence with resignation.

It would be an extremely one-sided representation of the atmosphere encountered by the researcher in the Halpatis' colonies, to describe it as a 'culture of poverty'. A militant mood rules, expressing itself in a variety of actions of an individual or collective nature, but even the latter are localized and of limited duration. Support from without is a necessary condition for giving an organizational form to a protest, but there are no signs that such support will be speedily forthcoming.

Concentration on the powerlessness of the rural poor easily leads to a distortion of perspective—to the supposition that the existing situation in itself excludes all hope of improvement. In this, emphasis falls too unilaterally on the immobilizing effect of the process of polarization, still continuing. Rural society is not caught up in an involutionary process of change which is basically static. The situation is extremely fluid with a high degree of upward and downward mobility at all social levels, though with a different direction at the top and at the bottom. The presence of the landless in such great numbers is in itself sufficient to arouse the aggressiveness of the propertied classes. The poverty-struck life of the rural underclasses feeds on the idea that they are essentially redundant—a kind of debris which weighs heavily in an otherwise 'healthy' social order. The exasperation provoked by their proximity is still further exacerbated whenever they begin to behave in a manner which, in the eyes of their superiors, smacks of presumption, such as when they begin to show signs of resisting the exploitation and oppression they undergo.

The discontent over the inferior social place assigned to them is making way, however, for a much more intransigent attitude, as it becomes apparent when even minimal claims to positions regarded as being the private domain of the higher social classes, and as determining the life-style of the latter, are not heeded to. Any claim to the right to exist by those people who have always remained in the shadow, however careful and modest, is quite accurately perceived as an attack on the existing social order. Members of the tribal castes in south Gujarat who try to hack out an upwards path for themselves through education, all too soon meet with opposition from the *ujliparaj*. The latter's already less-than-positive attitude towards social inferiors who do not know their place, shifts to straightforward aggression as it becomes apparent when they encounter competition from this quarter for the facilities and privileges which are distributed through the government machinery. The Scheduled Castes who were the first to apply for these were also the principal target for the violence of the *ujliparaj* that erupted at the beginning of 1981, especially in central and north Gujarat (Bose 1981: 715). The worst reign of terror appears to have arisen at places in the countryside where class oppositions between agricultural labourers and landowners were most pronounced, as one observer reported: 'The most aggressive and cruel in their attacks on the SC were Patidar landholders in Kheda, Ahmedabad and Mehsana. These are also the districts of concentration of an awakened SC population' (Desai 1981: 822).

It is of great significance that the economic and political struggle lying at the base of this confrontation runs along caste lines. Not only do the higher castes react to the threat they perceive, by falling back on this primordial loyalty but those in the vanguard of the lower castes on an upward course strengthen themselves likewise by emphasizing unity on a caste basis. Instead of a continuing differentiation, with a greater chance of division within the lowest echelons of the labour regime, it looks as though a process of compression is taking place as a result of pressure from above. In this way an alliance could be forced in the countryside between low upwardly mobile castes blocked in their aspirations, and backward tribal castes, such as the Halpatis.

Suffrage has had a mobilizing effect on the suppressed but voluminous underclass. The populist slogans which have been raised and repeated for years—such as the promise to ban poverty—have lost their magic but found a ready audience. These external accelerators have contributed to the increasing social consciousness. The numerical ratio is clearly to the disadvantage of the castes/classes which are defending their social pre-eminence. On the other hand they have firm control of power, and the state of the strong shows itself to be a state of violence against the weak, as I have already established. Incidents in which members of the landless population are the victims are daily events in many parts of India. A constant constituent of the news is that the open intimidation and terror perpetrated by the upper layer is seldom opposed with any force by the local authorities, but is rather often sanctioned and sometimes even encouraged by them.[3] Except in a few states

[3] For this, see the continuous stream of news items in *Economic and Political Weekly* for example. See also the general surveys such as Sharma 1978, in which a number of recent incidents have been collected.

with a somewhat more progressive political climate—a bloc to which Gujarat certainly does not belong—it would seem that this combination of formal and informal oppression is certainly not a thing of the past. On the contrary there is reason for suggesting that the contest has only just begun. This prediction is partly inspired by the confirmation that among those suffering this violence, resistance is slowly beginning to get under way—a reaction which in its turn leads to an even worse form of brutalization.

An end to the escalation of violence is not yet in sight and there seems to me to be little chance of resistance from below being brought under permanent control. Containment of tensions resides in the readiness to make concessions. Willingness to offer a better future to those forced to live in abject poverty undoubtedly has to be extorted through struggle. As the result of the break-down of a set of structural and cultural conditions which act as a brake on mobilization, I am quite critical of the common view that agricultural labourers will not be the first to initiate action. It remains to be seen whether they will form the weakest link in a chain of action for which a vanguard from other segments of the underclasses take the initiative. It is far from accidental that in the recent agitations in the Bardoli area, the Halpatis showed themselves to be more militant than the members of other tribal castes. It is precisely the identity of landlessness—of being neither tied to a small piece of land nor having any traditions of this—which serves to radicalize and prevent that inclination towards premature accommodation to which small landowners more easily tend to succumb.

Thus, when I state that there is little reason to anticipate the near future with optimism, I do so in the consciousness that, for the pauperized sections among the landless, the situation can hardly become any worse than it already is.

GLOSSARY

Adivasi—Collective name for tribal groups and castes
Anamat—Reservation
Antyodhaya—Lit. unto the last, upliftment of the poor
Ashram—Institution of social work on Gandhian lines
Athavisi—Moghul controlled area in south Gujarat consisting of 28 revenue circles
Athio—Local measure of flour, ca. ¾ kg.

Bahargam—To go outside, to migrate (abroad)
Bajri—Species of coarse grain
Bandh—Strike
Bani—Provision of loan leading to temporary transfer of land
Bhagat—Tribal priest and medicineman
Bhajan—Devotional song
Bhajan Mandali—Group coming together to sing devotional songs
Bhakti—Devotion, worship
Bhata—Brick-kiln
Bhencod—Sister fucker
Bhumiputra—Son of the soil
Bidi—Country cigarette
Bigha — Land measurement nearly ⅔ of an acre

Chaitra—April
Chakar—Farm-servant at the same time house-servant
Chhas—Skimmed milk, residue of the preparation of ghee (clarified butter)
Chhuta (majur)—Casual day-labourer
Chor—Thief

Dalal—Commission agent, trader
Dam—Value, money
Devi—Goddess (also called Mata) which inspired a tribal movement in the early twenties in south Gujarat
Dhaniyamo—Traditional name for master of farm servant
Dharma—Religion, duty
Dharmasala—Guest-house
Dhoti—Male cotton dress which covers the lower part of the body
Dhow—Sea-going boat

Ekada—Marriage circle; group of like-minded people

Falia—Hamlet, village street

Garasia—Predatory chieftains who extracted a tribute from the peasantry in early and pre-colonial period
Ghanti—Work-bench for diamond polishing
Ghar Jamai—Son-in-law living in the house of his father-in-law
Gherao—Action restricting personal freedom of movement

Gorat—Rich loamy soil
Govalio—Cowherd
Gram Sevak—Village level worker

Hali—Bonded farm servant
Halipratha—System of debt bondage previously prevalent among agricultural labourers of south Gujarat
Haphta—Instalment, now also used in the meaning of a regular bribe
Hijrat—Migration
Hitchko—Swing
Holi—Spring festival

Jarayat—High-level dry land
Jovar (Juvar)—Species of millet

Kachhada—Sari as worn by working-class women, i.e. tied between the legs.
Kaim majur—Permanent labourers coming daily or regularly
Kaka—Father's brother, Uncle in general
Kali Jamin—Black soil
Kaliparaj—Lit. black people, derogatary term to describe adivasis in south Gujarat
Kam—Work
Kartak—October-November
Kathiawadi—People from Kathiawad, the erst-while name of Saurashtra
Khadi—Hand-woven cloth
Khandadhio—Tribal equivalent of *ghar Jamai*
Khandeshi—People from Khandesh, a region in west Maharashtra
Kharif—the season of autumn
Khathelo—Wooden bed-frame with a rope or web base
Khavati—Lit. to eat, advance payment in kind or cash on work to be performed
Khedut—Peasant
Khursi—Lit. Chair, Political seat
Kisan Sabha—Peasant Union
Kodra—Species of coarse grain

Lal Jovar—Red millet of inferior quality
Lal Vavta—Red flag

Magshar—December-January
Mama—Mother's brother
Mamlatdar—Revenue official in charge of taluka administration
Mata—See Devi
Maund—Measure of weight equal to 20 kgs.
Morcha—Procession
Mukadam—Labour intermediary, jobber, foreman
Muth—Monastery

Nagli—Species of coarse grain
Nasto—Light breakfast
Nira—Non-fermented juice of (usually date) palm tree

Pan-supari—betel-leaf and arecanut
Panch—Consultative body, council
Panchayat—Local consultative body
Patel—Village police-man
Patala—Team of brick-kiln workers
Patalavala—Team-leader of brick-kiln workers

Phagan—March-April
Posh—February-March
Potalum—Piece of cloth in which various items are wrapped up
Pratinidhi sabha—Representative body, committee

Rab—Gruel
Rabi—The season of spring
Rojio—Permanent labourers coming daily or regularly
Rotlo—Flat, unleavened bread
Ryatvari—System of land settlement with each individual cultivator

Sadhu—Ascetic
Samjuti—Compromise
Sardar Senas—Vigilance corps named after Sardar (Patel)
Sari—Common female dress
Sarjela—Tribals who wanted to maintain the existing tribal culture
Sarkari mabap chhe—Government (officials) are our mother and father
Sati-Pati—Acceptance of 'pure' husband-wife relationships; militant anti-*ujliparaj* tribal movement in the eastern part of Surat District during the fifties
Satyagraha—Gandhian form of passive resistance
Savkar—Moneylender
Seer—Unit of weight, about 2 pounds
Sirpanch—Village headman
Sudharavun—Self-improvement
Swaraj—Freedom

Talati—Village accountant
Taluka—Sub-district

Udhad—Work allotted on contract
Ujliparaj—All Hindu castes without a recent tribal past
Updeshak—Social worker

Vaisakh—May
Varga Vigraha—Class war
Varjela—Reformist tribals
Varna—The four main caste segments into which traditional Hindu society was divided
Vasiduvali—Farm-maid who cleans the stable
Vavla—Plot of land in the past given to farm servant for his own cultivation
Vibagh—Area around Bardoli as perceived by the members of the dominant caste

Zim rakha—Watchman engaged for protection of crops paid collectively by the farmers

Yuvak Mandal—Youth club

ABBREVIATIONS

(Used in the Bibliography)

C.I.S.	Contributions to Indian Sociology
E.E.H.	Explorations in Economic History
E.P.W.	Economic and Political Weekly
E.S.	Economy and Society
I.E.S.H.R.	The Indian Economic and Social History Review
I.J.A.E.	Indian Journal of Agricultural Economics
J.B.B.A.S.	Journal of the Bombay Branch of the Asiatic Society
J.G.R.S.	Journal of the Gujarat Research Society
J.P.S.	The Journal of Peasant Studies
J.U.B.	Journal of the University of Bombay
M.A.S.	Modern Asian Studies
Q.J.E.	The Quarterly Journal of Economics
S.B.	Sociological Bulletin
T.M.	Tiers Monde
R.S.S.	Revision Survey Settlement
S.R.	Survey Report
N.S.	New Series

BIBLIOGRAPHY

BOOKS AND ARTICLES

ABRAHAM, A.
1979 'Sugar workers draw a blank', *E.P.W.* XIV, 2035–7.

AMIN, S. (ed.)
1974 *Modern migrations in western Africa*, London. Introduction: 65–124.

Anon.,
1974 'Beyond the ken of organised politics', *E.P.W.* IX, 131.

Anon.,
1972 *Gujaratne rajkiya ane sanskrutika itihas*, Ahmedabad.

Anon.,
1977 *History of rural development in modern India*, II, New Delhi.

Anon.,
1948 'Notes and comments', *I.J.A.E.* III, September.

Anon.,
1979 'Plight of migrant labour', *E.P.W.* XIV, 755.

BAKS, C.
1969 *Afschaffing van pacht; een onderzoek naar de sociale gevolgen van de afschaffing van pacht in twee dorpen van Zuid-Gujarat, India*, Diss. Universiteit van Amsterdam.

BANDYOPADHYAYA, N.
1977 'Causes of sharp increase in agricultural labourers, 1961–71: a case study of social-existence forms of labour in North Bengal', *E.P.W.* XII, A 111–26.

BARDHAN, K.
1977 Rural employment, wages and labour markets in India: a survey of research', *E.P.W.* XII, A34–64 (Review of Agriculture); 1062–1074; 1101–18.

BARDHAN, P.K.
1982 'Agrarian class formation in India', *J.P.S.* X, 73–94.

BATES, C.N.
1981 'The nature of social change in rural Gujarat: the Kheda district 1818–1918', *M.A.S.* XV, 771–821.

BAVISKAR, B.S.
1980 *The Politics of development: sugar co-operatives in Maharashtra*, Delhi.

BETEILLE, A.
1974 *Studies in agrarian social structure*, Delhi.

BHATT, A.
1970 'Caste and political mobilization in a Gujarat district', in: Kothari: 299–339.

BORRADAILLE, H.
1874 Discussion of Borradaille 1829 inquiry into Gujarat caste rules', *J.B.B.A.S.* X, 93–119.

BOSE, P.K.
1981 'Stratification among tribals in Gujarat', *E.P.W.* XVI, 191–6.
'Social mobility and caste violence: a study of the Gujarat riots', *E.P.W.* XVI, 713–16.

BREMAN, J.
1974 'Mobilisation of landless labourers; Halpatis of south Gujarat', *E.P.W.* IX, 489–96.
1974 *Patronage and exploitation; changing agrarian relations in south Gujarat, India.*, Berkeley/Delhi (1979).
1978 'Seasonal migration and co-operative capitalism; the crushing of cane and of labour by the sugar factories of Bardoli, south Gujarat', *E.P.W.* VIII, 1317–60; *J.P.S.* VII, 1978–9: 41–70; 168–209.

BROWN, J.
1972 *Gandhi's rise to power; Indian politics, 1915–22*, Cambridge.

BYRES, T.J.
1981 'The new technology, class formation, and class action in the Indian countryside', *J.P.S.* VIII, 405–54.

CHARLESWORTH, N.
1979 'Trends in the agricultural performance of an Indian province; the Bombay Presidency, 1900–1920', in: Chaudhuri & Dewey, 113–40.
1980 'The "middle-peasant thesis" and the roots of rural agitation in India', *J.P.S.* VII, 259–80.
1982 'The roots of rural agitation in India, 1917–1947; a reply to Hardiman', *J.P.S.* IX 266–76.

CHAUDHURI, K.N. & C.J. DEWEY (eds.)
1979 *Economy and society; essays in Indian economic and social history*, Delhi.

CHOKSEY, R.D.
1962 *Economic Life in the Bombay Gujarat (1800–1939)*, London.

CONNELL, J., B. DASGUPTA, R. LAISHLEY, M. LIPTON
1976 *Migration from rural areas: the evidence from village studies*, Delhi.

DANTWALA, M.L.
1937 *Marketing of raw cotton in India*, Bombay.

DAVE, J.
1946 *Halpati mukit; halipratha ane mukitdani hilachal*, Ahmedabad.

DESAI, I.P.
1971 'The slogan of a separate state by tribals of south Gujarat', in: *Indian Council for Social Science Research, Research Abstracts* no. 4, 7–20.

1977 'The Vedchhi movement', in: *History of rural development in modern India*, II, New Delhi.

1981 'Anti-reservation, agitation and structure of Gujarat society'; *E.P.W.* XVI, 819–24.

DESAI, M. B. & C. H. SHAH

1950 'Obstacles to grow more food (a study with reference to the Bardoli-Valod tract of the Surat District)', *I.J.A.E.* V, 4 ff.

DESAI, M. D.

1974 'Small farmers' development agency; experience in Surat district', *E.P.W.* IX, 1245–55.

DESAI, M. H.

1929 *The story of Bardoli, being a history of the Bardoli satyagraha of 1928 and its sequel*, Ahmedabad.

DHANAGARE, D. W.

1983 *Peasant movements in India 1920–1950*, Delhi.

DHOLAKIA, R. H. & P. M. PATEL

1978 'Relative growth of tribal population in Gujarat: 1961–71', *J.G.R.S.* XL, 30–8.

DJURFELDT, G. & S. LINDBERG

1976 *Behind poverty: the social formation in a Tamil village*, New Delhi.

DOSABHAI, E.

1894 *A history of Gujarat from the earliest period to the present time*, Ahmedabad.

ENTHOVEN, R. E.

1920 *Tribes and castes of Bombay*, Bombay.

EPSTEIN, T. S.

1973 *South India: yesterday, today and to-morrow*, London.

FISHER, J. H.

1951 'The harvest labor market in California', *The Quarterly Journal of Economics* LXV, 463–91.

FORREST, G. W. (ed.)

1887 *Selections from the letters, despatches and other state papers preserved in the Bombay Secretariat*, Home Series, 1, Bombay.

FRANKEL, F. R.

1978 *India's political economy 1947–77; the gradual revolution*, New Delhi.

G.O.

1980 'Sugar workers: round two', *E.P.W.* XV, 17–18.

GOUGH, K.

1978 'Agrarian relations in Southeast Asia, 1750–1976', *Review* II, 1978: 25–33.

GOVERNMENT OF GUJARAT

An assessment of the performance of SFDA, Surat District, 1971–1972 to 1973–1974, Directorate of Evaluation, Ahmedabad.

GUHA, R.
1982 'On some aspects of the historiography of colonial India', in: Guha, 1–8.
(ed.) 1982 *Subaltern studies I; writings on South Asian history and society*, Delhi.

HARDIMAN, D.
1976 'Politicisation and agitation among dominant peasants in early twentieth century India, some notes' *E.P.W.* IX, 365–71.
'The crisis of the lesser Patidars: peasant agitations in Kheda district, Gujarat, 1917–34', in: Low, 47–76.
1981 'A rejoinder to Charlesworth', *J.P.S.* VIII, 367–80.

HUNTER, W.
1892 *Bombay 1885–1890; a study in Indian administration*, London/Bombay.

JAYARAMAN, T. K.
1979 'Seasonal migration of tribal labour; an irrigation project in Gujarat', *E.P.W.* XIV, 1727–32.

JOSHI, H. & V. JOSHI
1976 *Surplus labour and the city; a study of Bombay*, Bombay.

JOSHI, P. C.
1979 'Emergence of the poor as a class', *E.P.W.* XIV, 355–6.

KALATHIL, M.
1978 'Industrial relations in a small-scale industry', in: Ramaswamy, 89–107.

KATTI, A. P.
1966 *Seasonal in-migrants in rural Shimoga*. Demographic Research Centre J.S.S. Institute of Economic Research, Dharwar.

KEATINGE, G.
1921 *Agricultural progress in Western India*, London.

KOSAMBI, D. D.
1956 *An introduction to the study of Indian history*, Bombay.

KOTHARI, R. (ed.)
1970 *Caste in Indian Politics*, New Delhi.

LAL, R. B.
1983 'Socio-religious movement among the tribals of South-Gujarat', in: Singh, 285–308.

LIPTON, M.
1977 *Why poor people stay poor; a study of urban bias in world development*, London.

LOW, D. A. (ed.)
1977 *Congress and the Raj; facets of the Indian struggle*, London.

MARLA, S. (ed.)
1981 *Bonded labour in India; national survey on the evidence of bonded labour*, New Delhi.

MARX, K.
1956 'Debatten über das Holzdiebstahlgesetz', in: *Karl Marx-Friedrich Engels Werke*, Band 1, 109–47.

MC ALPIN, M. B.
1975 'The effects of expansion of markets on rural income distribution in nineteenth century India', *E.E.H.* XII, 289–302.

MEHTA, B. H.
1934 'A summary survey of the economic life of an aboriginal tribe of Gujarat', *J.U.B.* II, 311–59.

MEHTA, J. M.
1932 *A study of the rural economy of Gujarat*, Baroda State Press.

MEHTA, S. M. & M.J. MEHTA
1966 'A study of the practice of slavery with special reference to Gujarat', *J.G.R.S.* XXVIII, 74–9.

MEILLASSOUX, C.
1973 'Are there castes in India?', *E.S.* II, 89–111.

MISHRA, S. C.
1952 'Commercialisation, peasant differentiation and merchant capital in the late nineteenth-century Bombay and Punjab', *J.P.S.* X, 3–51.

MUKHERJEE, R.
1981 Realities of agrarian relations in India', *E.P.W.* XVI, 109–16.

MUKHTYAR, G. C.
1930 *Life and labour in a south Gujarat village*, Calcutta.

MYRDAL, G.
1968 *Asian Drama; an enquiry into the poverty of nations*, 3 vols., New York.
1969 'L'état "mou" dans les pays sous-développés', *T.M.* X, 5–24.

OBEROI, A.S. & H.K. MANMOHAN SINGH
1980 'Migration flows in Punjab's agriculture'. *E.P.W.* XV, A2–12.

OMVEDT, G. (ed.)
1981 'Capitalist agricultural and rural classes in India', *E.P.W.* XVI, A 140–59.
1982 *Land, caste and politics in Indian States*, Delhi.

PANDIT, D.
1969 'The myths around sub-division and fragmentation of holdings: a few case histories', *I.E.S.H.R.* VI, 151–63.

PARULEKAR, G.
1975 *Adivasis revolt*, Calcutta.

PATEL, J. M.
1964 'Agricultural labour in a South Gujarat village', in: Vyas, 92–119.

PATEL, N.
1972 'A passage from India', *Transaction*, April, 25 ff.

PATEL S. D.
1965 'Rural community of south Gujarat', *J.G.R.S.* XXVII, 52–62.

POCOCK, D. F.
1972 *Kanbi and Patidar; a study of the Patidar community of Gujarat*, Oxford.
1973 *Mind, body and wealth; a study of belief and practice in an Indian village*, Oxford.

POPKIN, S. L.
1979 *The rational peasant: the political economy of rural society in Vietnam*, Berkeley.

RABITORY, N.
1975 'System v. expediency: the reality of land revenue administration in the Bombay Presidency', *M.A.S.* IX, 529–46.

RAGHAVAIAH, V.
1971 *Tribal revolts*, Nellore.

RAMASWAMY, M. E. A. (ed.)
1978 *Industrial relations in India*, Delhi.

ROBERTSON, E. P.
1865 *Glossary of Gujaratee revenue and official terms*, Bombay.

ROGERS, A.
1892 *The land revenue of Bombay*, 1, Bombay.

RUDRA, A.
1968 'Class relations in Indian agriculture', *E.P.W.* XIII, 916–23; 963–8; 998–1004.

SABERWAL, S.
1979 'Sociologists and inequality in India: the historical context', *E.P.W.* XIV, 243–54.

SANGHAVI, N.
1980 'Competitive populism', *E.P.W.* XV, 2127.

SAXENA, D. P.
1947 *Rururban migration in India; causes and consequences*, Bombay.

SCOTT, J. C.
1976 *The moral economy of the peasant: rebellion and subsistence in Southeast Asia*, New Haven.

SHAH, A. M.
1982 'Division and hierarchy; an overview of caste in Gujarat', *C.I.S.* XVI, 1–33.

SHAH, G.
1974 'Traditional society and political mobilization: the experience of Bardoli satyagraha (1920–1928)', *C.I.S.* VIII, 89–107.
1975 *Caste association and political process in Gujarat; a study of Gujarat Kshatriya*, Bombay.

1977 *Protest movements in two Indian States*, Delhi.

1982 'Rural politics in Gujarat', in: Omvedt, 134–55.

SHAH, P. G.

1958 *The Dublas of Gujarat*, Bombay.

SHARMA, U. (ed.)

1978 *When violence erupts*, Delhi.

SHUKLA, J. B.

1937 *Life and labour in a Gujarat taluka*, London.

SINGH, A. P.

1979 'Farm workers vs. rich farmers; class and caste in a Punjab village', *E.P.W.* XIV, 1753–4.

SINGH, K. S. (ed.)

1983 *Tribal movements in India*, II, Delhi.

SINGH, J. P.

1980 'Population mobility in India', *S.B.* XXIX, 33–62.

SPODEK, H.

1975 'Sardar Vallabhbhai at 100, *E.P.W.* X, 1925–36.

SRINIVAS, M. N.

1979 'Future of Indian caste', *E.P.W.* XIV, 237–42.

STOKES, E.

1978 *The peasant and the Raj: studies in agrarian society and peasant rebellions in colonial India*, Cambridge.

TAHMANKAR, D. V.

1970 *Sardar Patel*, London.

TODARO, M. P.

1981 *Economic development in the third world* (2nd. edition), New York.

TOOTHI, N. A.

1935 *Vaishanavas of Gujarat*, London.

VEEN, K. W. VAN DER

1972 *I give thee my daughter*, Assen.

VYAS, V. S. (ed.)

1964 *Agricultural labour in four Indian villages*, Sardar Patel University, Vallabh Vidyanagar.

1976 'Structural change in agriculture and the small farm sector', *E.P.W.* XI, 24–32.

WEBER, M.

1979 'Development tendencies in the situation of East Elbian rural labourers' (translated by K. Tribe), *E.S.* VIII, 172–205.

1924 'Entwicklungstendenzen in der Lage der ostelbischen Landarbeiter', in: *Gesammelte Aufsätze zur Sozialund Wirtschaftsgeschichte*, Tübingen.

1893 'Die Ländliche Arbeitsverfassung', in: *Verhandlungen des Vereins für Sozial-Politik*, Band 58, Leipzig.

YAGNIK, A.
1981 'Second phase in caste war', *E.P.W.* XVI, 977–8.

GOVERNMENT SOURCES

CENSUS REPORTS AND GAZETTEERS

1883 *Report of the Census of British India 1881*, III.
1883 *Report of the Census of the Baroda territories 1881*, Bombay.
1902 *Census of India 1901*, XVIII, Baroda, part 1, Bombay.
1911 *Census of India 1911*, XVI, Baroda, part 1, Bombay.
1922 *Census of India 1921*, XVII, Baroda State, part 1, Bombay.
1932 *Census of India 1931* XIX, Baroda, part 1, Bombay.
1941 *Census of India 1941*, XVII, Baroda, Baroda State Press.
1971 *Agricultural Census 1970–71*, Gujarat.
1982 *Census of India 1981*, Series-5 Gujarat, *Provisional Population Totals*, Government Press, Baroda.
1877 *Gazetteer of the Bombay Presidency*, II, Gujarat: *Surat and Broach*, Bombay.
1901 *Gazetteer of the Bombay Presidency*, IX, *Gujarat population, Hindus*, Bombay.
1923 *Gazetteer of the Baroda State*, 2 vols., Bombay.
1962 *Gazetteer of India*, Gujarat State, *Surat District*, Ahmedabad.

SURVEY AND SETTLEMENT REPORTS

1897 *Settlement report of the Bardoli taluka 1865–66* (included as appendix R. in R.S.S. of Bardoli taluka 1897).
1897 *Papers relating to the revision survey settlement of the Bardoli taluka*, 1895 S.R. no. 359, N.S., Bombay.
1900 *Papers relating to the revision survey settlement of the Jalalpor taluka of the Surat Collectorate*, S.R. no. 350, N.S., Bombay.
1907 *Settlement Report of the Vyara taluka of the Navsari Division 1906–1907*, Baroda.
1910 *Revision settlement report of Kamrej taluka of the Navsari Division 1909–1910*, Baroda.
1911 *Revision settlement report Palsana taluka 1910–1911*, Baroda.
1916 *Revision settlement report of the Mahuwa taluka of the Navsari division*, Baroda.
1927 *Second revision settlement of the Bardoli taluka and Valod Petha of the Surat district*, 1925, Bombay.

OTHER OFFICIAL DOCUMENTS

1974 *Assessment of the performance of SFDA, Surat District, 1971–72 to 1973–74*, Government of Gujarat, Directorate of Evaluation, Ahmedabad.

1920 *Baroda economic development committee 1918–19*, Report, Bombay.

1873–5 *Baroda enquiry commission*, 4 vols., Bombay.

1823 *Bombay Revenue proceedings 1823*, range 368, XXXVIII, 4816, letter of Collector of Surat, W.J. Lumsden, 9 April.

BROOMFIELD, R.S. & R.M. MAXWELL

1929 *Report of the special enquiry into the second revision settlement of the Bardoli and Chorasi talukas*, Bombay.

1968 *Classification of relatively more economically backward areas*, (in Gujarati), Government of Gujarat, Ahmedabad.

Collector Morrison's Report, 13 November 1812, 15 September 1819; 20 September 1820. Indian Office Library, London.

1837–8 *Correspondence between the Directors of the East India Company and the Company's Government in India on the subject of slavery*. Accounts and Papers, XVI, Slavery Session, 15 November 1837–16 August 1838.

1974 '*Final report on the survey of seasonal migration of labour in* Panchmahals district 1971–72', *The Bulletin of Economics and Statistics* XIV, 1–25, Bureau of Economics and Statistics, Gujarat.

1955 *Privileges provided by Bombay State Government for backward classes*, Government of Bombay, Bombay.

1900 *Report of the famine operations in the Baroda state for the year 1899–1900*, Baroda.

1979 *Report of the Gujarat State land commission*, Government of Gujarat, Ahmedabad.

1950 *Report of the Hali Labour Enquiry Committee*, M.L. Dantwala & M.B. Desai (not published), Bombay.

1966 *Report of minimum wages advisory committee for employment in agriculture*, Ahmedabad.

1927 *Royal commission on agriculture in India*, II, part 1, *Evidence taken in the Bombay Presidency*, London.

SHIRRAS, G.F.

1924 *Report on an enquiry into agricultural wages in the Bombay Presidency*, Government of Bombay, Labour Office, Bombay.

1983 *Socio-Economic review; Gujarat State 1982–83*, Bureau of Economics and Statistics, Government of Gujarat, Gandhinagar.

OTHER PUBLICATIONS

Mimeographed reports

BHATT, A.
Study of working and living environments of seasonal migrants. Gujarat Institute of Area Planning, Ahmedabad.

BLANKENBERG, F.
1981 *Sandhal padati: a traditional system of labour exchange in a changing village economy.* Comparative Asian Studies Programme, Rotterdam.

DESAI, B.D.
1979 *A socio-economic study of the milk producers of South Gujarat.* Centre for Social Studies, Surat.

DESAI, M.B. et al.
Changing farm production and organization in developing agriculture in a district in Gujarat. Research project no. 315 under P.L. 480 counterpart Funds, Final report 1967–72, 2 vols., Department of Agricultural Economics, M.S. University, Baroda.

DESAI, M.D.
1974 *Employment, income and levels of living of agricultural labourers; a study in the Surat District, Gujarat 1969–70.* Agro-Economic Research Centre, Sardar Patel University, Vallabh Vidyanagar.

GANDHI, R.D. & SHAH, C.H.
1978 *Rural seasonal migration*, Gujarat Institute of Area Planning, Ahmedabad.

GAUDE, J.
1976 *Causes and repercussions of rural migration in developing countries; a critical analysis.* Rural employment policy research programme. Working Papers World Development Programme Research, ILO, Geneva.

JAIN, S.A.C.
1983 *Impact of integrated rural development programme in Bardoli taluka.* South Gujarat University, Surat.

KUMBHAR, B.L.
1981 *Baseline survey for the Sarbhon project on rural crafts and nutrition centre* (taluka Bardoli, district Surat). Gujarat Institute of Area Planning, Ahmedabad.

KUMAR, S.S.
Planning for development of Surat District; first phase study, part III, *Water resources planning for irrigation use.* Gujarat Institute of Area Planning, Ahmedabad.

LAL, R.B.
1977 *Bonded labour in Gujarat (does it exist in Gujarat?)*, Tribal Research and Training Institute, Gujarat Vidyapith, Ahmedabad.

MANKODI, K. & T. GANGOPADHYAY
1983 *Rehabilitation, the economic and ecological costs.* Centre for Social Studies, Surat.

MURTHY, N.
1978 *Demography of tribal population in Gujarat.* Gujarat Institute of Area Planning, Ahmedabad.

PAHWA, A.K.
Planning for development of Surat District; first phase study, part V—*Industry.* Gujarat Institute of Area Planning, Ahmedabad.

PATEL, R.M.
1960 *Afawa (Surat District, Gujarat): an advanced village in traditional setting.* Sardar Patel University, Vallabh Vidyanagar.

PATHY, J.
1983 *Agrarian structure in tribal Gujarat and its implications for tribal policies.* South Gujarat University, Surat.

SAMANTA, B.B.
Planning for development of Surat district; first phase study, Part IV—*Agriculture.* Gujarat Institute of Area Planning.

SAMANTA, B.B., R. ROY, S.K. KUMAR, A.K. PAHWA, R.N. ROY, A. DESAI
1977 *Planning for development of Surat District.* Gujarat Institute Institute of Area Planning, Ahmedabad.

SHAH, G.
1977 *Socio-economic conditions of Chodhras; a restudy.* Centre for Social Studies, Surat.
1978 *Agricultural labourers, are they bonded?* Centre for Social Studies, Surat.

Theses

DESAI, K.I.
1979 *Tribals in a non-tribal setting; a sociological study of tribals in an urban community.* Ph.d. thesis, South Gujarat University, Surat.

DESAI, S.
1930 *Marriage and family in Gujarat.* Ph.D. thesis, University of Bombay.

KALATHIL, M.
1979 *The sociological implications of industrialisation in a locality in Gujarat.* Ph.d. thesis, University of Delhi.

NAIK, K.V.
1979 *Wage structure and economic condition of agricultural labourers in Navsari taluka.* M.Phil. thesis, South Gujarat University, Surat.

PARMAR, J.G.

1978 *Impact of sugarcane industry on rural economic development of Surat district.* M.Phil. thesis, South Gujarat University, Surat.

PATEL, R.D.

1973 *Class structure and agricultural resources of a village of Bardoli taluka.* M.A. thesis, South Gujarat University, Surat.

SAHOV, U.C.

1981 *A sociological study of child labour.* M.Phil. thesis, South Gujarat University, Surat.

SHAH, C.H.

1952 *Effects of world war II on agriculture in India (with special reference to Gujarat).* Ph.d. thesis, Bombay University.

WOOD, J.

1971 *The political integration of British and princely Gujarat: the historical—political variable in Indian state politics.* Ph.d. dissertation, Columbia University, New York.

UNPUBLISHED SOURCES

BANK OF BARODA

1972 *Bank Survey Report on Surat District*, May.

CHARLESWORTH, N.

1981 *The ryotwari land revenue system and the peasant economy in colonial India*, Paper presented to the second Anglo-Dutch conference on comparative colonial history, 23–25 september 1981, Leiden.

KHET VIKAS PARISHAD

1978 *Administrative report, Ahmedabad.*

GUJARAT KHET VIKAS PARISHAD

1981 *Report upto March 1980*, Khet Bhavan, Ahmedabad.

KUMBHAR, B.L.

Rural poor in India; ameliorative measures and results—a review. Gujarat Institute of Area Planning, Ahmedabad.

McEWEN SCOTT, A.E.

1973 *The invisible proletariat*, University of Essex, April.

PATEL, P.

1982 '*Impact of irrigation on power relations in a village: a case-study of Tundi*'. Centre for Social Studies, Surat.

Role of landed interests in the current agitation in Gujarat, n.d.

RUDOLPH, S.H. & L.I. RUDOLPH

Determinants and varieties of agrarian mobilization. Paper presented to the conference on agrarian productivity and power, organized by the South Asia Political Economy Project of the (U.S.) Social Science Research Council and the Indian Council for Social Science Research.

SHAH, G.

Ethnicity and politics: a study of scheduled tribes in Gujarat (manuscript), Surat.

Traditional society and political mobilization (manuscript), Surat.

INDEX